Jurispr

Jurispr   nd
theorie   ce,
philoso   ow
does la   of
rights?

This   ru-
dence.   de
range o

Fron   ent
thinker   ol-
ume ex   ral
questio

Suri Ra

Jurisprudence

Suri Ratnapala

CAMBRIDGE UNIVERSITY PRESS
Cambridge, New York, Melbourne, Madrid, Cape Town, Singapore, São Paulo, Delhi

Cambridge University Press
477 Williamstown Road, Port Melbourne, VIC 3207, Australia

www.cambridge.edu.au
Information on this title: www.cambridge.org/9780521614832

© Suri Ratnapala 2009

First published 2009

Cover design by Modern Art Production Group
Typeset by Aptara
Printed in China by Printplus

National Library of Australia Cataloguing in Publication data
   Suri Ratnapala
   Jurisprudence
   9780521614832 (pbk.)
   Includes index
   Bibliography
   Jurisprudence
340.1

978-0-521-614-832 paperback

To Vidura Ravindranatha, Rusri and Adrian Surindra

Contents

Acknowledgements

The birth of this book owes most to the people at the Cambridge University Press who foresaw its value, placed their confidence in me to deliver the work and patiently, kindly but relentlessly pressured me to complete it. I must mention first Jill Henry, the publisher who persuaded me to undertake this work amidst the enormous pressures of teaching and the somewhat different research expectations of my school and university. Jill's enthusiasm and commitment was maintained by her successors, Zoe Hamilton and Susan Hanley, whose encouragement and understanding helped me to sustain my effort. I am grateful to Kath Harper, for her sharp editorial scrutiny of the manuscript and the improvements that she offered.

I received useful insights from the anonymous reviewers and I am indebted to the scholars, both past and present, who have inspired me over the years, particularly in the classical liberal tradition.

Work of this nature consumes precious years of an author's life and is not possible without the sympathy and support of family. I owe them the greatest debt.

Suri Ratnapala
2009

Figures

1

Introduction

This book is about the social phenomenon that is known as law and its relation to justice. This is not a treatise on some branch of law such as contract law, tort law or the law of crime. It is about past and present theories concerning the nature of law and justice in general. However, it is
not possible to conduct an inquiry of this nature, let alone make sense of
the more important questions, without reference to actual legal systems and
actual laws. Hence, specific rules of law figure in discussions throughout this
book.

   Jurisprudence in the sense used in this book has been around since at least
the time of the philosopher Socrates (470–399 BC). Great minds have sought
answers to questions about the nature of law, right and justice, but questions
persist. This says as much about the complexity of these ideas as it does about
the limits of our language and reason. Theories that have proposed answers to
questions have themselves become subjects of ongoing debate. This book does
not pretend to have the last word on any of these questions, but neither does it
seek to avoid controversy. Its primary object, though, is to state in comprehensible
terms the major questions in jurisprudence, assess critically the contributions on
these questions made by various schools of thought, introduce the reader to
some new insights about legal systems and make its own contribution to this
conversation about law and justice. It does not matter that there is no consensus
about the meaning of concepts such as law and justice. There may never be.
We can make up our own minds after getting to know relevant theory, and
in so doing learn a great deal about the legal system and the society we find
ourselves in.

Rewards of jurisprudence

The study of jurisprudence brings immediate rewards to the lawyer. It hardly matters to a physicist or a chemist how anyone defines physics or chemistry. The physicist and the chemist are not constrained in what they do by definitions of their disciplines. They simply get on with being physicists or chemists. In contrast, it is critically important to a legal practitioner to be recognised as doing law, particularly by judges and clients. A practising lawyer is restricted, if not by a definition of law, at least by the way law is understood by judges and other officials who enforce the law. A good lawyer is one who knows when to argue strictly from statutes and precedents, when to re-interpret laws or distinguish precedents and when to appeal to policy, justice or the good sense of the judge. This is the stuff of jurisprudence. Make no mistake: jurisprudence sharpens legal professional skills.

There are rewards too for the social scientist and the philosopher. Law is part of the structure of society, whether modern or primitive. Law both shapes and is shaped by society. Law impacts on every human activity undertaken within society. Imagine going to work this morning. Decide whether you wish to drive or take the train. If you drive, the road rules will help you get to your office safely. If you take the train, the contract you make by buying a ticket will oblige the rail company to take you there. When you get to your office your employment contract (or some statute) will determine what you do and how much you get paid. Imagine just about any activity and you will find law in attendance – sometimes helping, sometimes hindering. For the sociologist, anthropologist, economist and just about any social scientist, it pays richly to consider the nature of law and the legal system.

Law raises critical issues in moral philosophy. The question of why a person should observe the laws of a society is a moral question. The statement 'The law should be obeyed because the law says so' does not take us anywhere. We must look outside the law to find the duty to obey the law. Law is normative in the sense that it lays down rules of conduct – what ought to be done and what ought not to be done. Basic laws of society, such as the rules against harming person and property and the rule that promises must be performed, are also moral rules. Particular laws, though, may offend the moral of sense of individuals. Some enactments – such as those that authorise war crimes and genocide – will shock the human conscience and draw universal condemnation. Are they laws, and, if so, are there moral obligations to obey them?

The remaining contents of this chapter are arranged as follows. First, the compass of jurisprudence is explained. Second, I discuss certain threshold issues that arise in any quest to understand the concept of law. Third, I provide a synopsis of each chapter's scope and content. Finally, I mention some salient issues in jurisprudence that are not addressed in this book but that represent future challenges for jurists and other students of law.

Jurisprudence

Jurisprudence is an imprecise term. Sometimes it refers to a body of substantive legal rules, doctrines, interpretations and explanations that make up the law of a country: thus, English, French or German jurisprudence refers to the laws of England, France and Germany. Jurisprudence may also refer to the interpretations of the law given by a court. We speak in this sense of the constitutional jurisprudence of the US Supreme Court and the High Court of Australia, and the jurisprudence of the European Court of Human Rights. Jurisprudence in this sense is not synonymous with law, but signifies the juristic approaches and doctrines associated with particular courts.

The subject of this book is jurisprudence in a different sense. This jurisprudence consists of scientific and philosophical investigations of the social phenomenon of law and of justice generally. It embraces studies, theories and speculations about law and justice undertaken with the knowledge and theoretical tools of different disciplines – such as law, history, sociology, economics, political science, philosophy, logic, psychology, economics, and even physics and mathematics. No discipline is unwelcome that sheds light on the nature of law and its relation to society.

The range of questions about law and justice asked within this jurisprudence is indefinite. What is law, and can it be defined? What are the historical origins of law? How do rules of behaviour emerge in a society even before they are recognised or enforced by the state? Is there a basic set of rules that make social life possible? How does law shape society? How does society shape law? What qualities must law possess to be effective? How do judges decide hard cases? Whence comes their authority? Is there superhuman natural law? If so, how do we find its principles? Why do people obey some laws even when they face no sanction for disobedience? Is there a duty to obey an unjust law? Can we make moral (or economic) judgments about particular laws or legal systems? What do we mean by justice? Is there a special brand of legal justice? Are there universal standards of justice? What is natural justice and what are its minimum demands? What do we mean by social justice? These questions are not just interesting in themselves, but are critical for understanding the phenomenon of law and its relation to justice. They are legitimate questions within jurisprudence as the discipline is understood in this work. Of course, it is impossible in a book of this scale to discuss all of the contributions from different disciplines or to consider all the important questions that have been raised, and can be raised, in relation to law and justice. The book's discussions are therefore selective. I explain the basis of the selection in the course of this chapter.

Legal theory

The term 'legal theory' is associated with theories seeking to answer the question: what is law? It is a specific project within jurisprudence. John Austin, the

19th century legal positivist (discussed in more detail in Chapter 2), thought that this was the only project in jurisprudence (Austin 1995 (1832), 18). Most British legal positivists since Austin have tended to limit their inquiries to the task of finding a universally valid definition of law or a set of criteria to distinguish law from other kinds of rules. The best known of the modern British legal positivists, Herbert Hart, devoted his book *The Concept of Law* to the challenge of showing how rules of law are different from: (a) commands such as those of a gunman who relieves you of your wallet; (b) moral rules that fall short of law; and (c) mere coincidences of behaviour that represent social habits or practices (Hart 1997, 8–9). Legal positivists prefer the term 'legal theory' to describe what they do.

It is worth mentioning that legal theory does not stop with the range of questions posed by the positivists. A theory is a testable hypothesis or proposition about the world. It is possible to theorise about many other aspects of the phenomenon of law, such as the law's origins, its emergent quality, its role as a factor of production, its psychological force, and so on. Hence, legal theory, when used in relation to the central themes of legal positivism, should be understood as limited to theories about the idea of law and its basic concepts.

Analytical and normative jurisprudence

Some writers have identified two species of jurisprudence – analytical and normative. Questions concerning the meaning of law in general and of the major concepts of the law are grouped within analytical jurisprudence, and questions focused on the moral dimensions of the law are left to normative jurisprudence (Davies & Holdcroft 1991, v). Analytical jurisprudence is roughly co-extensive with legal theory, as identified with legal positivism. Some scholars have further classified analytical jurisprudence into general and particular branches (Harris 1980, 4). General analytical jurisprudence is focused on the concept of law generally, and particular jurisprudence on the basic concepts of law that are common to most, if not all, legal systems. (See Figure 1.1.) These are the building blocks of legal rules and include concepts such as right, duty, liberty, liability, property, possession and legal personality.

It is important to keep in mind that these are labels of convenience. They are valuable if taken as navigational aids, but may mislead if treated as true categories. There is much analysis in normative jurisprudence and, as we will discover in our inquiries, there is much that is normative in various analyses of the concept of law.

Law

In every language there is a word for law, in the sense of rules of conduct that are considered obligatory by members of a community. The term 'law' is also used in science to state a theory about the physical world. In saying that every action has

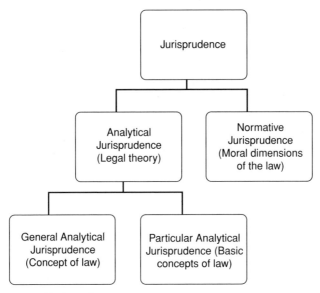

Figure 1.1 Types of jurisprudence

an equal and opposite reaction, Isaac Newton stated a law of nature. However, our immediate concern is not with this type of law, but with laws that prescribe rules of conduct in society. Law in this sense is common to all societies. There is no society that does not have rule breakers, and no society without discord. Yet it is hard to imagine a society where there are no common rules. Cohabitation and cooperation are not possible except on the basis of some common understanding of what behaviour is acceptable and what is not. The rules that indicate the right and wrong ways of behaving are generally identified by the term 'law' or a word of equivalent meaning. There are many kinds of law, such as moral law, religious law, laws of etiquette, customary law, common law, royal law, statute law, and so forth.

The modern state does not concern itself with all of these laws, but only with those that for reasons of policy it chooses to enforce. Thus, in the United Kingdom the coercive power of the state is not applied when a person fails to observe the widely accepted social rule of joining the queue to be served at a shop or restaurant. However, the state will enforce the rule against theft if a customer walks away with goods without paying for them. Lawyers will account for this difference by saying that only the latter case involves a breach of the law, properly so called. The law that they refer to is state law – the law that the state makes or chooses to recognise and enforce. An efficient and fair legal system enables citizens to identify with some confidence those rules that the courts or other state officials will recognise and enforce, and those that they will not. It makes sense in jurisprudence to pay special attention to the question of the formal criteria that legal systems use to identify state law. Nothing that I say in this book is intended to devalue this enterprise.

Excluding moral considerations from the concept of law (the possibility of which I leave as an open question at this point) is a very different exercise from excluding them from jurisprudence. The question of whether law has a necessary connection to morality is important, but it is only one among the many worthwhile questions we may ask about law.

The quest for a definition of law

Some influential thinkers in the tradition of legal positivism have attempted to define law. Thomas Hobbes, Jeremy Bentham and John Austin defined law as the commands of a political sovereign backed by sanctions (Hobbes 1946 (1651), 112; Bentham 1970 (1782), 1; Austin 1995 (1832), 24). Hans Kelsen defined law as norms validated by other valid norms within a system of norms that ultimately derives from a common basic norm (1967, 201). Joseph Raz held that 'law consists of authoritative positivist considerations enforceable by courts' (1995, 208). Such definitions do not work without supplementary definitions. Austin had to define 'sovereign', 'command' and 'sanction'; Kelsen explained what he meant by 'norm', 'basic norm' and 'validity'; and Raz explained what is meant by 'positivist considerations'.

The leading positivist, HLA Hart, however, found that nothing concise enough to be recognised as a definition can provide an answer to the question 'What is law?' (Hart 1997, 16). Hart identified the typical case of law as the result of the union of primary and secondary rules. Specifically, he argued that law comprises primary rules of obligation that are recognised as law according to the secondary rules of recognition accepted within that system. This was, to Hart, only the central case of law, and he acknowledged that 'as we move from the centre we shall have to accommodate . . . elements of a different character' (1997, 99).

Legal positivists, despite their differences, unite in the claim that they have a general theory that accounts for all occurrences of law in all cultures and times, and that also distinguishes law from all other types of norms and social practices. They claim, as part of this general thesis, that a law is a law irrespective of its moral standing. In other words, law has no necessary connection with morality. A law that authorises genocide does not cease to be law only by reason of universal moral condemnation. Hence, positivists in one way or another seek to establish the necessary and sufficient conditions for something to be called law. In this sense they are all defining law.

It is of paramount importance in a modern state to have a reliable set of indicators that identify the rules likely to be enforced through the power of the state. Identifying indicators of law and providing definitions of law are two very different undertakings. I will be supporting the view that the former is feasible, but the latter is not. Some of the most persistent debates in legal theory arise from the neglect of the nature of definitions. Some thinkers define the law without realising that they are doing it. Some others define the law without making clear what kind of definition they are giving.

There are different kinds of definition and it is important to know in what sense a theorist is seeking to define law. It is possible to give a *lexical definition* of the term 'law'. A lexical definition simply reports the sense in which the term is understood within a language community. The definition of a 'bachelor' as an unmarried man is a lexical definition. This is what English speakers understand by that word. A lexical definition of the concept of 'law' (more accurately, its vernacular equivalent such as *lex, loi, Gesetz, lag* or *legge*) will indicate the sense in which the term is understood within a given community. A lexical definition of law in a remote Australian Aboriginal community or in an Inuit tribe may be different from the lexical definition of law among English speakers in England or Australia. A lexical definition may be right or wrong, and can be empirically tested by asking members of a community what they mean by law. Sociologists and anthropologists are particularly interested in lexical meanings of law.

It is also possible to give the term 'law' a *stipulative definition*. A stipulative definition assigns a meaning to a term. Such a definition is neither right nor wrong. A law may variously define an 'adult' to mean any person who has reached the age of 16, 18, 20 or 25. The definition may be fair or unfair, practical or impractical, but it is neither right nor wrong as it does not pretend to report a fact. Stipulative definitions are common in legislation. Section 23 of the *Acts Interpretation Act 1903* (Cth) stipulates that a reference in an Act to a man includes a woman and a word in the singular includes the plural unless a contrary intention appears in the Act. Jeremy Bentham, the first and greatest of the British legal positivists and a founder of modern utilitarianism, defined the law as the command of the sovereign. As I show in Chapter 2, he was conscious that this was a stipulative definition and that law was understood very differently in his own community. He proposed this definition for the utilitarian reason that it promotes clarity and certainty, which is to the public advantage.

A jurist may also give the concept of law a *theoretical definition*. A theoretical definition is a special case of a stipulative definition. Whereas a stipulative definition can be completely arbitrary, a theoretical definition assigns a meaning to a term and justifies it by a scientific theory. Unlike a non-theoretical stipulative definition, which is neither right nor wrong, a theoretical definition can be shown to be wrong by disproving the theory. The statement 'Earth is the planet third closest to the Sun in a system of planets that orbit the Sun' is a theoretical definition of the Earth. The definition will be falsified if another planet is found closer to the Sun. A theoretical definition that cannot be falsified is purely stipulative. Many of the theories of law consciously or unconsciously construct theoretical definitions.

A definition – whether lexical, stipulative, theoretical or any other – is not of much use unless it enables us to identify with some precision the things that are included within the term. One way to do this is to give the 'extension' of the term. Extension is the naming of all items that belong within the term. It makes perfect sense for a father writing a will to define his family as 'my wife A and my children B, C and D'. On the contrary, it is impractical, if not impossible, to give the extension of a term such as 'Englishman' because there are just too many English men to name. Hence, it is necessary to state the 'intension' of the term.

The intension of a term specifies all the properties that are not only necessary but also sufficient to place something within the term. The intension of the term 'Englishmen' may be stipulated as 'all men born in England or who have a parent born in England'. The definition of a triangle as the figure formed by straight lines connecting three points (and only three points) on one plane is an intensional definition. Anything more or anything less will make some other kind of figure. Hart gave the example of a definition of an elephant as a 'quadruped distinguished from others by its possession of a thick skin, tusks and trunk'. This is an intensional definition, and so is the definition of Earth given previously.

Definitions are important in law as they are in mathematics, logic and empirical science. Geometry defines the notions of point, line, circle, triangle, square, and so forth. Without these we will not know that on a conceptual plane, a straight line drawn through the centre of a circle will divide it in half, or that the sum of every triangle adds up to 180 degrees, or that the diagonals of a square will bisect each other at right angles. The definition of the units of measurement is critical in empirical sciences. The kilogram, the basic unit of measuring mass, is determined by a piece of platinum-iridium kept in a vault in Sèvres, France. The metre is defined as the distance travelled by light in an absolute vacuum in 1/299 792 458 of a second. Likewise, definitions matter in law. Law makes little sense unless we have a clear understanding of the fundamental legal concepts such as right, duty, liberty, power, liability, and immunity. In fact, we cannot make any legal statement without deploying one or more of these concepts. The law also requires more concrete definitions. A law that imposes income tax must define what 'income' is. A law that protects minors must define a 'minor'. A law that excludes heavy vehicles from a city street must define a 'heavy vehicle'. Criminal offences must be defined with a high level of precision to make the criminal law workable and fair.

Legal positivists are not content with defining legal categories, and seek a universal concept of law. Anthropologists ask: what do the Barotse or the Trobrianders or the Koori people or the English understand by law? Legal positivists, in contrast, search for a definition of law that is both theoretical and intensional. In other words, they seek a definition that specifies the necessary and sufficient ingredients of law and that holds true for all societies at all times. Have they succeeded? We will find out in the chapters to follow. For the moment, it is worth mentioning one aspect of the challenge that awaits them.

Law is an inseparable part of society and society is a complex, dynamic and emergent order. Society comes about when individuals observe certain common rules of conduct that allow them to cohabit and cooperate with one another. These rules may exist in the form of state laws, customs, morals, religious precepts and various informal norms that people observe as matters of etiquette and civil behaviour. Thus, law in its broadest sense gives structure to society. There are different kinds of complexity. Law and society are examples of what scientists call emergent complexity. Take a look at an intricate work of art such as a filigree. The design may be extraordinarily complex, but the object is static. No part of it moves. Thus, it is complex but not emergent. Now consider a clock. It is a highly complex machine with many interacting parts that are in perpetual motion. It is not static like the filigree, but its behaviour does not change over time. Again, the clock does not have the property of emergence. Society, in contrast, changes over time as the individuals who compose it adapt to the changing world. It is therefore complex and emergent. The law, therefore, also has the property of emergent complexity. Defining such systems is not easy.

The arrangement of the contents of this book

I summarise the contents of this book in the following pages. The summaries are unavoidably oversimplified. The book is arranged in four parts:

Part 1 – Law as it is (Chapters 2, 3 and 4)
Part 2 – Law and morality (Chapters 5 and 6)
Part 3 – Social dimensions of law (Chapters 7, 8, 9 and 10)
Part 4 – Rights and justice (Chapters 11 and 12)

There is danger in placing philosophical ideas and theories in compartments. Many thinkers have written on both law and justice. Some, like Hobbes, Bentham, and the modern British positivists, have taken care to separate their views on law from their thoughts on justice and what the law ought to be. Some, particularly in the natural law tradition, regard law and morality as inseparable. Yet the division I have proposed is not completely arbitrary.

Part 1 contains chapters on legal positivism and legal realism. Legal positivists and legal realists entertain different conceptions of law, but they share the aim of explaining the law *as it is* as opposed to what the law *ought to be*. The two schools are also united by their insistence that the law has no necessary connection with morality. I begin this survey in Chapter 2 by discussing the most influential school of jurisprudence within the British Commonwealth – legal positivism. It is associated with a distinguished line of British thinkers, commencing with Thomas Hobbes and his followers Jeremy Bentham and John Austin. In more recent times scholars such as Herbert Hart, Neil MacCormick and Joseph Raz have refined the positivist message. That message can be summarised here only at risk of gross oversimplification. However, it may be said that at a minimum positivists share and defend the position that rules of law may be logically and factually separated from other rules of conduct such as moral and social rules, and that a universal test or set of tests can be stated for identifying law that transcends cultural differences. Positivists do not deny that law may enforce a community's morals, or even that in a particular legal system some moral test may determine whether a rule is recognised as law. Their contention is that a law that satisfies the formal criteria of validity is a law even if it is immoral. This chapter traces the evolution of British positivism to date, examines the central ideas of this school of thought and evaluates its influence on political and social life.

The greatest contribution to legal positivism outside the British tradition is that of Hans Kelsen, whose remarkable theory demands our closest attention, not the least because it is easily misunderstood. Kelsen set out to establish a science of legal norms that is independent and separate from the political and cultural forces that produce specific legal norms. Kelsen wrote: 'It is the task of the science of law to represent the law of a community, i.e. the material produced by the legal authority in the law making procedure, in the form of statements to the effect that "if such and such conditions are fulfilled, then such and such a sanction shall follow"' (1945, 45). Kelsen described laws as norms that are validated by other norms within a given system of norms. The whole system is sustained by political realities that, analytically speaking, lie outside the legal system. Kelsen's theory has intuitive appeal to legal practitioners and has played a major role in the resolution of legal disputes arising in the context of revolutionary overthrow of established legal order. Chapter 3 explains Kelsen's theory and, in the light of criticisms it has drawn, evaluates its intellectual and practical contributions to our understanding of the nature of law.

Legal positivism has been challenged by thinkers in the two realist traditions of jurisprudence: the American and the Scandinavian. While the two branches have much in common, their approaches and concerns differ. I discuss these schools of thought in Chapter 4, beginning with the Americans. American realism, as Karl Llewellyn pointed out, represents an intellectual movement rather than a school of thought or set of theories about law. American realists mount a serious challenge to the positivist conceptions of law by their deep scepticism of law as rules enacted by constitutionally authorised law makers. Realists share with legal positivists one premise: it is important to distinguish the law as it exists from the law as it ought to be. The realists study what the courts are doing, disregarding what the courts ought to be doing. The realist, though, soon discovers that what the courts do in fact is engage in value laden legal creativity.

While positivists and realists agree that it is important to separate the 'is' from the 'ought', they differ on how to ascertain the 'is'. The realists' most serious departure from legal positivism occurs at this point. The positivists look to the established law giving authorities (tyrants, parliaments, etc) to discover the law. The American realists liken this thinking to putting the cart before the horse. They look instead to judgments of courts, especially the appellate courts, to discover the law as it actually is. Legislative enactments and previous judicial precedents influence what courts do, but they are not the only influences that shape judicial decisions. In his famous article 'The path of the law', Oliver Wendell Holmes declared that 'the prophecies of what the courts will do in fact, and nothing more pretentious, are what I mean by the law' (Holmes 1897, 461). Most realists question the very possibility of rules. Law is represented by the actual behaviour of the legal system, not by how it ought to behave according to rules laid down by legislatures. In layman's language, the proposition is that it is idle to regard law as rules written in a law book when the law is what the higher courts say it is.

The Scandinavian realists mount a different sort of attack on legal positivism. Scandinavians point out that rules are not real things: they have no physical existence. No one has touched or felt a rule, or even seen one in the way we see a chair or an elephant. What we see are writings in a statute book. Parliament has declared that a person who takes property without the consent of the owner must be convicted of theft and punished. This is not a rule but a fact. The law consists of facts. Any talk of rules belongs in metaphysics. A collection of politicians gather in a house called parliament and decree this or that. This fact creates certain changes in the behaviour of people and of courts. American realists describe the law in terms of the decisions of officials, particularly those of the appellate courts. The Scandinavians look at law from the viewpoint of the person who obeys the law. They ask why the person obeys the law. Law is law, from the Scandinavian viewpoint, because of its psychological force in altering the way people behave.

In Part 2, I consider the theories that, directly or indirectly, assert the inseparability of law and morals. Chapter 5 is focused on the classical tradition of natural law theory, which asserts the presence of a higher form of law that deprives immoral human law of its obligatory force. The strongest version of natural law theory is expressed in the maxim *Lex injusta non est lex*, or 'unjust law is not law'. More accurately, this line of argument claims that at some point on the moral scale an enactment may be seen as so immoral or unjust that it loses its authority as law. The most famous modern formulation of this argument was provided by Gustav Radbruch, the German philosopher and one time minister of justice. In an article that is said to have inspired post-war courts to reject the defence of lawful orders raised by Nazi war criminals, Radbruch contended that 'where there is not even an attempt at justice, where equality, the core of justice, is deliberately betrayed in the issuance of positive law, then the law is not merely "flawed law", it lacks completely the very nature of law' (Radbruch 2006 (1946), 7). He maintained that large parts of Nazi law, measured by this standard, never attained the dignity of law. I trace this tradition from the early Greek philosophers through Roman legal doctrine, the theological teachings of St Augustine, St Thomas Aquinas and the schoolmen, natural rights theories, Hobbes, Locke and others, to its modern exposition by John Finnis.

The question of the possibility of separating law and morals is discussed further in Chapter 6. The chapter considers the work of two modern legal theorists, Lon Fuller and Ronald Dworkin, who maintained that the concept of law is imbued with morality of a certain kind. Fuller identified it as the inner morality of the law. Dworkin called it the law's integrity. Fuller regarded law as a purposeful enterprise whose aim is to subject human conduct to the guidance and control of general rules. The law's capacity to guide human actions depends on certain properties in its enactments. These properties are: generality, prospective operation, accessibility, clarity, consistency, reasonable constancy, possibility of observance, and congruence with official action. Rulers fail to make law to the extent that they fail to endow their enactments with these qualities. Fuller argued that these qualities are not just requirements of efficiency but constitute the inner morality of the law.

Dworkin examined the concept of law as it is understood in the Anglo-American culture. People expect integrity in their legal system. People's duty to obey the law, which is a moral duty, and the state's monopoly of power to enforce the law rest on the law's integrity. Integrity requires internal coherence and consistency based on the principle of treating like cases alike. Dworkin used the allegory of the chain novel (or a soap opera) to explain the role of the courts, who are the final arbiters of the law in the Anglo-American system. A chain novel may be written by successive authors developing the story as time goes by, yet readers expect some consistency and coherence in the unfolding story. A character must not be the hero in one episode and the villain in the next unless there is a credible explanation in the narrative. A story set in the countryside must not become overnight a story of inner city life. A disjointed chain novel leaves readers dissatisfied. Similarly, incoherent and inconsistent judicial action will destroy the faith that people have in the legal system. We can always pick up another novel to read, but few of us can choose another legal system to live under.

Part 3 moves the focus of the book to the law's social dimensions. I begin with a discussion of the sociology of law and sociological jurisprudence in Chapter 7. Law is a social phenomenon. It is the product of society, but at the same time it affects the way society is structured and functions. The sociology of law is the study of the connections between law and society. There are two kinds of sociology: positivist sociology and interpretive sociology. Positivist sociology applies the methods of empirical science to the study of social phenomena. Just as a natural scientist seeks to explain the causes of physical events such as ocean currents, earthquakes, weather patterns and pollution, a sociological positivist looks for the causes of social occurrences such as juvenile crime, family breakdown and drug addiction. Interpretive sociologists think that the social world is very different from the physical world and, hence, it cannot be understood purely by the methods of natural science. There are psychological, ideological and spiritual dimensions of human behaviour that cannot be measured like physical objects. Hence, interpretive sociologists take a more holistic approach and enlist other kinds of knowledge such as history, philosophy and psychology. I explain and discuss the sociological theories concerning law advanced by the pioneers in the field: Karl Marx, Max Weber, Émile Durkheim, Eugen Ehrlich and Roscoe Pound. The interpretive sociologist understands the law in a muc broader sense than lawyers do. The lawyer's law is made of the formal rules of state law expressed in statutes, orders, judgments and so forth. Sociologists treat the law of the state as only one specialised form of regulation among a much larger range of social control devices. Law includes, from the sociological viewpoint, customs, social practices, moral codes, and the internal rules of associations such as clubs, churches, cults, and even criminal syndicates.

I consider Karl Marx's view of the law as part of the superstructure of society. The foundation of society consists of the economic relations that determine how the goods that satisfy human wants are produced and distributed. The superstructure made of the state and its laws not only reflects this economic system but also reinforces it. As human communities progressed from tribal living to feudal society and the capitalist economy, the form of the law also changed to reflect and consolidate the features of each system. Marx predicted the inevitable self-destruction of capitalist society and its transformation by a transitional dictatorship into a stateless socialist society. The common ownership of the means of production and the abolition of class divisions would bring an end to the need for law and the state. History did not unfold the way Marx predicted, but his thinking continues to be influential as an ideology.

Max Weber, like Marx, was a student of economic and social history. Weber developed a theory about the progression of law from its ancient roots in tradition and magic to its current rational form. He identified the causes of the rational-isation of law with the needs of a capitalist economy and of the bureaucratic state. However, unlike Marx, Weber did not identify the law exclusively with the maintenance of the capitalist exchange economy and saw other purposes that the law fulfilled.

I follow the discussion of Weber's legal sociology with the work of Émile Durkheim, for whom law was the basis of social solidarity. Durkheim, like Marx, thought that law represented the contours of society, but unlike him did not see the law in oppressive terms. The division of labour plays a critical part in Durkheim's sociology. It determines the kind of law that a society has. In older societies, where there was little division of labour, law is found mainly in its repressive form. Criminal law is the main form of repressive law. In modern society, the more extensive division of labour calls for restitutive law. Every society has both kinds of law, but the restitutive kind predominates as society becomes economically sophisticated.

The chapter continues with a discussion of the sociological jurisprudence of Eugen Ehrlich, who was most famous for his idea of the living law. The centre of gravity of the law is not in parliaments or the courts but in the life of the people. Society emerges from the ground up as an association of associations. Its origins are in the genetic associations known as the family. Other associations are formed as people collaborate for mutual advantage. The process eventually leads to nationhood and government, and thence to international associations of the kind that we observe today. Ehrlich argued that legal norms exist in society before they are enacted as legal propositions by the state. Most people obey the rules of social life without compulsion. However, when on occasion the norms are violated, and resulting disputes cannot be resolved informally, the courts have to apply what Ehrlich called norms of decision, which consist of lawyer's law combined with moral and policy reasons that inevitably enter judicial calculation.

The chapter closes with an account of the sociological jurisprudence of Roscoe Pound. Pound recognised that there are narrow and broad meanings of law, but he was a jurist first. Whereas the previous thinkers came to the law from sociology, Pound went from law to sociology. The first task of the jurist is to know the law in the lawyer's sense. Pound considered the changing role of law in society, concluding that the law's role is the adjustment of competing interests with a minimum of friction and waste. The importance of his theory lies in his demonstration of the way interests are born outside the legal system and are transformed into legal relations, and in his message that legal institutions are shaped by the needs of the social and economic order, and not the reverse.

The discussion of the social dimensions of law is continued in Chapter 8, where I consider three major strands of radical jurisprudence that challenge the premises of both legal positivism and natural law theory. The chapter examines the body of theory produced by scholars of the movements popularly known as critical legal studies (CLS), feminist jurisprudence and postmodern legal theory. They are the views of thinkers who question the traditional understandings of the nature of law and its role in social regulation. Radical jurisprudence represents a brand of sociology of law that combines empirical observations of the law with normative critiques. The chapter commences with the central claims of liberal legal ideology that are challenged by radical theory. The common theme of the radical schools is that liberal law is fundamentally oppressive. The key reason is that law transforms abstract ideas ('man', 'woman', 'husband', 'wife', 'child', 'consumer', and so on) into legal categories in a way that 'reifies' by making them appear as real categories. A woman, for example, is cast into a stereotype that limits her role in the eyes of the law. CLS scholars argue, further, that this brand of legality papers over a serious contradiction in society as constructed by liberal law. A person desires individuality as well as togetherness with others. A society organised on liberal principles denies this dilemma by its celebration of individual rights and autonomy. According to CLS, liberal law systematically weakens the social bond and creates in persons a deep sense of alienation.

Feminist legal theory views this reification as the outcome of a male dominated culture. There are different interpretations of the female predicament under liberal law. Some feminist legal theorists argue that women, by nature, are different from men. Whereas men have a sense of separation from others, women view life in relational terms. They see themselves as carers, not competitors. The impersonal, abstract nature of law fails to accommodate the feminine and thereby disenfranchises women. Other feminist theorists take the opposite view: that the law draws illegitimate distinctions between the genders, keeping women out of positions either expressly (as in the case of combat ranks of the military) or by male oriented eligibility standards – for example, those that favour physical attributes as against intellectual abilities. Feminists such as Catharine MacKinnon present a straightforward uncompromising argument against male domination, and call on women to give up the equality quest and fight for ending oppression in the form of rape, sexual assault of children, endemic family violence, prostitution and pornography, and other modes of female subjection.

This chapter also investigates the postmodernist movement in legal theory, concentrating particularly on deconstruction and language game theory. The postmodernists, who have displaced critical legal studies as the major force in radical jurisprudence, question the liberal claim to objectivity of the law on epis-temological grounds. The recent origins of postmodernist theory are found in the thinking of Friedrich Nietzsche and Martin Heidegger, but in fact postmodernists reopen an ancient debate that started in the quarrels between the Sophists and Plato about the possibility of objective knowledge and universal values. In its most radical form deconstructionist theory holds that there is no reality outside texts. Words gain their meaning from their difference from other words, which themselves gain their meanings from their difference from yet other words, and so on. This process, Jacques Derrida argued, is one of infinite regression and hence words are 'undecidable' (1981, 280). Therefore, texts themselves lack objective meaning. Less radical language theorists regard language not as a wholly arbitrary system of subjective meanings but as something legitimated by the conventions of a speech community. These theorists argue that the stan-dards of truth and justice are products of specific 'language games', conventions, and shared normative understandings or community practices. Knowledge is not entirely subjective, but contingent. I consider the compatibility of this approach with the liberal notions of law and legality.

Chapter 9 discusses theories of law that explain the law's growth and function from the economic point of view. Until the pioneering work of Ronald Coase, Guido Calabresi, Henry Manne and others, economists paid little attention to law and lawyers tended to disregard the economics of law. Since then, the study of the development and efficiency of common law rules by transaction cost analyses has become widespread. The Coase theorem – that in conditions of zero transaction costs the allocation of rights would not matter, as parties would bargain towards the efficient solution – means, conversely, that in conditions of significant transaction costs the allocation of rights by law is critical from the point of view of social cost and wealth maximisation. These insights led Richard Posner to the theory that the common law, through the process of litigation, trends towards efficient rules. Even if this is the case, the law is often not the result of common law progression, but is the consequence of legislation emerging from the interplay of social and electoral pressures. I follow the discussion of transaction costs theory with explanations of the key ideas and achievements of the public choice theory, produced by economists who engage in micro-economic analyses of democratic decision making processes.

Chapter 10 is a discussion of the neglected but rich tradition of evolutionary theory in jurisprudence, from the 18th century evolutionist thinkers to contemporary institutional theorists. These theories explain the emergence of law in society and the way law is fashioned by the accumulation of social experience. The process of spontaneous order (of which the common law is a prime example) – also known as emergent complexity – has in recent times generated enormous excitement in the disciplines of economics, psychology, artificial intelligence, computer science and mathematics. Scientific insights into emergent complexity are shedding light on the ways in which order (hence, rules) arise out of seemingly chaotic interactions of elements (read 'persons' in the context of law) without the help of a designer (read 'legislator' in the case of law). According to this theory law predates rulers, governments, parliaments and courts, and law continues to be generated by the emerging coincidences of behaviour on the part of individuals pursuing different life aims. This chapter identifies the moments of evolutionary thinking in the classical and medieval periods and traces the systematic development of evolutionary jurisprudence by Matthew Hale, Bernard Mandeville and the 18th century Scottish moral philosophers. The chapter proceeds to examine the later development of this tradition by the Austrian school of economics and the new institutional economists. It concludes by assessing the relevance to jurisprudence of current scientific research into emergent complexity.

Part 4 consists of two chapters on rights and justice. A claim of justice is made not as a plea for compassion or charity but as a matter of right. It may be presented as a legal entitlement or a moral claim, but always as a right. A person who lacks legal rights under a contract because of some technical defect may have a moral claim to performance under it. Labour unions seeking higher wages do so in the name of moral rights. Hence, it is important to consider the concept of a right before discussing justice. In Chapter 11, I discuss the nature of rights and duties using WN Hohfeld's analysis of fundamental legal conceptions and their inter-relations. Hohfeld's system identifies the basic concepts or building blocks without which one cannot construct a sensible legal statement. The system is focused on law but is transferable to moral codes of conduct. I explain the Hohfeldian system of jural relations, and address its subtleties and some refinements proposed by other writers. The system is found to withstand the standard criticisms made against it.

Chapter 12 is on justice. Justice signifies a universally treasured value. No one wishes to be treated unjustly. Hence, a claim made on grounds of justice is a psychologically powerful claim. Yet 'justice' is a spectacularly imprecise term that serves many, often conflicting, causes. Justice may mean justice as virtue, legal justice in the procedural or substantive sense, distributive justice, or political justice. The term is used much too loosely, leading to serious confusion of our normative choices by obscuring the tensions between different conceptions of justice. This chapter is dedicated to explanation of the different conceptions of justice, with a view to providing readers with the theoretical knowledge necessary to engage fruitfully in the great debates about justice. A discussion of Aristotle's system of justice as virtue is followed by sections on legal and distributive justice. The second half of the chapter investigates two distinct theoretical traditions concerning political justice. One is the social contract approach. I discuss the contending theories presented by John Rawls and Robert Nozick within the social contract framework. The other approach is that of the evolutionary tradition in social theory, which originated in the work of the 18th century English and Scottish philosophers. These ideas are explored mainly through the thinking of David Hume and Adam Smith, and I conclude with a discussion of the central normative implications of the evolutionary view.

Old debates and new frontiers

The province of jurisprudence is vast. If jurisprudence is understood as the study of law and justice in all their dimensions, it is not solely the preserve of jurists. Historians, sociologists, anthropologists, economists, philosophers, psychologists and scientists have a great deal to offer to the discipline, as seen from their increasing interest and exciting contributions. Like other branches of intellectual inquiry, jurisprudence represents a process of discovery through observation, careful theorising and vigorous challenge. The phenomenal transformation of the world through the information revolution revives old debates in jurisprudence and opens new frontiers.

The convergence of legal systems and the emergence of new legal orderings as a consequence of globalised markets, the rise of international institutions, the proliferation of new technologies, the discovery of cyberspace and the emergence of new forms of property and of communication are generating new challenges for scholars seeking to explain the nature of law and the processes of legal change. Legal theories need to be reconsidered, and where necessary restated, in the light of these changes. Although the nation state remains strong and its coercive powers to regulate economic and social activity are mostly intact, a large part of the global trade is regulated by norms that originate in usage or in the quasi-legislative activities of international trade associations such as the International Chamber of Commerce. The World Trade Organisation (WTO) is a legislative body with enormous powers, not only over international trade but also indirectly over the structure of domestic economies and political institutions. Some countries need to make structural adjustments having significant social, cultural and political ramifications in order to meet WTO conditions. Numerous free trade agreements also have similar effects on partner nations. International commercial arbitration continues to expand as the principal mechanism for dispute resolution in world trade, with major centres of arbitration now spread across the globe. These factors suggest that the centre of gravity of legal systems is no longer so clearly located in national legislatures.

On the political side, the international human rights regime has been strengthened immeasurably, partly by being linked to global trade and partly by the construction of institutions such as the International Criminal Court. The international community has greater capacity to punish crimes against humanity after they are committed, but appears powerless to halt or pre-empt large scale politically perpetrated human tragedies such as those unfolding in Dafur in Sudan and in Zimbabwe. The so-called responsibility to protect (R2P) has not moved beyond theory.

Some of the most exciting prospects for jurisprudence lie in two new branches of science. One is in evolutionary psychology and cognitive science. These disciplines are shedding light on the psychology of rule following. A fundamental question in jurisprudence remains: why do people observe rules? The simplistic explanation that people obey the law for fear of punishment is long abandoned. Mutual convenience is a better explanation, but it is insufficient because people usually do not stop and calculate convenience before acting. These psychological disciplines hold out prospects of deeper understanding of legal systems. The other branch consists of the work of researchers in many disciplines working collaboratively or intra-disciplinarily to study the phenomenon of emergent complexity. The research in this field is adding to knowledge of complex systems, including the law, by revealing how self-ordering systems emerge and change over time. I outline the prospects that this emerging science holds for jurisprudence, but note that challenging work lies ahead.

PART 1
LAW AS IT IS

2

British Legal Positivism

Legal positivism is the most influential school of thought in jurisprudence. This is hardly surprising, as the idea of law as the creation of a human law giver that lies at its heart is a common intuition. Ask the person on the street whence comes the law, and expect to hear that law is the work of parliaments, monarchs or other rulers. Ask a lawyer what the law is, and anticipate an answer drawn from legislation and judicial precedents. The ancients may have regarded the law as received from divine sources but in the modern world, where most laws have a known human author, people think of law as the product of designing human minds.

British legal positivists regard the law as 'social fact', by which they mean that law is found in the actual practices or the institutions of society. Legal positivists have their significant disagreements but they share the common aim of helping people understand the law *as it actually is*. A survey of positivist writings on the nature of law reveals the following main themes:

1. Law is the creation of human agents. Even custom is not law unless it is recognised and enforced by a human authority.
2. The law *as it is* can be distinguished from notions of what the law *ought to be*. Law is social fact. It is found as rules declared by authorities such as legislatures and courts, or in the actual practices of those who enforce the law.
3. There are good practical reasons for distinguishing the law as it is from what the law ought to be. It will make the law more clear and certain, so that people have a better idea of their rights and duties and the community is better able to assess the worth of laws.

4.   It is possible to identify a set of formal criteria by which we may determine whether or not a rule is a law.

5.   There is no *necessary* connection between law and morality, though many laws are based on moral precepts. A law does not cease to be a law if it fails some moral test which is not in itself a law. The US Bill of Rights imposes several moral tests, but they are binding as law, not morals. A legal system may leave room for judges to introduce their moral standards in deciding controversies. According to legal positivists, that makes no difference to the positive character of the law. The court's judgments will produce law even if they fail our own moral tests. Thus, an immoral law may yet be a law in theory as well as in fact.

I propose to examine the history and theory of British legal positivism through the work of its principal proponents, considered in historical order. But first, it is worth saying something about the philosophical tradition of positivism to which legal positivism is related.

Positivism and logical positivism

Positivism

Positivism, as a philosophical method, is also known as empiricism. Auguste Comte (1798–1857) is regarded by many as the first true positivist. He sought to expel metaphysics (unverified belief systems) from the study of society. Comte argued that we can truly understand the nature and functioning of society only by the scientific method of empirical observation, theory construction and verification. Comte believed that our ways of thinking about the world have evolved through three stages: the theological, metaphysical and scientific (1975 (1830–42), 1, 21). In the beginning, people conceived of the world as divinely ordained. The authority of rulers in such a world is subordinate to divine will. In the metaphysical age that commenced after the French Revolution, the will of God was replaced by notions of natural rights. According to this worldview, people have rights by virtue of being born human, and these rights must not be abrogated by human rulers. Thus, the French philosopher Jean-Jacques Rousseau began his famous book *The Social Contract* with the words 'Man is born free but everywhere is in chains' (1968 (1762), 165). The existence of natural rights, though, is a moral claim that cannot be proved or disproved. In the modern era, many people turn away from metaphysics to find answers to questions by scientific study of the observable world. This is positivism. If you want to know the law concerning murder you try to find the law as it is authoritatively stated, or as it is actually enforced, as opposed to what the law ought to be.

Logical positivism

Logical positivism, also known as logical empiricism, is the philosophical program associated with the Vienna Circle[1] of the 1920s, and later with the British empiricists such as Bertrand Russell and AJ Ayer. Yet the roots of this intellectual tradition may be traced to the thought of the 18th century Scottish philosopher David Hume. Like positivists, logical positivists seek to eliminate metaphysics from knowledge statements. Any statement that cannot be 'verified' is metaphysical, and hence has no cognitive significance.

Nature of scientific knowledge

In his *Enquiries Concerning Human Understanding*, Hume explained the principle of verification thus:

> If we take in our hand any volume; of divinity or school metaphysics, for instance; let us ask, *does it contain any abstract reasoning concerning quantity or number?* No. *Does it contain any experimental reasoning concerning matter of fact and existence?* No. Commit it then to the flames: for it can contain nothing but sophistry and illusion. (1975 (1748), 165)

According to Hume, a statement makes sense only if: (a) it is true in the purely formal or abstract sense; or (b) it reports a fact or scientific law that can be verified by experience or experiment. Hume in this passage was referring to the two forms of scientific knowledge that philosophers today call *analytic* and *synthetic* (as illustrated in Figure 2.1). Analytic knowledge is abstract or formal. Mathematics

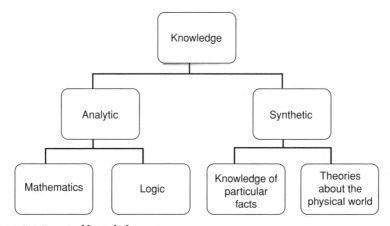

Figure 2.1 Forms of knowledge

---

1 The Vienna Circle was a group of physicists, mathematicians and philosophers who met regularly in Vienna and are considered the principal instigators of this school of thought. They were Moritz Schlick, Rudolf Carnap, Herbert Feigl, Phillip Frank, Kurt Gödel, Hans Hahn, Otto Neurath and Friedrich Waismann.

and logic are its two branches. A statement is true in the analytic sense if it is mathematically or logically correct within a given set of axioms. Take the case of mathematics. The statement $2 + 2 = 4$ is mathematically true whether we are talking of apples or oranges or elephants. The famous Pythagorean theorem that in a right angled triangle the square of the hypotenuse equals the sum of the squares of the remaining sides is mathematically correct according to the axioms of Euclidean geometry. Now consider simple logic. If we assume that all persons seek happiness it is logically correct to say that whoever is a person will seek happiness. The above statements do not convey knowledge of particular facts, but state the logical consequences that flow if certain facts are present.

Synthetic knowledge is of two kinds. It may be knowledge about a particular physical fact, or it may be a theory about cause and effect in the physical world. The statement that I have $10 in my wallet is a statement of particular fact. So is the statement that the Empire State Building is 1250 feet tall. These claims can be proved or disproved. You can count the dollars in my wallet and, with the right instruments, measure the height of the Empire State Building. In contrast, a theory about causation in the physical world cannot be proved but may only be falsified. Hume was the first to notice the problem of verifying statements about cause and effect. Where there is fire there is heat. We come to expect this not by direct proof but by experience. We expect the future to resemble the past not because of prescience but because of experience. We accept certain social practices and rules, not because we can 'verify' them but because experience has shown the value of observing them. Karl Popper in the 20th century made a sustained attack on the verification doctrine of the logical positivists. He said that we cannot prove our scientific theories but can only present them as conjectures or hypotheses. These conjectures we hold to be true until falsified by experience or experiment. The theory that the Sun circled the Earth was considered true from the dawn of the human race until Nicolaus Copernicus published his astronomical observations in 1543. The statement that 'all ravens are black' holds true only until a raven of a different colour is found. Logical positivism, despite these controversies, was a powerful intellectual force that touched all fields of inquiry, including legal theory.

Logical positivists argue that statements such as 'God is omnipotent' cannot be verified. As Rudolf Carnap observed, neither can Heidegger's claim that 'nothing nihilates'. According to the logical positivists, we are free to believe these things, but their inclusion in philosophy and science leads to confusion. Let us consider logical positivism in relation to law. The statement 'The law of England prohibits the smoking of cannabis' is a synthetic statement. It may be verified or refuted by consulting the relevant law books and legal practice. The statement 'If John smokes cannabis, he will break the law' is an analytic statement. Both statements may be verified. In contrast, the proposition 'Cannabis smoking ought to be lawful' cannot be shown to be true or false in a logical or empirical sense. It is simply a person's moral preference.

Legal positivism

Legal positivism bears resemblances to logical positivism, but differs in some ways. Legal positivism aims to identify the law *as it is*. This may seem easy, but is not. First, there is the question: what do we mean by law? The word 'law' (or its vernacular equivalent) has many meanings. We can dismiss immediately the sense in which natural scientists use the term 'law' – as in 'the second law of thermodynamics' or 'Newton's three laws of motion'. Scientific laws are theories about the natural world – why things happen the way they do. The law that concerns us is of a very different kind: namely, law that tells people what they may do, must do or must not do. We may call this 'normative law'.

There are many types of normative law. They include religious laws, moral laws, customary laws and laws of etiquette. Legal positivists offer theories on how we may distinguish law 'in the legal sense' from laws in the non-legal sense. These theories generally attribute the property of law only to those rules that are derived from a law making authority existing as a political or social fact. A rule may be universally observed in a society but will not be a law in the legal positivist's book unless it is made or recognised by established authority. Hart is an exception among legal positivists. He saw no reason to deny the name 'law' to the customary rules observed by primitive societies that had no legislatures or courts or other authority. He called these rules primary rules of obligation. Likewise, Hart regarded international law as law, even though the international community lacks the kind of law making bodies and law enforcement capacities that we expect of national legal systems (1997, Ch. X). He made the obvious observation that developed national legal systems generally display a set of secondary rules that regulate the recognition of primary obligation rules, their modification and their application (1997, 91). These secondary rules authorise certain bodies to make, declare or modify laws, and define their powers and procedures. In common law systems, the secondary rules define the law making powers of the legislatures and confer on the courts the authority to interpret and declare relevant law in particular cases that come before them. The secondary rules may be found in a written constitution or may exist, as in the case of the UK, in the form of custom.

The other major theme in legal positivism is the claim that law has no necessary connection to morality, although often enough the law will express the morality of the people it regulates. As Hart wrote, 'Here we shall take Legal Positivism to mean the simple contention that it is in no sense a necessary truth that laws reproduce or satisfy certain demands of morality, though in fact they have often done so' (1997, 185–6). The Austrian jurist Hans Kelsen (1881–1973) went further in making his case for a science of law. In his *Pure Theory of Law*, Kelsen argued that a legal rule and a moral rule are distinct, though they may often coincide in content. The norm 'Do not kill' is both a moral rule and a legal rule. The moral rule is moral because of its content. It is derived from a higher or more general moral principle. In contrast, the legal rule is legal not owing to its content but 'only because it has been constituted in a particular fashion, born of a definite procedure and a definite rule of law' (Kelsen 1935, 517–18). Conversely, a morally repugnant rule will be a law if it has been made according to the established procedures and criteria of validity.

The morality of a community may enter the law in several ways, but legal positivists insist that in each such case morality has legal force only because a competent authority such as a parliament or a court has converted the moral rule into a legal rule. A legal system may include a moral test of legality. This may be done in several ways. First, the moral principle against which laws must be tested may itself be enacted as a superior constitutional rule. The equal protection clause of the Fourteenth Amendment to the US Constitution commands that 'No State shall . . . deny to any person within its jurisdiction the equal protection of the laws'. Laws that violate this clause are unconstitutional and void. Equal treatment is a moral principle generally accepted in American society. Yet legal positivists treat the equal protection clause as setting a legal (not moral) test, because it is part of the positive law of the United States.

Second, a legal system may authorise a court to dispense justice according to some general notion of morality, without actually laying down specific moral rules that the court must apply. The Roman *praetor* had such power. In the 13th century, the English monarch authorised his principal spiritual advisor, the Chancellor, to grant equitable relief to plaintiffs who petitioned the monarch when justice was denied by courts because of the rigidities of common law forms of action. The Chancellor's sense of equity trumped law. The Chancellor's Court, like the Roman *praetor*, eventually narrowed its wide discretion to a set of self-imposed predictable rules. The legal positivists have no difficulty in regarding equitable rules as law, as they are made by authorised law makers.

Third, the open texture of language leaves judges with a measure of discretion in deciding cases. Many laws are clear and leave little room for judicial interpretation. A law that fixes the age of voting at 18 years or sets the maximum term of parliament as five years is hardly contestable. Most laws, though, are not of this type, but concern rules of conduct. It is not possible to devise a legal rule concerning conduct that resolves all future questions without going into endless detail. Such an infinitely complex law, if it can be written down, will be incomprehensible. This means that legal rules often leave grey areas (penumbras of uncertainty) where judicial discretion plays a decisive role. Legal positivists such as Hart think that in such cases the court acts as a legislator with the authority of parliament.

Legal positivists argue that in each of the above situations, moral standards attain legal status only through some form of official promulgation. This is the famed 'separation thesis' of legal positivism that is ceaselessly debated. In general, legal positivists separate the law from the materials from which the law is built, including morals, customs, folkways and policy (see Figure 2.2).

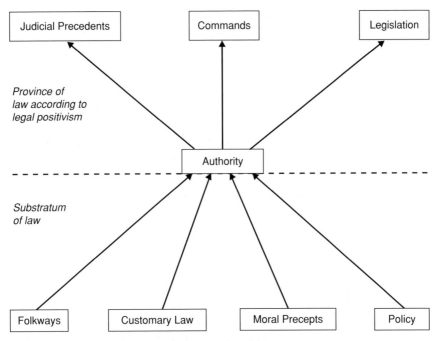

Figure 2.2 **Province of law according to legal positivism**

Scientific, normative and hybrid theories of legal positivism

A scientific theory offers an explanation of some aspect of the physical or cultural world within which we live. It seeks to explain the world as it exists. A scientific theory may be general, in the sense that it is said to be true for all times, places and cultures, or it may be special, in the sense that it holds true in specific conditions. A normative theory, in contrast, is about what ought to be done. Thus, scientific theory is about 'is' and normative theory is about 'ought'. Hobbes, Bentham, Austin and Hart, in my view, represent a hybrid strand of legal positivism. Their work at times suggested that the concept of law has an objective and universal (therefore scientific) meaning that allows law to be separated from other norms, such as social and moral rules that shape human behaviour. They seemed also to propose that, irrespective of scientific validity, societies should, for their own good, embrace the positivist concept of law. They argued that the public interest is served better if society does not confuse law with morality, and accepts as law only those rules and commands that satisfy formal requirements of validity irrespective of moral content. This version does not deny that a particular society may recognise as law only those rules that conform to certain moral standards. Instead, it makes the utilitarian argument that moral tests of legality cause more harm than good because they lead to the uncertainty of the law.

Legal positivism and legal realism

Legal positivism is not the only school of thought within jurisprudence that seeks to separate the law *as it is* from the law *as it ought to be*. Legal realists (whose theories we discuss in Chapter 4) have the same ambition. There is a critical difference, though, between the positivist and realist traditions in legal theory. Positivists define law with reference to formal criteria of legal validity, whereas realists conceive the law as it is actually experienced by people. A positivist will treat the ban on littering the town square as law because it has been enacted by a law making authority designated by the legal system. It does not matter that everybody ignores it and no one is prosecuted. A realist will say that the ban is not law because law enforcers ignore it and it has no practical effect. Hence, the two schools differ radically in the way they identify the law as it is. What they genuinely share is the conviction that there is no necessary connection between law and morality and that a morally repugnant rule can have the force of law.

Modern legal positivists are not intellectual clones of the 17th and 18th century proponents. They have healthy quarrels but agree on three basic premises: (1) law exists as social fact; (2) law is the product of human authority; and (3) there is no necessary connection between law and morality.

In what follows I discuss the history and philosophy of British legal positivism, its modern refinements and the principal criticisms that its central ideas attract.

Thomas Hobbes and *Leviathan*

The idea that the ruler's will is law (*voluntas principis*) recurs throughout the history of Western political thought. It was particularly influential in the 16th and 17th centuries, during which the feudal kingships of western Europe were transformed into absolute monarchies. Monarchs claimed the right to absolute political power by divine right. France's Louis XIV famously declared '*L'état, c'est moi*' (I am the state). The absolutist theories were not about law but about political power. They claimed that the monarch might make law at will. They did not say that customary law and natural law were fictitious, only that the monarch's judgment was final on all questions of law. *Voluntas principis* was more a political claim than an objective description of the phenomenon of law.

We find in the work of Thomas Hobbes (1588–1679) the first clear theory of law based on the notion of sovereign power. Hobbes was a royalist who was dismayed by the destruction wrought by the English Civil War (1642–49) and the arbitrary rule of the Rump Parliament that followed the defeat and execution of Charles I in 1649. The turmoil and chaos of those times convinced Hobbes that only strong central government could secure the safety and wellbeing of the people. Hobbes spent most of the turbulent decade in self-exile in Paris, during which he wrote his greatest work – *Leviathan*, published in 1651. The book remains one of the most powerful justifications of absolute power. Whereas other contemporary defenders of royal absolutism appealed to the divine right to rule, Hobbes made a utilitarian case for recognising an 'uncommanded commander' whose will is law.

Hobbes concluded from his observation of human nature that people will be in perpetual conflict unless they are subject to a supreme political authority. Individuals on the whole have equal strength. ('For as to the strength of body, the weakest has strength enough to kill the strongest, either by secret machination or by confederacy with others that are in the same danger with himself' (Hobbes 1946 (1651), 80). Hence every person will lay claim to everything, including the control of other persons. The result will be war among individuals and hopeless misery. Hobbes, memorably, put it this way:

> Whatsoever therefore is consequent to a time of war, where every man is enemy to every man, the same [is] consequent to the time wherein men live without other security than what their own strength and their own invention shall furnish them withal. In such condition there is no place for industry, because the fruit thereof is uncertain: and consequently no culture of the earth; no navigation, nor use of the commodities that may be imported by sea; no commodious building; no instruments of moving and removing such things as require much force; no knowledge of the face of the earth; no account of time; no arts; no letters; no society; and which is worst of all, continual fear, and danger of violent death; and the life of man, solitary, poor, nasty, brutish, and short. (1946, 82)

We know that the history of humankind was not remotely like this. Many past and present societies have prospered without the protection of absolute rulers. Equally, many societies have been impoverished and destroyed by absolute rule. However, we should mention in Hobbes' defence the following points.

First, Hobbes was right in saying that civilisation is impossible in conditions of perpetual conflict. It is difficult to conceive of humanity flourishing without security of life, liberty and property. This is commonsense that history repeatedly confirms. Second, Hobbes advocated *absolute* power but not *arbitrary* power. He considered absolute power to be the remedy for the arbitrariness of a self-help system. According to Hobbes, 'the end of obedience is protection' and the 'obligation of subjects to the sovereign ... is understood to last as long, and no longer, than the power lasteth by which he [the sovereign] is able to protect them' (1946, 144). Hobbes maintained that the natural right of individuals to protect themselves can never be relinquished by covenant. Although sovereignty is intended to be immortal, 'yet is it in its own nature, not only subject to violent death by foreign war, but also through the ignorance and passions of men it hath in it' (1946, 144). Hobbes here was saying that sovereignty can be destroyed not only by the subjugation of the nation by a foreign power but also by the sovereign's own corruption. Hobbes' sovereign is not necessarily an individual. It could be a group or even an elected parliament. A sovereign (whether one or many), when ruled by passion or ignorance, may govern in its own interests or prove too incompetent to protect the interests of its subjects. Such a sovereign loses its right to obedience. Unfortunately, history shows that Hobbes' confidence that absolute power will deliver safety of life, liberty and property of the individual subjects was seriously misplaced.

Hobbes' theory is conspicuously missing in most discussions of legal positivism. Even Hart's *The Concept of Law* has little to say about Hobbes. Perhaps it is because Hobbes defined the law with a moral purpose in mind. As James Boyle put it, 'Hobbes was shoring up the power of a centralised state by appearing to deduce, from the very definition of law, the need to subordinate all forms of normative authority to the power of the sovereign' (1987, 385). Hobbes argued strenuously that the only effective way for people to escape the misery of their natural condition was by conceding all political power, including a monopoly of law making power, to a supreme commander. Hobbes, unlike later positivists, was not preoccupied with the demonstration of law as scientific fact. For Hobbes, the greater good demanded that people equate the law to the command of the sovereign. Subjects have a moral duty to obey the law so made, except in extreme conditions when a weakened or corrupt sovereign can no longer offer them protection.

Jeremy Bentham: law and the principle of utility

The English jurist and philosopher Jeremy Bentham (1748–1832) is the greatest historical figure in British legal positivism. In *An Introduction to the Principles of Morals and Legislation* Bentham laid the groundwork for a theory of law as the expressed will of a sovereign. (This book first appeared in a private printing in 1780, but was published only in 1789.) Bentham developed this theory in great detail in a sequel entitled *Of Laws in General* (1970a (1782)). This work, though completed in 1782, was only discovered lying among his papers at the University College, London, in 1939, and an authoritative edition of it appeared only in 1970. As Bentham's book collected dust, a work titled *The Province of Jurisprudence Determined* by one of his disciples, John Austin, rose to prominence and became the most influential treatise on legal positivism. The debt that Austin owed to Bentham was enormous, patent and acknowledged. Yet Austin's work in some respects pales in the company of Bentham's two books.

Principles and *Laws* together reveal Bentham's thinking about the law. Bentham, like Hobbes, did not think that law everywhere was regarded as the legislative will of a sovereign. Bentham regarded the term 'law' as a socially constructed fictitious entity. He knew that even in his own country the law, as commonly understood, was found mainly in the form of common law that was not the creation of a political sovereign. He wrote:

Common law, as it styles itself in England, judiciary law as it might aptly be styled every where, that fictitious composition which has no known person for its author, no known assemblage of words for its substance, forms every where the main body of the legal fabric: like that fancied ether, which, in default of sensible matter, fills up the measure of the universe. Shreds and scraps of real law, stuck on upon that imaginary ground, compose the furniture of every national code. What follows? – that he who, for the purpose just mentioned or for any other, wants an example of a complete body of law to refer to, must begin with making one. (Bentham 1970b, 8)

Bentham regarded this authorless, unpromulgated and uncodified body of rules that made up English law as being unworthy of the name 'law'. He dismissed similarly the idea of a higher natural law. He called such law 'an obscure phantom, which, in the imaginations of those who go in chase of it, points sometimes to *manners*, sometimes to *laws*; sometime to what the law *is*, sometimes to what the law *ought* to be' (Bentham 1970b, 298).

Bentham reasoned that a system of law that derives its rules exclusively from the clearly expressed legislative will of a sovereign will produce clearer and more certain laws than the rules generated by the common law system. His preference for legislation was grounded in utilitarian moral philosophy, of which he was a principal instigator. There is no better short statement of this philosophy than Bentham's own memorable words at the beginning of *An Introduction to the Principles of Morals and Legislation*:

Nature has placed mankind under the governance of two sovereign masters, *pain* and *pleasure*. It is for them alone to point out what we ought to do, as well as to determine what we shall do. On the one hand the standard of right and wrong, on the other the chain of cause and effects, are fastened to their throne. They govern us in all we do, in all we say, in all we think: every effort we can make to throw off our subjection, will serve but to demonstrate and confirm it. In words a man may pretend to abjure their empire: but in reality he will remain subject to it all the time. The *principle of utility* recognises this subjection, and assumes it for the foundation of that system, the object of which is to rear the fabric of felicity by the hands of reason and of law. Systems which attempt to question it, deal in sounds instead of sense, in caprice instead of reason, in darkness instead of light. (1970b, 1–2)

Bentham's notion of pleasure included not only carnal pleasures but also the more sublime forms of satisfaction gained from intellectual and spiritual pursuits, noble deeds and self-sacrifice. He drew from this his famous principle of utility, which states that an action ought to be approved or disapproved according to its tendency to increase or diminish the happiness of the party whose interest is in question. Bentham was convinced that a system of law that derives its rules exclusively from the commands of a sovereign authority, when measured by the yardstick of public utility, is superior to the common law system. Whereas the former produces clear, authoritative and certain laws, the latter generates a cumbersome and illogical mass of precedents that serve the interests of lawyers but not of the public. Bentham proposed the codification of all laws.

Bentham's assault on the common law overlooked its virtue as a dynamic, adaptive and natural outgrowth of a people living in relative freedom. He overestimated the capacity of a comprehensive code to supply clear answers to novel controversies that are a permanent feature of our ever changing world. It is possible to argue that comprehensive codification fails Bentham's own test of utility. I will return to these issues in later chapters, but first let us understand Bentham's theory of law and its importance in jurisprudence.

Bentham's definition of law

Bentham offered a detailed definition of a law in Chapter 1 of *Of laws*. It was not a lexical definition in the sense that it described how 'law' was understood by people (especially lawyers) in his time. It was a stipulative definition, stating what he thought ought to be the accepted meaning of 'law'. The definition, though convoluted, was meticulously crafted and avoids some of the defects that taint Austin's later effort. It also anticipated many of the refinements that modern legal positivists introduced. Bentham wrote:

> A law may be defined as an assemblage of signs declarative of a volition conceived or adopted by the *sovereign* in a state, concerning the conduct to be observed in a certain *case* by a certain person or class of persons, who in the case in question are or are supposed to be subject to his power: such volition trusting for its accomplishment to the expectation of certain events which it is intended such declaration should upon occasion be a means of bringing to pass, and the prospect of which it is intended should act as a motive upon those whose conduct is in question. (1970a, 1)

Bentham made his own incredibly laboured elaboration of this definition in *Of laws*. The work is breathtakingly lucid and elegant in some parts and frustratingly dense and complex in other parts. There is much to quarrel with philosophically about Bentham's thesis, but as a technical exposition of the structure, manifestations and operation of the law in the legislative form it has no parallel. We do not have the luxury of engaging with the detail of his analysis, hence must focus on its main features.

Source of law – the sovereign within a state

A law is an expression (assemblage of signs) of the will (volition) of a sovereign within a state. Law in this sense requires a state (political order) that establishes sovereign authority. A society that lacks the superstructure of a state and has no sovereign hence has no law in the sense of Bentham's definition, though it may have law in a different sense. Bentham meant, by 'sovereign', 'any person or assemblage of persons to whose will a whole political community are (no matter what account) supposed to be in a disposition to pay obedience: and that in preference to any other person' (1970a, 18). Thus, the sovereign may be an elected parliament, an oligarchy, or even a tyrant who secures the people's obedience by naked force.

Bentham, unlike Austin later, suggested that the sovereign's power may be limited by 'transcendent laws', by which he meant constitutional rules (1970a, 64). Austin was forthright on this question. The constitutional rules that constrain the sovereign are merely rules of positive morality. Bentham struggled to explain the idea of legally limited sovereignty. He discussed the issue in relation to a sovereign who is an individual. The sovereign prince may set limits on his own power by a royal covenant (*pacta regalia*). A covenant that seeks to bind his successor will only be a 'recommendatory mandate' that becomes covenantal only when adopted by the successor (1970a, 64–5). Bentham recognised the absurdity of a person giving themselves a binding order. I cannot enforce my New Year resolutions except by the power of my own will and good sense. Similarly, the effectiveness of a sovereign's self-command depends on the sovereign's will and good sense. It will be effective as law only if the sovereign is subject to an outside force, such as a superior court with power to invalidate laws – in which event the sovereign is not sovereign. Bentham says that a sovereign's self-imposed limitations are enforced only by force of religious or moral sanctions. These forces are no match for the political will of the sovereign (1970a, 70).

The will of the sovereign

The content of the law may be established by the sovereign by *conception* or by *adoption* (Bentham 1970a, 21). Conception is where the substance of the law is conceived by the sovereign itself, as when the Queen in Parliament enacts a statute that lays down a new rule of conduct. Adoption is where the sovereign confers validity on a rule made by another person. This may happen in one of two ways. First, the sovereign may adopt laws already in existence and made by other persons. Bentham called this 'susception'. Thus, sovereigns may adopt the laws created by their predecessors, thereby providing for the continuity of the legal system. Second, sovereigns may declare that they will adopt laws made in the future by another person. This is 'pre-adoption'. What we call delegated legislation today falls within this category. This is the case where an Act of Parliament authorises an official to make laws and bestows validity upon them. Such an official, in Bentham's language, has the power of 'imperation' (1970a, 22).

Not every expression of sovereign will generates law as it is commonly understood. Sovereign will becomes law only when it takes the legislative form. Thus, administrative orders, military commands and judicial decisions, in Bentham's view, are not laws. Bentham thought that in the case of Britain the will of the sovereign always takes the legislative form. The British sovereign is a corporate body comprising the Crown, the Lords and the Commons. He observed: 'it would be hardly possible for that complex body to issue any order the issuing of which would not be looked upon as an act of legislation' (1970a, 5). Thus, the Crown in

Parliament was making law even when it enacted the bill of attainder that condemned the Earl of Stafford to death and when it exiled the Earl of Clarendon. In contrast, Bentham regarded a royal decree of the absolute monarch of France, to banish a citizen or to send him to the Bastille, not as an act of legislation but as a judicial act or a preventive order of the executive. Why did Bentham think that the former were legislation but not the latter, even though the two sovereigns had the same extent of power and the orders were indistinguishable in content? He stated that such *lettres de cachet* were not regarded in France as legislation but as *ordres souverains* (sovereign orders) (1970a, 6). If so, what counts as legislation (and hence as law by Bentham's definition) depends not on the nature of the act but on local usage and understanding as to what constitutes a legislative act. Here again, Bentham conceded that his definition of law was not universally valid but was stipulative.

Subjects and objects of a law

A law is about conduct – what a person or class of persons may do, must do or must not do in given circumstances. A statement that does not impose a duty on a person or confer a liberty is not a law. According to Bentham, generality is not a necessary quality of a law. Subjects of the law are the persons to whom the law is directed. A law may be directed at a single person, commanding that person to do or not do a specified act (1970a, 34, 77–80). A law has effect only on persons who are subject to the sovereign's power. Thus, the law of England will not control the French sovereign or his subjects.

The objects of a law are the acts or forbearances that the sovereign aims to secure by enacting the law. If a law states 'No trader shall export wheat in a foreign owned vessel', the subjects of this law are traders and its object is to ensure that exported wheat is only carried by vessels owned by nationals.

Forms of law

Bentham, unlike John Austin much later, did not commit the error of identifying law exclusively with the commands to do or not do something. Hence, he identified law with *mandates*. He was aware that many enactments do no more than declare or clarify the law and that some laws actually grant persons freedom to do as they please. Law, in its most commonly known sense, is made up of mandates. Mandates include commands and prohibitions as well as non-commands and permissions (Bentham 1970a, 16, 97–98). Bentham made a painstaking classification of the different kinds of mandates that may issue from the sovereign. I explore this taxonomy in Chapter 11.

Parts of a law

Bentham observed that a law is different from the statutory instruments such as Acts of Parliament that create law. Take, for example, the law prohibiting murder in the State of Queensland. Section 291 of the *Criminal Code* prohibits unlawful killing unless it is authorised, justified or excused by law. Authorisations, justifications and excuses for killing are found in other parts of the Code and in other laws. Section 302 sets out the circumstances when killing is murder. Section 305 prescribes life imprisonment for murder. The *Supreme Court Act* empowers the Supreme Court to conduct trials of persons charged with murder. Thus, the law prohibiting murder is made up of provisions in many statutes. The law draws its components from several different statutes.

Bentham's contempt for the common law

Bentham's definition of law is stipulative. It identifies law exclusively with legislation enacted by a sovereign, although by his own admission that was not the common understanding of his time. Bentham embraced this definition for the utilitarian reason that it would produce greater happiness of the greater number.

Bentham argued that customary law and the common law lacked the 'signs of law'. A law, in Bentham's view, is known beforehand. It must set a standard by which conduct of people can be judged by courts to be legal or illegal. Adjudication is primarily a process of deduction from established law and found facts. Bentham saw in customary and common law the opposite process. The court determines whether an act is legal or illegal and people infer a rule of conduct from the court's decision. The rule is drawn inductively from the observation of what courts actually do. The law in its legislative form applies generally, whereas a judicial order binds only the parties. Bentham concluded that customary laws 'are nothing but so many autocratic acts or orders, which in virtue of the more extensive interpretation which the people are disposed to put upon them, have somewhat of the effect of general laws' (1970a, 158). He likened the common law process to the old Turkish practice of hanging a baker who was caught selling under-weight bread. The silent act of hanging had the desired effect on cheats. Bentham wrote: 'Written law is the law for civilised nations; traditionary law, for barbarians; customary law, for brutes' (1970a, 159).

Bentham was conscious that customary law and common law cannot be eliminated from a legal system without the comprehensive codification of all branches of the law. He pursued the cause of codification with passion and industry, producing three major works on the subject: *Papers relative to codification and public instruction* (1817), *Codification proposal, addressed to all nations professing liberal opinions* (1822–30) and *First lines of a proposed code of law for any nation compleat and rationalised* (1820–22). These have recently been consolidated in one volume (Bentham 1998).

History shows that Bentham failed in his mission, within his own country and in other parts of the English-speaking world. Bentham did not inspire the codes of civil law countries, as they pre-dated his writings. The civil law codes have their origins in the French Civil Code (*Code civil des Français*) enacted by Napoleon I in 1804. The failure of the codification movement in England is not surprising. Bentham misconceived the nature of English common law. Common law, contrary to Bentham's hyperbole, provided guidance for conduct for both the people and the courts. The common law courts did not create the common law willy-nilly. In the large majority of cases, the courts enforced a known rule, articulated in precedents and followed in practice by most people. The common law possessed a virtue that Bentham simply failed to notice. It was the capacity for incremental legal change to reflect social evolution – something that a legislative process riddled with factional conflict lacks. In England, the common law was regarded not just as law but as a system of law that was the product of English genius. On Bentham's own greatest happiness principle, the English common law has done rather well in upholding the legitimate expectations of the people.

John Austin's command theory of law

In 1832, 50 years after Bentham's *Of Laws in General* was completed, John Austin published *The Province of Jurisprudence Determined* (1995 (1832)). In 1819 Austin moved to London from Suffolk with his family and became a neighbour of Bentham and James Mill, the pioneers of utilitarianism. He became a close friend of Bentham, whose thinking shaped his jurisprudence. *Province of Jurisprudence* contains the first 10 of the series of lectures on jurisprudence that Austin delivered at the University of London from 1829 to 1833. The lectures were not popular and had to be discontinued because of falling attendance. The published version, though, became the most influential text in English jurisprudence for more than 100 years.

Austin, like Hobbes and Bentham before him, embraced the idea of law as sovereign command. Like Bentham, he acknowledged that the term 'law' means different things to different people, but he argued that we would all be better off if we learned to distinguish between different kinds of laws. Austin was by no means Bentham's intellectual clone and we must note the important differences between them. Austin's work came under the most searching scrutiny in the latter part of the 20th century. His theory of law was dissected and heavily criticised by scholars within and outside the legal positivist tradition. Many of the criticisms are well made but it is evident that even the sternest critics, Hart and Kelsen, owed significant debts to Austin in their own work.

Austin's utilitarianism

The principle of utility was, for Bentham, the only basis of moral judgment. Bentham's moral theory was wholly materialistic. He argued that God's will is unknowable and what can be gathered from the scriptures is only 'that which is presumed to be his will on account of the conformity of its dictates to those of some other principle' (1970b, 31). Thus, Bentham rejected the notion that the scriptures were a source of law. Conversely, Austin regarded the law of God as revealed in the scriptures to be a primary source of moral rules. He accorded to these laws the status of 'laws properly so called' (1995, 38). Austin thought, as Aquinas did, that there is a part of the law of God that is unrevealed and must be discovered through reason. As God wills the greatest happiness of all his creatures, reason leads us to the principle of utility. Austin wrote: 'From the probable effects of our actions on the greatest happiness of all, or from the tendencies of human actions to increase or diminish that aggregate, we may infer the laws which he has given, but has not expressed or revealed' (1995, 41). Austin devoted his Fourth Lecture to the defence of his thesis that utility is the index to the discovery of divine pleasure.

Austin, like Bentham, reasoned that aggregate happiness is served by identifying the law with sovereign will. However, he was unwilling to exclude from the category of 'law' the moral dictates of the scriptures. Hence, he created a sub-set of 'laws properly so called' – named 'positive law' – to signify laws made by the sovereign and its delegates. Positive law, Austin determined arbitrarily, is the only concern of jurisprudence. Positive law or 'the law simply and strictly so called' is the 'law set by political superiors to political inferiors' (Austin 1995, 18). The revealed law of God is the subject of theology.

Austin, unlike Kelsen later, did not set up a science of law that banished the history, philosophy and sociology of law to other disciplines. However, in limiting its province to sovereign law he sought, unsuccessfully, to remove from jurisprudence the study of customary law, international law and natural law.

Austin's respect for the common law

Austin's other major disagreement with Bentham concerned the role and worth of the common law. He did not share Bentham's disdain for the common law, although he agreed with Bentham that judges are the mere agents of the sovereign, authorised to adjudicate disputes and to supply a rule where one is needed. In Bentham's ideal world the law is fully codified and the courts have no role in legal development. Austin's utilitarianism led him to the opposite conclusion: that judicial law making is not only inevitable but is also an unambiguous public good. His complaint about the judiciary was not that they legislated but that they legislated too cautiously. In his pointed criticism of Bentham, Austin wrote:

> I cannot understand how any person who has considered the subject can suppose that society could possibly go on if judges had not legislated, or that there is any danger whatsoever in allowing that power which they have in fact exercised, to make up for the negligence or the incapacity of the avowed legislator. That part of the law of every country which was made by judges has been far better made than that part which consists of statutes enacted by the legislature. (1995, 163)

Austin rightly rejected the robotic view of the judicial function. The world is simply too complex and dynamic for the law to be exclusively the product of a legislature whose members are preoccupied with immediate affairs of state and electoral politics. Questions arise in courts before legislatures are seized of them, and judges cannot refuse to judge for want of legislative direction. Moreover, as discussed presently, the language by which statutes lay down the law is open-textured and their application in cases at the margins (penumbral cases) depends on judicial choice. Only legislation of infinite and self-defeating complexity can possibly create a robotic judge. Even in civil law systems, where the law is extensively codified and the Code is pre-eminent, there is a need for judicially established principles (*jurisprudence constante*). The more important question concerns the limits of judicial discretion. Judges cannot legislate at will without destroying public confidence in the courts, and thereby their political and moral authority. Courts that defeat legitimate expectations of litigants, formed in reliance on legislation, common law and custom, are unlikely to retain the fidelity of the community that they are meant to serve. I return to this issue at many points in this book.

Austin's taxonomy

Austin sought to isolate what he thought was the proper subject of jurisprudence through painstaking classification of all that answers to the name 'law'. This includes – in addition to the laws of the political sovereign – divine law, moral laws, customary laws, laws of private associations, laws of households, and international law. Only some of these, according to Austin, are 'laws properly so called'. The criterion for a law to be 'properly so called' is that it derives from authority. The others are laws by analogy – laws only in the figurative sense. They resemble proper laws to varying degrees but are merely the opinions of persons as to what ought or ought not to be done.

Laws properly so called and positive law

Proper laws derive from authority, and there are two kinds of authority in Austin's legal universe: the authority of the Christian scriptures and the authority of the political superior. The scriptures are the source of the divine law – that which is set by God for his creatures. The political superior is the direct or circuitous source of human law properly so called, which Austin termed 'positive law'. Austin excluded the unrevealed part of the law of God from the class of laws properly so called, because it is founded on opinion and not text. He was not troubled by the fact that the meaning of scriptures is also often a matter of opinion that historically has divided the faithful. Austin considered the positive law to be the exclusive concern of jurisprudence, and the laws of God as the subject of theology (1995, 109).

As already mentioned, the common law, according to Austin, is law made by sovereigns through their delegates, the judges. Sovereign commands may be express or tacit. Sovereigns can change the common law at will but often allow it to stand during their pleasure. Austin wrote: 'Now when customs are turned into legal rules by decisions of subject judges, the legal rules which emerge from the customs are tacit commands of the sovereign legislature' (1995, 36). Elsewhere he stated that the sovereign is 'the author of the measureless system of judge-made rules of law, or rules of law made in the judicial manner, which has been established covertly by subordinate tribunals as directly exercising their judicial functions' (1995, 199). I discuss the fictional nature of this proposition later.

In his Fifth Lecture, Austin introduced a further subdivision of positive law. He distinguished laws set directly by the political superior or sovereign from laws set by private citizens in pursuance of their legal rights. The laws set directly by the sovereign include laws made by authorised officials or 'subordinate political superiors' such as ministers, judges and other agents of the state. As to laws made by private citizens in pursuance of their legal rights, Austin gave the examples of rules made by guardians for their wards and by slave owners for their slaves. The provisions in the will of a testator and the rules of a corporation would also be of this kind. The testator and the corporation are not agents of the state. However, since all legal rights are established by laws of the sovereign, the ultimate source of these private laws remains the sovereign. Austin's legal universe takes roughly the form shown in Figure 2.3.

Laws improperly so called

In Austin's theory, not all norms are proper laws, but only those that have been authoritatively established by God or by the sovereign. There are many kinds of law improperly so called. The common denominator of this class is that they are based on opinion and not authority. They resemble proper laws to varying degrees. Austin made a broad distinction within laws improperly so called. Some of them resemble proper laws closely and are called laws with reason. Others are only remotely analogous and are called law by 'caprice of the fancy' (Austin 1995, 108). They are laws only in the figurative sense. Austin termed the former 'laws by analogy' and the latter 'laws by metaphor'.

The kind most remote from proper law are the laws of science, which in Austin's lexicon are laws by metaphor. They do not command anything to be done or not done, but predict the effects of physical causes (Austin 1995, 149). They are called laws because they resemble proper laws whose commands usually are obeyed. (It should be mentioned that scientists take the opposite view: that their laws are the true laws as they predict cause and effect with certainty, whereas the laws of the legal system are imitations as their consequences are less certain.)

Laws by analogy are, in Austin's taxonomy, not law but positive morality. This class includes non-obligatory rules of social etiquette, household rules and moral rules. It also encompasses customary law, international law and constitutional

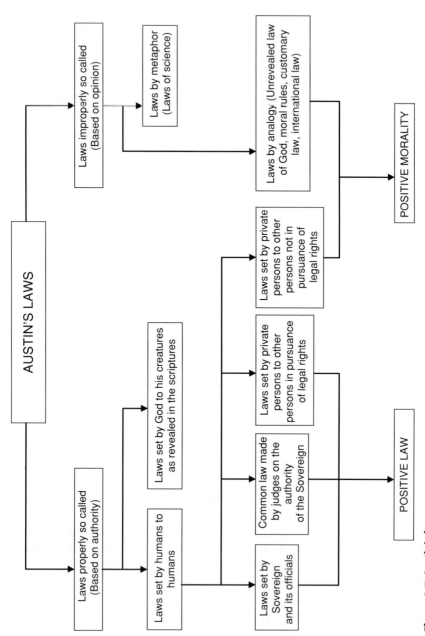

Figure 2.3 Austin's laws

law, which are considered to be binding according to general opinion. Austin recognised that customary law comprises rules that are spontaneously adopted by a community whose members live by them, and that their effect may be identical to that of positive law. Yet these rules do not fit within his category of 'laws properly so called', because they derive their force not from sovereign or divine command and sanction but from opinion and fear of social disapproval. Hence, they remain positive morality until transformed into legal rules by legislation or judicial recognition.

The law of nations (international law) is consigned to positive morality, as it does not flow from the will of a sovereign but 'consists of opinions and sentiments current among nations' (Austin 1995, 124). Austin thought that the great pioneers in international law such as Hugo Grotius and Samuel von Pufendorf confused the practice of nations (positive international morality) with their own ideal of a law of nations (1995, 160). What about treaties by which nations accept obligations towards other nations? These obligations depend once again on a custom – that treaties should be honoured in good faith (*pacta sunt servanda*).

The stipulative nature of Austin's taxonomy is palpable when we consider the role of customary law. Sometimes a custom is so useful and valued in society that it demands recognition as positive law. Sometimes a custom that has outlived its social utility may be so entrenched that it can only be extinguished by positive law. Austin acknowledged that a customary law (whether domestic or international) may have the same practical effect as a positive sovereign law (1995, 125–6). But in his legal universe it is not positive law, because it does not flow from the will of a determinate sovereign. No political sovereign, no law. Hence, international law, in Austin's lexicon, can become positive law only under a global empire whose rulers command the obedience of all subordinate states.

Austin's positive law

Positive law, according to Austin, comprises the commands of a political sovereign supported by sanctions on those who disobey. There are three key elements of this concept of law: (1) a political sovereign, (2) command, and (3) sanction. In Austin's theory a society that does not have a political sovereign does not have law in the strict sense of positive law. It will have what Austin termed 'laws improperly so called' or positive morality. Austin regarded the political sovereign as a necessary feature of an independent political society. Where there is no sovereign, there is no independent political society, and *vice versa*. Later positivists have found all these elements wanting, in reason and fact.

Sovereign
Austin wrote:

> Or the notions of sovereignty and independent political society may be expressed
> concisely thus. – If a determinate human superior, not in a habit of obedience to a like

superior, receive habitual obedience from the *bulk* of a given society, that determinate superior is sovereign in that society, and the society (including the superior) is a society political and independent. (1995, 166)

According to this description a sovereign possesses five essential attributes.

1. The sovereign is a determinate human superior

The sovereign, according to Austin, is a determinate human superior. It may consist of a single person, as in an absolute monarchy, or a group of persons, such as the Crown, Lords and Commons in the United Kingdom. In every case, one or many, the persons who make up the sovereign must be identifiable. This is one of the main reasons for Austin's view that customary law is not positive law. Customary law is the product of generally held opinion of an indeterminate community of persons. The persons who create customary law and the persons who are obliged by customary law are to a large extent the same individuals.

The sovereign must not only be determinate, it must be human. The law of God as revealed in the scriptures, according to Austin, is law properly so called but is not positive law, as it is not promulgated by a human superior.

2. The bulk of the people habitually obey the sovereign

This is common sense. It is an indispensable condition of a stable and functioning society that its rules are observed by most of the members most of the time. Widespread disobedience of the law usually means that political authority and the legal system have become ineffective. Such a state, according to Austin, is the state of nature. What is the position when the society is torn by civil war? Austin's answer is simple. If each warring section of the society habitually obeys its own separate political superior, the original society is no longer one but two independent societies. This is usually the case during secessionist wars where a region asserts its independence from the rest of the country. During the American Civil War (1861–65) the United States divided into two nations – the Union and the Confederacy. If, during civil strife, no person or body commands habitual obedience of any part of the country, there is a state of nature or anarchy (Austin 1995, 169). This is likely to happen when there is an attempt to overthrow a legal regime by violence and a struggle for supremacy follows. There is no Austinian positive law until the supremacy of one faction or the other is established.

3. The sovereign is not in the habit of obedience to any other human superior

The monarch of a kingdom within an empire, or the government of a state or province within a federation, will not be sovereign, according to Austin's definition, because its authority is subject to the will of a superior. Bentham did not insist on this element.

4. The sovereign's power cannot be legally limited

It cannot be limited by positive law, although it may be constrained by positive morality. Austin maintained that constitutional rules are rules of positive morality that the sovereign may disregard. He thought that a legally limited sovereign was a contradiction in terms. His sovereign, by definition, has no superior. If a sovereign's power is limitable it is because there is a superior power that can impose limits. In that case the superior power is the real sovereign. Yet we know that political authority in some countries is effectively limited by constitutional provisions enforced in a variety of ways, including judicial review by courts having power to invalidate unconstitutional acts of the legislature and the executive. As Herbert Hart pointed out in his blistering criticism of the command theory of law, even the British sovereign (the Crown in Parliament) is constituted by the law, including the law of royal succession. Law is thus prior to sovereignty (Hart 1997, 54). The sovereign of the United Kingdom, the Crown in Parliament, has reconstituted itself on a number of occasions, most recently by the *House of Lords Act 1999*. Each change was brought about by an Act of Parliament that was enacted according to the existing law. Hart's point is that the search for a legally unlimited sovereign is doomed.

Austin also asserted that a sovereign cannot place legal limitations on itself or its successors. Any such limitation is merely a recommended principle or maxim (Austin 1995, 213). A sovereign, as defined by Austin, may abrogate or disregard any self-imposed limitation. If the limitation is binding, then the sovereign is not the sovereign but some other superior by whose will it is binding. This is a much more interesting question in constitutional law and theory.

In the 19th century, the British Parliament enacted the Constitution Acts that created a legislature in each of the Australian colonies. The legislatures were given power to make law generally for the peace, order and good government of the colonies. They were not sovereign legislatures, as they remained subject to the laws of the Imperial Parliament. In 1865 the Imperial Parliament enacted the *Colonial Laws Validity Act*. Section 5 of that Act allowed the colonial legislatures a measure of power to impose procedural limitations in relation to a defined class of laws. Yet highly respected judicial opinions in Australia have asserted that, irrespective of the 1865 Act, the power to make law generally includes the power to diminish that power (*Attorney-General (NSW) v Trethowan* (1931) 44 CLR 394 at 418, 428; *Clayton v Heffron* (1960) 105 CLR 214 at 250). The ultimate test of this theory must be in relation to the British sovereign, the Crown in Parliament, which is the epitome of the Austinian sovereign if ever there was one. Can the Crown in Parliament limit its own power or reconstitute itself?

The question arose in *Jackson v HM Attorney-General (Fox Hunting Case)* [2005] 3 WLR 733. Lord Steyn and Baroness Hale of Richmond answered in the affirmative. The facts were as follows. The Crown, Lords and Commons acting as Crown in Parliament passed the *Parliament Act 1911*, which removed the power of the House of Lords to reject money bills and reduced its power to reject other bills. Under this Act, the House of Lords could delay general legislation for two years, after which the Crown and the House of Commons (Crown in Commons) might enact the bill without the Lords' consent. In other words, Parliament was redefined as Crown in Commons for certain purposes. This is impossible in Austinian theory, unless Crown in Commons is regarded as a subordinate agent of Crown in Parliament. In 1949, Crown in Commons acting under the 1911 Act enacted the *Parliament Act 1949* to reduce further the power of the Lords. The *Parliament Act 1949* thus amended the *Parliament Act 1911*. According to the 1949 Act, the Lords' competence to resist a bill ended after one year. The *Hunting Act 2004* (which banned fox hunting with hounds) was passed by the Crown in Parliament under the procedure set by the *Parliament Act 1949*, against the wishes of the Lords. If the 1949 Act was invalid, so too would be the *Hunting Act 2004*. The appellants, who were a group of fox hunters, argued, as Austin would have, that the Crown in Commons was a subordinate body created by the sovereign, which is the Crown in Parliament, and that the 1911 Act could only have been amended by the triumvirate of Crown, Lords and Commons. The argument failed. During the course of his judgment Lord Steyn stated:

> But apart from the traditional method of law making, Parliament acting as ordinarily constituted may functionally redistribute legislative power in different ways. For example, Parliament could for specific purposes provide for a two-thirds majority in the House of Commons and the House of Lords. This would involve a redefinition of Parliament for a specific purpose. Such redefinition could not be disregarded. (761)

Baroness Hale of Richmond agreed, saying that '[if] Parliament can do anything, there is no reason why Parliament should not decide to re-design itself, either in general or for a particular purpose' (783).

How would Austin respond if he was with us? He might say that the judges simply got it wrong, since the sovereign cannot legally limit its power by reconstituting itself, or otherwise. Alternatively, he might say that the true sovereign, the Crown in Parliament, remains sovereign because it can repeal the 1949 Act. If this is not possible, he might argue that the judiciary, the Commons and Crown colluded to perpetrate a political revolution by which Crown in Commons was installed as the political superior. This was a key argument that the Attorney-General advanced in defence of the 1949 Act. Three of their Lordships conceded as much when they observed that the validity of the 1949 Act had been politically accepted by all parties for more than half a century (Lord Bingham of Cornhill at 750; Lord Nicholls of Birkenhead at 757; Lord Hope of Craighead at 773). Revolution or not, the decision has confirmed that the *Parliament Act 1949* is binding on the Crown in Parliament, the alleged sovereign of Britain.

5. Sovereignty is indivisible

The final attribute of Austin's sovereign is indivisibility: according to him, the notion of a divided sovereign is absurd. However, in many modern states power is divided among the legislative, executive and judicial branches of government.

Power is also divided territorially in the case of federations. There is much overlap and power sharing among the branches, and under the constitutions of many countries no one branch appears supreme. But not so in Austin's view. In Austinian theory judicial and executive actions are simply different ways of executing sovereign commands. Officials and judges are mere delegates or ministers of the ultimate law making body, the legislature. This is not the reality in countries where there are written constitutions and where courts have full powers of judicial review. The United States Supreme Court can and does invalidate federal or state law that in its opinion offends the Constitution. This does not make the Supreme Court the political superior. The Supreme Court cannot assert its power of review except on the application of a person with standing. Congress and the Executive can also interpret the Supreme Court's rulings. The system is one of political checks and balances, and it is hard to see an Austinian sovereign in the United States.

What of federations, where power is distributed between a central government and regional units and neither the regions nor the centre is the political superior? It is silly to suggest that great federations like the United States, Australia, Canada, Germany and Switzerland are for this reason lawless. Austin was seized of this problem, but could offer only a weak, though clever, response. The regional units and the federal government, Austin claimed, are jointly sovereign in each and every unit and in the federation (1995, 206). A regional unit is simultaneously a part of the sovereign (aggregate) body and a subordinate entity that is a delegate or minister of the federation. The will of the aggregate body is determined according to the federal compact and enforced by the courts of the units and the federal state. This is a painful fictionalisation of the actual workings of a federation such as the United States or the Commonwealth of Australia. Austin was saying that in a federation the sovereign is the constituent body, the body competent to change the constitution. If so, a federal sovereign rarely speaks, and when it does it speaks only about the constitutional compact. It is far more sensible to say that there is no Austinian sovereign at all in such federations, as the centre and the regions are without exception limited by the constitutional demarcation of powers. The dismissal of constitutional limitations as positive morality is another illustration of the stipulative nature of Austin's taxonomy.

The problem of the sovereign in representative democracy

Representative democracy complicates the task of identifying the sovereign. In some countries the legislators and ministers of state are directly or indirectly elected by enfranchised members of the society. In Austin's own country, England, the sovereign is the Crown in Parliament (Monarch, the Lords and Commons). The House of Commons is elected by those who have the right to vote at general elections. So are they part of the sovereign? Austin thought so. The members of the House of Commons are the delegates of those who elect them. Austin wrote: 'speaking accurately, the members of the commons' house are merely trustees for the body by which they are elected and appointed: and consequently, the sovereignty always resides in the king and the peers, with the electoral body of the commons' (1995, 194). Here is the problem. According to Austin, the sovereign cannot be both the commander and the commanded. If the sovereign is in the habit of obedience to the electorate, it is not the sovereign. At any rate, the electorate is the master of the most powerful component of the Crown in Parliament, the House of Commons, and thereby also installs the executive. Who, then, is the sovereign? It cannot be the electorate, as the electorate is the creature of Parliament, which has power to enfranchise or disenfranchise people. Our search for the sovereign in representative democracy ends in hopeless circularity.

Command, duty, sanction

Positive law, according to Austin, is produced by a sovereign's command. A command is not a request but an imperative that creates a duty by the presence of a sanction. A command involves: (1) a wish or desire conceived by a rational being that another rational being shall do or forbear; (2) an evil in case of non-compliance; and (3) intimation of the wish by words or other signs (Austin 1995, 24). A command cannot be separated from duty and sanction. They are aspects of a single event. Where there is a duty there is a command, and where there is a command there is a duty. In each case the duty arises from the existence of a sanction for breach.

Laws producing commands may be general, in the sense that they constitute rules of conduct applying to classes of persons or events. The rules of criminal law are general commands. They are impersonal and are not directed to particular individuals. Commands may also be occasional or particular. A command by which an individual's property is appropriated to the state is a particular command. In each case the command creates positive law.

Austin noted three kinds of commonly termed laws that are not imperative. These are not laws properly so called, but may be justifiably included within jurisprudence. (1) Declaratory laws do not create new duties but clarify or interpret existing legal relations. Austin conceded that imperative rules may be enacted under the guise of a declaration. (2) Laws to repeal law are not imperative commands. It should be noted that the repeal of some laws may create new duties or revive old ones. The repeal of a law exempting some part of a person's income from tax creates a liability to the tax. (3) Laws of imperfect obligation lay down rules without attaching a sanction for their breach (Austin 1995, 31–2). The statutory duty of the city council to keep the streets clean will fall within this category. It must be noted that laws that create rights and liberties in individuals are imperative, and hence, by Austin's definition, are laws properly so called. They are imperative because they create correlative duties on the part of another. Thus, a law that grants me the liberty to drive my car brings about a whole range of duties on the part of others to respect my liberty.

Law and morality

Austin distinguished positive law from positive morality. Positive morality is an aspect of morality generally. It is moral to be kind to fellow beings, to practise temperance, to give to charity and generally to be virtuous. These are moral *values* but not moral *rules*. In Austin's system, positive morality is made up of moral rules that resemble positive law. In every society, though, there are moral rules derived from moral values. Many rules of positive morality are co-extensive with rules of positive law. Rules against murder, rape, robbery, theft, and cheating are just a few obvious examples. What happens when a rule of positive law offends a rule of positive morality? We can give a legal answer or a political answer. In Austin's view, the legal answer is that positive law prevails. The political answer depends on how the conflict plays out in society. There are occasions when a rule of positive law is so obnoxious to the moral sense of the society that its enforcement is successfully resisted. In such instances the rule remains legally valid but is without practical effect.

Austin, unlike Bentham, was a man of faith and steadfastly maintained that the sovereign is bound to obey the divine law. This, though, is a moral duty and if the sovereign legislates against divine law it will nevertheless be law. Austin wrote: 'Now to say that human laws which conflict with the Divine law are not binding, that is to say, are not laws, is to talk stark nonsense' (1995, 158). Any other view is not only wrong but pernicious, as it can lead to anarchy (1995, 159).

Austin's achievement

Austin provided a taxonomy of things commonly called laws, and offered a definition of positive law as the true subject of jurisprudence. He gave no valid reason for so limiting the province of jurisprudence. In fact, his own *Lectures on Jurisprudence* was a treatise on the nature of all types of laws, including the law of God, customary law and international law. Despite the stipulative and often arbitrary nature of his definitions and classification, Austin's system sheds a great deal of light on the legal universe. The inaccuracies of his system are manifest and manifold and his casuistry is patent. But he presented a comprehensible model that offered 20th century legal positivists a clear set of ideas to adopt, criticise and refine.

Austin's theory, like those of Hobbes and Bentham, is ultimately a thesis in utilitarian moral philosophy. The utilitarian case for the rigid separation of law and morality rests on the belief that the object of knowing and improving the law is impeded by denying that bad laws are laws. Austin, like Bentham, sought to demystify the law, to make it more clear, certain and comprehensible. His contribution to this cause is undeniable. Austin was more insightful than Bentham in some respects. His recognition of the worth of judicial law making is an example. Austin consigned constitutional law, customary law and international law to the category of positive morality, but acknowledged their regulative force.

In Austin's scheme many rules of positive morality are the equals of positive law. So, does the name matter? As Shakespeare's Juliet said,

> What's in a name? that which we call a rose
> By any other name would smell as sweet . . .

Herbert Hart's new beginning: the burial of the command concept of law

Herbert Lionel Adolphus Hart (1907–92) was Professor of Jurisprudence at the University of Oxford from 1952 to 1969. His work, particularly *The Concept of Law*, dominated British jurisprudence in the final decades of the 20th century. Legal positivism's critics were mostly those outside that tradition, until Hart arrived. Hart sought to rescue legal positivism from the factual and conceptual traps into which Bentham and Austin had led it. Like Bentham and Austin, Hart was a utilitarian in philosophical outlook, and like them he saw public benefit in separating law from rules of other kinds. But unlike Austin and Bentham, he realised that this cannot be done by identifying law exclusively with the commands of a sovereign. To do so is seriously to misunderstand the nature of law and the legal system. The command theory does not account for all the different kinds of rules that we justifiably call law.

The first part of Hart's book is a sustained criticism of the command theory. The command theory is premised on the existence of a sovereign commander whose power is unlimited and cannot be legally limited. Hart argued, correctly, that in many legal systems, including that of Britain, there is no such sovereign. The British sovereign is a creation of law, including the rules of royal succession. It is practically unreasonable to say that these rules are rules of morality but not law. The idea of law as a command that people obey because of the threat of sanction misses an important quality of law – the reflective acceptance of the law as binding by the people to whom it is directed. A person may compel another to obey a command by threatening evil, as when a robber demands my wallet by threatening to shoot me. But the robber is not making law but violating the law. Bentham and Austin would have agreed that the robber's command is not law because the robber is not the sovereign. Hart's answer is that a sovereign is no different from a robber if people obey their commands solely due to fear of sanction. It is misleading to understand law in this way.

Hart called his theory a version of soft positivism. It is 'soft' in two ways. First, it accepts that law may exist in society as a matter of practice and observance, even if it is not officially declared to be law. This is the practice thesis. Second, it accepts that the legal system may permit a court to apply a moral standard in resolving a case before it. This does not mean that morality trumps law, but only that the rules of recognition in the legal system allow the court discretion to take morality into account in identifying the law or in creating new law.

Rules and obligations

The key to understanding Hart's positivism is to appreciate the nature of obligation. There are occasions where we feel obliged to do or not do something, as when the robber threatens to shoot us if we don't hand over the money. However, it is very odd to say that we have an *obligation* in that situation. Hart argued that the concept of law as sovereign command backed by a threat overlooks the element of obligation that characterises law. We know that in some societies people are terrorised into obeying the commands of rulers. This is the robber situation writ large. Yet in normal society there are a vast number of rules that people observe, not because they fear retribution but because they think that it is right to do so. These rules are used by individuals to justify their actions, to make claims of right and to criticise the conduct of others. People count on these rules to be observed in going about their lives. This is an important insight. If most people do not voluntarily observe the law most of the time, there is something seriously the matter in society. Perhaps there is no society at all, as society is founded on shared rules of behaviour. This lack of observance is not the case in normal society. There are many laws that individuals do not like, but in viable societies most people will agree that the rules made according to certain accepted processes ought to be obeyed. Hence, a theory that identifies law solely with sovereign commands is flawed from the start.

The idea of a rule implies an obligation, but not all rules are thought to be obligatory. Rules of social etiquette and rules of grammar are rules. They are not just convergent habits but expected ways of doing things in a given society. But there may not be a sense of obligation attached to them. The sense of obligation arises from social pressure. The point at which a rule becomes a rule of obligation is uncertain, but the fact that it happens is not. There are degrees of social pressure. Where the pressure is generated by common hostility that produces feelings of guilt or shame but stops short of physical sanctions, we find moral rules imposing moral obligations. When the pressure takes the form of physical sanctions there is a primitive or rudimentary kind of law imposing legal obligations. The sanctions may be socially implemented even in the absence of a government. Ostracising, stigmatising and other forms of punishing existed in societies long before any kind of government was established. Obligation rules arise out of the common belief that they are necessary to maintain social life or a prized feature of it (Hart 1997, 87). They generally take the form of negative injunctions that limit the freedom of individuals for the common good: for example, thou shall not kill; thou shall not steal; thou shall not dishonour thy promises.

External and internal aspects of a legal rule

Hart argued that the appreciation of the sense of obligation allows us to perceive the internal aspects of a legal rule in addition to its external manifestation. He claimed that the command theorists had lost sight of the internal aspect. The external aspect of a rule is its objective existence. The internal aspect of a rule reveals the sense of obligation to observe the rule. I may say: 'It is the law in the Kingdom of Saudi Arabia that persons must not consume alcohol'. I make a statement of observed fact and thereby capture the external aspect of the rule. However, I do not engage with the internal aspect of the rule as I do not have a sense of obligation to follow the rule. On the contrary, when I say that I have an obligation under Queensland law to observe speed limits when driving my car, I am not only stating the law as fact but I am expressing a sense of obligation not to drive faster than the speed limits. A person looking at a society from an extreme external point of view may only see regularities of behaviour. The proverbial Martian may conclude after observing a controlled intersection that vehicles are likely to stop when the red lamp lights up, and think no further about it. This is the extreme external point of view. A less extreme external point of view may make the Martian realise that the drivers of the vehicles accept the 'stop on red light' rule as binding. This is sometimes called the hermeneutic view. Drivers may see the rule from the fully internal point of view and may believe that they ought to stop at the red light even if there is no risk of an accident or of being arrested and punished. Hart conceded that often people do not accept a rule but follow it to avoid sanction, but observed that the challenge for the legal theorist 'is to remember both these points of view and not to define one of them out of existence' (1997, 91). He accused the proponents of the predictive theory of obligation of this very sin. Predictive theory, associated with the school of American realism (discussed in Chapter 4), rejects the notion of rules altogether and regards law as made up of predictions of what the courts actually do. According to predictive theory, the lawyer's task is to predict how a citizen's case will be decided by the court.

Neil MacCormick, another British positivist, noted that Hart's explanation of the internal point of view conflates two distinct points of view that need to be separated if we wish to understand accurately the concept of a rule. MacCormick accepted that the focus on the purely external aspect of a rule hopelessly distorts its nature. However, he pointed out that an inquiring external observer (unlike a robotic Martian) may understand that members of a society consider a rule as binding from a reflective internal point of view, although the observer may not have reason to accept the rule. I do not accept the rule that a person must not drink beer, but I can understand that most citizens of Saudi Arabia accept the rule willingly as worthy of observance. What I have is not an external point of view but a non-volitional *cognitively* internal point of view. In contrast, most Saudi Arabian citizens may accept the rule voluntarily and hence have a *volitionally* internal point of view. It is the shared volitionally internal point of view that gives rise to a rule (MacCormick 1979, 288–98). Raz also identified a third kind of viewpoint between the external and the internal. This is the detached viewpoint expressed in statements that lawyers and law teachers typically make in explaining the law on some matter (Raz 1979, 153). A person may use normative language without normative commitment (e.g. in France, drivers must drive on the right side of the road). Hart accepted this refinement of his theory, conceding that it is possible for lawyers (and anyone else for that matter) 'to report in normative form the contents of a law from the point of view of those who do accept its rules without themselves sharing that point of view' (1983, 14).

Legal positivists and legal realists alike are empiricists who wish to rid the law of metaphysics and ground it firmly in fact. Hart was also an empiricist, but believed that the nature of a rule was only partly revealed by observation of its external effects. We do not mystify the notion of law by acknowledging its psychological dimension; we illuminate it.

Primary and secondary rules of obligation: emergence of a legal system

Every society, even the most primitive, displays obligation rules. It is hard to conceive a social order that does not rest on some commonly accepted rules of conduct. Some rules – such as those against murder, theft, violence and the breaking of promises – are ubiquitous. Others are indigenous. These are primary rules of obligation that arise spontaneously and pre-date the establishment of formal legislatures, courts and governments. Primary rules of obligation in primitive society are not simply regularities of habits or convergent practices of individuals. They are rules considered by members to be binding and enforced by social sanctions. Unlike the early positivists, Hart had no doubt that these may properly be called laws.

Small social groups bonded by kinship and shared beliefs living in a stable environment may survive by these rules alone. But as society gets larger and more complex, the shortcomings of a rudimentary set of laws based on diffused social pressure become evident and the need for a different type of rules is felt. Hart called these 'secondary rules of obligation'. There are three chief defects in a primitive system of laws. First, there is no authoritative means of resolving doubts about the meaning and application of laws. This is not a serious problem in close-knit groups who live by a few simple rules in a stable environment where disagreements can be resolved consensually. Legal uncertainties increase in larger societies, where most members are strangers and life is complex. Second, primary rules of obligation in primitive societies are relatively static. New rules crystallise slowly through convergence of practice and the build up of pressure to conform. Conversely, old rules that outlive their value linger while the pressure to conform dissipates slowly. The lack of a legislative body prevents society from deliberately adapting laws to changing conditions. Third, primitive society has nothing resembling courts that can authoritatively resolve disputes arising from the violation of laws, and no specialised agency to enforce judgments and mete out punishments.

Developed societies have secondary obligation rules that address these defects. The secondary rules provide for the authoritative recognition of legal rules, for changing legal rules and for adjudicating disputes concerning the observance of legal rules. These rules typically establish courts, legislatures and executive governments. They define the powers of these bodies, lay down procedures for the exercise of powers and prescribe criteria for the recognition of primary legal rules. Rules of this type, by their union with primary legal rules, bring about a legal system. Whereas primitive society has a *set* of laws, modern society has a *system* of laws (Hart 1997, 234). Hart used the terms 'set' and 'system' in an arbitrary way. That laws can emerge spontaneously and exist as self-ordered systems without the assistance of secondary rules is well known in the evolutionary tradition in social theory, which began with the Scottish moral philosophers Hume, Smith and Ferguson and others and has continued to this day through the works of the Austrian school in economics and of modern complexity theorists. (I discuss this jurisprudential tradition in Chapter 10.) However, terminology notwithstanding, Hart's distinction allows us to see clearly the function and value of secondary rules of obligation.

In most countries the secondary rules of obligation are set out in a written constitution. In the United Kingdom they are part of the customary constitution. Written or unwritten, their existence depends on acceptance by legislators, courts, executive government, public service and other officials on whose conduct the legal system depends. Whereas primary rules of obligation apply to all people, secondary rules have particular application to officials. Official acceptance is the critical internal aspect that makes these rules possible. Figure 2.4 represents Hart's view of the universe of law.

The rule of recognition

Secondary obligation rules typically stand in a hierarchical relation to each other. This relation is determined by a superior rule that Hart called the rule of recognition. In most countries the rule of recognition is stated in the constitution. In England, it is accepted that the common law overrides custom and that laws of Parliament override common law. This does not mean that the Queen in Parliament is a sovereign in the Austinian sense. Austin's sovereignty is unlimited and illimitable. The Queen in Parliament is a superior source of law but it is also the creation of the rule of recognition. Hart also rejected Austin's view that common law is tacit sovereign commands, or that legislation is the ultimate source of all law. The common law is law, however precarious its existence. It is not derived from legislation, although legislation may alter it (Hart 1997, 101).

The rule of recognition provides the ultimate criterion for verifying the validity of laws. When parliament enacts laws and when judges find rules to be valid according to the rule of recognition, they are not obeying anyone's command. It is possible to say that they are obeying the rule of recognition by stretching the meaning of 'obey'. It is more exact to say that they are accepting and observing, from the internal point of view, the obligatory effect of the rule of recognition.

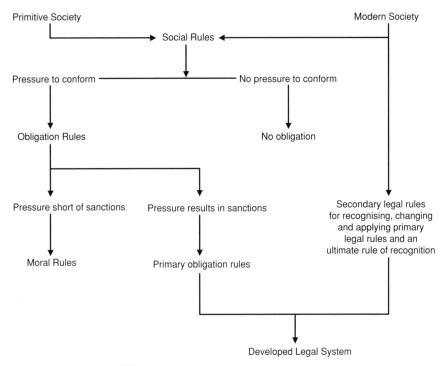

Figure 2.4 Hart's positivism

A legal system in the modern sense arises when two conditions converge. First, the primary rules that are considered valid by the rule of recognition are generally obeyed by citizens. Second, the rule of recognition is accepted by officials as the standard of official behaviour. (It must be noted that Hart sometimes used 'rule of recognition' to refer to all the rules concerning recognition, change and adjudication, and at other times to refer to the ultimate rule among these. I use the term in the latter sense for clarity.) The rule of recognition may change through peaceful transition, as when Britain granted its colonies degrees of self-government and finally independence. It could also change through foreign conquest or by violent domestic revolution, as frequently observed in parts of the world where stable constitutional democracy has not taken root. The primary rules of obligation may remain largely unaffected while the struggle over the rule of recognition goes on. This was not the case, though, in Russia and China, where communist revolutions simultaneously overthrew existing regimes and fundamentally changed the country's primary legal rules.

International law

According to the theory of law as sovereign command, international law is not proper law but is, if at all, positive morality. The theories that postulate that law comprises rules derived from a common fundamental norm (such as Hans Kelsen's 'pure theory of law', discussed in the next chapter) must find a basic norm that validates all international law rules. This is not easy to locate in the absence of a global legislature or court comparable to those of municipal (national) legal systems. International law does not qualify as a legal system even by Hart's own theory, as it lacks an authoritative rule of recognition. Yet Hart had no difficulty in treating international law as law properly so called because he believed that there can be *law* without a *legal system*. International law rules resemble the primary rules of obligation in a primitive society. They are law because sovereign states consider them as obligatory and use them to press their claims and to evaluate and criticise the conduct of other states. The argument that international law is not law for want of effective enforcement is dismissed as based on the discredited command theory. Hart took more seriously the practical observation that there can be no law where there is free use of violence. A society of individuals who possess nearly equal strength can descend to lawlessness unless individual use of force is restrained. International law leaves room for self help and war. Often, even collective actions fail to stop aggression. So what sustains international law? Hart argued that the high risks that war carries even for the most powerful aggressors provide a natural deterrent against international anarchy (1997, 219).

Law and morality

Hart's famous debates with Lon Fuller and Ronald Dworkin about the separation of law and morality are discussed in Chapter 6. However, this discussion of British legal positivism should not be concluded without a brief explanation of Hart's position on this subject.

Hart, like his precursors in the positivist tradition, denied any *necessary* connection between law and morality. Legal positivists appreciate the many ways in which the law is connected to morality. Their argument is that the validity of a law does not depend on such a connection. Positivists offer scientific and moral reasons for keeping the morality and the validity of law separate. Their scientific thesis is: it is simply not true that all rules regarded as law satisfy a moral test. This is an assertion of observed fact. There are many laws in the law books that we may condemn as immoral. Yet we recognise them to be laws and in many cases we observe them willingly. The moral case is that we can make the law better if we clear up the confusion between the legality and the morality of laws. If we recognise that a morally bad enactment is a law, we can do something about it. If we deny that it is a law, it may never get fixed. As we shall see in later chapters, neither the scientific nor the moral thesis is free of controversy.

In considering Hart's position on law and morality we must keep in mind the important distinction between 'law' and 'legal system'. Hart was careful to distinguish the question of the validity of particular laws from the question of the efficacy of whole legal systems. A legal system exists when citizens generally accept and observe the primary legal rules of obligation and officials similarly accept secondary rules of recognition, change and enforcement of laws. Acceptance is the basis of a legal system. A legal system that does not provide the most basic conditions for the survival of individuals may lose the fidelity of the people that sustains it. These are conditions that secure life, liberty, property and the performance of contracts (Hart 1997, 199). They are secured by forbearances of a moral kind that the law demands. We are unlikely to find anything resembling a legal system where these conditions are lacking. Hart agreed that a legal system requires a minimum content of natural law. The legality of particular laws that offend the morals of the community is a different question. A society may have law with or without a legal system. A legal system that is effective may produce laws that many consider to be morally repugnant. Yet they will be valid laws if they satisfy the criteria set by the rule of recognition. In his debate with Lon Fuller over the punishment of the German 'grudge informers' who for personal reasons procured the death or imprisonment of others under the Nazi regime's monstrous laws, Hart took the view that there was nothing to be gained by denying the legality of the Nazi laws. In such cases, he argued, it is better to say 'This is law, but too iniquitous to obey or apply' (1997, 210). We may have a moral duty to disobey inhuman laws but we do not advance clear thinking by denying them the status of law. I consider these views more fully in Chapter 6.

There is an internal aspect to both primary and secondary rules of obligation. An important question is whether the internal aspect of a legal rule necessarily adds a moral dimension to the rule. The internal aspect reflects the sense of having an obligation, as opposed to 'being obliged' by fear of sanction. This sense of obligation may be a moral sense, but Hart insisted that it need not be so. 'Not only may vast numbers be coerced by laws which they do not regard as morally binding, but it is not even true that those who do accept the system voluntarily, must conceive of themselves as morally bound to do so, though the system will be more stable when they do so' (1997, 203). Allegiance to the system may be based on 'calculations of long term interest; disinterested interest in others; an unreflecting inherited or traditional attitude; or the mere wish to do as others do' (1997, 203).

Hart saw the many ways in which law may be connected to morals. But these were, for Hart, not *necessary* but *contingent* connections. The common stock of legal rules that we associate with civilised living are also moral rules. They include the rules against murder, assault, theft, robbery, rape, depriving freedom and damaging property and the rules concerning the keeping of promises. Morality constantly influences law making by legislators and judges. In some countries the constitution lays down moral tests in the form of fundamental rights and freedoms that every law must pass in order to be valid. These tests, Hart and other positivists argue, are enforceable not because of their morality but because they constitute an established rule of recognition. The language of law is open textured and hence leaves judges with discretion to take morality into account in identifying the existing law. Alternatively, the law may direct judges to make new law according to their own judgment (Hart 1997, 254). Rules of statutory interpretation and the notions of legality, natural justice, procedural fairness and equity also import morality into judicial reasoning. But to Hart and other positivists these connections are only contingent, and not conceptual (1997, 268).

Hart's positivism is soft positivism. He stated that 'It will not matter for any practical purpose whether in deciding cases the judge is *making* law in accordance with morality (subject to whatever constraints imposed by law) or alternatively is guided by his moral judgment as to what already *existing* law is revealed by a moral test for law' (1997, 254). It mattered for Joseph Raz. According to Raz, judges are either applying law or developing law. No moral judgment is involved in the application of law. Judges may be guided by morality in developing law in much the same way as legislators, but in doing so they are not discovering law but making law. Morality, for Raz, can never be part of pre-existing law (1979, 49–50). Individuals engage in moral judgments in deciding what ought to be done or not done. The function of the law 'is to mark the point at which a private view of members of the society, or of influential sections or powerful groups within it, ceases to be their private view and becomes (i.e. lays a claim to be) a view binding on all members notwithstanding their disagreement with it' (Raz 1979, 51). The law, by authoritatively stating the rule to follow, relieves people of the interminable discussions about right conduct. Law, once made, admits no further moral arguments.

British positivism's contribution to jurisprudence

British legal positivism's contribution to jurisprudence is extensive and profound. Legal positivism at birth was part of the wider 18th century intellectual movement known as the Enlightenment, which turned away from tradition, superstition and irrationality to embrace empiricism and science. The command theory of law, despite its factual inaccuracies and theoretical shortcomings, serves to demystify the law by showing that law is based in fact and not belief. The theory is intuitively appealing to lawyers and laymen and with small refinements provides a useful way of understanding the legal universe. It can be said that Bentham and Austin made Hart and Kelsen possible. Twentieth century British positivists removed much of the coarseness from the theory.

Legal positivism's empiricism has exposed it to the suspicion that it is insensitive to the moral dimensions of social life. This is ill-founded. Legal positivism is the child of utilitarian moral theory, which seeks to advance the public good. Its message is that we can make the law better if we do not confuse it with morality. Positivists cannot be accused of confusing legal duty and moral duty. An unjust law is law, but a citizen may have moral reasons for disobeying it. Hart, Raz and other modern positivists have shown that the span between legal positivism and natural law thinking is not as great as once thought.

Jurisprudence, however, does not begin and end with the definition and description of formal law. Legal positivists concede that theirs is not the only prevalent conception of the law. There are many matters of interest about the law that are left untouched by legal positivism. How does the normative content of the law emerge? What are the history, anthropology and sociology of law? How do we measure the worth of particular laws? Do citizens have a moral duty to obey or disobey the law? Do judges have a moral duty not to enforce heinous laws of the kind enacted by the Nazi regime? How do we find the moral standards by which we may identify such a duty? Is the meaning of legal texts objectively ascertainable or are they socially constructed? These are interesting and legitimate questions that must not be banished from the province of jurisprudence. In the chapters that follow I address these questions and also consider the most important criticisms of legal positivism.

3

Germanic Legal Positivism: Hans Kelsen's Quest for the Pure Theory of Law

British legal positivism was founded on empiricism. Empiricist legal theorists reject metaphysical or mystical explanations of law and assert that law exists as social fact and nothing more. The main inspiration for Germanic legal positivism is not empiricism but the transcendental idealism of the German philosopher Immanuel Kant (1724–1804). Whereas British legal positivists regard law as fact distinct from morals, their Germanic counterparts seek to separate law from both fact and morals. This chapter discusses Germanic legal positivism principally through the work of its most famous proponent, Austrian legal philosopher Hans Kelsen.

Kelsen (1881–1973) was born in Prague but moved with his family to Vienna at the age of two. He taught at the universities in Vienna and Cologne and at the University of California at Berkeley. Kelsen was the author of the Austrian Constitution and the designer of the Austrian model of judicial review adopted by many countries.

The key elements of Kelsen's theory are these. Facts consist of things and events in the physical world. Facts are about what there *is*. When we wish to know what caused a fact we look for another fact. A stone thrown in the air comes down because of the force of Earth's gravity. There are seasons because the Earth's axis is tilted at 23.5 degrees. A norm, unlike a fact, is not about what there is but is about what *ought* to be done or not done. Whereas facts exist in the physical world, norms exist in the world of ideas. Facts are caused by other facts. Norms are imputed by other norms. The requirement that a person who commits theft ought to be punished is a norm. It does not cease being a norm because the thief is not punished. (He may not get caught.) The norm that the thief ought to be punished exists because another norm says so. Not all norms are laws. There are also moral norms. Legal norms are coercive; moral norms are not. Moreover, a legal norm has the quality of 'validity'. A legal norm is valid if it is endowed with validity by another norm. Whereas physical things arise from causation, legal norms arise from validation by another valid norm. A norm that confers validity upon another norm owes its own validity to another norm, and so on. This regression cannot go on infinitely. Kelsen conceived the idea of a basic norm (*Grundnorm*), a kind of First Cause of the legal system beyond which we cannot speculate in a legal sense. The basic norm is presupposed. A legal norm exists because of a chain of validity that links it ultimately to the basic norm. The legal system is a system of legal norms connected to each other by their common origin, like the branches and leaves of a tree. This is only a thumbnail sketch of Kelsen's theory. Its intricacies and implications remain to be considered in the following pages.

Kelsen's writing is remarkably lucid in some parts but maddeningly dense in others. It seems at times that language fails to adequately express the subtleties of his theory. It is easy to misunderstand his theory of law. It is not possible to gain an accurate understanding of the pure theory without a reasonable grasp of the philosophy on which it is based – transcendental idealism. In particular, the claim of purity of the pure theory can be understood only through this mode of thought. (Note that the term 'idealism' is used in these pages in the philosophical sense explained hereafter, and not in the more commonplace sense of commitment to ideals.) Kelsen claimed that, despite its conceptual subtlety, he was merely making lawyers conscious of what they intuitively or subconsciously do in practice (1967, 204–5). This is partly true.

From empiricism to transcendental idealism

David Hume (1711–76) is considered the father of British empiricism, but he also provided the inspiration for transcendental idealism. Immanuel Kant, the instigator of the latter school, confessed that it was Hume's writings that interrupted his dogmatic slumber (1883 (1783), 6). Hume made two famous observations about the limits of human knowledge. First, he observed that there is an unbridgeable gap between the physical world *as it is* and the way we *perceive* it. There are two reasons for this. The first is that 'nothing is ever present to the mind but its perceptions, impressions and ideas . . . [t]o hate, to love, to think, to feel, to see; all this is nothing but to perceive' (Hume 1978 (1739–40), 67]). When we think of something we are actually thinking of other thoughts. We do not know what causes these perceptions to occur in our minds. But this does not matter since we have no choice but to live in this world of perceptions 'whether they be true or false; whether they represent nature justly, or be mere illusions of the senses' (1978, 84) We form systems of ideas (theories) by connecting perceptions. Here, according to Hume, we run into the second problem. We cannot actually prove the causes of things, although we expect from experience that certain events cause certain other events. By repeatedly observing that there is heat near a fire, we conclude that fire is the cause of heat. This is not proof. We see fire and we feel heat but we do not see or feel the causal relation. Hume argued that we can never prove that something cannot come into existence without a cause or productive principle. Hence, the idea that everything has a cause cannot be intuitively self-evident or known *a priori*. Hume did not deny that things are caused by other things. His sceptical point was that our belief in causation is based not on intuition but on experience. Hence, knowledge about the world is hypothetical and fallible. Hume's theory works like this. I hear a sound. This is an impression. I assume from past experience that the sound is that of my kettle whistling as the water boils. When I check, the kettle is cold. Looking out of the window I see branches swaying and realise that I heard the sound of the wind among the trees.

Hume's second important insight concerning human knowledge was that it is impossible logically to derive what ought to be done from observed facts. This is the error of trying to derive the 'ought' from 'is' (Hume 1978, 469). Suppose we know as a fact that in a particular society all persons speak. It does not follow that John, who is a member of that society, *ought* to engage in speech. John, for instance, may have taken a vow of silence. If we say that John ought to speak because everyone else speaks, we draw an illicit inference of ought from fact. If we say that John has a duty to speak we must find some other source of obligation.

Hume was a sceptic but not an idealist. Idealism in its strict form is the belief that thoughts or ideas are all there is and that nothing exists outside our minds. Hume did not deny the existence of things; he only doubted our ability to know them as they really are. Hume's insights, particularly those concerning causation, shook the philosophical community and awoke Immanuel Kant from his intellectual slumber. In his seminal work, *Critique of Pure Reason*, Kant agreed with Hume that we cannot know objects as they really are. In other words, we cannot know the thing in itself (*Ding an sich*). But Kant firmly believed that things exist outside our minds. These he called *noumena*. What we know are only the impressions that things create in our minds. These he called *phenomena*. There is thus a noumenal world of things and a phenomenal world of our impressions about things. Our knowledge is of the latter world. However, Kant argued that we possess a form of *a priori* knowledge, or knowledge that is prior to any experience. This knowledge shapes our experience. Kant thought that we cannot think of any object except in relation to time and space. Hume thought the reverse – that we have a sense of time and space only because we perceive separate objects (1978, 35). Kant said that we cannot conceive of something that has no cause. As noted previously, Hume argued that we can. Kant had not read Hume's *Treatise* when he published the *Critique* in 1781 (Wolff 1960, 117). Hume never read the *Critique*, as he died in 1776. Hence their disagreement was never resolved, but that does not matter for the present discussion.

Kant, like Hume, was not an idealist in the strict sense: he believed that there are real things in the world although we cannot experience them directly. He sought to distance himself from idealism by describing his system as *transcendental idealism*. The term 'transcendental' to Kant meant *a priori* (pre-existing) and transcendental idealism referred to his theory of *a priori* knowledge – knowledge that we have independent of experience. He wrote: 'I call all representations pure, in the transcendental meaning of the word, wherein nothing is met with that belongs to sensation' (1930, 22).

Kant also adopted Hume's insight about the impossibility of deriving 'ought' (*sollen*) from 'is' (*sein*). (Kelsen wrongly assumed that Kant was the first to discover the distinction (Kelsen 1998 (1923), 4). The error is inconsequential to our discussion.) Kant argued that scientific questions as to what is the case must be addressed by *pure reason*. This is the process of observation and logical deduction. Thus, we conclude from observations that the sum of the angles of a triangle happens to be 180 degrees irrespective of the dimensions of the triangle. Copernicus observed that the Earth moves in an elliptical orbit around the Sun. Moral questions cannot be answered in this way. A moral question is about what one ought to do or not do. Should a physician assist in euthanasia? Can war be justified, or adultery? Here we need to engage in *practical reason*. Kant searched for a universal and indisputable principle of moral judgment – a categorical imperative. In the *Groundwork of the Metaphysics of Morals* he set out this principle as follows: 'I ought to never act except in such a way that I can also will that my maxim should be a universal law' (1947, 70).

From transcendental idealism to the pure theory of law

Transcendental idealism is the epistemological foundation of Kelsen's 'pure theory of law', which presents law not as fact but as norms that exist in the realm of ideas. Facts are about what there *is*, whereas norms are propositions as to what *ought* to be done or not done. Kelsen said of his theory: 'It is called a "pure" theory of law, because it only describes the law and attempts to eliminate from the object of this description everything that is not strictly law: Its aim is to free the science of law from alien elements' (1967, 1). Specifically, Kelsen claimed that his theory is pure on two counts. First it distinguishes law from fact. As Paulsen remarked: 'At its core, Kelsen's legal theory does not consort with facts at all' (1998, 24). Second, it distinguishes law from morals. Kant's thoughts provided inspiration on both counts. The chief ingredients of Kelsen's pure theory are supplied by Kant's two distinctions between:

(a) the world of things (*noumena*) and the world of ideas (*phenomena*); and
(b) what *is* (*sein*) and what *ought* to be done or not done (*sollen*).

Law as norm

Kelsen applied the Kantian distinctions with the following results. The physical acts that give rise to law (passing of a statute, delivery of a judgment etc) belong in the world of things or fact. They occur in time and space so we perceive them with our senses. The question of whether these acts represent a legal norm (an 'ought') cannot be answered simply by observing the facts. It requires a mental inquiry about what the facts mean in a normative sense (Kelsen 1967, 2–4). For example, a group of persons assemble in a building called the Parliament House and engage in a debate about a document called the Terrorism Bill, which states that a person who commits an act of terrorism shall be punished by life imprisonment. (This actually means that terrorists *ought* to be punished, as the Act cannot guarantee that they *will* be caught and punished.) At the end of the debate there is a vote and a majority of the assembled group approve the Bill. The document is then certified as an Act of Parliament. What we have observed is not the law but a series of facts. The question for the legal scientist is whether these facts can be interpreted as giving rise to the norm that acts of terrorism ought to be punished with life imprisonment. What creates the norm is not Parliament's say-so but another norm that states that the will of Parliament expressed in a particular way ought to be obeyed.

Nature of norm

Kelsen wrote: 'Norm is the meaning of an act by which a certain behaviour is commanded, permitted or authorised' (1967, 5). A norm may take the form of a rule or a specific command. A police officer's order to stop traffic, the minister's order under the *Land Acquisition Act* to acquire a person's property and a judge's decree in a civil case are all norms. Kelsen's theory obliterates the distinction between rules and orders. A norm, according to Kelsen, need not supply a rule of conduct that can be known beforehand – a necessary condition for achieving the rule of law. However, not every expression of will directed to a person is a norm. An armed robber's demand that I hand over money is not a norm, whereas a tax collector's demand of money is a norm. The *subjective* meaning of the two acts is the same. Each wills that I hand over money. But only the latter demand has *objective* meaning in Kelsen's sense. It is objective because an antecedent valid norm authorised the demand (Kelsen 1967, 8). Thus, we may say that a norm is an 'ought' proposition that is objectively recognised. I may state in writing that in the event of my death my wife and child ought to be given all my property. This is an expression of my *subjective* will. It does not oblige anyone else to respect my wishes unless it is also *objectively* regarded by the community as binding. That is, others have cause to recognise my will as binding on them (Kelsen 1967, 4). For instance, if my writing is not witnessed as the law requires, my intent is not binding on others. Likewise, the subjective intent of the people who approved of the *Terrorism Act* will not be objectively valid

The world of norms

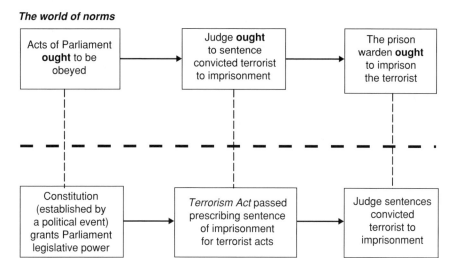

The world of fact

Figure 3.1 Transcendental idealism in the pure theory of law

unless it was expressed according to established legal requirements. Did the assembled group constitute Parliament? Was the enacting procedure correct? Is Parliament authorised to make law on the subject of crimes? The answers depend on other norms. Section 51 of the Australian Constitution states that Parliament shall, subject to the Constitution, have power to make laws for the peace, order, and good government of the Commonwealth with respect to the subjects enumerated in that section. A lawyer may conclude from this and other provisions of the Constitution that the provisions of an Act of Parliament on a prescribed subject ought to be observed by citizens, courts and officials alike. This type of inquiry takes place in the world of ideas. The transcendental character of Kelsen's theory is illustrated in Figure 3.1.

The vertical lines in the above figure do not indicate that the norms above the horizontal line are logically derived from the facts below the horizontal line. That is impossible. As first Hume and then Kant noted, an 'ought' cannot be inferred from an 'is'. Kelsen would explain that the norm above the line is simply an interpretation of the legal meaning of the fact below the line. Parliament by enacting the *Terrorism Act* wills that terrorists be punished by imprisonment. The enactment of the *Terrorism Act* is the event and not the norm. Its meaning is that terrorists *ought* to be imprisoned. This is the norm. But this norm flows not from the event but from another norm in the Constitution – that Parliament's enactments ought to be carried out. A natural scientist observes a physical event and concludes that another physical event *will* occur. A legal scientist observes a physical event and concludes that another physical event *ought* to occur. The natural scientist is directed to this scientific conclusion by a scientific law. The legal scientist is directed to this normative conclusion by another norm.

Kelsen used the term 'imputation' to signify the effect of a norm. We speak of causation in relation to the natural world. One physical event causes another event. Norms are not material things and one norm cannot cause another. A norm creates a duty to behave in a certain way by *imputing* a sanction to the breach of that duty (Kelsen 1967, 81).

Commands, authorisations and permissions

We typically associate the law with commands to do or not do something – for example, that we ought to repay our debts or that we ought not to commit theft. According to Kelsen there is no norm where there is no 'ought'. Yet many laws at first sight seem to lack an 'ought'. An Act of Parliament authorises (but does not compel) the minister to make regulations. My driving licence permits (but does not compel) me to drive my car on public roads. The *Social Security Act* grants me the right to receive a pension if I am unemployed or disabled but does not compel me to do anything. How do we explain these laws as norms? According to Kelsen, each of these laws has normative force. Such laws, in effect, say that people ought to 'endure' the actions of another person (Kelsen 1967, 16–17). The law under which I hold my driving licence means that people (including the police) ought to respect (endure) my liberty to drive. The law that authorises the minister to make traffic regulations means that the minister's regulations ought to be obeyed. The law that entitles me to a pension means that some official ought to pay me a sum of money.

Legislation, legal norm and statement of the law

It is vital to distinguish three elements of the legal process in order to gain an accurate understanding of Kelsen's theory. They are as follows:
1.   legislation, judicial precedent or custom – this is a fact
2.   the legal norm – this is the 'ought' proposition that results from the inter-
      pretation of the legislation, precedent or custom
3.   the statement of the rule of law.
Legal norms represent the meaning we give to a particular series of facts. The statement in a statute that something ought to be done is not a norm but a fact. The norm is the meaning we give to this fact when considered with certain other facts. The Queensland Parliament enacted the *Criminal Code Act 1899*. Section 291 of the Act states: 'It is unlawful to kill any person unless such killing is authorised or justified or excused by law'. Other provisions of the law describe authorisations, justifications and excuses for killing. Section 302(1) states that a person who unlawfully kills another under the circumstances set out in that section commits murder. Section 305(1) states that 'any person who commits the crime of murder is liable to imprisonment for life'. Provisions of other Acts determine how a person is charged and tried and, if found guilty, how sentence is imposed and executed. From all of this we glean the norm that a person ought

not to commit murder. The coercive (hence legal) nature of this norm is evident only when all the interlocking provisions are taken into account.

Kelsen also drew an important distinction between a legal norm and the statement of a rule of law. A legal norm is a command. Hence it is neither true nor false. I ask you to leave my property. My statement is neither true nor false. It is simply the expression of my wish. Similarly, an Act of Parliament states: 'A person convicted of murder shall be sentenced to life imprisonment'. It is the expression of the will of Parliament. It may be valid or not valid, but not true or false. On the contrary, the statement 'According to the law of England murder is punishable by life imprisonment' can be true of false. The former statement in the statute *prescribes* behaviour. The latter statement *describes* what the law is (Kelsen 1967, 73).

Raz usefully pointed out that statements about the law may be morally committed or detached (1986, 89–91). Committed statements affirm in a moral sense the rules, rights and duties under the law. A person who says 'You have no right to enter my property' may be making a moral statement about the law. This kind of statement has no place in the science of law, according to the pure theory. Detached statements are those typically made by lawyers, who state the law without expressing a moral commitment. The position is as follows.

Act of Parliament	A person convicted of murder shall be sentenced to life imprisonment.
Legal norm	The court ought to sentence a person convicted of murder to life imprisonment.
Morally committed statement of the law	Persons who commit murder are rightly sentenced to life imprisonment.
Detached statement of the law	It is the law in England that a person convicted of murder is liable to be sentenced to life imprisonment.

Distinguishing legal and moral norms

Legal order as a coercive order

Kelsen, like other legal positivists, denied that there was a necessary connection between law and morality. A law that gives effect to a moral rule is law not because of its moral content but 'because it has been constituted in a particular fashion, born of a definite procedure and a definite rule of law' (Kelsen 1935, 517–18). A norm in the sense of an 'ought' could be legal or moral. Often it is both. The rule against theft is moral as well as legal. Law is not the only regulative system in society. Moral norms play an important role in guiding behaviour.

Moral norms, like legal norms, have both subjective and objective existence. A vegetarian may say that all persons ought to abstain from eating animal products. This is subjectively true for the vegetarian, but it has no objective existence in a society of committed meat eaters. Hence, it is not a moral norm of that society. On the contrary, my wish that people ought not to inflict gratuitous cruelty on animals will be objectively true in most civilised societies, and therefore be a moral norm in those societies.

Kelsen also argued that law and morals cannot be distinguished according to their respective content. The only kind of moral norm that cannot be a legal norm is one that is addressed wholly to a person's own mind, such as: 'Suppress your inclinations' (Kelsen 1935, 62). Kelsen regarded such morals rules as incomplete. A positive (complete) moral rule deals with both internal and external behaviour. So does a positive legal rule (Kelsen 1935, 60).

It is also not possible to distinguish moral and legal rules by the way they are created. There are two ways in which legal rules come about: by custom and by the will of a law making authority. Positive moral rules are also established by custom, or by the will of a moral authority such as a divine being, a prophet or a church. According to Kelsen, moral prescriptions derived from purely philosophical speculation have no force as rules unless they gain currency in society. That happens by force of custom or authority.

Legal and moral norms also cannot be distinguished by the methods of their application. Moral systems lack the kind of specialised enforcement agencies (courts, police etc) that we associate with legal systems. Yet, as Kelsen observed, primitive legal systems also lack such organs (1935, 62). How then can we distinguish legal from moral norms? The difference, according to Kelsen, lies in the fact that the legal order is a coercive order, whereas the moral order is not:

> The fundamental difference between law and morals is: law is a coercive order, that is, a normative order that attempts to bring about a certain behaviour *by attaching to the opposite behaviour a socially organised coercive act*; whereas morals is a social order without such sanctions. The sanctions of the moral order are merely the approval of the norm-conforming and the disapproval of the norm-opposing behaviour and no coercive acts are prescribed as sanctions. (1935, 62; emphasis added)

This statement requires two clarifications. First, according to this view what is needed for a society to have law is the means of applying 'socially organised' coercion. Such means may exist (as in primitive societies) without specialised agencies such as courts and governments. This allows Kelsen to dispense with the requirement of a sovereign and to recognise that primitive law and international law are actually law.

The second clarification is that a law may exist even if no coercion is *in fact* applied. The thief may not get caught, or if caught and tried may be acquitted for want of evidence or because of judicial error. The moral norm states: 'A person ought not to commit theft'. The legal norm states: 'If a person commits theft, they ought to be punished'. The legal norm, like the moral norm, is not a statement of fact. It does not assure that what *ought to* happen will *in fact* happen.

Legal order is a dynamic order

Legal and moral order can be distinguished in another respect. Whereas moral order may be static or dynamic, legal order is always dynamic. Kelsen pointed out that legal order is dynamic in the sense that the content of its norms is variable depending on the will of the norm creating authority. In contrast, the content of the norms of a static order is in a sense predetermined as they derive from the content of a higher norm. The lower norms are subsumed by the higher norm. This is the case with some moral systems. As Kelsen explained:

> From the norm to love one's neighbour one can derive the norm not to harm one's fellow man, not to damage him physically or morally, to help him in need and – particularly – not to kill him. Perhaps one might reduce the norm of truthfulness and love for one's fellow man to a still higher norm, such as to be in harmony with the universe. On this norm a whole moral order may be founded. Since all norms of an order of this type are already contained in the content of the presupposed norm, they can be deduced from it by way of logical operation, namely a conclusion from the general to the particular. This norm, presupposed as the basic norm, supplies both the reason for validity and the content of the norms deduced from it in a logical operation. (1935, 195)

It is important to notice that not all moral systems are static in the sense just described. Norms of a customary moral system may change as society adapts to changing circumstances. Moral systems founded on the authority of a church may also be changed legislatively. (Consider the changes with respect to homo-sexuality, divorce and contraception in some churches.) Kelsen's point is that legal order, unlike moral order, is always dynamic in the sense that the con-tent of its norms is not predetermined. The norm creating authority determines what norms to create and with what content. Parliament may or may not pro-hibit polygamy or the consumption of cannabis. Parliament may outlaw trade monopolies or create a trade monopoly. The legal order is dynamic in this sense. This is not to say that the norm creating authority has unlimited discretion to determine the content of norms. The discretion of Parliament may be limited by constitutional provisions. The legislative discretion of the Australian Parliament is limited by the separation of powers doctrine and the federal distribution of powers, as well as the express and implied rights and freedoms guaranteed by the Constitution. Likewise, the powers of ministers and local authorities to make subordinate laws are constrained by the terms imposed by parent legislation. The key point is that norm creating authorities have discretion to determine content within the limits of their jurisdiction. A higher norm confers jurisdiction but does not dictate content.

Validity and the basic norm

Legal order differs from moral order because of its coercive character. This is an incomplete explanation of legal order. An armed robber's command that I hand over my wallet is coercive and so is the tax collector's command that I pay the state a part of my income. The reason the tax collector's command is law is that it is 'valid'. The robber's command is not law because it is not valid. So what is 'validity'?

In Kelsen's theory a valid norm is a norm that exists, and a norm that exists is valid (1945, 30). A norm's existence is obviously different from the existence of a physical thing like a chair or an animal. A norm is incorporeal. We cannot see it, hear it, touch it or smell it. So how do we know it exists? As Hume and Kant pointed out, an 'ought' (which is what a norm is) cannot be derived from an 'is'. It can only be derived from another 'ought', or norm. Thus, a norm is valid if it has been made in accordance with another valid norm. That is to say, it has been issued by a person or body that is authorised to do so by that other norm, in accordance with procedure stipulated by that norm. That norm is valid if it is made as authorised by another valid norm, and so on. Ultimately this chain of validity stops at a norm whose validity cannot be derived from another valid norm. It simply has to be presupposed if we are to make sense of the legal system. Let us see how this system works in practice.

Consider the norm that the prison warden ought to imprison X. This norm is valid because a judge has stated that X ought to be imprisoned after X was found guilty at the trial. The judge's order is valid because according to the *Crimes Act* a person found guilty (after trial) of the offence of doing Y ought to be sentenced by the judge to imprisonment. The *Crimes Act* is valid because according to the Constitution the commands of an Act of Parliament ought to be obeyed by judges. In the case of some legal systems the inquiry may extend further. The Constitution's validity may be derived from another Constitution. The validity of the Australian Constitution at the time of its commencement in 1901 was derived from the norm established by the *Commonwealth of Australia Constitution Act*, a statute enacted by the British Parliament.[1] That norm was valid because of the basic norm of the British Constitution that commands of the British Parliament (Crown in Parliament) issued in the form of Acts of Parliament ought to be obeyed by subjects. The last mentioned norm, it is found, is not derived from another valid norm. It was established by the political events that followed the Glorious Revolution of 1688. It is what Kelsen called the basic norm that must be presupposed. Kelsen described the basic norm thus:

> Coercive acts ought to be performed under the conditions and in the manner which the historically first constitution, and the norms created according to it, prescribe. (In short: One ought to behave as the constitution prescribes.) (1945, 201)

So how did the basic norm arise? The basic norm that the will of the Crown in Parliament expressed in the form of an Act ought to be obeyed was established following the political settlement that occurred after the Revolution of 1688, under which William of Orange and Mary of Scotland jointly took the throne of England and Scotland after conceding supreme legislative power to the Parliament at Westminster. However, following Kant and Kelsen (and before them Hume) we acknowledge that the basic norm (an 'ought' or *Sollen*) cannot be

---

1 I consider the legal position as it was in 1901 for simplicity. The basic norm of the Australian legal system has since changed, owing to political and legal developments that occurred after Federation.

derived from the historical event of the Revolution Settlement (an 'is' or *Sein*). Yet it is highly improbable that the basic norm would exist if the historical event had not happened. The Kelsenian explanation would be along the following lines. The actors that brought about the political settlement after the Glorious Revolution willed that the norms expressed by the Crown in Parliament ought to be obeyed as supreme law. This was the subjective meaning of what they did and said. This meaning was generally accepted within the polity; hence it became an objective norm. If key actors or the populace generally did not accept this norm, it would not have become the basic norm. This acceptance was not logically necessary. It was simply a political fact.

Basic norm of customary law systems

The reader will recall that according to 'command theories' of law (discussed in Chapter 2) customary law is not law until it is converted to law by the direct or indirect command of the political sovereign. In practical terms, it means that a customary law is not law until it is enacted by Parliament or recognised and enforced by a court of law. This view of the law leads to the necessary conclusion that a society that lacks a sovereign political authority lacks law. According to this view of the law many tribal societies are lawless. Hart's rejection of the 'command concept' of law allowed him to appreciate that law was a feature of all societies, primitive as well as modern. Primitive societies have laws in the form of primary obligation rules. Modern societies have in addition secondary obligation rules (rules of recognition) that enable primary rules to be authoritatively recognised, changed and enforced by specialised organs of the state such as parliaments and courts. Hart thought that it is the presence of the secondary rules that brings about a legal system. A primitive legal system has a *set* of laws but not a legal *system* (Hart 1997, 234).

Kelsen, like Hart, recognised that primitive society possesses legal norms. However, Kelsen's theory of the legal order was more abstract than Hart's idea of a legal system, and was broad enough to encompass both customary and developed legal systems. The existence of the basic norm is not dependent on the existence of formal norm creating authorities such as parliaments and courts. Every norm, including the basic norm, is the result either of deliberate human action or of custom. It is possible to locate the basic norm of a customary legal order. Kelsen explained:

> In a social community, a tribe, it is customary that a man who marries a girl pays a certain amount to her father or uncle. If the groom asks why he ought to do this, the answer is: because in this community such a payment has always been made, that is, because there is a custom to make this payment and *because it is assumed to be self-evident that the individual member of the tribe ought to behave as all other members customarily do.* This is the basic norm of the normative order that constitutes the community. (1967, 197; emphasis added.)

Logic of presupposing the basic norm

Validity of norms can be expressed in the form of syllogisms (Kelsen 1967, 202). A syllogism consists of a major premise, a minor premise and a conclusion derived from the two premises. A popular illustration is as follows:

Major premise: All humans are mortal.

Minor premise: Socrates is human.

Conclusion: Socrates is mortal.

The syllogistic process of reasoning in relation to norms is illustrated in the following example:

Major premise: People ought to behave according to the subjective commands of the City Council. (Objectively valid norm)

Minor premise: The City Council has commanded that people ought not to throw litter on the city streets. (Subjective command)

Conclusion: People ought not to throw litter on the street.

The major premise in the above syllogism can be questioned. Why should people behave according to the subjective wishes of the City Councillors? The answer is provided by another syllogism.

Major premise: All persons and authorities ought to behave according to the subjective commands of Parliament. (Objectively valid norm)

Minor premise: Parliament has commanded that people ought to behave according to the subjective commands of the City Council. (Subjective command)

Conclusion: People ought to behave according to the subjective commands of the City Council.

The reader will notice that in this scheme, the major premise of one syllogism is the conclusion of the higher syllogism. Ultimately, we encounter a major premise that cannot be stated in the form of a conclusion of yet another syllogism. It is possible that the major premise 'All persons and authorities ought to behave according to the subjective commands of Parliament' is such a premise because it is stated in the Constitution, which exists as cold, hard political fact. The major premise, therefore, cannot be stated in the form of the conclusion of another syllogism. If so, it has to be presupposed or else all the normative conclusions are false. Hence, Kelsen called the basic norm 'the transcendental-logical presupposition' (1967, 201).

Effectiveness and validity of the basic norm

A legal system is founded on a specific basic norm. We cannot arbitrarily choose a norm to be the basic norm. This is because the basic norm cannot be presupposed as valid if it is not effective. What is the point in saying that the basic norm of the United Kingdom is that one ought to behave as the Queen commands if the courts and everybody else only obey the commands of Parliament? Kelsen stated: 'The basic norm refers only to a constitution which is actually established by legislative act or custom, and is effective' (1967, 210). The basic norm, like all other norms, is an interpretation of a set of facts. Without facts there are no norms. This is not a contradiction of the 'is' and 'ought' distinction. The basic norm is not derived from facts but is an interpretation of them.

All norms of a legal system derive their validity ultimately from the same basic norm, just as the leaves and branches of a tree arise from the same root base. The effectiveness of the basic norm depends on the effectiveness of the norms that are derived from it. Imagine a country where the basic norm of its legal system is that one ought to behave as the Dictator commands. The Dictator's commands are so terrible that people stop obeying them and the Dictator is not strong enough to force the people to obey them. There comes a point at which the norm 'One ought to behave as the Dictator commands' is no longer effective. As Kelsen wrote, 'A constitution is "effective" if the norms created in conformity with it are by and large applied and obeyed' (1967, 210). If they are widely disregarded, a different norm may emerge as the basic norm.

It is important to keep in mind that effectiveness is a condition of validity but is not validity itself (Kelsen 1967, 213). This is the consequence of the 'is' and 'ought' distinction. The effectiveness of the norm is part of reality. It furnishes a reason for the legal scientist to think that a norm, in the form of an 'ought', exists. But the reality does not always accord with the norm. A norm may be valid even when it fails on occasion to be effective in shaping conduct. Consider the norm 'One ought not to drive at more than 100 kph on the motorway'. If this norm is totally disregarded by motorists and never enforced by the police the norm is wholly ineffective, giving us no reason to think that the norm exists at all. What does not exist cannot be valid. But if most motorists observe the speed limit most of the time, the occasional infringement will not render the norm invalid, even though it is evident that the norm is ineffective from time to time. It is in the nature of norms that they are capable of being violated. If a norm is not capable of violation, if it is always fully effective, it is not a norm but a law of nature – an 'is' statement and not an 'ought' statement.

Logical unity of the legal order and determining whether a norm belongs to the legal order

The legal order, according to the pure theory, is a hierarchical order. Every norm of a legal order exists because of validity conferred on it by another norm within that order. The validity of every norm is ultimately derived from the basic norm. Hence, the legal order has a logical unity. A lower norm cannot contradict or violate a higher norm from which it derives validity. Kelsen argued that the logical unity of the legal order also makes the conflict of norms at the *same* level logically impossible.

In the physical world it makes no sense to say that something exists and it does not. Unicorns exist or they do not. Earth orbits the Sun or it does not. In the words of Aristotle: 'It is impossible for the same man to suppose that the same thing is and is not. One cannot say of something that it is and that it is not in the same respect and at the same time.' (1968 (350 BC), 163) A statement about the physical world is either true or false, but not both.

A norm is neither true nor false. 'A person ought not to commit adultery' is not about what *is* but about what *ought not* to be done. Hence it is neither true nor false. However, the statement 'It is a norm of the legal order of this country that a person ought not to commit adultery' is either true or false, but not both (Kelsen 1967, 205–6). Its truth or falsity can be determined by consulting statutes and judicial precedents. It is possible that in a different legal order adultery is permitted. It is also possible that the same legal order may prohibit adultery during one period and permit the practice during another period. In such cases there is no conflict of norms. But adultery cannot be permitted and prohibited in the same legal order at the same time and in identical circumstances. It is physically possible that different norm creating authorities within the same legal order may issue contradictory commands. Parliament may prohibit something and the High Court may permit it. Federal and state parliaments may pass conflicting laws. A legal order, being a hierarchical order, usually has norms to resolve these conflicts. Thus, in Australia the High Court's ruling will override a law of Parliament and a valid federal law overrides an inconsistent state law. It is also physically possible that the same norm creating authority may unintentionally enact conflicting norms.

Conflicting norms may operate simultaneously in the practical sense. There are unconstitutional laws that no one has tested in a court. There are regulations in the statute book that are *ultra vires* the parent statutes. These may never be annulled, for want of challenge. This does not mean that the higher order norms are invalidated. The conflicting norms will have practical operation despite their logical inconsistency. What the pure theory says is that logically they cannot remain in conflict within the same legal order because all norms derive their validity ultimately from the same basic norm. A court that faces a conflict of norms will first look at the constitutional status of each norm. A higher order norm will override a lower order norm. If the conflict is between norms of the same hierarchical level, the court will seek to resolve it through interpretive methods. For example, a later law is presumed to prevail over a conflicting earlier law (*lex posterior derogat legi priori*). A special law is presumed to prevail over a more general law that conflicts with it (*lex specialis derogat legi generali*). These rules of interpretation are logical rules. If the norm creator issued a command in 2007 and another in 2008 on the same subject, it is logical to presume that the later command represents the norm creator's current wish. Similarly, it is logical to presume that the norm creator's special command is intended to qualify its more general command. What happens if the conflict remains irreconcilable after all the interpretive options are exhausted? In practice, the court will adopt one norm in preference to the other, or formulate a new norm. What the court will not do is refuse to resolve a question that is properly before it simply because the relevant norms are irreconcilable. The court's decision in this type of case amounts to an act of legislation. The court's authority to legislate on such occasions is referrable to the norms conferring jurisdiction upon it. The resolution of such conflicts is part of the routine business of courts. What if there is an irreconcilable conflict within the same command, as when a norm creator says 'One must do X' and also 'One must not do X'? According to Kelsen, this command 'is simply meaningless and therefore no objectively valid legal norm exists' (1967, 208).

We are entitled to question whether logical unity is a necessary attribute of a legal order. We may embrace a different notion of a legal system, as I do elsewhere in this book. However, if we are thinking about the legal order as conceived by the pure theory, it is evident that logical unity is an essential feature of the legal order and that the order breaks down if conflicts of norms are not resolved when they occur.

Membership of a legal order

Branches belong to the same tree if they arise directly or indirectly from the same root system. Similarly, according to the pure theory, norms belong to the same legal system if their validity flows directly or indirectly from the same basic norm. The unifying factor in the case of the tree is the common root system, and in the case of the legal system it is the common basic norm, as shown in Figure 3.2.

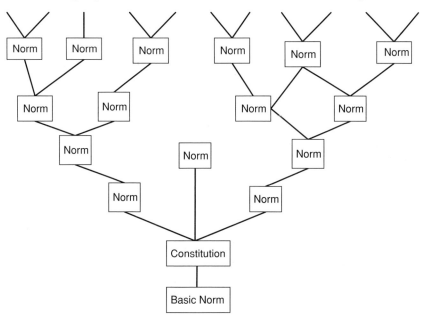

Figure 3.2 The tree of norms

How can we determine in practice whether a norm belongs to a legal system? Consider a judge called upon to decide whether driver X is guilty of the offence of failing to stop on the red light at an intersection. The judge must decide whether there is a valid norm that X *ought* to stop on the red light. The judge observes that the *Traffic Act* requires motorists to stop on the red light, but that does not provide a complete answer to the question. The answer is found in the higher norm (in the Constitution), which states that Acts of Parliament ought to be observed. The judge will not generally ask the question: what validates the Constitution? However, the answer will be found in the norm that the Constitution ought to be obeyed. In other words the judge traces the validity of the norm about stopping at red lights to the basic norm of the legal system. If the norm cannot be so linked to the basic norm it is not a part of the legal order. The relation to the basic norm is the indispensable criterion for a norm to belong to the legal order.

The criticism of Joseph Raz

Raz disagreed with the last mentioned proposition and argued that the basic norm 'does not contribute anything to the criteria of identity and membership' (1980, 104). According to Raz, since all norms of a legal order are traceable to the constitution, the various chains of validity end there. Hence, he claimed: 'The tree diagram can exist even if the basic norm is omitted from it' (1980, 104). This argument is correct only if Kelsen's theory is abandoned. The constitution *of itself* is a fact. Constitutional norms are the meanings that the legal scientist gives to the constitution. The legal scientist gives normative force to the rules of the constitution only because a superior norm confers validity upon them. That superior norm is the basic norm. We must remember that Kelsen's tree is the tree of norms, not of facts. The norms established by the constitution are valid because the basic norm dictates that one ought to behave as the constitution prescribes. It is the basic norm that enlivens the constitution and hence all other norms that derive their validity from the constitution. Without it the tree collapses. We may reject Kelsen's pure theory on any number of grounds, but within that theory the basic norm is indispensable.

Raz developed a concept of a legal system resembling Kelsen's theory but dispensing with the basic norm. He stated that legislative power need not be created by law and that the first constitution is law because we know that it belongs to an efficacious legal system (Raz 1980, 138). He also insisted that the powers of the authors of the first constitution can be conferred upon them by an ordinary law of the legal system (1980, 138). Raz's theory can be supported, but only if we ignore the 'is/ought' problem and assume that legislation directly creates norms. The existence of a legislative enactment is a fact, whereas a norm is an 'ought'. Kelsen's point (following Hume and Kant) is that an 'ought' cannot be derived from a 'fact'; it can only be derived from another 'ought'. The pure theory results from the uncompromising observance of this disconnect. The need for a basic norm arises because norms cannot be derived from facts. The first constitution, of itself, cannot create norms of obligation. The norms of the constitution are obligatory because the basic norm states that the first constitution (whether made with or without legal authority) ought to be obeyed.

Raz, like most legal positivists, conceived the law as fact and the legal system as a system of legal facts. This conception can be justified on the utilitarian ground that it simplifies the explanatory model and aligns it better with the way people think about the law and legal system. Lay persons do not care about Hume's empiricism or Kant's transcendental idealism. They do not care about the relation of 'is' and 'ought' or about the purity of legal theory. They want to know what the rules of the game are so that they can get on with their lives as best they can. Law as fact makes more intuitive sense, and in that sense *may* be of greater utility than the pure theory. This does not mean, however, that the pure theory is logically wrong.

Legitimacy and revolution

In an ongoing legal order, a norm remains valid until it is terminated by its own terms or by a higher norm. Some laws contain 'sunset clauses' according to which they cease to operate after the expiration of a prescribed period. Generally, though, norms established by a law remain valid until repealed by another norm enacted by another valid law. In other words, a valid norm remains valid until it is terminated in the way prescribed by the legal order founded on the basic norm. Kelsen called this the principle of legitimacy (1967, 209). The basic norm itself may be transformed in the manner prescribed by the basic norm. In other words, the basic norm may be changed legitimately. Written constitutions usually contain special rules by which they may be changed. The Australian Constitution may be amended by a procedure that requires approval by a special majority at a national referendum (section 128).

However, it is possible that a constitution may prohibit certain kinds of constitutional amendment. Article 79(3) of the German Constitution states that 'Amendments to this Basic Law affecting the division of the Federation into Länder, their participation on principle in the legislative process, or the principles laid down in Articles 1 and 20 shall be inadmissible'. Articles 1 and 20 guarantee basic human rights and the democratic structure of the state. In short, the most fundamental values of the German Constitution are said to be unalterable. The Indian Supreme Court has taken the view that the basic features of the Indian Constitution cannot be altered by recourse to the amending procedure (*Kesavananda Bharathi Sripadagalvaru v The State of Kerala* AIR 1973 SC 1461). It is generally regarded by constitutional scholars that the *Act of Union 1707* cannot be repealed by the UK Parliament. This Act united the Parliaments of England and Scotland and hence is constitutive of the current sovereign Parliament of the United Kingdom (Smith & Brazier 1998, 77). Similarly, scholarly opinion takes the view that the UK Parliament cannot limit its own sovereign power (Smith & Brazier 1998, 78; *Vauxhall Estates Ltd v Liverpool Corporation*

[1932] 1 KB 733). Where a constitution or some aspect of it cannot be changed by a constitutional process, such change may nevertheless occur by way of a revolution.

Revolution

Sometimes the basic norm of the legal order changes by means not authorised by the basic norm. This can happen in a number of different ways – sometimes violently, sometimes by peaceful and consensual means. It happens when one state conquers another and imposes its own sovereign power over the conquered state. The establishment of Crown sovereignty over Britain's colonies subordinated local legal systems to the English law and constitution. It happens when a region of a country secedes from the whole and establishes its own legal order. Recent examples include the separation of: Bangladesh from Pakistan (1971); Eritrea from Ethiopia (1993); Slovenia (1991), Bosnia-Herzegovina (1991) and Croatia (1995) from Yugoslavia; East Timor from Indonesia (1999); and Kosovo from Serbia (2008). The basic norm also changes when an empire or federation breaks up into independent states. The basic norm may also be displaced by domestic events, as when the constitution is overthrown in a *coup d'etat* or by a popular uprising. The English Revolution of 1688, the American Revolution of 1776, the French Revolution of 1789 and the Russian Revolution of 1917 are monumental historical examples of such constitutional change.

Consensual revolution

The basic norm can be changed by peaceful and consensual means. Such change is revolutionary when the new basic norm does not derive its validity from the old basic norm. The constitutional evolution of the Australian Commonwealth provides a good illustration of revolution by consensus.

The Australian Constitution is a part of an Act of the UK Parliament passed in 1900 – the *Commonwealth of Australia Constitution Act 63 & 64 Victoria (Chapter 12)*. The Constitution was alterable by the UK Parliament, as it was not bound by its own laws. In 1931, the UK Parliament enacted the *Statute of Westminster*, which declared that no Act of Parliament of the United Kingdom shall extend to a dominion unless that dominion requested it and consented to it (section 4). The Statute was adopted by Australia in 1942 and from that date the UK Parliament refrained from making law for Australia in the absence of a request. In theory, the UK Parliament could have repealed the *Statute of Westminster*, but any UK law made for the Commonwealth of Australia without a request would have been regarded as ineffectual by Australian courts. The ultimate source of legislative power for the Commonwealth of Australia became the Australian Constitution. The reason for this change was the political reality that Australia would no longer recognise UK law directed at the federation. The power to legislate on request remained until it was relinquished by the UK Parliament by the *Australia Act 1986* (UK). This is the position even though, as a sovereign legislature, the UK Parliament is not bound by its own previous laws, and may repeal them or may legislate against them. The UK Parliament has lost competence in relation to Australia through a revolutionary process in which it was a willing participant.

A revolution may also occur peacefully, when an independent nation makes a collective decision to adopt a new constitution in a manner unauthorised by the existing constitution. Such constitutions are known as autochthonous constitutions. The current US, Indian and Irish constitutions and the 1972 Sri Lankan Constitution were adopted by autochthonous processes. The US Constitution was adopted by the Constitutional Convention in Philadelphia in 1787 and ratified by conventions in the different states. The Indian Constitution in 1950 and the Sri Lankan Constitution in 1972 were adopted by specially created constituent assemblies. Ireland's 1937 Constitution, though enacted by the existing parliament (Dáil Éireann), was approved at a referendum as an autochthonous (independently established) constitution. In each case the new constitution marked a break with the past. Australia's Constitution is not an autochthonous constitution, although it was drafted by constitutional conventions and approved at referenda held in the several colonies. The draft so approved was enacted into law by the UK Parliament, ensuring legal continuity. The continuity was broken only by the political effects of the *Statute of Westminster Adoption Act 1942* and the *Australia Act 1986* (UK).

Revolution by force

The basic norm of a legal order may be displaced by force. The American, French and Russian revolutions are among the best known historical illustrations. In each case the existing basic norm was changed by violent struggle. In some cases the change is swift and decisive and in other cases the struggle for legal supremacy may stretch over many months or even many years, with the basic norm remaining in a state of uncertainty.

The American Revolution and the establishment of the US Constitution are remarkably instructive of the fluctuations of the basic norm in revolutionary conditions. The 13 British colonies that became the United States of America were subject to British law. Hence, the legal order of each colony was founded on the basic norm of the British Constitution. Though the colonists were subject to the laws of the British Parliament they were not represented in it. In 1775, following accumulated grievances, the colonies established their own governments in defiance of the British Crown. The British government's efforts to maintain its sovereignty by military force led to the War of Independence (also known as the Revolutionary War), which lasted six years. Significant events concerning the legal order occurred during this period of conflict. The colonies formed the Second Continental Congress, which on 4 July 1776 adopted the famous American Declaration of Independence. The Congress then proceeded to draft Articles of Confederation that were finally ratified by all states in 1781. The Articles established a confederation called the 'the United States of America'. However, under Article 2, the states retained their separate sovereignty. States adopted their own separate constitutions. There was no certainty during this time about the basic norm of each state, as the outcome of the Revolutionary War remained uncertain. Eventually, the British forces were defeated, with substantial help from France, and in the *Treaty of Paris 1783* Britain recognised the independence of the American states. A period followed in which each of the 13 states functioned as independent political entities loosely confederated with each other. Each state had its own legal order based on its distinct basic norm. In 1787, the Congress of the Confederation invited delegates from each state to a convention in Philadelphia for the purpose of discussing improvements to the Articles of Confederation. Delegates from all the states except Rhode Island attended. After deliberation, the delegates agreed to expand their mandate and proceeded to draft a new constitution for the United States of America. They agreed that the Constitution would be binding on the ratifying states if a minimum of nine states ratified it. On 21 June 1788, New Hampshire became the ninth state to ratify the Constitution. The Constitution commenced its operation on the swearing in of George Washington as the President on 30 April 1789.

The change in the basic norm by revolution usually means that the courts of the country recognise it. This may happen in one of two ways. The courts may accept the new reality and interpret the events as creating a new legal order founded on the new basic norm. In 1958, the President of Pakistan in a *coup d'etat* proclaimed the annulment of the country's constitution and assumed supreme power. There was no effective political resistance to this move. When the legality of the action was questioned, the Chief Justice of Pakistan, the Honourable Muhammed Munir, declared that the effect of the 1958 annulment of the Constitution by the President 'is not only the destruction of the existing Constitution but also the validity of the national legal order' (*The State v Dosso* [1958] 2 PSCR 180, 184). In 1966 the Prime Minister of Uganda, in complete disregard of the 1962 Constitution, assumed all state powers and proclaimed a new constitution. There was no political opposition to this action. The Chief Justice of Uganda, Sir Udo Udoma, declared: '. . . our deliberate and considered view is that the 1966 Constitution is a legally valid constitution and the supreme law of Uganda; and that the 1962 Constitution having been abolished as a result of a victorious revolution in law does no longer exist nor does it now form part of the Laws of Uganda, it having been deprived of its *de facto* and *de jure* validity' (*Uganda v Commissioner of Prisons; Ex parte Matovu* [1966] EA 514).

In Kelsenian terms, the superior courts of Pakistan and Uganda regarded the revolutionary acts and the absence of resistance to them as reasons for recognising a new basic norm. From one point of view the courts were interpreting the normative significance of certain political realities. From another point of view, the judicial rulings were themselves revolutionary acts that contributed to the effectiveness of the new basic norm.

Effects of revolution on existing law

A revolution in the *legal sense* is about changing the basic norm of the legal order. Not all attempted revolutions succeed. Some have temporary success when their leaders gain and hold power for a period before the old order is restored. The short-lived Confederacy of the United States and the white minority regime of Southern Rhodesia offer historical examples. In 1861, 11 southern states broke away from the American Union and established the Confederacy, which lasted until its defeat in the Civil War in 1865. In 1965 the white minority government of the British colony of Southern Rhodesia (now Zimbabwe) unilaterally declared its independence from the UK and ruled the country until 1979, when the nation returned to British sovereignty.

The legal situation must be considered in relation to the following scenarios:
1. The attempted revolution has failed and the basic norm remains unchanged.
2. The revolution has succeeded, there is no opposition to the new regime and a new basic norm is established.
3. The revolution is in progress and the outcome is uncertain owing to resistance.
4. The old order is restored after the initial success of the revolution.

An attempted revolution fails and the existing basic norm is unchanged

A revolution in the legal sense is a direct and deliberate violation of the basic norm. Revolutionary activity almost certainly will violate many other criminal laws, such as those concerning treason and mutiny. If the attempted revolution fails, the basic norm stands and so do all the norms that derive their validity from it. Hence, the commands and statutes of the revolutionaries have no legal effect. The fate of the revolutionaries will depend on how the authorities deal with them under existing norms. Often it is harshly.

The revolution succeeds and a new basic norm is established

A revolution changes the basic norm of the legal order, but it is unusual for the new rulers to make wholesale changes to the laws of the land. Many of the existing laws, particularly the private law, will remain unaffected. Thus, contracts of the past will continue to be enforced, property owners will retain title, torts will remain actionable and crimes will be punishable. The Bolshevik Revolution of October 1917 in Russia was an exceptional case. The revolutionary forces led by Vladimir Lenin aimed not only to take supreme power but also to radically change the laws of the land in order to socialise the means of production, exchange and distribution. They succeeded in establishing the first communist state. Similar revolutions followed in many countries where communist or workers' parties took power. In each case the laws were fundamentally altered. The Islamic Revolution in Iran in 1979 also brought about radical legal change. However, it is more often the case that the new regime leaves the bulk of the general laws untouched.

What is the source of the post-revolution validity of the old laws? The ousted basic norm no longer supports them. Kelsen's answer is simple. If the old laws are regarded as valid it is because the new constitution has validated them expressly or tacitly (Kelsen 1967, 209). The content of these norms remains unchanged but the reason for their validity changes as the old basic norm is displaced by the new.

The revolutionary struggle is in progress and there is uncertainty about the basic norm

As noted previously, a revolutionary struggle may last many months or even years. The revolutionary group may even gain temporary control of the machinery of government. There will be uncertainty during such periods as to what the basic norm is, and hence uncertainty about the validity of specific laws. Courts that derive their authority from the old constitution may have to consider the validity of three types of laws or purported laws.

1. Existing non-political law

The first category comprises non-political laws that existed at the commencement of the revolution, which are validated by the basic norm that the revolution seeks to overthrow. In other words, these are the laws of the old regime. Of these existing laws, some are political and some non-political law. Non-political law here refers to private law governing matters such as contract, torts, property, marriage, succession, criminal law protecting person and property and the laws of evidence and procedure. Political law refers to the constitution and other laws that concern the powers of government and the political system. (The distinction between political and non-political law is one of convenience and is not always easy to draw, as shown by communist and Islamic revolutions.)

A rebel regime that is striving forcibly to change the political laws may not have an immediate interest in changing non-political laws. In such cases, as Kelsen suggested, the non-political laws may be deemed to be tacitly adopted by the rebel regime, and hence may be valid under both contending basic norms. A key reason for judicial willingness to recognise and enforce non-political law in these circumstances is the avoidance of hardship to innocent individuals.

2. Non-political law enacted by the rebel regime

The second category comprises laws of a non-political nature made by a rebel regime that is in temporary control. There are sound practical reasons for courts to apply the non-political laws of a rebel regime, chief among them being the avoidance of general lawlessness and hardship to individuals. Assume that the rebel regime makes a law that dispenses with the need for consideration in forming an enforceable contract, and that many contracts are concluded by persons relying on this enactment. It will be manifestly unjust if these contracts are not enforced because they are invalid according to the old law. Again, if the criminal laws against theft, murder, assault and other injuries are not enforced because they have been modified by the rebel regime, the society will descend into chaos. This is, of course, a moral reason for enforcing the law. Is there a legal reason in the Kelsenian sense?

It is conceivable that the norm enacted by the rebel regime is validated by a norm of the legal order that the rebels are seeking to overthrow. This reasoning is known as the 'doctrine of necessity'. As the Privy Council stated, the doctrine holds: '. . . when a usurper is in control of a territory, loyal subjects of the lawful Sovereign who reside in that territory should recognise, obey and give effect to commands of the usurper in so far as that is necessary in order to preserve law and order and the fabric of civilised society' (*Madzimbamuto v Lardner-Burke* [1969] 1 AC 645, 726). The origin of the doctrine is found in Hugo Grotius' *De Jure Belli ac Pacis*:

> Now while such a usurper is in possession, the acts of government may have a binding force, arising not from a right possessed by him, for no such right exists, but from the fact that the one to whom sovereignty actually belongs, whether people, or king, or senate, would prefer that measures promulgated by him should meanwhile have the force of law, in order to avoid the utter confusion which would result from the subversion of laws, and suppression of the courts. (1927 (1625), 159)

This rationale was adopted by the US Supreme Court in a number of cases considering the validity of laws enacted by the Confederate states during the Civil War. In *Texas v White*, the Court stated:

> It may be said, perhaps with sufficient accuracy, that acts necessary to peace and good order among citizens, such for example, as acts sanctioning and protecting marriage and the domestic relations, governing the course of descents, regulating the conveyance and transfer of property, real and personal, and providing remedies for injuries to person and estate, and other similar acts, which would be valid if emanating from a lawful government, must be regarded in general as valid when proceeding from an actual, though unlawful government; and that acts in furtherance or support of rebellion against the United States, or intended to defeat the just rights of citizens, and other acts of like nature, must, in general, be regarded as invalid and void. (74 US 700, 733 (1868))

The doctrine of necessity (or implied mandate) allows the courts to justify the enforcement of rebel laws, on the authority of a norm of the old legal order to which the courts owe allegiance.

3. Political law enacted by the rebel regime

The most difficult problems for the courts arise in relation to political laws enacted by a rebel regime for the time being in control of the machinery of government. The usurper in this scenario is in temporary command but has not gained lasting control of the state. Judges derive their jurisdiction from the old constitution, to which they have pledged loyalty. The ultimate source of their authority is the basic norm of the legal order challenged by the rebels. Consider a decree that abolishes the parliament and grants legislative power to the commander of the rebel forces. This decree directly violates the constitution. If the court gives effect to the decrees of the commander, it will in effect recognise a new basic norm and thereby advance the revolution. (This new basic norm would be something like: 'The commander's decrees ought to be obeyed'.) The alternatives are for the judges to refuse enforcement of the commander's decrees (and risk retribution) or to stand down as judges. If the court is not physically situated within the territory controlled by the rebel regime, the judges will be less intimidated, but their decisions may be ineffective so long as the rebel regime controls the organs of enforcement.

Madzimbamuto v Lardner-Burke vividly illustrates the legal issues. Southern Rhodesia (later Zimbabwe) was a British colony administered under a constitution (*Constitution 1961*) that granted a high degree of autonomy to the local legislature and executive. The UK Parliament retained the power to legislate for the colony, including the power to amend the *Constitution 1961* at will. The highest appellate court of the colony remained the Privy Council sitting in London. The majority of the people of the colony were black Africans, but the government was dominated by minority whites led by the Prime Minister, Ian Smith. Britain was planning to grant the colony independence under a constitution that would have led to black majority rule. On 6 November 1965, Madzimbamuto was detained lawfully under a detention order made under emergency regulations in keeping with the *Constitution 1961*. The regulations were effective for three months and could have been extended only with the approval of the Legislative Assembly (*Constitution 1961*, s72). On 11 November 1965, Ian Smith and his Cabinet made a 'Declaration of Independence' that Southern Rhodesia was no longer a Crown colony but was an independent sovereign state. The Governor (Queen's representative in the colony) responded immediately with a public statement that the Declaration of Independence was unconstitutional, and on 16 November 1965 the UK Parliament passed the *Southern Rhodesia Act 1965*, which reaffirmed UK sovereignty over Southern Rhodesia, nullified the enactments of the Smith regime and suspended the power of the Legislative Assembly. The UK government, with the support of the international community, instigated a range of measures to reverse the revolution, including trade embargoes on the colony. The rebel regime disregarded the *Southern Rhodesia Act* and established itself as a *de facto* government. Although the state of emergency expired on 4 February 1966, Madzimbamuto continued to be held under new purported emergency regulations made by the rebel regime. When his detention was challenged, the High Court of Southern Rhodesia agreed that the Declaration of Independence was unlawful but that it was necessary for the court to give effect to the emergency regulations of the rebel regime because it was the only effective government in the colony. This argument was supposedly based on the doctrine of necessity.

The applicant appealed to the Privy Council. The majority of the Council (Lord Pearce dissenting) firmly rejected the High Court's reasoning and allowed the appeal. They held that the practical difficulties of ruling against the usurper did not absolve the court from upholding valid law. The doctrine of necessity was overridden by the express commands of the sovereign UK Parliament:

> Her Majesty's judges have been put in an extremely difficult position. But the fact that the judges among others have been put in a very difficult position cannot justify disregard of legislation passed or authorised by the United Kingdom Parliament, by the introduction of a doctrine of necessity which in their Lordships' judgment cannot be reconciled with the terms of the Order in Council. It is for Parliament and Parliament alone to determine whether the maintenance of law and order would justify giving effect to laws made by the usurping Government, to such extent as may be necessary for that purpose. ([1969] 1 AC 645, 730–1)

Lord Pearce, in a dissenting opinion, spelled out the limits of the doctrine of necessity. The acts of the usurper may be recognised as valid so far as they:

(a)   are directed to and reasonably required for ordinary orderly running of the state

(b)   do not impair the rights of citizens under the lawful 1961 Constitution, and

(c)   are not intended to and do not in fact directly help the usurpation and do not run contrary to the policy of the lawful sovereign (at 732).

Contrary to the majority view, Lord Pearce concluded that the detention orders, though unlawful, should be recognised (hence validated) under the doctrine of necessity. A principal reason was that the continuation of the emergency rule was consistent with the UK government's policy of seeking the reversal of the revolution through non-disruptive means (at 741–2). Lord Pearce's disagreement with the majority was not about the rule but about its application to the facts. These opinions, when put into Kelsenian terms, hold that the doctrine of necessity refers to a norm derived from the constitution under which the courts were established. Its validity is traceable to the basic norm of the old constitution, not the usurper's constitution. It must therefore yield to the overriding acts validly made under the old constitution. In *Madzimbamuto* the Privy Council explained the content of this norm as it exists in the legal order of the UK and its colonies. In another legal order, there may not be a norm of necessity, or the norm may have a different content.

The old legal order is restored after the initial success of the revolution

A rebel regime may be successful over a period of time but be eventually overthrown, with the result that the old regime is reinstated. In this scenario, the courts are no longer under the physical control of the usurper. In the previous scenario we considered the norm that would validate a usurper's enactment while the usurper was still in control. Here we consider the norm that would validate the usurper's enactment after the usurpation has ended. The first is a case of contemporaneous validation and the second a matter of retrospective validation. Why should the two cases be treated differently? Lord Pearce in *Madzimbamuto* offered the following explanation:

If acts are entitled to some retrospective validity, there seems no reason in principle why they should not be entitled to some contemporaneous validity. It is when one comes to assess the question of public policy that there is a wide difference between the retrospective and contemporaneous. For during a rebellion it may be harmful to grant any validity to an unlawful act, whereas, when the rebellion has failed, such recognition may be innocuous. (at 733)

Lord Pearce suggested that the courts are more likely to validate rebel acts if the rebellion is at an end. The statement is consistent with Kelsen's view that the question of validity of a usurper's enactment is determined by a norm of the prevalent legal order. The judges' decision to confer or refuse validity to a rebel enactment will be valid law if it is authorised by a valid higher norm ultimately derived from the basic norm of the restored legal order.

International law

International law, according to the command theories of Bentham and Austin, is not law but positive morality. The principal reason for this view is that there is no global sovereign whose commands are habitually obeyed by nations. This was true in the time of Bentham and Austin and remains true today. The United Nations is not a global sovereign. Hart, who rejected the command concept of law, argued that international law is law in the same way that the law of primitive societies is law. Primitive societies lack specialised law making and law enforcing agencies, but display the operation of certain legal rules through diffused social pressure. Kelsen also compared international law to primitive law, but claimed that international law and national law are parts of a unified system of law derived from a single basic norm. Kelsen therefore took a monist view of international law, in opposition to the dualist view that regards international law and national law as separate systems of law.

The dualist view holds that international law is the law governing relations among states, and national law is the law regulating relations among individuals and between state and individuals. They are separate and independent systems of law (Triepel 1958 (1899); Anzilotti 1928). In many states, rules of international law do not become part of national law unless and until they are adopted as valid law by the appropriate law making authority of the state. The United Kingdom and Australia are among these states. A treaty ratified by the Australian or UK government will not be binding on citizens or officials unless its provisions are given domestic effect by an Act of Parliament. It is true that courts of these countries sometimes make use of international law principles and treaty obligations in interpreting statutes or developing the common law. Even in such instances, international law enters the state legal system not by its own force but by an act of state in the form of a judicial decision.

Dualism holds that a norm of national law and a norm of international law may contradict each other without the one invalidating the other, just as the laws of one nation may contradict laws of another nation without invalidating them. In Australia it is an offence to drive a car on the right-hand side of the road, whereas in the United States it is an offence to drive on the left-hand side of the road. Yet each law is valid within its own sphere of operation. Dualists argue that international law and national law similarly operate in different spheres, and hence may make contradictory demands without invalidating each other. International law, they say, binds states in relation to other states, whereas national law binds states and their citizens in relation to each other.

Kelsen disagreed with this reasoning and maintained that international and national law operate within the same sphere in relation to the same subjects. He argued that the state is not some separate metaphysical entity but a collection of individuals assembled and regulated by national law, like any corporation. All law regulates human behaviour. State responsibility at international law is actually individual responsibility. Kelsen wrote: 'That international law obligates and authorise states means this: it does not obligate and authorise individuals directly, like the national legal order, but only indirectly through the medium of the national legal order (whose personification is "the state")' (1967, 325). Modern international treaties sometimes create offences such as piracy, slave trading and terrorism that can be committed by persons acting not as agents of the state but as private individuals. Treaties have also established special *ad hoc* tribunals to try particular types of offences committed by individuals. They include the Nuremberg and Tokyo tribunals created following the Second World War, and the more recent UN tribunals on the Yugoslav and Rwandan conflicts. In 2002, the permanent International Criminal Court (ICC) was established under the *Rome Statute of the International Criminal Court*, with jurisdiction over crimes of genocide, crimes against humanity, war crimes and crimes of aggression. Some writers consider these treaties as international instruments that directly regulate the conduct of individuals (Starke 1998, 542). Even so, the apprehension, trial and punishment of offenders are achieved through the agency of different states.

If the rules of international law are regarded as moral rules (as Bentham and Austin did) the problem disappears, because in positivist legal theory law and morals occupy different fields. If so, we can say that the state has a moral obligation to behave as international law directs, but no legal obligation to do so. If, however, a rule of international law is considered to be law that is binding on a state, it cannot also be not binding on that state. A rule cannot be law and not law at the same time. (This is the principle of non-contradiction that Kelsen applied to law, following Kant.) How does a rule of international law become binding on a state? It can be binding because: (a) national law is subordinate to international law; or (b) national law recognises and gives domestic effect to the rule of international law. In each case international law becomes part of the single hierarchy or system of norms. Kelsen argued that the pure theory of law enables us to see the logical unity of national and international law. I will examine this argument presently, but first will address a threshold question.

As previously discussed, a legal order according to the pure theory is a coercive order. This is what distinguishes law from social and moral rules. Kelsen claimed that the international legal order is a coercive order. The coercive element in international law is found in the legal right of reprisal. A state whose right is violated by another state is permitted by international law to punish the offender by reprisal or use of force. Self-help is a legitimate means of rights protection at international law. International law also permits collective action to enforce its rules. Kelsen argued that in this respect international law resembles primitive law, where ostracism, self-help and group sanctions are means of enforcing the law (1967, 326). This is a questionable analogy, as I will presently argue.

Logical unity of national and international law: Kelsen's monist view

Kelsen argued that the unity of national and international law is seen whether primacy is accorded to international law or national law. I argue that unity, according to the pure theory, can be shown, if at all, only by acknowledging the supremacy of national law.

Does unity result from the primacy of international law?

According to this point of view, national legal systems are validated by a norm of international law. The norms of international law are ultimately validated by the basic norm of the international legal system. Many of the rules of international law today are found in treaties that nations have concluded among themselves. The United Nations Charter itself is a multilateral treaty. Other rules are made by international organisations established by treaty, such as the International Labour Organisation (ILO) and the World Trade Organisation (WTO). Yet all treaties derive their validity from a higher norm of customary international law expressed in the maxim *pacta sunt servanda* (agreements must be observed). Hence, as shown in Figure 3.3, the basic norm of the international legal system is something like: 'States ought to behave as international custom directs'. That is, if the international legal system is a system of law according to the pure theory. But is it?

In actual practice, national laws and state actions are frequently at odds with international law. The laws of many countries, for example, violate civil and political rights guaranteed by the *International Covenant on Civil and Political Rights* (ICCPR). Nations at war do not always observe the rules of international humanitarian law. States routinely violate WTO and ILO rules with impunity. Kelsen claimed that such conflicts do not negate the logical unity of the international and national legal systems. He compared the situation to that of unconstitutional laws remaining valid within state legal systems:

> The situation is exactly analogous to a situation within the state's legal order, without, on that account, causing any doubt as to its unity. The so-called unconstitutional statute,

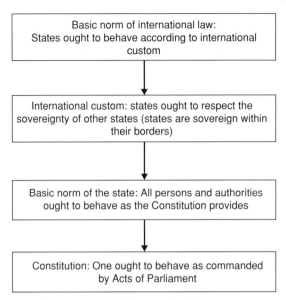

Figure 3.3 Monist version 1: primacy of international law

too, is and remains a valid law, without the constitution having to be suspended or changed because of it. The so-called illegal decision, too, is a valid norm and stays valid until its validity is abolished by another decision. (Kelsen 1967, 330)

Kelsen argued that a national law that violates international law is valid until it is annulled. However, the offending state commits a delict (wrong) under international law for which all its citizens are collectively liable to sanction (Kelsen 1967, 328). The fact that there are no effective means of annulling the offending national law or inflicting punishment, in Kelsen's view, does not affect the validity of international law. This analogy of international law with constitutional law is misleading.

We say that an unconstitutional law will be effective until and unless it is annulled when there is a credible means of annulling the law. If a constitution does not provide any means of invalidating a law that violates it, it is idle to talk of the unconstitutionality of the law. There are constitutions that do not invalidate inconsistent laws. The constitutions of the United Kingdom and New Zealand are of this type. Similarly, it makes little sense to say that a national law is voidable for inconsistency with an international legal norm when the international legal order provides no means of invalidating the national law or of punishing the offending state. As Hart pointed out, not only national laws but national constitutions may defy international norms (1998, 574). The British Constitution, for example, permits Parliament to legislate contrary to international law.

Kelsen's comparison of international law with primitive legal systems is again faulty. Diffused pressures may be effective within a close-knit and interdependent group such as an extended family or tribe. Not so in the global community

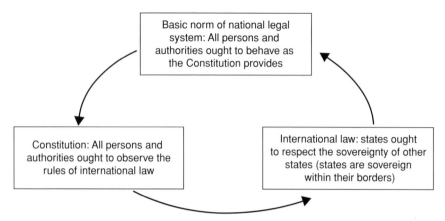

Figure 3.4 Monist version 2: primacy of national law

of sovereign and unequal states, where member states selectively adopt and abandon rules according to national convenience and their capacity to resist pressure from other nations. In most primitive societies the norm 'One ought to behave as custom directs' is effective and hence serves as the basic norm. In the community of nations, the norm 'States ought to behave as international custom directs' has much less effect. According to the pure theory the basic norm is an effective norm, and the effectiveness of the basic norm depends on the general effectiveness of the norms derived from it. If there is no effective basic norm at the international level, there can be no unity of international legal norms, and hence no unity of international and national legal systems.

Overall, Kelsen's attempt to ground the unity of national and international legal systems in the primacy of international law is doomed by the demands of his own pure theory.

Does unity result from the primacy of national law?

Kelsen's alternative explanation (illustrated in Figure 3.4) presupposes the sovereignty of a particular state and the primacy of its legal system. The legal system of a sovereign state may confer validity on the norms of international law. Such domestic recognition may be extended to all the norms or specific norms of international law. Recognition of international legal norms may occur in different ways. As Kelsen stated: 'Such recognition may take place either expressly by the act of the legislature or of the government or tacitly by the actual application of the norms of international law, by the conclusion of international treaties, or by respecting the immunities established by international law, etc' (1967, 335). International law so adopted becomes valid law only within the adopting state. If all states recognise a rule of international law it becomes valid for all states.

Three points must be made concerning this mode of integration of international and national law:

1.   According to this view of the unity of international and national law, the basic norm of the unified legal order is the basic norm of the national legal order. The norm that confers validity on the international legal norm is ultimately derived from the basic norm located in the constitution of the state.

2.   An international legal norm forms part of the national legal order only while its validity continues to be recognised by a valid national legal norm. An international legal norm may be invalidated by a subsequent valid national law.

3.   Not all states recognise the same norms of international law at the same time. Hence, international law has no claim to universal validity.

The monist view of international law founded on the primacy of national law is consistent with the pure theory and with state practice of many nations. According to this view international law is law, but only to the extent of its recognition by individual states. Whether a particular rule of international law is recognised by the state is a question that is answered by referring to the laws, judicial decisions, customs and practices of that state.

The reader should bear in mind that the foregoing discussion considered the legal status of international law according to the pure theory. There is an alternative way of conceiving at least some parts of international law as law by looking outside the pure theory. A few thoughts in this direction are offered below.

An evaluation of the pure theory of law

Kelsen's pure theory of law enriched jurisprudence. Kelsen was the first legal positivist, long before Hart, to abandon the concept of law as sovereign command. Hart, in my view, did not sufficiently acknowledge his debt to Kelsen. Kelsen introduced a new dimension to legal theory by compelling us to think of the distinction, and also the relation, between fact and norm, between legislative act and its normative effect. Kelsen offered an internally consistent model of the legal system that in some respects reflects the intuitive thinking of lawyers and law makers. Tracing a law's validity back to the constitution is normal legal reasoning. So is the idea that valid laws form an internally consistent system of laws. Kelsen's theory, unlike his predecessors', recognised the laws of primitive societies and of the international community as law.

Criticisms of Kelsen are often directed at the concepts and the internal consistency of his theory. Critics may question the adequacy of his theory to explain legal systems as they actually exist. Kelsen's idea of law as a norm to which a sanction is attached does not easily account for some kinds of laws. Procedural and evidentiary laws, laws creating organisations, laws conferring liberties and rights and laws repealing other laws fit uncomfortably within the pure theory. His arguments for the logical unity of the international and national legal orders are unconvincing at the present time in history.

Purity of Kelsen's theory

Kelsen claimed that his theory is pure on two counts. It distinguishes law from morals and law from fact. Did Kelsen succeed in separating law from morals? According to Kelsen's theory a legal norm exists because it is valid. It is valid because its making is authorised by another valid norm and so forth. Ultimately it is validated by the presupposed basic norm. A legal norm may (and often does) imitate a moral norm or draw its content from the content of a moral norm. This imitation does not convert the moral norm into a legal norm or the legal norm into a moral norm. What is the nature of the duty to obey each of these norms? Let us consider the norm 'Do not steal', which, as we know, is a moral norm as well as a legal norm in most countries. Let us call the moral norm Norm M and the legal norm Norm L.

There is a moral duty to obey Norm M because it is a moral norm. There is a legal duty to obey Norm L because it is a legal norm validated in Kelsen's theory by the basic norm. However, two further questions may be asked to test Kelsen's claim that law is totally separate from morality.

Given that the content of Norm L is identical to the content of Norm M, is there a special moral duty to observe Norm L?

The answer to this question according to Kelsen's theory is as follows. There is a legal duty under Norm L not to steal in addition to the moral duty under Norm M not to steal. A breach of Norm L attracts a sanction prescribed by law, such as imprisonment. This sanction may not be imposed if the thief is not caught or the prosecution fails to make the case. The thief who escapes the state sanction may still suffer some other kind of social or psychological sanction for his breach of the duty under Norm M. (An acquitted thief may be shunned by society and may suffer from feelings of guilt and pressures of conscience or faith.) The coincidence of the content of Norms L and M does not defeat Kelsen's separation thesis.

Is there a general moral duty to obey a valid legal norm?

A moral system may contain a general moral duty to obey valid legal norms. Kelsen does not deny that such a moral duty may exist. His position is that the moral duty should not be confused with the legal duty. The duty to obey a legal norm arises not from a *moral* norm but from a higher valid *legal* norm. Ultimately the legal duty to obey Norm L is imposed by the basic norm of the legal system.

Here is the ultimate problem for Kelsen's thesis concerning the separation of law and morals. The basic norm depends for its existence on efficacy. Efficacy of the basic norm depends on whether the particular legal norms derived from it are generally observed. Assume that the basic norm of a legal system is: 'Do as the Dictator commands'. If the Dictator's commands are ignored and the Dictator is powerless to enforce them, the basic norm of the dictatorship will cease. Is it possible to argue then that the existence of the basic norm depends on the moral attitudes of the people?

The moral attitudes of the people may be part of the state of affairs that makes the basic norm possible. This does not mean that the law is not separate from morality in Kelsen's scheme. The basic norm is not derived from this factual situation but is a mental construction of this state of affairs. The legal duty to observe the basic norm arises from this construction. This duty exists apart from any moral duty that one may have to observe the basic norm.

Separation of law from fact

Kelsen, following Hume and Kant, holds that an 'ought' cannot be derived from an 'is'. This logical proposition has not been contradicted. The law when understood as an 'ought' statement is eternally distinct from fact. The 'ought', however, cannot exist unless there are facts. Consider the norm that a court ought to impose a fine on a motorist convicted of a traffic offence under the *Traffic Act*. This norm exists because the following conditions exist:

1.   It is validated by a higher valid norm such as: 'Acts of Parliament ought to be observed'
2.   Parliament has passed the *Traffic Act*.

The second condition is a fact. The norm is separate from this fact in the sense that it is a mental construction of what the fact means. Nevertheless the relation between fact and norm is patent.

The same reasoning applies to the basic norm. The basic norm is presupposed because there is no higher norm from which it is derived. Nevertheless a basic norm must be effective. The state of effectiveness is a state of fact. The basic norm is a construction of this state of fact. The relation between fact and norm is again clear.

Kelsen's view that law is separate from fact is correct in the sense that legal norms are not derived from fact but are interpretations of fact. However, from another viewpoint law has an indispensable relation to fact inasmuch as the content of a legal norm is always an interpretation of a fact.

Explanatory weakness of the pure theory

Perhaps the most serious criticism of Kelsen is that his theory gives an elegant but misleading account of the law because of the particular definition of law on which it is based. FA Hayek remarked that this definition 'is postulated as the only possible and significant definition, and by representing as "cognition" what are simply the consequences of the definition adopted, the "pure theory" claims to be entitled to deny (or represent as meaningless) statements in which the term "law" is used in a different and narrower sense' (1982, II, 49). A theory is as good as its explanatory value. The pure theory defines a norm to include not only rules capable of guiding future behaviour, but also every *ad hoc* command that a person in authority issues. A tyrant's order to the executioner to hang an innocent man is as much a norm as the rule that persons ought to observe their contracts. Lumping together rules, commands, decrees and judgments under the term 'legal norm' serves the purposes of Kelsen's chosen theory, but at the cost of obscuring some important features of law as a social phenomenon. The concept of the rule of law (*Rechtstaat*) loses meaning when the distinction between a rule of conduct and arbitrary command is obliterated. Kelsen was not a friend of dictatorship. He was in fact a fugitive from the Nazi regime. Yet, according to the pure theory, Germany was a law governed society under Hitler's *Reich*.

Kelsen equated the existence of a legal norm with validity, and defined validity as derivation from a basic norm. Many of the fundamental rules of social life (rules that made social life possible) existed before governments, parliaments and courts were established. The idea that these rules are valid today because they are derived from the basic norm of the current legal order is fictitious. The spontaneous emergence of new norms governing conduct that have no derivation from authority is an ongoing feature of social order. The rules of cyberspace and electronic transacting are but one illustration of this phenomenon.

Alternative concepts of legal systems

Hart provided an alternative view of a legal system (see discussion in Chapter 2). A legal system, according to Hart, arises when a society develops secondary legal rules. These rules establish ways to formally recognise primary legal rules, to make new legal rules (or modify existing ones) and to adjudicate disputes concerning their application. In practice, they establish legislatures and courts and determine their powers and procedures. The overriding rule among them is the rule of recognition. In Hart's system, legal rules – whether they are primary or secondary rules – exist because they are accepted by persons not simply through coercion but through a sense of obligation.

Legal positivist concepts of legal systems offered by Bentham, Austin, Kelsen, Hart and Raz have an important common element. It is that legal systems arise directly or indirectly out of the deliberate acts of human agents. There is an alternative conception of legal systems, which proposes that legal systems can and do arise spontaneously, as a result of human actions but not of deliberate human design. The roots of the spontaneous order tradition are commonly traced to the thinkers of the Scottish Enlightenment, principally Hume, Ferguson and Smith. Its later revival owes much to the work of the Austrian school in economics and modern institutional theory. The elaboration of this jurisprudential tradition is undertaken in Chapter 10.

4

Realism in Legal Theory

In the previous two chapters I discussed the two most influential versions of legal positivism. In this chapter I explain and consider the theories of the jurisprudential school known as the legal realists, who challenge legal positivism in important ways. Realists are also positivists in the sense that they seek to explain the law *as it is* as opposed to what the law *ought to be*. Realists agree with the positivists that law's connections with morality are only contingent or coincidental. An immoral rule may still be law. Theirs is a very different complaint: namely, that positivists misrepresent the nature of law by their undue focus on its formal features.

Legal realism refers mainly to two schools of thought. One is known as American realism and the other as Scandinavian realism. Scholars of both traditions reject the more formal descriptions of the law given by legal positivists, but differ in what they see as the chief defects of positivist theory. The American realists claim that the law in real life is very different from the law stated in the law books. The real law, they say, depends on how appellate courts interpret written words and how trial courts determine the facts in particular cases. There is uncertainty at both ends.

Scandinavian realism is a movement that started with Axel Hägerström's attempt to find a scientific theory of law that did not involve metaphysical explanations. Hägerström and those who followed him down this path found that the force of law could not be explained by physical facts alone. They claim that, however hard you try, it is not possible to find a corporeal thing that corresponds to concepts such as property, right or duty. Law, they say, exists by the psychological effects caused by certain facts. Whereas American realism is mainly about getting the facts right about law making, Scandinavian realism concentrates on

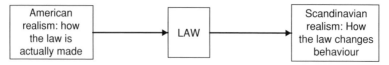

Figure 4.1 American and Scandinavian realisms at a glance

the psychological pressures that make people observe the law. This is illustrated in Figure 4.1.

The theorists even within each school do not speak with one voice, and the differences among them need to be examined. First, though, we must understand what sort of jurisprudence the realists criticise before we consider the nature of their criticisms. The main target of legal realism has been the attitude known as legal formalism. Legal formalism is often identified with legal positivism but, as observed below, this is only true of the most extreme versions of positivism.

Legal formalism and legal positivism

Legal formalism treats law as a closed and gapless system of rules that can be applied logically, without the need to take into account any policy or moral considerations. It treats the law as a system similar to mathematics. Mathematicians may calculate the time it takes a spacecraft launched from Earth to reach the planet Mars. They will need information such as the speed of the spacecraft, gravitational forces and planetary positions, but policy plays no part in their calculations. Legal formalism holds that a solution to a legal problem can be found by a similar process of deduction from known rules and established facts. According to the formalist view, policy plays a part in the making of law but has no role after the law is made.

It is hard to find a legal positivist today who would espouse formalism to this degree. Legal positivists, no doubt, think that law consists of rules and commands issued by recognised law makers such as monarchs, dictators, parliaments and judges. This means that the law is usually found written on paper or, in the modern age, in some form of electronic file. This is the idea of law that most lawyers and lay people have. It reflects the way lawyers, judges and law teachers usually go about the business of identifying and explaining the law. A law teacher instructs students to search for the law in statute books, law reports and commentaries written by legal scholars. Legal practitioners look to these sources to advise their clients and to argue their cases. Judges justify their decisions by the rules found in these written materials, or so they maintain.

However, modern legal positivists recognise that there is more to law than this. The most carefully crafted law will leave room for argument. There are a number of reasons for this. First, language by nature has limitations. There is only so much precision that language can achieve. As Hart pointed out, legal language has an open texture (1997, 128). Take the word 'adult'. It will suggest different ideas in different contexts. A person may be an adult for the purpose of being admitted to an adult movie, but not be an adult for the purpose of universal adult franchise. 'Reasonable care' will mean different standards of care in different activities. A surgeon's standard of reasonable care will be much higher than what is expected of a law professor. Even within one activity, opinions will differ on what is reasonable. Language consists not only of individual words, but also of combinations of words forming phrases, clauses, sentences and so forth. These combinations create further indeterminacy. Second, law makers cannot think of every question that may arise concerning the application of the law that they make. It is just too hard. Third, even if law makers can think of every question that can arise today, they cannot foresee what new questions may arise in the future. Law makers who used the word 'vehicle' in the 19th century would not have envisaged aeroplanes and spacecraft. The meaning of legal language changes because the world in which we live changes over time.

Facts are the other source of uncertainty about law. Even if all parties are agreed as to what the law means, they may disagree about the facts in issue. Take the case of motorist X, who is charged with the offence of driving on the prohibited side of the road. Assume that the prosecution, the defence and the judge all agree that the law requires motorists to drive on the left-hand side of the road. Yet X may deny that he drove on the right-hand side. Evidence will have to be found and evaluated to determine this question, and there is no certainty about the outcome. In more complex cases, large numbers of facts have to be proved and inferences drawn from the proven facts.

Modern legal positivists do not dispute any of this. They agree that the law can never be a mechanical process. What they say is that the law, despite the uncertainties at the edges, provides the general standards that make social life possible. Judicial discretion is unavoidable, but under the doctrine of precedent it serves rather than defeats the generality and predictability of the law. Hart explained the legal positivist position in this way:

> The open texture of the law means that there are, indeed, areas of conduct where much must be left to be developed by courts or officials striking a balance, in the light of circumstances, between competing interests which vary in weight from case to case. None the less, the life of the law consists to a very large extent in the guidance of both officials and private individuals by determinate rules which, unlike the application of variable standards, do *not* require from them a fresh judgement from case to case. This salient fact of social life remains true, even if the uncertainties may break out as to the applicability of any rule (whether written or communicated by precedent) to a concrete case. Here at the margin of rules and in the fields left open by the theory of precedents, the courts perform a rule producing function which administrative bodies perform centrally in the elaboration of variable standards. (1997, 135)

The American realists took a more radical view of the law, and some among them doubted the existence of legal rules at all. The American realists, though, were writing before Hart restated the central ideas of legal positivism. Hart's reformulation of legal positivism owes much to the realist critique of formalism.

American realism

A few general comments

Despite their serious differences, American realism and legal positivism share one important belief. It is that we must not confuse 'the law as it is' with 'the law as it ought to be'. They part company on the question of how we find 'the law as it is', as illustrated in Figure 4.2. The positivists, according to Hart, look to established primary rules and to secondary rules of recognition that designate law making bodies. American realists are sceptical about the degree to which rules represent the law. They seek to investigate how courts actually reach their decisions, given that rules are imprecise by nature and the discovery of facts is an imperfect process. Some realists regard law finding as an exercise in predicting how judges (or other officials) will decide legal disputes.

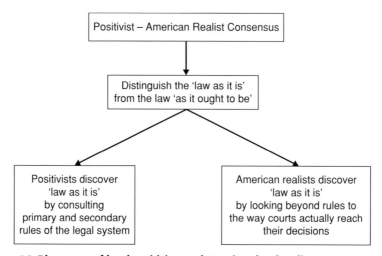

Figure 4.2 Divergence of legal positivism and American legal realism

It is important to note that the separation of law and morals in American realism is more ambiguous than in legal positivism. Most realists think that the degree of uncertainty inherent in rules allows judges to make moral decisions. The realists consider this judicial leeway to be a virtue of the law, as it allows greater consideration of justice. They also wish courts to use their discretion systematically to improve the law. The realists' separation of 'is' and 'ought', as Karl Llewellyn observed, is a temporary divorce (1962, 55). The divorce lasts while the scholars are discovering what courts actually do. The scholars will find that courts actually make moral decisions clothed in the language of logic. All that the divorce means is that at the initial stage of the inquiry the realists keep their own views of what the courts 'ought to do' separate from what the courts 'actually do'. The realists, on discovering that the courts in fact engage in law making, recommend that the courts drop their formalistic pretences and engage in systematic and informed law reform.

Some writers, such as Jerome Frank, have observed two types of sceptics among American realists: rule sceptics and fact sceptics. Rule sceptics pay more attention to the uncertainties of the rules that make up the law. They are preoccupied with the work of appellate courts, which are the final arbiters of the law. Fact sceptics are more concerned with the uncertainties that attend the discovery of facts on which a judgment depends. Their focus is mainly on the work of trial courts (Frank 1949, viii–ix). There are many authors within the school of American realism; for want of time and space I have focused the following discussions on the work of three of the most influential among them: Oliver Wendell Holmes Jr was the instigator of the realist movement; Karl Llewellyn synthesised much of the work of the rule sceptics; and Jerome Frank was a principal thinker among the fact sceptics.

Oliver Wendell Holmes Jr and the birth of American realism

Realist thinking was introduced to American jurisprudence by Oliver Wendell Holmes Jr (1841–1935). Holmes the lawyer must not be confused with his famous father Oliver Wendell Holms Sr, who was a physician, poet and essayist. Holmes Jr was called to arms during the American Civil War and served with distinction on the side of the Union before becoming a lawyer, Harvard law professor, philosopher and judge. He served on the Massachusetts Supreme Court for 20 years and on the US Supreme Court for 30 years. He had an enduring interest in history, philosophy and science – disciplines that he brought to bear on his writings. His thought was influenced by the British empiricists, American pragmatists such as William James, John Dewey and Charles Sanders Peirce, the historian Henry Maine and the evolutionary biologist Charles Darwin. Holmes was the flawed genius of American jurisprudence. We cannot notice his flaws without understanding his merit.

Holmes' most famous writing is his 1885 speech at the dedication of the Boston Law School's Rich Hall, which was later published by the *Harvard Law Review* under the title 'The path of the law'. It is reputed to be among the most widely read law review articles ever. It is also Holmes' most extravagant and undisciplined statement, and readers who try to gather Holmes' legal philosophy solely from this speech are likely to be seriously misled. Holmes' views on law were formed in the 1870s, during his teaching years at Harvard College and later at the Harvard Law School. However, we must look to his earlier writings to gain a firmer grasp of his legal philosophy. The following four themes run through Holmes' jurisprudence:

1. The law is an evolutionary process. It is the product of experience and not logic. It reflects society's adaptation to a changing world.
2. Courts play a vital role in the evolution of the law by actively reforming the law to suit changing conditions. Decisions of the appellate courts are

presented as logical deductions from established rules, but in fact they are legislative in nature. Courts make new law for new conditions.

3. Statutes depend for their efficacy on the courts and hence they are not law until enforced by the courts.

4. Law, for the above reasons, turns out to be nothing more than predictions about how courts will decide a dispute.

The evolutionary character of law

Holmes' evolutionary view of the law is first evident in the constitutional law lectures that he delivered at Harvard College in 1871–72. Holmes criticised Austin's theory that law is the command of a political sovereign, anticipating by nearly a century most of Hart's arguments in *The Concept of Law*. Holmes observed that law may exist independent of and even in opposition to sovereign will. He wrote that 'other bodies not sovereign, and even opinion, might generate law in a philosophical sense against the will of the sovereign' (Holmes 1871, 723).[1] Austin, as the reader will recall from Chapter 2, claimed that custom and common law become law only by the tacit command of the political sovereign when they are adopted by the courts. Holmes dismissed this as fiction. He noted that 'custom and mercantile usage have had as much compulsory power as law could have, in spite of prohibitory statutes' (1871, 724). Custom has performed its regulatory function before the courts are asked to recognise it as law.

This is a quintessentially evolutionary view. The law grows spontaneously as the result of human actions, even without the direction of law makers. This insight echoes the evolutionist thinking of the Scottish Enlightenment, discussed in Chapter 10. It recalls Adam Ferguson's famous saying that 'nations stumble upon establishments, which are indeed the result of human action, but not the execution of any human design' (1966 (1767), 122). Holmes fully unveiled his evolutionary conception of the law in his 1880 Lowell Lectures at Harvard University, which were later published as *The Common Law*. In his first lecture Holmes decried the tendency to treat the law like a mathematical system of axioms and corollaries. 'The law embodies the story of a nation's development', and to know what it is 'we must know what it has been and what it tends to become' (Holmes 1963 (1881), 5).

There are two problems with law's adaptation to change. One is that there is always some lag between change and the law's response to it. The second is that rules of law tend to remain in place after the reasons for their existence have ceased. Holmes described the evolutionary process of the law thus:

> The customs, beliefs, or needs of a primitive time establish a rule or a formula. In the course of centuries the custom, belief or necessity disappears, but the rule remains. The reason which gave rise to the rule has been forgotten, and ingenious minds set themselves to inquire how it is to be accounted for. Some ground of policy is thought of,

---

1 This quote is from Holmes' account of his own lectures given in the 'Book notices' section of volume 6 of the *American Law Review*, of which he was editor.

which seems to explain it and to reconcile it with the present state of things; and then the rule adapts itself to the new reasons which have been found for it, and enters on a new career. The old form receives a new content, and in time even the form modifies itself to fit the meaning which it has received. (1963, 8)

Holmes sought to demonstrate his theory by the history of tort and crime. He argued that early liability rules arose from the desire for revenge. Why else did ancient law require the dog that bit the plaintiff to be handed to the plaintiff tied on a log four cubits long? Or banish the rock that made the plaintiff trip over and break his collarbone? In more modern times, why do our courts attach strict liability to the circus owner for damage caused by an escaped lion, or vicarious liability to the pizza café owner for the accident caused by the delivery boy, even when in each case the owner is faultless? The most telling example is the admiralty rule under which admiralty courts order the arrest and sale of a ship to pay for damage caused by collision, even when the owner had leased the ship and had no control over it whatsoever. Holmes quoted Chief Justice Marshall: 'This is not a proceeding against the owner; it is a proceeding against the vessel for an offence committed by the vessel; which is not the less an offence, and does not the less subject her to forfeiture, because it was committed without the authority and against the will of the owner' (1963, 27). Courts of the present age have given policy reasons for strict liability and vicarious liability that are far removed from the original revenge motive. The law that initially served one purpose is now serving another.

Liability rules have not always evolved in this way, but Holmes' central point is this. Law is the product of social and economic forces. Law adapts and acquires new meanings to suit the convenience of the times. Holmes saw in the law's progression one of the most important features of evolution, whether biological or cultural. It is that adaptation is never perfect. The world does not stand still, so by the time a thing adapts to the world the world has moved on. This also means that the law can never be fully logical. As Holmes put it: 'The truth is that law is always approaching, never reaching consistency . . . It will become entirely consistent only when it ceases to grow' (1963, 32). This is a profound observation that anticipated a key insight of the modern science of emergent complexity, a topic that is discussed in Chapter 10.

Judicial role in legal evolution

The appellate judge takes centre stage in Holmes' theory of law. Social forces may provide the stuff of the law, but for the realist in Holmes what matters in the end are the concrete decisions of the appellate courts as to what the law is. (As discussed presently, there are other realists who focus more on the evidence aspect of legal disputes and consequently place the trial judge and jury at the centre of their investigations.) The final arbiter of the law (as opposed to facts) in common law systems is not the legislature but the judges of the highest court of appeal. In the United States, that court is the state Supreme Court or the US

Supreme Court, depending on the kind of case. In Britain it is the House of Lords, and in Australia it is the High Court of Australia.

Holmes did not help his own cause by not being careful to distinguish what judges ought to do from what they in fact do. He switched back and forth between descriptions and prescriptions without warning. At some points he appeared to contradict his own injunction to keep 'the law as it is' separate from 'the law as it ought to be'. This is particularly evident in *The Path of the Law*. However, a careful reading allows us to separate Holmes' descriptive account from his prescriptions.

Appellate judges, according Holmes, perform a legislative function in attuning the law to 'what is expedient for the community concerned'. However, they do so unconsciously and without admitting the legislative nature of what they do:

> Every important principle which is developed by litigation is in fact at the bottom the result of more or less definitely understood views of public policy; most generally to be sure, under our practice and traditions, the unconscious result of instinctive preferences and inarticulate convictions, but none the less traceable to views of public policy in the last analysis. (Holmes 1963, 32)

Judicial legislation and the certainty of the law

Holmes' prescriptive thesis was that judges should shed their pretence and should legislate overtly. Judges should recognise their inevitable duty to weigh 'considerations of social advantage' in stating the law (Holmes 1897, 467). Holmes believed that the judges do this anyway, often unconsciously. The real foundation of the judgment is left unexpressed because judges dislike discussing policy and clothe their decisions in the language of logic.

Holmes' prescription is easier said than done. A litigant who takes a dispute to a court expects a judgment according to law, not policy. If the law is based on a judge's view of right policy, public faith in the law and the judicial system will quickly decline. More importantly, it will deny people the guidance of the law as regards right and wrong conduct. Holmes was aware of this problem. He wrote: 'Finally, any legal standard must, in theory, be capable of being known. When a man has to pay damages, he is supposed to have broken the law, and he is further supposed to have known what the law was' (1897, 89). This is the reason that, in the field of negligence, the broad test of reasonable care (the prudent man test) has been progressively replaced by precedents on specific classes of acts and omissions. Yet the judicial method that Holmes commended does not easily reconcile the opposing needs of legal adaptation and legal certainty.

Holmes, as well as those who followed, paid insufficient attention to the way in which judges adapt the law to the changing world. They do not explain how community expectations or 'public policy' filter into the law through the judicial sieve. If judges legislate, they do so in a very special way. They cannot decide what is good for the community on the basis of their personal convictions. The court receives the signals of community good from the community's own practices and expectations. The arguments of the litigants before the court in the end are not about policy, but about the legitimacy or reasonableness of their expectations.

The court decides what expectations are reasonably held according to the practice of the community. Expectations change as the conditions of social life change. Holmes was right to observe that in some areas of the law, the community expectations may be unclear so that judges are left with legislative discretion. Even in these areas, however, the courts ought to adopt a policy that is most consistent with the grown system of rules. If the Court of Exchequer in *Rylands v Fletcher* (1868) [1] LR 3 HL 330 had decided that the loss should be borne not by the party that introduced the dangerous substance to the neighbourhood but by the party that was most able to bear the loss, the system of rules upon which British society and commerce functioned would have been instantly destabilised.

Holmes was aware of these constraints on judicial discretion. His language unfortunately tends to hyperbole, and consequently gives false impressions of his theory. A more nuanced account of the role of the judge in common law is offered by another evolutionary theorist, FA Hayek, whose jurisprudence I discuss in Chapter 10.

Law as prophecy: the trouble with the 'Bad Man' point of view

Every lawyer owes certain duties to the client. Foremost among them is the duty to advise the client about the chances of success if the case goes to court. The lawyer therefore tries to predict the court's answer to the client's claim. There is no controversy here. However, in 'The path of the law', Holmes made the extraordinary claim that law consists only of predictions of what the courts will do in particular cases: 'The primary rights and duties with which jurisprudence busies itself again are nothing but prophecies' (1897, 458). These prophecies lie scattered within statute books and law reports; the lawyer's job is to generalise them and reduce them to a manageable system (1897, 458).

Holmes' remarks were so extravagant that one might wonder whether he got carried away by the occasion or whether judicial office had coloured his judgment, for by this time he was a judge. The remarks are not only untrue but they also contradict Holmes' own view of the law, written before he became a judge! As noted previously, Holmes believed that law has its origins in the life of the community and exists before it is recognised and enforced by courts. The law has already done its work before it gets noticed in the courts. Holmes was right only if he was merely identifying an important aspect of legal practice, and not the law generally.

The view of law as prediction led Holmes to his famous 'bad man' thesis. If the law is nothing but predictions of what the courts will do, the best way to discover the law is to see it from the viewpoint of a really bad man. Holmes' logic is this: the good man does not try to test the law, but the bad man is always trying to get away with what he can. Holmes wrote:

> If you want to know the law and nothing else, you must look at it as a bad man, who cares only for the material consequences which such knowledge enables him to predict, not as a good one, who finds his reasons for conduct, whether inside the law or outside of it, in the vaguer sanctions of conscience. (1897, 459)

The 'bad man' viewpoint is focused on wrongs. How many years will I get if I get caught? How can I swindle my employer? How can I avoid paying for the goods that I bought? A good man or woman will also want to know the law *as it is* in order to be law abiding. Hart pointed out that in our daily lives we observe rules as standards of conduct and not simply as predictions (1997, 137). Besides, there is much more to law than the punishment of wrongs. Good men and women want to know how to bequeath property, how to set up a charity, how to establish a trading partnership or a corporation. The legal process, as W Twining observed, is viewed from different standpoints by different actors; the bad man's standpoint is not that of the judge, or the prosecutor, or the legislator (1973, 285). The bad man test is not always the most direct or reliable route to finding the law.

Law as prophecy is about what courts and other authorities do when faced with a dispute or claim. However, as Holmes himself noticed before his judicial career, the law has a life outside the courts. Hart's comparison of the law with the rules of a game is vivid and compelling. Children and adults play various games, such as cricket, football, hockey or netball, for their enjoyment. These games are often played without umpires or referees. The game is possible because the players by and large voluntarily observe a set of rules. Try to imagine a game of football or netball without any rules, and you will see a completely different activity. The introduction of an official to oversee the game and to enforce its rules does not change the rules that pre-existed (Hart 1997, 142). The law is like that.

Holmes was right to reject formalism and the idea of law as commands of sovereign bodies. His error was to identify the law with the commands of a different sort of sovereign, the appellate court.

Karl Llewellyn and the Grand Style

Karl Llewellyn (1893–1962) held chairs in law at the universities of Yale, Columbia and Chicago. He is best known for his book *The Bramble Bush: On our law and its study*, first published in 1930, which became the most read introductory legal text in American law schools. Llewellyn's most important writings on jurisprudence are conveniently collected in one volume, *Jurisprudence: Realism in theory and practice*.

Llewellyn observed that traditional jurisprudence failed to investigate one of the most important aspects of the American legal system: the way that courts balance the contending demands of the two ideals of law – certainty and justice. Like other rules sceptics, Llewellyn mocked the idea that rules provide unfailing guidance to judges, leaving them only the task of its mechanical application. However, Llewellyn valued rules and the certainty they bring to the law. His point was that mathematical certainty is not in the nature of law. He considered, moreover, that the degree of uncertainty is not a vice but a virtue of the law. Llewellyn's key ideas about the law may be summarised as follows.

Rules and discretion

Rules are porous and judges have discretion in understanding and applying the law. Llewellyn followed Holmes in pointing out that society is always in flux, so law is ever catching up with society. The probability is 'that any portion of law needs re-examination to determine how far it fits the society it purports to serve' (Llewellyn 1962, 55). The courts bear primary responsibility for this re-examination.

Law and morality

Llewellyn shared with other American realists the belief in a temporary divorce between law and morality. The realists' quest is a moral one: to help improve the law. However, to improve the law they must know 'the law as it is' as opposed to what they would like the law to be. Realists then discover that 'the law as it is' is shaped by moral (policy) considerations that the courts apply in the guise of logic. At this point the realists remarry law and morality. They want the courts to take their marital duties seriously, i.e. to actively align the law with justice and be frank and open about what they do. Law's liaison with justice should not be a clandestine affair but an open and scrutable partnership.

Distrust of rules as descriptions of what courts do

Llewellyn, like other rule sceptics, did not believe that rules fairly represent the way courts actually decide cases (1962, 56). A lawyer who wants to find out what the courts actually do must engage in the systematic study of opinions (judgments) of the courts. When realists express scepticism of rules, they are referring to the rules written down in statutes and past judicial precedents. The offence of murder is defined in the *Criminal Code Act*. The good lawyer will not stop at the definition in the Act, but will study the judgments of the appellate court to see how, in particular kinds of cases, the courts have understood and applied this definition. Again, consider a judgment that explains a common law rule. The good lawyer will not be guided solely by the words of one majority judgment, but will explore a line of decisions to see how the courts have worked the rule in practice.

Llewellyn thought that these are the reasons realists regard the law as generalised predictions of what the courts will do (1962, 158). Why do some realists think that these predictions are not actually rules? Realist lawyers discover, by deep and systematic study of opinions, the way that the rule operates in practice – which may be different from how it is stated in the law books. If so, have they not found the real rule? The realist argument is that all we can do from the study of precedents is predict, because we cannot be certain that what is established in past opinions will be followed in the next case. I can think of three reasons why a rule may not be followed. First, the later court may not wish to follow the rule because it does not respect the law and believes that it has arbitrary power to depart from it. The court in such a case acts like a common criminal.

The rule remains, but it is violated. Second, the later court may think that the earlier opinions got the law badly wrong, and hence the established view should be rejected or revised. In this case the existing rule is replaced by a new rule. Third, a later court may think that the earlier line of precedents was correct in the social conditions that prevailed, but that conditions have changed, and with them the expectations of the members of society. Therefore the old rule set by past precedents must be modified or replaced. In theory, every rule is susceptible to this kind of change. This is why the law is an evolutionary process.

The question for the realist, then, is this: can we ever call something a rule which is not static, but is dynamic and adaptive and hence changes over time? If we cannot, then we must abandon altogether the notion that society is governed by rules. The word 'rule' then will apply only in mathematical and logical systems or in natural science. If so, we will deprive ourselves of the use of the concept of a 'rule' in social contexts, though it has been the basis of society from the beginning of human history and long before there were courts or parliaments.

Llewellyn, to be fair, did not deny the existence or utility of rules. His major thesis was that we miss something about the nature of law if we regard the law as sourced only in rules. He believed that rules, properly understood, serve the dual purpose of promoting legal certainty while allowing judicial freedom to do what is just.

In fact, Llewellyn wanted to make rules sharper. He recommended grouping cases and fact situations into narrower categories than had been the past practice. The reason is obvious. Consider the rule that a surgeon should take reasonable care during an operation and afterwards. Surgeons who wish to avoid liability will want to know much more about this rule. They would like to know, in relation to particular types of surgical cases, what type of advice, tests, procedures and post operation care will suffice to dispel a claim for damages if there is a mishap. This can be discovered only by seeing how the courts in the past have treated surgical misadventure in different kinds of situations. One would hope that this is what a good textbook on torts or medical law today provides.

Law reform

American realism had two major aims. The first was to gain a better factual understanding of what the law is and how it works. Realists thought that traditional positivist theory did not do this very well. However, most realists – Llewellyn among them – were not content just to describe the process of law but wished to make the law better, to serve its social purpose. This involved evaluating the effects of the law as it stands. Llewellyn urged judges and lawyers to evaluate the law constantly by considering its effects.

The American realists did little to develop a theory about how we may evaluate the effects of law. Holmes, in his Boston speech on 'The path of the law', asked students to study political economy so that they could find out the costs and benefits of particular legal rules. This kind of inquiry entered law school curricula only with the rise of the 'law and economics' movement in the second half of the

20th century, and even then only in a few schools. The law reform agendas of many American realists were driven by their own perceptions of what was wrong with American society, particularly its market based economy. History shows that their views did not have much traction in the courts or in the public mind.

The Grand Style

In 1959, during the course of an address to the annual meeting of the Conference of Chief Justices, Llewellyn unveiled his views about the Grand Style or manner of reason. He believed that the appellate courts of the United States were at their glorious best during the first half of the 19th century, when the Grand Style of judicial reasoning was dominant. The judicial lustre began to fade in the latter part of that century and by 1909 its practice was all but dead. Llewellyn saw a revival of the tradition at the time he spoke, and used his address to encourage its restoration. So what is this admirable Grand Style?

The style, in essence, is to test each decision against life wisdom, and where necessary to vigorously recast precedents in the light of that wisdom. Llewellyn explained:

> In any event, as overt marks of the Grand Style: 'precedent' is carefully regarded, but if it does not make sense it is ordinarily re-explored; 'policy' is explicitly inquired into; alleged 'principle' must make for wisdom as well as for order if it is to qualify as such, but when so qualified it acquires peculiar status. On the side both of case law and of statutes, where the reason stops there stops the rule; and in working with statutes it is the normal business of the court not only to read the statute but also implement that statute in accordance with purpose and reason. (1962, 217)

In simpler terms, judges working in the Grand Style give themselves the authority to reshape the law according to their wisdom, provided that the grounds for doing so are explicitly stated and discussed.

The trouble with Llewellyn's formulation is its elasticity. Most judges may be able to associate with the style by giving their own interpretation to these words. What 'does not make sense' to one judge may make perfect sense to another. Reason may lead different judges to different destinations and 'reason may stop' at different points for different judges. The formulation is consistent with what people understand as judicial activism as well as judicial restraint. Llewellyn, though, was proposing by these words a much larger role for the appellate judge than the legal culture of countries such as England and Australia currently permits.

Fact sceptics

Jerome Frank, a fact sceptic, derided rule sceptics as living in an artificial two dimensional legal world of rules and predictions. The world of the fact sceptics, he claimed, is three dimensional, with the third dimension made up of facts in dispute (1949, ix). The fact sceptics also practise rule scepticism, for they distrust what the rule books say on the state of the law. Their primary interest, though, is in the incurable uncertainties that attend the trial aspect of cases. Frank explained the aim and spirit of fact scepticism as follows:

> No matter how precise or definite may be the formal legal rules, say these fact skeptics, no matter what the discoverable uniformities behind these formal rules, nevertheless it is impossible, and will always be impossible, because of the elusiveness of the facts on which decisions turn, to predict future decisions in most (not all) lawsuits, not yet begun or not yet tried. The fact skeptics, thinking that therefore the pursuit of greatly increased legal certainty is, for the most part futile – and that pursuit, indeed, may well work injustice – aim rather at increased judicial justice. (1949, ix)

The idealised view of the law is something like this. The law consists of rules that are knowable in advance. When a legal dispute arises, and it ends up in court, the judge or the jury ascertains relevant facts. Facts are established by evidence heard by the judge or jury. The court then applies the law to the facts so found and reaches the judgment.

Every lawyer knows that reality is different from the ideal. Facts cannot be proved beyond all doubt. The law expects only certain imperfect standards of proof to be met. Even in a criminal trial, the prosecution's burden is to prove the commission of the offence beyond a reasonable doubt. There are sound reasons for these imperfect standards. Facts must be based on evidence, and evidence is given by witnesses or found in documents and material things such as a blood stained knife with the accused person's DNA on it. There may not be witnesses. The recollections of witnesses may be affected by a large number of factors, such as impaired sight or hearing, inaccurate observation, misinterpretation of observed facts, and fading memory. Judges and juries also have to draw inferences from the established facts through guesswork.

The common law rules of evidence and the requirements of natural justice and due process seek to make the trial process fairer and more reliable, but the system remains human – imperfect and prone to error. All this is commonplace for the competent lawyer. Frank, though, raised two other causes of legal uncertainty that lawyers usually do not talk about: namely, (a) prejudice or bias on the part of judges and juries; and (b) the breakdown of the distinction between rules and facts in judicial reasoning.

Effects of prejudice

There are different kinds of prejudices that may affect the way judges and juries decide questions of fact. There may be overt prejudice on grounds such as race, gender, religion or political views. Where bias is demonstrable, the decision may be overturned. However, there are other biases of judges and jurors that are not easy to detect. Appearance, dress, mannerisms and habits of parties and witnesses may have a positive or negative influence. This is why lawyers pay attention to how their clients and witnesses present themselves in court. Frank commented:

Concealed and highly idiosyncratic, such biases – peculiar to each individual judge or jury – cannot be formulated as uniformities or squeezed into regularised 'behaviour patterns' . . . The chief obstacle to prophesying a trial court decision is, then, the inability, thanks to these inscrutable factors, to foresee what a particular trial judge or jury will believe to be the facts. (1949, xi)

Frank was scathing of juries and 'judicial jury worshippers'. He regarded jurors as 'hopelessly incompetent' fact finders. Judges' instructions to the jury he dismissed as 'an elaborate ceremonial routine' which today seems like 'debased magic spells or cabalistic formulas' (1949, 180–2). The reason for this harsh judgment is the fact that juries are neither specialised nor accountable. They do not have to give reasons for the general verdicts (guilty or not guilty) that they declare. Faith in juries is not universal, even in the common law world. Frank was not saying anything new here, as his views of juries were shared by respected mainstream commentators. Much more interesting are his thoughts on the rule–fact distinction.

Dissolution of the rule–fact distinction

According to the common (idealised) accounts of the law in action, the court comes to findings of facts and then applies relevant legal rules to the facts so found. Frank argued that this is not the way judges often decide cases. He claimed that in their preoccupation with rules, traditional legal theorists and rule sceptics fail to notice that rules and facts are often indistinguishable in the thought processes of judges and juries (1949, xiii).

Frank argued that judges come to a decision about the right outcome and then work backwards to the appropriate rule. Justices Holmes, Cardozo and Hutcheson had previously made this point. Frank gave an interesting demonstration of this judicial tendency. A drunken driver runs over a man and causes him serious injury. In some American states, such as Georgia, these facts are construed as 'assault with intent to kill', and in others, such as Iowa, are held to be 'reckless driving'. Thus, different rules are applied to the same fact type in different states. A study reveals the reason. In Iowa, 'reckless driving' carries a harsher penalty than in Georgia. If Georgian courts wish to give a similar penalty, they must construe the same facts as constituting the graver offence of 'assault with intent to kill'. Frank considered this to be evidence that courts first determine what punishment the driver deserves and then find a rule that allows the selected punishment to be imposed (1949, 101–2).

This means that facts, crucially, determine the choice of rule. When facts come to light in the course of the trial, the judge begins to think about what justice demands or what the decision ought to be. In the final analysis the judge is guided by intuition. As Hutcheson wrote, a judge 'waits for the feeling, the hunch, that intuitive flash of understanding that makes the jump-spark connection between question and decision' (1928–29, 278). Justice Cardozo said much the same when he talked of the law's 'piercing intuitions, its tense, its apocalyptic moments' (1928, 59).

However, we must be cautious in embracing these ruminations. These are words of self-proclaimed realists, but they are more romantic than realistic. This kind of agonised pondering relieved by lightning bolts of wisdom may be what happens in really hard cases, but such cases are not so common that this account reflects normal practice. The routine work of trial courts is quite humdrum. The facts are reasonably clear and so are the rules. The judge acts very much according to the official script, by applying known rules to believable facts.

Frank's comments on juries are more persuasive and enlightening, though again not very original. Juries are instructed on the applicable law, but they have the freedom to give a verdict that they believe is right, even against the legal instructions they receive from the judge. Usually they are asked only to give a general verdict saying that an accused person is guilty or not guilty of the offence charged. They do not have to give reasons for the verdict and, except in the most unreasonable verdicts, their decisions are rarely reversed on appeal. In reality, they mix up facts and rules and produce a composite decision on the charges.

The legacy of American legal realism

American realism as a distinct movement was not long lived, but it continues to influence jurisprudential scholarship directly and indirectly. Its influence within the United States is considerable, for a number of reasons. First, the great champions of American realism initially were highly respected serving judges such as Holmes, Cardozo and Hutcheson, who were justifying their own judicial philosophy. They said things about judicial conduct that others would have been hesitant to express. Second, the US Constitution bestows on the federal judiciary, and in particular on the US Supreme Court, a political status that is unknown in other common law countries. This is partly because of the constitutional structure of divided powers and the limitations on legislative power cast by the American Bill of Rights. The court therefore has greater capacity to heed the realist doctrines. Third, the realists' appeal for critical examination of legal rules for their social effects provided inspiration for late 20th century American legal theorists on both the left and the right. On the left, the critical legal studies movement saw legal rules and doctrines as supportive of the hierarchical structure of society and markets. On the right, the law and economics movement began to evaluate laws for economic efficiency, examining in particular their role in increasing or decreasing transaction costs. Legal realism's influence on the courts of other common law countries has been variable but modest. British and Australian courts have been touched only lightly by American realism.

However, legal positivism owes a large debt to American realism that is rarely acknowledged. American realism jolted legal positivism out of its complacency by questioning widely held assumptions about the nature of rules. It should be remembered that Holmes exposed the weaknesses of the command theory of law long before Hart. Realism prompted the rethink of legal positivism that was brilliantly undertaken by scholars like Hart and Raz. It forced positivists to distance themselves from formalism and to reconsider the nature of legal language and judicial discretion. It may even be true to say that Holmes made Hart possible.

Scandinavian realism

American realists were preoccupied with the way law is made in practice, and how it ought to be made. The central concern of Scandinavian realism is to explain how the law changes the behaviour of people. They seek to explain scientifically the force of the law, free of the metaphysical (mystical) element imbedded in traditional explanations. Their scientific inquiry leads to the finding that the force of the law is produced by the psychological effects caused by the ritualistic modes of law making, such as the process by which parliament approves legislation or a judge pronounces a judgment. So, did the Scandinavian realists who pursued a non-mystical account of the law's force end up with a mystical explanation? The answer depends on what we mean by facts. If the psychological effects produced by legal procedures and concepts are facts, then the realists can justly claim to have provided an empirical explanation of law.

Scandinavian realism is known in the Anglophone world mainly though the writings of four scholars who best represent this important school of thought: Axel Hägerström, Karl Olivecrona, Vilhelm Lundstedt and Alf Ross. The following discussion is based on their writings.

Hägerström and the mystical force of law

Scandinavian realism was born of the inquiries concerning law and morals undertaken by the Swedish philosopher Alex Hägerström (1868–1939). Hägerström was not a lawyer but a philosopher with a deep interest in law. He held a chair in philosophy at the Uppsala University in Sweden until his retirement.

Hägerström was a philosopher in the empiricist tradition. He wished to study social phenomena such as law with the rigorous methods of the empirical sciences. He wrote his major works in the 1920s, and as a critic of the command theory of law preceded Hart by several decades. His investigations led to the conclusion that concepts such as property, right and duty could not be explained in the way that we explain natural objects and events. Hägerström's writing is very dense and his arguments are complex, as are his examples. The key message, though, is quite simple.

According to Hägerström, any concept that does not correspond to a physical thing is meaningless. The concept 'chair' has meaning because it corresponds to a real object that we can see and touch. Hägerström argued that concepts such as 'right', 'duty' and 'property' are meaningless because there are no facts that correspond to their existence. What does the statement 'I have the right of property to my house' mean? The state will use its coercive power to help me protect my house from the acts of others in certain circumstances – for example, if I have not let the house to a tenant – or the state will allow me to use force to protect it. The fact of state protection does not correspond to my right of property. The state intervenes only if an unauthorised person interferes with my possession, and there is no guarantee that the state will always assist (Hägerström 1953, 1–2). What if the invader disputes my title and I cannot prove it? So is there any set of facts that correspond to 'right of property'? I can say that the fact of my peaceful enjoyment of the house corresponds to the 'right of property'. In that case I will have no right when I really need it, which is when someone disturbs my peaceful enjoyment. Hägerström wrote: 'This insuperable difficulty in finding the facts which correspond to our ideas of such rights forces us to suppose that there are no such facts and that we are here concerned with ideas which have nothing to do with reality' (1953, 4). This is true if one looks for exact correspondence. I argue below that Hägerström's insistence on exact correspondence for anything to qualify as real reveals his fundamental misunderstanding of the nature of society and law – but let us first complete his account of what law is.

If legal words have no basis in reality and if they do not refer any real thing, do we have law at all? The answer, according to Hägerström, is that not only do we have law, but civilised life is not possible without law. What, then, is the nature of law, and how does law guide people's behaviour? Hägerström correctly said that the law's force on people cannot be explained by the physical laws of nature, but only by its psychological effects. Here is a simple explanation.

If I pour water into my kettle and place it on a fire the water will boil in a few minutes. The causal connections are evident. The fire heats the kettle, which then heats the water to boiling point. All this happens according to the laws of nature. Now, Parliament passes an Act which provides that a pedestrian should not cross the road until a green light signals permission to do so. Consequently most people cross the street only on the green light signal, even if it is safe enough to cross the road when the light is red. The connection between the Act of Parliament and the pedestrians' behaviour is not physical like the connection between the fire and the water in the kettle. What if a policeman standing by physically restrains a person from crossing before the green light appears? Here the physical link is between the policeman and the pedestrian, not between the Act and the pedestrian. The policeman may be obeying a different law that requires police officers to physically prevent unlawful acts. In that case the link between the law and the policeman's behaviour is not physical. In each case, the effect of the law on the actor is mental. Hägerström concluded that legal concepts exert mysterious forces that the laws of nature cannot explain. They 'belong to another world than that of nature' (Hägerström 1953, 5). Legal concepts and forms thus have a magical quality. They are magical not in the sense of the dark arts of witches and sorcerers, but in the sense that they move people by words and forms that are meaningless when put to empirical test.

How does this magic work in practice? Take the case of legislation. If a group of private individuals gather in a hall and proclaim that all persons in Australia should drive on the right-hand side of the road, they would be dismissed as lunatics. However, if the group are the elected representatives of the people and they assemble in Parliament House and make the same statement according to certain procedures, the people are likely to obey it as law. The magic is not in the content of the law but in the form of the law. Legislators know how the legal system works. They know that when a right is enacted there will follow in society a change in behaviour. One class of persons will obtain a benefit and another class will give it. They also know that anyone who meets the requirements of procedural law will gain a judgment and that the judgment will be enforced. Although rights are contingent on certain facts, whether the facts actually exist is beside the point if procedurally the plaintiff meets the conditions for a judgment (Hägerström 1953, 316).

Similarly, in a court case the judge knows that the judgment will produce certain consequences. The judge's decree is a means of psychological compulsion in the case. The effect comes about not because the right exists but because of the judge's pronouncement. Hägerström rejected the common view that a remedy to enforce a right exists because the right exists. Since rights have no empirical existence, the judge can never take account of any right that exists prior to the judgment. What we call a right is nothing but the changes in the social behaviour brought about by the judgment.

Inadequacy of Hägerström's theory

The error at the heart of Hägerström's theory is that of trying to understand social phenomena like law by the methods of linear science. Society is a complex and dynamic order. It is not like a chair or other object. It is not even like an individual animal, although animal life also represents complex order at a different level. Society comprises groups of interacting individuals. As the modern science of complexity (discussed in Chapter 10) reveals, rules of behaviour can arise spontaneously as a result of the interactions of individuals, even without legislatures and courts. These rules are honed by the accumulation of experience. They establish rights and duties. These rules pre-date authority.

Hägerström thought that the idea of a right is meaningless because it does not correspond to a stable fact or state of affairs. In other words, anything as unstable or contingent as a right has no existence. This is clearly wrong, and is a result of what scientists call linear thinking. We can understand a right as a kind of relation between two persons. It can be in relation to a thing such as a house, or a contract such as a contract of service. The fact that this relationship is unstable (because the house may be invaded or the hired plumber may not do his job) does not mean that the relationship is unreal. Uncertainty is a feature of complex life systems, and society is one such system. The fact that a right is not always respected or enforced does not mean that there is no such thing as a right. On the contrary, if there are no rights and duties society will not exist; nor will

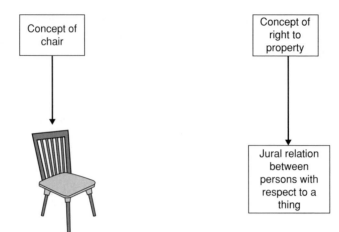

Figure 4.3 Idea and fact

courts or legislatures. In Figure 4.3, the set on the left shows the connection of the concept of a chair to the stable object to which it refers. The set on the right shows the connection between the concept of a right to property and the jural relationship to which it refers. The fact that this relationship is not corporeal and is variable does not mean that the concept of property right is meaningless.

Hägerström's error can be shown in another way. When he said that a right is nothing but a change in the social behaviour brought about by a court's judgment, what does it really mean? A change in social behaviour can be effected only if there was prior social behaviour. Social behaviour is always prior to any court's judgment. If there is no prior social behaviour there is nothing for the court to change. Social behaviour is not random but patterned. Rights and duties arise from the expectations created by these behavioural patterns.

Hägerström attributed the people's observance of the law to the magical or mystical forces generated by legal words and forms. This belief also arose directly from his linear view of the world. He thought that only things that can be perceived with our sensory organs are real. The factors that make people voluntarily observe the law are magical because they cannot be physically sensed. This belief arises from a primitive monist view that the world consists only of physical things and events. In contrast – as Karl Popper explained in his famous 1978 Tanner Lecture at the University of Michigan – our universe actually consists of three interacting worlds: (1) the world of physical objects and events; (2) the world of mental objects and events; and (3) the world of the products of the mind and culture such as scientific theories and art. Popper provided a fuller explanation of the three world theory in his book *Objective Knowledge* (1972). As Popper pointed out, these are inseparably interacting worlds. The facts that correspond to the concepts of right, duty and property are to be found in the second and the third worlds and are as real as the facts of the physical world.

What Hägerström put down to magic, Hart and Alf Ross regarded as the reflective acceptance of rules by thinking human beings. The internal aspect of rules is a critical dimension missing from the work of the Swedish realists, but clearly present in their Danish counterpart, Alf Ross.

Hägerström's followers: Karl Olivecrona

Hägerström's philosophy was embraced and developed by his student, Karl Olivecrona (1897–1980), who was Professor of Jurisprudence at the University of Lund in Sweden. Olivecrona was a controversial figure who believed that a monopoly of force is the fundamental basis of law.[2] His views are summarised below.

The binding force of law

Olivecrona recognised that law belongs to the natural world of cause and effect. Law is produced by natural causes – the actions of human beings – that have natural effects in the form of actual influence on the conduct of judges and individuals. Law cannot be part of the natural world of cause and effect and also be apart from it. However, the law's effect is psychological. The binding force of the law is an idea in human minds. There is nothing in the outside world that corresponds to this idea (Olivecrona 1939, 16–17). The important thing to note here is that Olivecrona regarded the psychological effects of law as part of the natural world, and not of another world as Hägerström thought.

Olivecrona was otherwise faithful to Hägerström's view of the binding force of law. The constitution is held in reverence. Rules made in accordance with the constitution have a psychological effect on judges and people. The general attitude towards the constitution places some persons (legislators etc) in positions where they can put pressure on people to direct their actions. They gain a psychological mechanism to influence actions.

The content of a rule of law

Olivecrona rejected the idea that a rule of law is a command. A command implies a personal relationship between the one who commands and the person commanded. Such a relationship is lacking when the legislature makes general laws. He preferred the term 'independent imperative', though at other times he used 'legal performatives'. The content of the law consists of imagined actions of imagined people (such as judges) in an imaginary situation. The action that is the crime is imagined by the legislator, and the punishment is the imagined response of the judge.

Force

Although Olivecrona rejected the command theory of law, he regarded force as the basic ingredient of law. Law consists mainly of rules about the application of force. Rules may contain patterns of conduct for citizens, but the patterns are only an aspect of the rules about force. Rules of civil and criminal law are at one

---

2 In a 1940 pamphlet, *England eller Tyskland* (*England or Germany*), Olivecrona argued that only German hegemony could guarantee the peace and unity of Europe.

and the same time rules for private citizens and rules for officials about the use of force. Thus the rule 'A person must not commit murder' means that: (a) persons must not commit murder, and (b) if a person commits murder, the court must impose life imprisonment if the charge is proved, and the officials must forcibly imprison the accused person.

Morality and law

While many believe that morality influences law, Olivecrona proposed the opposite: that law shapes morality. Law has always been there, hence a child grows up in a moral environment conditioned by law. He maintained that law is a primary factor in the development of morals. Law's effectiveness depends on its moral influence, but the moral influence of law is required only for a limited number of fundamental rules. As for the rest, it is enough that the idea of a moral obligation to abide by the law is sustained and that it is not damaged by unreasonable laws or arbitrary jurisdiction. Olivecrona's views reflect the law of an older time, when the moral law was indistinguishable from the legal law. In ancient times, law was the community's traditional morality. Olivecrona conceded that, ultimately, the law rests on the moral duty to obey the law, a duty that will cease if the law fails to serve its fundamental social purpose.

The idea that law is the source of morality finds expression in Vilhelm Lundstedt's explanation of the Scandinavian realist position on justice. The statement that a claim is just, Lundstedt argued, contains a tautology insofar as it is based on material law. All legal claims are just. The only kind of justice external to the law arises in cases where the law does not provide a clear answer. Then there is a balancing of interests, but that is nothing but a question of evaluation. The common sense of justice does not support material law but receives its entire bearing from the law. Legal machinery takes feelings of justice into its service and directs them in grooves and furrows advantageous to society and its economy (Lundstedt 1956, 51).

Alf Ross's revision of Scandinavian realism

Alf Ross (1899–1979) was a Danish moral and legal philosopher. He was schooled in the jurisprudential tradition of the previously considered Swedes, but developed a brand of realist thinking that drew him very close to the positivism of Hart. The most serious defect in the Scandinavian attempts to describe the law by the methods of empirical science was their failure to reveal the nature of a rule, or what Hart termed the internal point of view that makes a rule obligatory. Ross attempted to address this aspect by his description of norms and legal rules.

Norms

Ross pointed out that a norm has two aspects: (a) a directive to do or not something; and (b) the correspondence of the directive to some social facts. One without the other cannot be a norm. The norm 'Drive on the left-hand side of the road' contains a directive to behave in a certain way. However, if everyone drives on the right-hand side of the road, it really has no existence. It is an empty statement. Hence, Ross defined a norm as 'a directive which corresponds in a particular way to certain social facts' (1968, 82). There is a norm that a person should not steal what belongs to another. It corresponds to the fact that people usually do not steal.

Note, however, that a norm corresponds to social fact in a particular way. This particular way refers to the fact that people observe the directive consciously, with a sense of obligation. Thus, not every social practice or regularity of behaviour reveals a norm. Most people sleep at night out of biological urge. People generally celebrate Christmas by setting up a Christmas tree, but they do not feel that they ought to do it. Bricklayers observe certain technical practices when they build a wall. They do so out of practical necessity and not out of a feeling of social or moral obligation. Hence, these regularities are not norms (Ross 1968, 84). Persons must feel that the directive is 'binding'.

The word 'binding' can refer two kinds of situations. It can mean being coerced by threat of punishment to do or not do something. This is the fear of sanction. Ross rejected this idea. It does not account for many kinds of norms that people observe even in the absence of sanctions. The other meaning of 'binding' is the feeling of obligation, experienced internally, that the norm is valid (1968, 86–7). If a norm is binding in the latter sense, it cannot be discovered solely by external observation of behaviour.

Legal rules

The definition of a norm given above is consistent with both law and moral rules. What is special about law that distinguishes legal rules from other norms? The existence of a norm does not depend on sanction. However, that does not mean that society may not establish institutional systems to impose sanctions for breaches of particular norms recognised as deserving of sanction. Legal rules are a special type of norms about the use of coercion. They contain directives to those in authority. Typically they are addressed to the courts in the form of laws that prescribe punishments for crimes, or other types of sanctions for breaches of other kinds of law. Their effectiveness depends on: (a) allegiance of officials to the constitution and the institutions under it; and (b) non-violent sanctions of disapproval and criticism that are implied in this attitude (Ross 1968, 90–1). Since they are directed to officials, legal rules are not generally enforced but are followed voluntarily. A court usually does not have to be coerced into doing justice according to law.

Are there then two sets of legal norms – one addressed to the citizen (primary norms) and the other addressed to authorities (secondary norms)? From the logical point of view, there are only secondary legal norms that prescribe how cases are to be decided. These norms stipulate the conditions under which violent coercion may be applied. From the psychological point of view, there are two sets of norms. Primary norms are those followed generally by citizens whether or not there is coercion. They may be obeyed because of both interested feelings (fear of sanctions) and disinterested feelings (respect for law and order) (Ross 1968, 91–2).

Ross's theory of law just described has only a tenuous connection with the Hägerström legacy. He was empiricist in presenting law as social fact, free of the metaphysical baggage of natural law thinking. However, Ross explored more thoroughly what Hägerström left unexplained as the magical or mystical force of legal forms. He did so in ways remarkably similar to Hart's positivism. Ross's philosophy of law leaves room for spontaneously grown norms of society to be recognised as law. His definition of legal norms as special norms directed to officials about the application of coercion is too narrow and artificial, and his system will stand even if the definition is widened to include the primary norms of behaviour to which sanctions are applied by the state.

Assessment of Scandinavian realism

Scandinavian realism, except for the work of Alf Ross, has not made a significant or lasting impact on the jurisprudence of the common law world. Even so, its contribution must not be undervalued. The Scandinavians drew attention to an aspect of the phenomenon 'law' that had not been the subject of serious study previously, and unfortunately remains neglected to date in the jurisprudence of Anglophone countries. Whereas the American realists galvanised our thoughts about the realities of law creation, the Scandinavians illuminated the way law serves its function by altering human behaviour. This is the psychological dimension of law. Laws are not corporeal things. We cannot hold them in our hands. They are not even ideas about real things (Kant's phenomena). They are ideas about how persons should *behave* in the real world in relation to material things and events. The force of the law, though, is real and observable as empirical fact. People usually change behaviour as the law commands, even if there is no fear of punishment. The Scandinavians deserve much credit for drawing our attention to the incorporeal but real nature of law.

Hägerström's view that there is no such thing as a legal right was flawed by his failure to notice that the real world consists not only of tangible things but also of mental constructs. Popper and later philosophers of science recognised the place of ideas in the real world. Hägerström's followers refined his insights, and in Ross's work we find a more realistic and useful theory that explains the nature and function of law. The Scandinavians, despite their shortcomings, revealed an aspect of law that offers rich intellectual rewards for scholars willing to explore the psychology of law.

PART 2
LAW AND MORALITY

5

Natural Law Tradition in Jurisprudence

From a purely factual standpoint the history of the natural law idea teaches one thing with the utmost clearness: the natural law is an imperishable possession of the human mind. In no period has it wholly died out.

Heinrich A Rommen (1955, 215)

The idea of a higher moral law that positive human law must not violate has a long and continuous history in both Western and Eastern thinking. It is found in Greek philosophy at least from the time of Heraclitus of Ephesus (c. 535–475 BC). It has a central place in Judeo-Christian doctrine as set out in the writings of Augustine, Thomas Aquinas and the Scholastics. It lived in the natural rights discourses of Grotius, Hobbes, Locke, Pufendorf and others. In Vedic (Hindu) philosophy the moral law of governance is revealed in the *Dharmasastra*. In traditional Sinic culture, Confucian philosophy subordinated law to ethics. The religious *Sharia* is a powerful influence on the law of Islamic nations. In our age, basic human rights are posited as universal higher norms binding on nation states. In Western philosophy such higher moral law is commonly known as natural law.

Natural law is so called because it is believed to exist independently of human will. It is 'natural' in the sense that it is not humanly created. Natural law theories are theories about the relation between the moral natural law and positive human law. Natural law theories vary in aims and content but they share one central idea: that there is a kind of higher (non-human) 'law', based on morality, against which the moral or legal validity of human law can be measured. Natural law theory in its most uncompromising form proclaims Saint Augustine's doctrine that unjust law is not law – *lex injusta non est lex*. We discover, though, that this is not a central tenet of some other natural law theories. Most natural law theorists maintain that the duty to obey the law is ultimately a moral duty.

One of the difficulties about understanding the natural law tradition has much to do with the modern legal mindset. Lawyers think of the law as rules enforceable in a court of law. Hence, if natural law is to make any sense to the modern legal mind, it must be capable of judicial recognition and enforcement even against positive state law. Natural law thinking, though, represents a much broader philosophical program. It investigates the moral principles that ought to govern political action, law making and adjudication as well as the personal lives of citizens (Finnis 1980, 23). The 'law' that natural law theory speaks of has a much wider meaning than the positive law of the state.

An examination of all the strands of natural law thinking would take up a large volume. Hence, I focus this chapter mainly on the classical tradition of natural law thinking in Western legal philosophy. This has been the most influential and most examined version of natural law theory. The chapter begins with several conceptual clarifications that will be helpful for a systematic presentation of the subject. It is followed by a discussion of some of the key historical contributions to this tradition by Western philosophers, from antiquity to the modern era. The chapter concludes with the discussion of John Finnis' restatement of the classical doctrine.

Law of nature, natural right and natural law

The terms 'law of nature', 'natural right' and 'natural law' signify distinct concepts, though they have important connections. They are sometimes used interchangeably, leading to misunderstandings. Hence it is helpful to begin our discussion by distinguishing these concepts.

Law of nature

A law of nature, in the strictest sense, is a scientific theory about the physical universe and how it functions. The law of gravity states that all objects with mass attract each other. Hence, an object thrown into the air will fall to earth. The second law of thermodynamics postulates the irreversibility of natural phenomena. Heat will flow from a hot object like my stove to a cold object like my saucepan, but the reverse is impossible. These are examples of the most exact type of the laws of nature. They take the form: 'If A, then B'. They are accepted as inflexible laws until refuted by evidence.

Human life is governed by the laws of nature. Human beings, like all other organisms, cannot exist without food, oxygen and other life sustaining conditions. This is because of unchangeable laws of nature. No food, no life. An organism's physical development and functioning are determined by the genome – the genetic instructions encoded in DNA. Some would regard this as a law of nature. Laws of nature also have much to do with human behaviour. The human race, like all other living species, reproduces. Hence, most human individuals reaching adulthood have a natural inclination to sexual procreation. Humans have natural instincts such as desire, love, compassion, hate, jealousy and fear. The human race is also a social species in the sense that by nature humans tend to live in interacting groups that we call society. We owe a great deal of our knowledge of these aspects of human existence to the biological, psychological, behavioural and social sciences – the so-called 'soft' sciences.

Laws of nature, whether they are of the precise kind (as studied in the physical sciences) or of the tentative kind (as examined in the soft sciences), are not normative laws. They inform us about the world *as it is* but not about how we ought to behave. On the contrary, natural law is about norms of behaviour.

Natural rights

Human existence depends on life sustaining conditions. Therefore, some philosophers argue that a person is endowed with certain natural rights and liberties simply by virtue of being born. These are the rights that are necessary for existence as a human being. The most basic of these are the right of self-ownership and the liberty of self-preservation. Thomas Hobbes wrote in *Leviathan*:

> *Jus Naturale*, is the Liberty each man hath, to use his own power, as will himself, for the preservation of his own Nature; that is to say, of his own Life; and consequently, of doing anything, which in his own Judgment, and Reason, hee shall conceive to be the aptest means thereunto. (1946 (1651), 91)

Similarly, John Locke wrote that every person 'hath by Nature a Power, not only to preserve his Property, that is, his Life, Liberty and Estate, against Injuries and Attempts of other Men; but to judge of and punish the breaches of Law in others' (1960 (1690), 341–2). Locke and Hobbes were speaking of a state of nature, by which they meant the conditions before there was civil government. Since these rights are inherent in all persons they must have existed before the establishment of kings, parliaments and courts – that is, before positive law. In other words, there were human rights before there was human law. If they are not derived from human law they must be conferred by a 'natural law', so the theory goes.

Natural rights are sometimes identified with the law of nature, particularly in the older literature. They are certainly not part of the laws of nature in the scientific sense discussed previously. A law of nature is about what *will* happen. If there is fire there will be heat. A person will die if deprived of food. On the contrary, a natural right is about what *ought or ought not* to happen. A law of nature cannot be violated. (If violated, it ceases to be recognised as a law of nature.) Natural rights can be and frequently are violated. A person has a natural right to live. Yet we know that murder happens and in some places people are put to death by law.

Natural law

The idea of natural law is different from that of natural right, but they are closely related. It is difficult for us to think of a right that is not based in law. If I have a right to live, it is because others have a duty not to deprive me of my life. This duty is created by a law of some kind. Legal positivists will say that it is unlawful to take another's life because the law of the state forbids it. Natural law theorists will say that the duty not to take human life exists even in the absence of positive law. It exists by virtue of natural law. The relation between natural law and natural right is similar to the relation between positive law and legal right. Whereas a legal right is derived from a positive law a natural right is derived from a principle of natural law. Natural law, though, is not coextensive with natural rights. Some natural law theories have broader aims than the preservation of natural rights. Theological versions of natural law theory, for example, may enthrone religious law over human law.

Some Greek philosophers, who will be mentioned presently, believed that universal moral rules are part of the unchanging law of nature. However, a law of nature in the modern scientific sense is about the way the universe is, whereas natural law is about what ought to be done or not done. There are two important implications of this. First, natural law cannot repeal or change the law of nature. Second, as we noted in the previous chapter, a rule of natural law cannot be logically derived from a law of nature, because an 'ought' does not flow logically from an 'is'. Although the law of nature and natural law are logically distinct, they have important practical connections. The law of nature sets the conditions for life on Earth. These conditions can be destroyed by natural causes or by human action. A person may be killed or maimed by disease or natural disaster. Natural law has nothing to say about such matters except perhaps to demand that persons help victims of disaster. Natural law's concern is with human actions. Natural law asks human actors not to engage in acts that deprive persons of their natural rights.

What, then, is natural law? The common element in all versions of natural law is that it is a kind of universal law that is not humanly created. Beyond this, the notions of natural law differ with respect to its source and the nature of the obligations it creates. The rest of this chapter is an exploration of these aspects.

Two great questions in natural law theory

There are two questions that any credible natural law theory must address:
1.   How do we discover the natural law?
2.   What effect has natural law on human law?
These two questions cannot be entirely separated. If a rule or principle has no binding effect (legally or morally) it is not a law in a practical sense. Yet the questions address different aspects of natural law theory that are worth keeping in mind as we continue our discussions.

Discovering natural law

At the heart of all natural law theory is the belief that there are universal moral laws that human law may not offend without losing its legal or moral force. A natural law theory cannot leave this question to the subjective moral judgment of each person. If each individual is free to decide which laws they are morally bound to obey (or are morally bound to disobey), there may soon be no laws at all and society may descend to a Hobbesian state of nature. (Imagine what would happen on the roads if each motorist was free to decide which traffic rules to follow and when, or if individuals were free to exempt themselves from the law of homicide according to their own moral judgment.) Hence, the first challenge of a natural law theory is to demonstrate how universally valid moral laws can be discovered.

Philosophers of classical antiquity identified natural law rules with the eternal order of the universe. Theologians trace natural law to divine will. Natural rights and social contract theorists consider the rules of natural law as dictated by the indispensable conditions of human life. Other theorists derive natural law from self-evident values and practical reason. This chapter will consider each of these viewpoints.

The effect of natural law on rulers and subjects

Theories of natural law also differ with respect to their effect on human actors. Some theorists regard natural law as creating moral obligations only. According to these, law makers have moral obligations not to make laws in violation of natural law and individuals may have no moral obligation to obey an immoral law, though they may face legal consequences for disobedience. Other theories accord superior legal force to natural law, such that a human law that violates natural law has neither moral nor legal validity (*lex injusta non est lex*). Figure 5.1 offers a highly simplified snapshot of the main variance among natural law theories.

Fusion of law and morals in early societies

Most people today who live in politically organised states associate law with enactments of law makers of one sort or another. They distinguish between legal rules, which can be enforced with the assistance of the courts, and moral rules, which are sustained by social pressures and the good sense of individuals. This has not always been the case. In fact, the notion that law can be made by a legislator is alien to many traditional societies that lack the paraphernalia of the state. A tribal society that has no law maker is organised according to customary rules of behaviour. It is evident that the people in older societies considered that

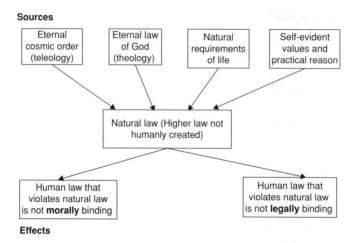

Figure 5.1 Variance of theories concerning sources and effects of natural law

certain customary rules of conduct were binding upon them, although it was impossible say how those rules were established. These customary rules may not be the kind of rules that courts in modern states would enforce. However, from the viewpoint of the people who observed them, they were obligatory in the same way that we in modern society consider legislation to be obligatory.

In the natural history of humankind, deliberate law making is a relatively recent activity. The anthropologist Edmund Leach pointed out that in the context of human history as a whole, law making is unusual (1977, 7). FA Hayek reminded us that humans lived in groups held together by common rules of conduct for something like a million years before they developed reason and the language needed to articulate those rules (1982, vol. 1, 74). It is not easy to separate law and morals when the law takes the form of social custom. Fritz Kern, in his classic work *Kingship and Law in the Middle Ages*, explained the difference between the modern and the medieval conceptions of law:

> According to the modern view, there is only one way in which the ideal law, Antigone's law of the Gods, can lawfully or constitutionally prevail over the positive law, the law of the State: by the enactment of new positive law ... The medieval conception is in complete contrast. Here the law is sovereign, not the State, the community, the magistracy, the prince, or any other person or body which we should contrast with the law. The State cannot change the law. To do so would be to commit something like matricide ... The medieval world was filled with theoretical respect for the sanctity of the law – not for the prosaic, dry, flexible, technical, positive law of today, dependent as it is upon the State; but for a law which was identified with the sanctity of the moral law. (1970, 154–5)

It is not a coincidence that in many languages legal right and moral right are expressed by the same word. The English word 'right' signifies what is right in law as well as what is morally right. As P Vinogradoff observed, that is also the case with the Latin *ius*, the German *Recht*, the Italian *diritto*, the Spanish *derecho* and the Slavonic *pravo* (1927, 1). The Sanskrit word *dharma* has both legal and moral connotations. These words go back to a time when the legal law and the moral law were for the most part one and the same.

The great law codes of the ancient world were attributed to mythical law givers. These legendary kings, heroes and prophets claimed to have received the law from divine sources (Kern 1970, 157). Historians generally agree that ancient 'law givers' – such as Ur-Nammu, Hammurabi, Solon, Lykurgus and the authors of the Roman Twelve Tables – did not intend to invent new law but to declare existing law. The ruler's duty in medieval feudal society was to uphold the law, not to make or remake it (Carlyle & Carlyle 1903–38, vol. 1, 172, 244; Ullman 1966, 150–1). When rulers legislated they purported to purge the law of its corruptions. This was the theory. In practice the ruler made law out of practical necessity, without actually repudiating the myth that the law could not be violated. As Kern stated, if the law of the mythical law giver stood in the way of desirable innovations, it would simply be regarded as perverted by corrupt tradition, and hence capable of improvement (1970, 160). According to this theory, there was no higher natural law by which the validity of the law could be adjudged. The law was the moral law, binding on ruler and subject alike.

The idea of a higher 'natural' law made sense only when law separated into state law and moral law. This bifurcation occurred when rulers gained political power to alter the law at will, and the realisation dawned that not all law was unalterable and unchanging divine law (Rommen 1955, 4). As states grew, law became associated with the will of authorities such as legislatures and courts. Once human authorities were conceded the power to actually make law, as happened in the Greek city states, the need to curb that power was obvious. No appeal could be made to the law itself, as the law was what the law maker willed. Only a higher law was capable of setting aside the human law. The Greeks formulated a theory of natural law in accordance with their understanding of the universal good.

Natural law thinking in Greek philosophy

Greeks believed in the existence of a higher natural law that human law or human actions must not offend. Natural law is just law, and just law is that which is in harmony with the universal laws of nature. Aristotle (384–322 BC) fairly represented the Greek view of natural law when he wrote:

> There are two sorts of political justice, one natural and the other legal. The natural is that which has the same validity everywhere and does not depend upon acceptance; the legal is that which in the first place can take one form or another indifferently, but which, once laid down, is decisive: e.g. that the ransom for a prisoner of war shall be one mina, or that a goat shall be sacrificed and not two sheep . . . (1976 (350 BC), 189)

Thus, man-made laws may differ from state to state but the natural law is the same everywhere (Aristotle 1976, 190). Laws of nations can differ without violating universal natural law. Aristotle compared the different rules of justice established by local legislation or convention (custom) to the standards for measuring commodities such as wine and corn. (Even today, the same corn will be measured in kilograms in most countries but in pounds in the United States.) The ethical goal of individuals and societies is to live according to the general laws of the universe. Hence, the laws of a society, whether customary or enacted by rulers, ought to conform to the higher law. There was a belief that the defiance of an unjust law was morally justified. The dramatist Sophocles (496–406 BC) captured this view in the memorable words of the heroine Antigone, who ignores a royal order and gives her brother an honourable burial. When King Creon exclaims: 'And still you had the gall to break this law?' Antigone replies:

> Of course I did. It wasn't Zeus, not in the least,
> Who made this proclamation – not to me.
> Nor did that Justice, dwelling with the gods
> Beneath the earth, ordain such laws for men.
> Nor did I think your edict had such force
> That you, a mere mortal, could override the gods,
> The great unwritten, unshakeable traditions.
> They are alive, not just today or yesterday:
> They live forever, from the first time,
> And no one knows when they first saw the light.
> (Sophocles 1984 (c. 441 BC), 81–2)

Unquestioned belief in higher law was an almost universal feature of ancient societies, and its hold on the Greek communities of the classical age was not surprising. The interesting jurisprudential question is: why did great philosophers of this period embrace this view? The explanation is found in the philosophical outlook known as teleology. It is not easy to understand the Greek theory of natural law without knowing the central idea of teleology.

Teleology

Philosophers look at nature in different ways. According to one view nature has no design, plan or purpose. It takes its own uncharted course. It is true that nature obeys certain universal laws, but these laws do not exist for a purpose. Rain does not fall so that farmers can grow crops. Farmers learned to grow crops where there was rainfall. The leopard does not have spots so that it can be a successful predator. The leopard is a successful predator because of the advantage of having spots. I do not have eyes so that I can see things. I see things because I have eyes. This view is known as metaphysical naturalism, mechanism or accidentalism. Charles Darwin's theory of evolution by random variation and selective retention (discussed in Chapter 10) epitomises the naturalistic view.

In sharp contrast, the teleological view holds that everything happens for a purpose. Nature is not random – things do not happen by chance but according to an overall design. Saint Thomas Aquinas wrote of teleology: 'Every agent acts for an end, otherwise one thing would not follow more than another from the action of the agent, unless it were by chance' (*Summa theologica* I, Q 44, art. 4; Aquinas 1947, 232). This means that every object and life form, including human beings, has a purpose in existing. How does something have a purpose? There cannot be a purpose without someone or something determining the purpose. Therefore teleology inevitably leads to the conclusion that the universe and everything within it functions according to a divine or supernatural plan. The contrast between the teleological and naturalistic worldviews is often illustrated by the opposing views of Aristotle and Lucretius about the organs of the human body:

- Aristotle in *De partibus animalium* (*On the parts of animals*): 'Nature makes the organs to suit the work they have to do, not the work to suit the organ' (IV, xii, 694b; 1972 (350 BC), 413)
- Lucretius in *De rerum natura* (*On the nature of natural things*): 'Since nothing at all was born in the body that we might be able to use it, but what is born creates its own use' (IV, 833; 1947 (50 BC), 1, 405).

According to teleology, there are two kinds of purpose at work in every object – external and internal. Externally, every object serves the purpose of another object. Soil and water allow grass to grow, grass feeds cattle and cattle provide us with beef to eat. Internally, every object tends towards the perfection of its own nature. A tree will grow roots, branches and leaves. A lion will learn to roar, be brave, hunt and do what lions do. A stone thrown into the air will fall to earth. Human affairs, according to teleology, are no different. Parents will procreate, love and nurture their offspring. Citizens will discharge their civic responsibilities. Traders will trade fairly. Rulers will rule justly. We know that reality is sometimes different. Some plants do not grow, a stone projected into outer space may not fall to earth, a lion may turn out to be timid, a parent may neglect children, a trader may cheat and a ruler may become a tyrant. Some of these failings can be explained by external causes (e.g. without rain a plant may not grow to a tree). Human beings, though, are capable of intentionally violating the order of nature. These universal laws are violated, not only by common criminals but also by great and noble people in their excessive pursuit of the good. Such violations are called *hubris*. When violations occur, some kind of Olympian law punishes *hubris* and restores the eternal order. A famous example of the punishment of *hubris* from Greek mythology comes from the Persian Wars (499–448 BC). The Persian king Xerxes sought to subjugate all of Greece. His forces had to cross the Hellespont, the narrow channel of sea that separates Asia Minor from Europe, known today as the Dardanelles. He ordered a bridge to be built across the Hellespont by linking a large number of ships, thus defying nature. Not long after, his naval fleet was partly destroyed by storms and then crushed in the battle at Salamis.

The best known teleological philosophers of Athens were Socrates, Plato and Aristotle. Much of what the world knows of Socrates' philosophy has been gathered from Plato's reports of Socrates' dialogues with his followers. Teleology took on concrete shape in Plato's theory of ideal forms. Everything in this world has an ideal form that exists on a heavenly plane. What we perceive by our senses in this world are imperfect copies of the ideal forms. Physical things exist only to the extent that they imitate the pure idea of the thing. The perfect circle exists as an *idea*. The circle that I draw is an imitation of the idea that can never be perfectly achieved, even with the most precise instrument. The more the figure deviates from the perfect form the less it is a circle, and at some point it ceases to be a circle. Likewise there is the idea of a perfect straight line, a perfect square, a perfect elephant, a perfect citizen, a perfect ruler, a perfect law, perfect justice, and so forth. Perfection of one's nature is the highest good.

Teleologists thought that it is the natural tendency of human beings to live according to the order of nature. They believed that it is only by living in harmony with universal law that a person can find the state of true happiness or wellbeing known as *eudemonia*.

Deciding what is natural: the Sophist challenge

The teleological worldview, even if true, offers only a partial solution to the first problem of natural law theory: namely, how do we determine the universal laws by which a person ought to live and the state ought to be organised? It is not a sufficient answer to life's problems to say that every thing and every being has a tendency to move towards the perfection of its nature. Individuals face moral dilemmas about what is right and wrong. Society is ever divided about questions of what is just. Teleology is unhelpful here. What is considered natural in one place or age may be considered unnatural in another place and another time. Discrimination according gender, skin colour, language, religion, caste, class or sexual preference has been regarded as natural in some societies at different times. Most modern states outlaw such discrimination as being unnatural. Greek society entrenched many social divisions that are considered unnatural today. The greatest teleological philosophers, Plato (c. 427–348 BC) and Aristotle, regarded slavery as part of the natural order and slaves as property, only a notch above livestock. Plato said of slaves: 'the human animal is a difficult possession; for it is stiff-necked, and evidently not willing at all to be or become easily managed in terms of the inevitable distinction in deed between slave, free man, and master' (1980 (360 BC), 7). Aristotle considered slaves to be an animate article of property (1905 (350 BC), 9–10). In the civilised world today, slavery is condemned as inhuman and contrary to nature (see, for example, Article 4 of the *Universal Declaration of Human Rights*).

Teleological reasoning had its contemporary critics. Epicurus (writing two and a half millennia before Bentham) argued that the principle of utility was the only rational basis of moral judgment. The most serious challenge to the teleological philosophers was posed in the second half of the fifth century BC by the Sophists.[1] The Sophists were itinerant teachers who, unlike the philosophers, made healthy profits out of teaching. They became famous for training aspiring politicians in the art of rhetoric and for propagating controversial views. Many of them were foreigners with no particular loyalty to Greek institutions. Teleology promoted the belief that the laws of a state generally reflected the order of nature. Sophists would not have a bar of this. Sophist thinking was based not on teleology but on untempered rationalism. Sophists regarded the hierarchical structure of Greek society as unnatural and Greek laws as artificial constructs that served the interests of the powerful, contrary to natural law. Hippias pre-empted Rousseau, Marx, Locke, Paine and the United Nations by 2500 years in preaching the oneness of all humanity. Alcidamas declared: 'God made all men free; nature has made no man a slave' (Rommen 1955, 9). What was needed, the Sophists argued, was not piecemeal law reform but radical overhaul of the system. All of this was subversive of the stability, order and ethical foundation of Athenian society.

The philosophers had two responses to these attacks, one simple and the other sophisticated. The simple answer was that the natural order was embodied in the laws of the 'polis' (the city state), as they were god given. Heraclitus of Ephesus, writing before Socrates, claimed that 'all human laws are fed by one divine law' and 'the people ought to fight in defence of the law as they do of their city walls' (Fragment 44; Bakewell 1907, 34, 6). Plato began his book *The Laws* by putting into the mouths of three strangers the view that the laws of their cities were god given (1980 (360 BC), 3). The best person in a city is 'one who throughout his life served the laws more nobly than any other human being' (Plato 1980, 115). Rommen observed that Socrates, Plato and Aristotle had a 'strong belief in the excellence of the existing laws of the polis as well as in the conformity of such laws to the natural law' (1955, 19). Socrates' reverence for the laws of the polis was so great that he willingly carried out his own execution (by drinking hemlock) after a jury found him guilty of the charge of criticising Athenian democracy. What these philosophers meant by the laws of the polis were not the politically expedient laws of the rulers. Athens at the time of Socrates and Plato was governed successively by corrupt oligarchies and democracies. Plato lamented in his Seventh Letter that 'law and morality were deteriorating at an alarming rate' (1980, 16). Aristotle, in his *Politics*, was critical of contemporary democracies and oligarchies. The laws that the philosophers identified with natural law were the fundamental and enduring laws of the polis known as *nomoi* (singular: *nomos*). Nevertheless,

---

1 The first of this group was reputed to be Protagoras. Others included Gorgias, Prodicus, Hippias, Thrasymachus, Lycophron, Callicles, Antiphon and Cratylus.

even these laws needed a more sophisticated defence against the Sophist charge that they entrenched power and privilege and denied human rights to different classes. The sophisticated argument was that the natural law is discoverable by reason.

Role of wisdom

Socrates, Plato and Aristotle identified moral rectitude with justice. The moral man was the just man and the moral state was the just state. The key question, then, is what makes a just person and a just state? According to the teleological worldview, every thing and every being has a position and a purpose in the overall scheme of the universe. Hence, a just person is one who lives according to their position. Socrates put it bluntly when he said that 'justice consists of doing the things that belong to oneself and not interfering with other people' (Plato (1974, 204).[2] The question remains: how do we figure out what is just conduct? The Greeks did not have a single God or a Holy Book. They had a pantheon of gods and most believed in various oracles, of which the Oracle at Delphi is the most famous. Hence, the philosophers turned to the examination of the human mind to discover justice.

Plato

Plato argued that the mind is made up of three elements. The first is *reason*. which is the capacity to calculate and decide. This is the reflective element. The second is *appetite*. It is a form of irrational and instinctive impulse. Plato nominated thirst, hunger and sexual arousal as primary examples of this mental aspect (1980, 215). The third element is *spirit*. Indignation, stubbornness, blind courage and recklessness are examples of spirit. It is different from appetite because it is an attitude and not an instinct. It is different from reason because it is not logical and calculating.

The three elements are often in conflict. Imagine that your bakery sold you a loaf of bread that you later discover is underweight. You are naturally annoyed. The next day is a public holiday and all food shops are closed except this bakery. Appetite makes you hungry and reason tells you to go to the cheating baker but your indignation tells you not to go there again. This is the kind of conflict that has to be resolved within the mind. Plato believed that spirit, though irrational, is usually on the side of the right: it is the natural ally of reason (1980, 217). A just person, according to Plato, is one who will not allow these three elements to trespass on each other's functions but bundles them into a 'disciplined and harmonious whole. Such a person is ready for action of any kind ... whether

---

2 Plato's method was to explain his ideas through a series of dialogues or debates between his teacher and friend, the philosopher Socrates (469–399 BC), and his critics and followers. The real Socrates left no writings and his thoughts and words are known only as reported by his students and followers, of whom the most notable by far was Plato. The words that Plato puts into the mouth of Socrates are generally treated as Plato's own. Hence the Socrates of Plato's writing is sometimes called the Platonic Socrates.

it is political or private' (1980, 221). The knowledge that allows a person to harmonise these elements is wisdom, hence wisdom is the key to just conduct (Plato 1980, 221).

What makes a just state? The corrupt and violent politics of his time convinced Plato that the existing constitutions of the Greek city states were unreformable. In his Seventh Letter he wrote:

> I was forced, in fact, to the belief that the only hope of finding justice for society or for the individual lay in true philosophy, and that mankind will have no respite from trouble until either real philosophers gain political power or politicians become by some miracle true philosophers'. (1980, 16)

In keeping with the teleological outlook, Plato regarded the just state as one that ensures that each class of persons 'does its own job and minds its own business' (1980, 206). Only true philosophers acting as social guardians could achieve this. In *The Republic*, Plato set out the details of what he thought would be the ideal (and therefore just) state. What is true of the individual mind, Plato thought, is true also of the state. The state has to balance the elements of reason, appetite and spirit. These elements are represented by three classes: reason by the guardians (philosopher-rulers); appetite by the entrepreneurs; and spirit by the auxiliaries (the military class). The guardians are those who have the wisdom to harmonise these elements. Plato's model state was the first blueprint for an authoritarian communist state. In Plato's republic, there is no marriage and no families. Children are raised and educated by the state and assigned to the different classes according to ability. Education, like everything else, is determined by the state.

Unfortunately Plato missed three central problems of political theory. First, assuming that we need social guardians, how do we identify them? Second, how do we make sure that wise men and women who become rulers govern wisely? Third, if the guardians become corrupt, how may they be replaced? The fact that the rulers are philosophers was, for Plato, a sufficient safeguard against misrule and injustice. However, these guardians are not gods or angels, but fallible and potentially corruptible human beings like the rest of us. History endlessly exposes the fallacy of entrusting absolute power even to the wisest and the best. It is for this reason that the Scottish philosopher David Hume wrote that 'in contriving any system of government, and fixing the several checks and controuls of the constitution, everyman ought to be supposed a *knave*, and to have no other end, in all his actions, than private interest' (1985 (1742), 42).

In any case, Plato's justice is not what people today associate with natural law. It subordinates the rights of individuals to the stability of a state organised according to an inflexible class division. As such, it is hard not to accept Karl Popper's damning conclusion that Platonic justice served 'the cause of the totalitarian class rule of a naturally superior master race' (1993, 119).

Aristotle

Aristotle is the most influential philosopher of the classical age. His discussion of the 'intellectual virtues' established the framework for natural law reasoning, which persists to this day. Aristotle rejected Plato's theory of ideal forms and his version of the ideal state. He believed in the eternal natural order of the universe, and that justice conforms to the laws of this order. Like Plato, he believed the polis to be part of this natural order and that a person could live the good life only by participating in the polis. Like Plato, he believed that the state takes precedence over the individual. However, unlike Plato, Aristotle did not believe that the best form of government is the rule of philosopher-guardians. He acknowledged the advantages of a system where political power is shared among the monarchical, aristocratic and popular elements of society. Importantly, truth for Aristotle was not the preserve of any class or sect. Truth is there to be discovered by those who have the intellectual virtues.

Aristotle noted that two kinds of knowledge are involved in the search for principles of right conduct. The first is knowledge of things that are invariable. This is knowledge about the universe as it is (Aristotle 1976, 204). There is no choice in these matters. Something is or something isn't. (Earth orbits the Sun or it doesn't; fire causes heat or it doesn't.) The second type of knowledge concerns matters that are variable. Societies have different laws and moral codes that are shaped by cultural, geographical and historical factors. Some societies allow the death penalty, abortion, euthanasia, homosexual marriage and polygamy while some others don't. Aristotle called this kind of knowledge *calculative*, in the sense that it involves the weighing up of choices for action. This is the origin of the distinction between pure reason and practical reason that Aquinas, Kant and later Finnis adopted.

Aristotle identified five modes of thinking that help in the discovery of truth, whether it is about the physical world or about right conduct. First, there is scientific inquiry (*episteme*). Science reveals the world as it is. Science can be demonstrated and it can be taught. The law of gravity can be explained and demonstrated by simply throwing something in the air and taking some measurements. More complicated experiments will demonstrate other natural phenomena. Second, there is intuition (*nous*). Scientific inquiry can only proceed on certain first principles and assumptions that must be taken as self-evident. Something cannot exist and not exist at the same time. Time is irreversible. Two plus two is four. Deductions from factual premises must be taken to be true. (If all humans are mortal, then Socrates the human is mortal.) Apart from logic, there are assumptions that we need to make to answer any question of fact. For example, we must trust the evidence of our senses until it is disproved. (Even laboratory experiments depend on sensory observations.) This kind of knowledge cannot be demonstrated but must be intuitively grasped. Third, there is art or technical skill (*techne*). This is about the right way to craft something. A bridge cannot be built in any way we like – or a ship, or a telescope. A violinist cannot play a tune simply by reading the notes in a music sheet. The creator must have, in addition to scientific knowledge, certain artistic or technical skills that come from experience and innate ability. Fourth, there is prudence or practical wisdom (*phronesis*). Prudence is not about finding facts or producing things but about what is to be done or not done (Aristotle 1976, 210). It includes farsightedness and regard to consequences of actions. It is a quality required for the proper management of a household or a state (Aristotle 1976, 209.) Fifth, there is wisdom (*sophia*). Whereas prudence is concerned with practical (variable) matters, wisdom is about universal and eternal things. Wisdom combines intuitive understanding of the indemonstrable first principles and scientific knowledge. It is 'knowledge of what is by nature most precious' (Aristotle 1976, 212). A prudent person may lack wisdom and one who is wise may not be prudent.

The problem is that the wisest of persons can disagree on important questions. As wise as he was, Aristotle considered as *just* anything that tended to conserve the happiness of a political association, including laws that discriminated among the different classes (1976, 173). He even justified slavery as part of *universal justice* as revealed by wisdom. The wise men and women of today would have none of this. There was also a notion of *particular justice* in Aristotle's scheme. Particular justice had two forms: distributive and rectificatory. Distributive justice was distribution according to merit. Distributive justice, for Aristotle, was not what the socialists of our age demand. Merit might mean wealth in an oligarchy, excellence in an autocracy and free birth in a democracy (Aristotle 1976, 178). Thus, even in a democracy those born to slavery had the rough end of distributive justice. Distributive justice put each person in their assigned place in society. Aristotle's rectificatory justice was more like the notion of justice administered by modern courts. It was concerned with correcting harm caused by wrongs such as tort, crime and breach of contract through compensation, equity and, in the case of crime, by punishment (Aristotle 1976, 179). Rectificatory justice did not allow a slave or woman to find emancipation. It only ensured treatment that befitted their inferior position. Rectificatory justice reinforced distributive justice. (See further discussion in Chapter 12.)

Reception of natural law in Rome

After the passing of the three giants of teleological philosophy – Socrates, Plato and Aristotle – the message of natural law was sustained by the Stoics, from whom it was received by Roman jurists and orators. Stoics were a school of philosophy founded by Zeno of Citium (334–262 BC). The school's name derives from the *Stoa Poikile*, the painted colonnade at the Agora of Athens where Zeno taught his students. Zeno preached that reason is natural to the human mind and that reason, unless corrupted by passion, accords with the natural order of the world. Passion gets in the way of reason, hence to discover the natural law through reason persons must subdue their passions and become sage. In some respects the Stoics were shockingly rationalistic. Chrysippus saw no reason to abstain from incest or cannibalism (Long & Sedley 1987, 430–1). He did not propose killing people for food, but thought it irrational to waste body parts of dead or amputated persons if they were edible. Only a few fragments survive of Zeno's *Republic*. It appears, though, that he approved Chrysippus' views on incest and cannibalism, saw no point in building temples and court houses, favoured communal wives and wished to get rid of the Athenian educational curriculum (Long & Sedley 1987, 430, 433).

Apart from their more outrageous proposals, the Stoics had a profoundly positive bearing on the natural law tradition. Stoicism rescued natural law from the stifling grip of Platonic thinking that deified the polis, entrenched privilege and consigned slaves, women and foreigners to sub-human status. The polis by this time was disappearing – swallowed up by Alexander's empire in the east and by the Roman republic in the west. The Stoics preached that class divisions were not natural but man made. In a decadent age when slavery increased exponentially and gladiators were forced into mortal combat with each other or with wild beasts for popular entertainment, Stoics argued for equality of the human race. Epictetus called slavery 'an abysmal crime' and Seneca said that citizens and slaves were blood relations equal under natural law (Rommen 1955, 24–5). Stoicism entered Roman jurisprudence initially through the writings of the great Roman orator, lawyer and senator, Marcus Tullius Cicero (106–43 BC). Its influence grew under Emperor Marcus Aurelius (161–180), who was himself a Stoic scholar and a sagely figure. We owe to Cicero the most precise and unambiguous statement of the Stoic natural law idea. In *On the Republic* he wrote:

> True law is right reason, in agreement with nature; it is of universal application, unchanging and everlasting; it summons to duty by its commands, and averts from wrongdoing by its prohibitions. And it does not lay its commands and prohibitions on good men in vain, though neither have any effect on the wicked. It is a sin to try to alter this law, nor is it allowable to attempt to repeal any part of it, and it is impossible to abolish it entirely. We cannot be freed from its obligations by senate or people, and we need not look outside ourselves for an expounder or interpreter of it. And there will not be different laws at Rome and at Athens, or different law now and in the future, but one eternal and unchangeable law will be valid for all nations and all times, and there will be one master and ruler, that is God, over us all, for he is the author of this law, its promulgator, and its enforcing judge. Whosoever is disobedient is fleeing from himself and denying his human nature, and by reason of this very fact he will suffer the worst penalties, even if he escapes what is commonly called punishment. (Cicero 1928 (54–51 BC), 21)

In this remarkable passage, Cicero captured all the elements of the Stoic natural law theory: (1) Natural law reflects the cosmic order of nature and is not man made. (2) We do not need wise men to tell us about the natural law, for reason reveals its principles. (3) Natural law is moral law; hence it cannot be repealed or altered by legislation. (4) Natural law is morally binding on rulers and subjects alike, though it can be and is violated by state law. (5) State law may excuse immoral acts, but those who commit them pay a heavy moral price in the form of the debasement of their own human nature.

The Stoics did not end slavery. (Even Cicero owned a slave – his secretary.) However, Stoic natural law ideas had a civilising influence on Roman law. Early Roman law treated women, children and slaves as the disposable property of the *paterfamilias*, the male patriarch of the family. The condition of slaves, freemen (*libertini* – emancipated slaves) and women improved gradually as Stoic thought filtered into Roman jurisprudence through the *ius gentium* (law of nations) and *ius naturale* (natural law). Roman law was both written and unwritten. The written law (*ius scripta*) comprised mainly the statutes of various *comitia* (representative assemblies) and the Senate, the magisterial and imperial edicts and the written opinions of select jurists (*responsa prudentium*). Edicts were statements clarifying the law. *Responsa prudentium* were answers to specific legal questions given by learned jurists who were legally authorised to give opinions, which were binding as law. The unwritten law (*ius non scripta*) was made up initially of the customary private law that was the heritage of Roman citizens – the *ius civile*. The *ius civile* literally meant the law of the citizens. It had no application to foreigners (*peregrini*) and freemen. This created a serious problem as Rome expanded from a village to a city, and then to an extended republic, and finally to an immense empire that embraced most of what is now Europe, England, Asia Minor and North Africa. The empire, at its zenith, had about 4 million citizens and 50 million non-citizens, including slaves, freemen and people of the diverse Roman colonies. As the peoples of the empire began to interact, Roman magistrates (*praetors*) faced the bewildering challenge of administering justice between citizens and foreigners and among foreigners from different nations. They noticed that all nations shared a common stock of fundamental laws, such as those concerning person and property and the honouring of contracts. This body of laws became known as the *ius gentium* (law common to all nations), and this law was applied to civil disputes involving non-citizens.

The apparent universality of these laws led some jurists, including Rome's two greatest law codifiers, Gaius and Justinian, to equate the *ius gentium* with the *ius naturale*, the natural law of reason that the Stoics spoke about (Buckland 1963, 53). This position was unsustainable because there were many laws of the *ius gentium* – such as those legitimising slavery – that the *ius naturale* of the Stoics condemned. However, it is likely that, at least until the end of Emperor Hadrian's rule (117–138), the two were regarded as the same (Buckland 1963, 53). Principles of the *ius gentium* and the *ius naturale* initially applied only to non-citizens, but were received eventually into the *ius civile* through law reform. There were two ways in which this occurred. First, the jurists providing *responsa* were influenced by Stoic natural law ideals. The *responsa* were a primary source of law. Second, the *praetors*, in formulating their own edicts, were guided by the opinions of jurists. The introduction of the concept of equity (*aequitas*), which allowed judges to ameliorate the harsher consequences of the law, was a notable case of Stoic law reform (Buckland 1963, 55; Rommen 1955, 28).

Christian natural law

It is not in the least surprising that natural law of the teleological kind became the bedrock of Christian jurisprudence. Belief in an omnipotent, omniscient and rational Creator leads naturally to the idea of a higher law to which all creatures are subject. Moreover, if God is responsible for all things and God is rational, the universe must be ordered according to a divine plan in which all things have a divinely determined purpose. Christian natural law theory was developed first by Saint Augustine of Hippo, and later by generations of Christian philosophers known as the Scholastics or schoolmen, of whom the greatest was Saint Thomas Aquinas. The Scholastics were so named because most of them studied in cathedral schools. They were scholar monks who sought to rationally justify their faith, and in that quest were greatly influenced by the classical masters, particularly Aristotle and the Stoics.

Saint Augustine of Hippo

Christian natural law is present in the New Testament. Saint Paul wrote that even Gentiles by nature followed God's law, which showed that the law was 'written in their hearts, their conscience also bearing witness' (Romans 2:14–15). However, the first systematic exposition of a Christian theory of natural law had to await the arrival of the Christian philosophers, of whom the first major figure was Saint Augustine (354–430). Augustine was an African, born in Tagaste (in present day Algeria), who rose to become the Bishop of Hippo and Christianity's first great scholar. As a student of rhetoric, he became familiar with Stoic philosophy, mainly through the writings of Cicero. The Stoics considered the natural law as part of the authorless eternal order of the universe. The universe for them was not random, but functioned according to a kind of cosmic reason. Stoics, like most Greeks and Romans of the classical age, had no concept of a single responsible creator God. Cicero's god was not the personal god of monotheistic faith but the impersonal god that represents the laws of the cosmic order. The classical world had many gods, who were themselves subject to universal law. Cosmic reason governed gods, humans, animals, plants and all objects.

In the Christian cosmology there is no law above God. God is the creator of the universe and all its laws. God is not like a computer programmer who writes the laws of a universal program and allows it to run its course. The Christian God keeps watch over his creation and intervenes at will. Augustine supplanted the impersonal cosmic reason with the reason of the purposeful personal God. The eternal cosmic law (*lex aeterna*) is God's law. Augustine wrote: 'eternal law is the divine reason and the will of God which commands the maintenance of the natural order of things and which forbids the disturbance of it' (*Contra Faustum*, XXII.27; Chroust 1944, 196). God created human beings and endowed them with reason. Human reason, though, is seriously limited and is only capable of an imperfect understanding of the eternal law. However, a part of the eternal law is imprinted on the human soul. We can discover it within us by searching our souls with the torch of reason. The law so discovered is the natural law (*lex naturalis*). Natural justice is that which is in accordance with the natural order. Injustice is the lack of concord with this order. Augustine stated two cardinal principles of natural law: (1) give unto each person their proper due; (2) do nothing unto another he would not have done unto himself (*Epistola*, 157, 3, 15; Chroust 1944, 199).

Augustine thought that at the beginning there was no human law, as the natural law was sufficiently recognised and observed by people. Inevitably, the natural law became obscured as reason was corrupted by vice. Human law became necessary to restore the natural law with the force of political authority. It is also the case that the natural law is general and abstract. The state, by its enactments, works out the application of the general natural law to the variable conditions of social life. Augustine, unlike some of the early Church Fathers, did not regard the secular state as a consequence of original sin. Instead he viewed the state as the product of man's social instinct, which is a natural and divinely ordained aspect of the created universe (*De Civitas Dei*, XV, 16; Chroust 1944, 201). The state thus is a natural part of the divine eternal order.

Human law's role is to serve the natural law and, through natural law, to serve the eternal law. Wise and virtuous people do not need human law, as they live by the natural law without any compulsion. Hence, human law is not made for the righteous but for the wicked (*Epistola* 153, 6, 26; Chroust 1944, 202). The role of human law is not to make people good but to prevent people being bad. Human law cannot eliminate all evil, only the worst excesses.

The problem is that not only citizens but also the state can be, and often is, wicked. A wicked state in fact can cause more harm to the natural order, whatever that may be, than a wicked individual. The state from time to time makes diabolical laws. Augustine was very clear about unjust laws. A law is unjust when it is at odds with the natural law, and such laws should be ignored by everyone (*Epistola*, 105, II, 27; Chroust 1944, 200). In other words, unjust laws create no legal or moral obligation.

Saint Thomas Aquinas

In the Middle Ages, natural law theory was maintained by the Canonists, the ecclesiastical lawyers concerned with the governance of the Church. Around 1140, Gratian, a scholar monk at Bologna, the great centre of legal learning, produced the *Decretum Gratiani*, the first of a series of six collections of canon law that became the *Corpus Juris Canonici*. (The *Corpus* remained as the law of the Roman Church until 1917, when it was replaced by the *Codex Juris Canonici*, promulgated by Pope Benedict XV.) The opening words of this first collection state: 'Mankind is ruled by two laws: Natural law and Custom. Natural Law is that which is contained in the Scriptures and the Gospel'. Elsewhere it is asserted that natural law 'came into existence with the very creation of man as a rational being, nor does it vary in time but remains unchangeable'. As to its force, the *Decretum Gratiani* states:

> Natural law absolutely prevails in dignity over customs and constitutions. Whatever has been recognised by usage, or laid down in writing, if it contradicts natural law, must be considered null and void. (I, viii, 2; D'Entrèves 1951, 34)

The Canonists were mainly concerned with the positive law of the Church, and not with philosophy. The best exposition of Christian natural law theory is that of the Dominican philosopher Saint Thomas Aquinas (1225–74). His work was profoundly influenced by Augustine and Aristotle, whom he refers to as 'The Philosopher'. Yet Aquinas was a great thinker in his own right, whose views about law are found in his monumental work *Summa Theologica*. Aquinas came to prominence as Europe emerged from the Dark Ages. The Church was under challenge by the secular state. Aquinas sought to maintain the spiritual and political supremacy of the Church through rational argument. Augustine had laid the foundation for this task, but Aquinas turned to Aristotle for the framework of his philosophy. The early patristic doctrine of the Church held that the coercive authority of the state was the consequence of original sin. There was no need for authority in the age of innocence. The state was installed after the fall as a penalty and remedy for sin. Hence, obedience to human law is a part of Christian duty. However, Aquinas argued, following Aristotle and Augustine, that the political state is not a punishment but is natural even in the state of innocence. The natural needs of man are the rational basis of the state. The state is part of a divine order, as God is responsible for both needs and their satisfaction. Aquinas painted an essentially teleological picture of the universe, but as a Christian he maintained that the world was ordained and controlled by God. The controlling principles of the universe supplied the ultimate criteria by which human laws must be judged. Aquinas identified four types of laws: eternal, natural, divine and human.

Eternal law

The universe is the creation of God. God is rational by nature, so the universe cannot be random. The laws that govern the universe are known as the eternal law, which controls both animate and inanimate things. All things that are subject to this law derive from it certain inclinations towards those actions and aims that are proper to them (I-II, Q 93, art 6; Aquinas 1947, vol. 1, 1008). The eternal law has two branches. One branch comprises the laws of nature that in the modern era are the subjects of the physical, biological and social sciences. These are the laws according to which the universe functions. The other branch comprises laws of behaviour, the moral law that distinguishes right and wrong conduct.

Aquinas maintained that the eternal law is not knowable as it truly is, and most scientists today would agree. Scientists generally concede that we may never discover all the laws of the physical world or develop a so-called theory of everything. Science has the modest aim of progressively extending human knowledge of the universe by observation, theorising and testing. From the Christian standpoint, to know the eternal law is to know God, and no one can read God's mind. The human mind can only comprehend the likeness of eternal law by the effects that it produces. Observations of the motion of celestial bodies, the behaviour of animals and plants, and the instincts, feelings and desires of human beings provide insights about the eternal law. Aquinas uses the Sun to explain the impossibility of knowing the eternal law. We do not know what the Sun is really like. We only have an imperfect idea of its nature gained by observing its effects on Earth (I-II, Q 93, art 2; Aquinas 1947, 1004).

If every person is subject to the eternal law, how can there be wrongdoers? Aquinas' answer has two aspects. First, human beings have imperfect knowledge of the eternal law and therefore are prone to error. Moreover, 'prudence of the flesh' (passion) corrupts reason and leads to wickedness. Second, the eternal law rewards good people with happiness and punishes the bad ones. 'Accordingly, both the blessed and the damned are under the eternal law' (I-II, Q 93, art 6; Aquinas 1947, 1008). The question of why God did not program all human beings to have perfect knowledge of the eternal law is left unanswered in the *Summa Theologica*.

Natural law

Inanimate things and irrational animals are governed by the first branch of the eternal law – the laws of nature. They obey these laws without knowing them. Thus, a rock thrown in the air falls to the ground, and a lion in the wild hunts by instinct. There is no great difference in the Thomist system between the behaviour of a rock and of a lion. Non-human animals have a limited capacity to calculate, as in survival techniques, but not to reason. (Findings in ethology, behavioural ecology and evolutionary psychology dispute this view of animal cognition, but that debate is best left to the discussion of evolutionary jurisprudence in Chapter 10.) The second branch of the eternal law, concerned with right conduct, has relevance only to entities that have the capacity for reason and moral judgment. These are human beings. One of the great paradoxes of creation is that only human beings endowed with the rational faculty are capable of disobeying the eternal law.

Human beings, like all things, obey the first branch of the laws of nature even if they have no knowledge of them. (Most people have at best a dim understanding of biology but they survive by obeying its laws as when they breathe, eat, drink, sleep, engage in humour and have sex.) However, a person cannot obey the moral commands of the eternal law without knowing what they are. If I do not know what the law commands, how can I observe it? The idea of eternal moral law makes sense only if it is knowable. Aquinas argued that human beings have a share of the eternal reason that enables them to discern what is good and evil. Human beings, in this way, participate in the eternal law: 'this participation of the eternal law in the rational creature is called the natural law' (I-II, Q 91, art 2; Aquinas 1947, 997). Aquinas went on to clarify that irrational creatures also partake of the eternal law, but not in a rational manner, 'wherefore there is no participation of the eternal law in them, except by way of similitude' (1947, 997). We may gather from all of this that natural law is that part of the moral eternal law that rational human beings understand by their God given reason, which is denied to physical objects and other animals.

Divine law

The term 'divine law' refers to the specific moral rules set out in the Ten Commandments (the Decalogue) and other authoritative Scriptures. Aquinas addressed the question of why divine law is necessary, given that the eternal law and the natural law of reason guide human conduct. He gave four reasons.

First, natural law only helps human beings to live up to their natural human nature. A person, unlike an irrational creature, can also aspire to a higher super-natural existence by following the divine law. Aquinas wrote: 'But to his super-natural end man needs to be directed in a yet higher way; hence the additional law given by God, whereby man shares more perfectly in the eternal law' (I-II, Q 91, art 4; 1947, 998).

Second, human reason, which is the means to understanding the natural law, is prone to error. Hence the cardinal rules of the eternal moral law need to be expressly stated. Aquinas wrote:

> Secondly, because, on account of the uncertainty of human judgment, especially on contingent and particular matters, different people form different judgments on human acts; whence also different and contrary laws result. In order, therefore, that man may know without any doubt what he ought to do and what he ought to avoid, it was necessary for man to be directed in his proper acts by a law given by God, for it is certain that such a law cannot err. (1947, 998)

Third, human law makers can only legislate in relation to external effects of acts, but cannot govern what is not seen. 'Consequently human law could not sufficiently curb and direct interior acts; and it was necessary for this purpose that a Divine law should supervene' (Aquinas 1947, 998).

Fourth, human law cannot punish or forbid all evil without hurting the common good. Aquinas, following Augustine, stated that by trying to do away with all evils, we 'would do away with many good things, and would hinder the advance of the common good, which is necessary for human intercourse ... in order, therefore, that no evil might remain unforbidden and unpunished, it was necessary for the Divine law to supervene, whereby all sins are forbidden' (1947, 998).

Morality has two dimensions. One consists of not doing wrong to others. This is what is classically known as justice. 'Thou shall not murder' and 'Thou shall not steal' belong to this category. The other category relates to virtue. The commonly identified virtues include chastity, temperance, charity, diligence, forgiveness, humility and courage. It is not feasible for the state to promote these by banning their opposites, namely: lust, selfishness, gluttony, sloth, wrath, impatience, greed, pride and cowardice. Aquinas, like Augustine before him, was astute enough to recognise that if all persons were compelled to be saints, there might not be, for example, any commerce or industry or art. Hence it is necessary for the divine law to supervene, whereby all sins are forbidden. Of course, if all persons followed all of the divine law in letter and spirit, the consequences for society would be equally problematic. The general point, though, is well made: that the state cannot compel persons to be virtuous without causing serious social harm, and that some things are best left to the individual's good sense.

Human law

Human law is the law established by custom or by the legislative acts of the state. Aquinas considered the moral basis of legislative authority. As mentioned above, human beings have knowledge of natural law by virtue of having a share of divine reason. Aquinas held that the moral authority for human law making is found in that part of the eternal law which reason reveals to man in the form of natural law. There are two ways in which human law is derived from the natural law. First, just as a scientist proceeds from indemonstrable first principles to particular conclusions, the law maker may derive logical consequences from the self-evident premises of natural law. Thus, the rule 'Thou shall not murder' is logically derived from the natural law precept that a person must not harm another person. Here the law maker has no discretion, as logic rules the matter. The law of homicide is a direct application of the natural law (I-II: Q5, art 2; Aquinas 1947, 1014–15). Second, human law may determine the way natural law applies to particular types of cases. It is a principle of the natural law that wrongdoers ought to be punished. Human law makers in different societies and in different periods may prescribe different punishments for the same offence. Here the law is determined by human discretion (Aquinas 1947, 1014–15).

The effect of unjust human laws

The essential point that Aquinas made is that whichever way human law is derived, its moral justification is in serving the natural law and hence also the eternal law. Aquinas stipulated three pre-conditions for the recognition of an enactment as a law at all. They are that the law is: (1) made for the common good; (2) made by the whole people or by God's vice regent for the whole people, who is the monarch ruling by divine right; and (3) promulgated (I-II, Q 90, arts 2, 3, 4; 1947, 994–5). Thus, a statute that serves the ruler's private interest may not be a law. Aquinas perhaps was thinking of some form of plebiscite when he referred to a law made by the whole people. Since law is made by the whole people or the vice regent of God, the commands of a usurper will not be law. A law has to be known by those to whom it is addressed. These are only the formal requirements of law. A law that is formally valid may yet fail the ultimate moral test.

Consider this example from recent history. An elected representative legislature enacts and promulgates a law that requires persons of a minority religious group to be exiled or executed. The majority of the people think that the law promotes the common good. Legal positivists are likely to say that the enactment is a law properly so called even though it is monstrously evil. Legal positivists may not condone the enactment but will argue that nothing is gained by denying the law's validity. (See discussion of this issue in Chapter 6.) Aquinas took the opposite view: that such a statute is not a law but a perversion of law (*non lex sed legis corruptio*).

> I answer that, as Augustine says 'that which is not just seems to be no law at all': wherefore the force of a law depends on the extent of its justice. Now in human affairs a thing is said to be just, from being right, according to the rule of reason. But the first rule of reason is the law of nature, as is clear from what has been stated above. Consequently every human law has just so much of the nature of law, as it is derived from the law of nature. But if in any point it deflects from the law of nature, it is no longer a law but a perversion of law. (I-II, Q 95, art 2; Aquinas 1947, 1014)

Aquinas conceded that law makers cannot be as precise as scientists in deriving particular conclusions from indemonstrable general principles: 'Human laws cannot have that inerrancy that belongs to the demonstrated conclusions of sciences' (I-II, Q 91, art 3; 1947, 998). Nevertheless, the central message is clear. Law makers have no business other than to serve the natural law by working out the logical implications and the practical applications of its precepts.

Does a person have a duty to obey an immoral or unjust law? Aquinas adopted the general legal doctrine that a command of an authority need not be obeyed if it is against the command of a higher authority. Since the authority of God is supreme over secular authority, human law that offends the natural law (or the divine law) is not binding on persons. 'Wherefore if the prince's authority is not just but usurped, or if he commands what is unjust, his subjects are not bound to obey him, except perhaps accidentally, in order to avoid scandal or danger' (II-II, Q 104, art 6; Aquinas 1947, vol. 2, 1646). Aquinas conceded that practical reason may sometimes dictate that a person ought to obey an unjust law if disobedience would destabilise a legal system that is generally just.

In summary, the Thomist theory of law affirms that law properly so called is law that is derived directly or indirectly from the eternal law of God and that does not violate the eternal law. The individual is directly and indirectly under the command of the eternal law. Apart from the physical laws of nature that govern all things, human beings are duty bound to obey the divine law of the scriptures and the moral precepts of the natural law that are imprinted in the form of reason. Individuals also have a moral duty to obey the laws of the state that do not violate the natural law or the divine law. The universe of the law according to Aquinas may be presented as in Figure 5.2.

Aquinas – Universe of Law

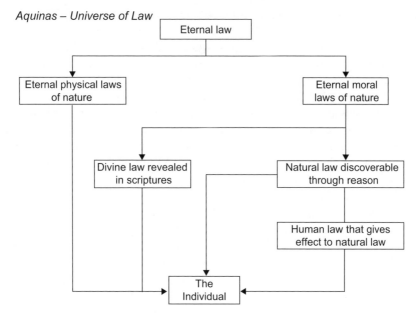

Figure 5.2 Aquinas' universe of the law

Theological beginnings of a secular natural law

A rethinking of theological natural law was bound to happen as Christians engaged with the world outside Christendom. Societies that Christian explorers discovered in the Americas and Asia had different gods, many gods or no gods at all. A natural law founded exclusively on Christian faith was not very natural to these peoples. Philosophers sought a basis of natural law theory that appealed to humankind generally. The seeds of a secular natural law tradition, though, had already been sown before the great discoveries, during the theological debates of the 13th to 17th centuries.

Greek natural law was based on cosmic reason. In Christian thought cosmic reason became divine reason. Aquinas, like Aristotle and other classical philosophers, ranked *reason* above *will*. Human law that flows from the will of rulers is subordinate to the natural law that flows from God's reason. Moreover, God does not and cannot legislate contrary to his own reason because God by definition is perfectly rational and good. Thus, God cannot will that man must hate God, commit murder, steal, tell lies or break promises. According to this train of thought, if we accept the existence of a perfect God, we must accept that divine reason rules. The later Scholastics and the Lutherans after them recognised two problems with this approach. The first was that God's rationality can be judged only with prior reason. Otherwise, God's reason must be taken on faith. The second problem was that human reason can lead different persons to different conclusions. Is abortion wrong under any circumstance? Is lying justified to save a life? Can there be a just war? Is adultery immoral, and what of adult homosexuality? We know that there is disagreement on these questions, even among the wisest. Hence, in practice, there is a need for a human authority to rule on disputed questions. According to the Catholic Church, that authority is the pope. This is the doctrine of papal infallibility. But what happens if the Church and the papacy are corrupted and divided and they lose their moral authority? This was the situation in the 14th century that led to the Papal Schism (known also as the Western Schism), when there were two popes – Urban VI in Rome and Clement VII in Avignon – both claiming to represent God on Earth.

The Conciliar Movement was a reaction to that state of affairs. Conciliarists, inspired by the writings of William of Ockham and Marsilius of Padua, argued that the universal Church consists of the congregation, not the papacy, and matters of doctrine should be resolved by a council elected by the faithful. This would have led to a form of theological democracy where the council, like a parliament, legislated on moral questions. It was a radical attack on the orthodox doctrine and it generated a long intellectual and political struggle. The papacy prevailed in the end, and at the Council of Constance (1414–18) the infallibility of the pope on all matters was confirmed. However, the deeper intellectual message of the Conciliarists did not die. Part of this message was that certain moral principles had to be accepted out of sheer necessity.

Scottish theologian John Duns Scotus[3] (1266–1308) was a major inspiration to Conciliarism. He argued that there were two kinds of natural law. One is natural law in the strict sense, and the other is natural law broadly speaking. Natural law in the strict sense consists only of the moral propositions that are self-evident and the necessary conclusions from them: *principia per se nota ex terminis* (*Ordinatio* IV, dist 17; Frank 1997, 202). These, he thought, were contained in the first two commands of the Decalogue concerning fidelity to God. God must not be hated or disrespected, and no other god should be worshipped. There is some doubt whether the command to observe the sabbath is strict natural law, but the commands not to commit murder, adultery, theft, or perjury and not to covet others' wives or property are not self-evident but are only 'exceedingly in harmony' with what is self-evident (Frank 1997, 203). These are natural laws in the broad sense. According to Duns Scotus, private property is not absolutely necessary, and in the state of innocence when everyone was perfectly nice to each other, all things were held in common. This is not the case in a community of sinners, who are likely to take more than their fair shares of material goods. Therefore the law allocating resources to private ownership 'is exceedingly consonant with peaceful living' and hence it is a natural law in the broader sense (Frank 1997, 204, 220). Thus, Duns Scotus

---

3 John Duns is more commonly known as Duns Scotus, meaning Duns the Scot.

acknowledged a concept of natural law based on the realities of social life and human need.

His English contemporary, William of Ockham (1288–1347), was a Franciscan friar whose prodigious intellect earned him the epithet *Doctor Invincibilis* (Invincible Doctor), and his method the name 'Occam's Razor'. Ockham's work got him into serious trouble with the Church in Avignon and he was excommunicated in 1328. Ockham thought that there were three kinds of natural law. The first kind is the laws that are true for all time and all places. They are the laws that we can derive logically from self-evident propositions such as: 'Exercise your will according to reason' and 'Avoid all blameworthy acts'. Ockham nominated the rules 'Do not lie' and 'Do not commit adultery' as belonging to this category. The second type of natural law consists of natural equity that prevailed in the age of innocence, when everyone behaved perfectly without the need for legal compulsion. We can forget about this type, as the age of innocence ended long ago when Adam and Eve committed the 'original sin'. The third kind of natural law is the moral law of our own era. This kind of law may be deduced by evident reason, the law of nations and from human behaviour (*Dialogus de imperio ac pontificia potestate* III, tr 2, p 3, c 6; Luscombe 1982, 715). Such natural law can be overridden if there is some special reason why it cannot be observed. Thus, a person may take another's property against the eighth commandment in case of extreme necessity (*Short Discourse*, 2, 24; William of Ockham 1992 (1340), 690).

Richard Hooker (1554–1600) argued that general principles of natural law are self-evidently known or gathered from the 'universal consent of men' and the fact that 'the world hath always been acquainted with them' (Hooker 1977, I, viii, 3, I, vii, 9). Francisco Suarez (1548–1617) contended that there cannot be a law unless it is willed by a superior; hence natural law is what is willed by God. However, he conceded that certain acts are objectively good or wicked independently of divine law. Human acts may in addition 'have a special good or wicked character in relation to God, in cases which furthermore involve a divine law . . .' (*De Legibus*, II, 6, 17; Suarez 1944 (1612): 202). Suarez, like William of Ockham, believed that in times of extreme need private property reverts to common use. Like Ockham, he maintained that when rulers become tyrants they forfeit the authority conferred on them by social contract and political power returns to its original natural source, the community (Haakonssen 1996, 18). Suarez was also the first Scholastic to think systematically about international law (*ius gentium*). He recognised that the *ius gentium* is the product of custom resulting from the actions of states.

The work of these Church Fathers represented a move away from the older tradition of seeking to know the mind of God through reason. According to these thinkers, natural law principles, though set by God, are discernible by rational deduction from human experience. They foreshadowed the theories of natural rights and social contract that were to become the cornerstones of the secular natural law theories that sprouted in the 17th and 18th centuries.

Rise of secular natural law: natural rights and social contract

Five factors encouraged the emergence of secular natural law theory in the 17th and 18th centuries. The first was the need for a natural law theory that was 'natural' in all societies irrespective of faith. The second was the need to counter the growing moral scepticism within Europe itself. The third was the gathering force of the Enlightenment, which disputed the traditional authority of church and state and questioned all metaphysical or mystical teachings. The fourth was the Lutheran belief that it is not possible to know the rational mind of God. If we knew the mind of God, we would be his equal. The fifth was the need to find a moral basis for the binding force of the *ius gentium* (international law) in a Europe deeply divided by religious and colonial wars. Some of the greatest intellectuals of the 17th century – among them Hugo Grotius, Thomas Hobbes, John Locke and Samuel von Pufendorf – turned their minds to this project.

The natural law theories that flowed from their speculations had two common themes. The first was that human beings have natural needs. They need protection from physical harm, they must have material resources to live and they need freedom to pursue their chosen life ends. The second theme was that human beings are also social animals by nature. They survive and prosper in cooperative social groups. This means that individuals must respect the natural needs of other individuals. Hence there must be a set of laws that secure the basic human rights that allow persons to survive and pursue their individual life ends without harming others. The second theme is concerned with the way these rights are recognised and protected. All these scholars attributed the existence of these rights to some form of social agreement.

Hugo Grotius

Hugo Grotius (1583–1645) was a Dutch scholar widely regarded as the greatest jurist of his age, and viewed by many as the father of the discipline of international law. No previous scholar apart from Suarez had paid serious attention to international law. The Roman *ius gentium* referred to the stock of civil laws that were common in all nations. These were laws that governed the relations between individuals, such as the laws prohibiting murder, theft and breach of contract. In contrast, what Suarez and then Grotius identified by the *ius gentium* was the law that governed relations among nation-states. Grotius' treatise *De Jure Belli ac Pacis* (*The Law of War and Peace*) was the result of his inquiry about the rights and duties of states towards each other in times of war and peace. The starting point of his inquiry was the question of how rights and duties exist at all. The answer lies in the nature of humans as social animals. Human beings, like other animals, have instincts of self-preservation. Unlike other animals, they also have an instinctive desire for social life.[4] Human beings have three additional attributes: capacity for language, a sense of what belongs to each other (what is yours and what is mine) and acting in accordance with general principles of conduct (*Prolegomena*, para 7; Grotius 1957 (1625), 11–12). The maintenance of social order in accordance with human intelligence is the source of law properly so called (para 8; Grotius 1957, 12). Grotius declared that these propositions 'would have a degree of validity even if we should concede that which cannot be conceded without utmost wickedness, that there is no God, or that the affairs of men are of no concern to him' (para 11; 1957, 13). Grotius believed that the free will of God is another source of law, but his key point in the *Prolegomena* was that there is a law that is natural to humankind irrespective of faith. This natural law confers upon the individual rights to self-preservation compatible with similar rights of others.

Thomas Hobbes

In *Leviathan*, Thomas Hobbes (1588–1679) famously described life in the state of nature as 'solitary, poor, nasty, brutish and short' (Hobbes 1946 (1651), 82). Hobbes believed (wrongly) that before the establishment of law and government people lived in a state of nature where every person was at war with every other person. This was because without the restraint of law every person had total freedom and a right to everything, including the bodies of each other. Hobbes wrote:

> The notions of right and wrong, justice and injustice, have there no place. Where there is no common power, there is no law; where no law, no injustice. Force and fraud are in war the two cardinal virtues. (1946, 83)

However, all is not lost. People by nature do not like conflict, and seek peace. They seek peace out of passion and reason. 'The passions that incline men to peace are: fear of death; desire of such things as are necessary to commodious living; and a hope by their industry to obtain them' (1946, 84). Reason allows men to identify convenient articles of peace – terms of a social contract that allows individuals to live in safety and harmony. These articles are otherwise called the laws of nature (1946, 84). Hobbes' 'laws of nature' were expressed normatively (as 'ought' propositions), but he presented them as scientific laws because without them human life is invariably at peril. Hobbes identified the following laws of nature in Chapters XIV and XV of *Leviathan* (1946, 84–105):

1. Persons have a duty to strive for peace to the extent that it is possible. However, every person retains the right to defend themselves against aggression.
2. Persons have a duty to give up their claims to total liberty and rights to everything that they held in the state of nature, provided that others too

---

4 This is not strictly true, as there are many other social species in the animal world. Animal societies, though, are less complex than human societies.

are willing to do the same. However, the liberty to defend oneself remains with the individual. This is the social contract.

3.   Persons should abide by the terms of the social contract, or else people will return to the state of nature. The very notion of justice arises from this obligation to observe the terms of the social contract. Hobbes wrote: 'The definition of injustice is no other than the non performance of covenant. And whatsoever is not unjust is just.'

4.   Persons owe gratitude to those who benefit them. Hobbes struck upon an important insight about human society. The observance of the negative rules of justice is a necessary condition of social life, but it may not be sufficient. Social cooperation declines if there is no reciprocity of goodwill among individuals. We should also remember that Hobbes was writing at a time when there was no state-provided social security and private charity was the sole means of dealing with personal misfortune.

5.   Every person should try to accommodate themselves to the rest. This is about 'give and take', about making reasonable adjustments for the sake of good relations.

6.   A person should forgive a wrongdoer who repents because forgiveness promotes peace.

7.   Revenge should never be to even the score but to deter future wrongs.

8.   Persons should not 'by deed, word, countenance, or gesture, declare hatred or contempt of another'.

9.   Every person must be acknowledged for the purpose of the covenant to be the equal of every other person by nature.

10. As a consequence of the previous law, no person at the time of entering into the covenant should reserve for themselves any right that they will not grant to others. Hobbes was clear that persons may retain certain rights and liberties, such as the right to govern their own bodies, air and water and the freedom of movement without which a person cannot live.

11. The things that cannot be divided, such as the resources of rivers and seas, are to be held in common. Interestingly, Hobbes accepted the law of primogeniture, which allows estates to be inherited by the firstborn to the exclusion of other children.

12. It is a law of nature that any dispute concerning rights must be determined by an impartial judge whose independence must be respected by all parties.

The rest of the rules are concerned with the independence and fairness of adjudication. Hobbes' laws of nature are logical deductions from two premises: (1) human beings have the natural right to live and to strive for their own betterment; and (2) human survival and flourishing depends on cooperation within society. Hobbes believed that these laws of nature can be maintained only by a sovereign body such as England's Crown in Parliament. He theorised that people enter into a covenant whereby they give up their autonomy to a sovereign power that is capable of protecting their rights and administering justice. Individual autonomy is surrendered to the sovereign in exchange for the sovereign's protection. Sovereign power is terminated when the sovereign is unable to provide this protection because of weakness or corruption. (See discussion in Chapter 2.)

Samuel von Pufendorf

Samuel Pufendorf (1632–94), born into a Lutheran family in Saxony, seemed destined to the clergy like his father until drawn to law and academic study. Pufendorf sought to reconcile the natural law founded on the survival needs of man with divine providence. The result of this effort is found in his major work, *On the Duty of Man and Citizen According to the Natural Law*. Pufendorf, like Grotius, commenced with the special nature of man. A paradox of human existence is this. On the one hand, the human individual is helpless without fellow humans. It takes a family to raise a child and a community to make civilised living possible. On the other hand, human beings, owing to their intelligence and manual dexterity (we can fashion weapons), have more capacity for evil than the brutes. A lion will kill only for food or in defence. As we all know, humans engage in deceit and wanton crimes against each other.

The only solution to this problem is sociability. Grotius thought that sociability is part of human nature. Hobbes thought that the human desire for survival compels people who are unsociable in nature to become sociable under the covenant establishing law and government. Pufendorf argued that apart from instinct and convenience, human beings have a moral duty to be sociable. Hence the fundamental natural law is that every person must cherish and maintain sociability, as far as possible. From this it follows that all things necessary for sociability are ordained by natural law, and all things destructive of it are prohibited (I, 3, 9; Pufendorf 1991 (1673), 35–6). All other rules are derived from this fundamental law.

Pufendorf held the view that the imperatives of social living give content to the natural law, but their binding force is owing to God's command. This is because, like the positivists, he thought that a law must flow from some competent authority. No legislator, no law. Sociability is enjoined on man by God. 'This is the origin of that quite delicate sense in men who are not totally corrupted, which convinces them that when they sin against the natural law, they offend Him who has authority over men's minds, and who is to be feared even when there is nothing to be feared from men' (I, 3, 11; Pufendorf 1991, 36–7).

John Locke

John Locke (1632–1704), the British philosopher, medical practitioner and political theorist, is considered the first great British empiricist by virtue of his ground breaking treatise, *Essay Concerning Human Understanding*. His political thesis concerning the limitation of sovereign power, set out in the *Two Treatises of Government*, became the authoritative statement of Whig political theory, which inspired the English constitutional settlement following the Glorious Revolution of 1688. Locke's important contribution to natural law theory is intimately connected with his political theory, and is found in the *Second Treatise*.

Locke's theory also begins with humans in the state of nature. However, unlike in the Hobbesian version, Locke's state of nature is not a state of war. The state of nature is ruled by the law of nature. Human beings are God's creatures and hence are his property. No person may therefore harm themselves or any other person (Locke 1960 (1690), 289). Every person has the right to life, liberty and property. A person owns their own body and mind and any property converted to use through their labour. This is the fundamental natural law. There is one serious problem with the state of nature. There is no civil government, hence every person is their own law interpreter, judge and enforcer. In the state of nature I determine what my right is, pronounce judgment in case of a dispute and enforce it to the best of my ability. So long as resources are plentiful in the state of nature conflicts are few and manageable. However, as life becomes more complex and commerce develops, the need for civil government arises.

Hobbes, in *Leviathan*, argued that only a sovereign authority with unlimited power is capable of establishing order and protecting the people. He saw no need for any precautionary limits on power. Locke, on the contrary, believed that it was the absence of limits on power, particularly those set by the separation of powers, that causes the inconvenience in the state of nature. Locke's people, like those of Hobbes, enter a covenant by which they concede to a supreme authority the power to protect life, liberty and estate. However, unlike Hobbes' covenant, which is a contract among individuals themselves, Locke's contract is between the individuals and the sovereign. Also unlike the Hobbesian folk, the Lockean people give the sovereign only a limited mandate. Power is conceded to the sovereign on trust in return for the specific undertaking that the sovereign will govern in a manner that avoids the principal causes of misery in the state of nature. Locke wrote:

> ... the power of the Society or Legislative [the supreme authority] constituted by them [the people], can never be suppos'd to extend further than the common good; but is obliged to secure every ones Property by providing against those three defects above-mentioned that made the State of nature so unsafe and uneasie. And so whoever has the Legislative or Supreme Power of any Common-wealth is bound to govern by establish'd standing Laws, promulgated and known to the People, and not by Extemporary Decrees; by indifferent and upright Judges, who are to decide Controversies by these Laws; And to employ the force of the Community at home only in the execution of such Laws, or abroad to prevent or redress Foreign Injuries, and secure the Community from Inroads and Invasion, And all this to be directed to no other end, but the Peace, Safety, and publick good of the People. (1960, 371)

Locke was more explicit than Hobbes about what will happen if the sovereign violates the natural rights of the people. The people retain the right of resistance to the sovereign: 'The Legislative being only a Fiduciary Power to act for certain ends, there remains still in the People a supream Power to remove or alter the Legislative, when they find the Legislative act contrary to the trust reposed in them' (Locke 1960, 385). When the legislature violates the trust, 'the trust must necessarily be forfeited, and the Power devolves into the hands of those that gave it, who may place it anew where they shall think best for their safety and security' (Locke 1960, 385).

Legacy of the natural rights theorists

Only four of the major natural rights theorists were discussed here, for reasons of economy. These theorists were followed by others, such as Jean-Jacques Rousseau, Richard Cumberland, James Harrington, Frances Hutcheson, Algernon Sydney and John Trenchard, to name only a few. The idea of inviolable natural rights became the central plank of the constitutional movements of the 18th and 19th centuries. It inspired the *Declaration of American Independence*, the US *Bill of Rights* and the French *Declaration of the Rights of Man and of the Citizen*. The rules derived from natural rights theory supply the most important provisions of the *Universal Declaration of Human Rights* and the international treaty law on human rights. Although debate continues about the ways and means of promoting these rights domestically and internationally, there is little disagreement about the moral case for their protection.

Natural rights theory marked a break with the theological tradition and created a foundation for a cross-culturally accepted set of ideas about fundamental rights of all human beings. The older Aristotelian–Thomist tradition of natural law, however, did not die. Its modern face is presented by John Finnis' masterful restatement.

John Finnis' restatement of classical natural law

In his book *Natural Law and Natural Rights*, John Finnis undertook a major restatement of the classical natural law theory, with the intention of clarifying its central ideas and defending the tradition against its critics. His restatement represents further development of the thought of Aristotle and Aquinas.

The central task that Finnis set himself was to persuade readers that there are universal basic values or goods that may be discerned through practical reason and from which we may derive our moral rules. Finnis agreed with Hume that it is not possible logically to infer the 'ought' from the 'is', meaning that we cannot derive a principle of how we ought to behave from observed facts of how things are. Finnis argued, however, that not every natural law theorist, and certainly not Aquinas, is guilty of that error (1980, 33). He pointed out that according to Aquinas the first principles of natural law that specify basic forms of good and evil are self-evident and indemonstrable. Finnis asserted, following Aquinas, that the basic goods may be non-inferentially grasped by persons who are old enough to reason. He pointed out that human intelligence operates in different ways when determining: (a) what is the case; and (b) what is the good to be pursued. In determining what the case is, we use inferential logic to derive conclusions from observed facts. In deciding what ought to be done, we engage in practical reasoning. Practical reasoning enables us to understand the basic self-evident principles (*prima principia per se nota*) from which we may infer what is right and wrong (Finnis 1980, 33–6).

Basic values

The starting point of Finnis' theory is the assertion that there are seven basic values or goods that are self-evident and that cannot be reasonably denied. They are also irreducible in the sense that they cannot be broken down to more basic goods. Basic values are not the same as basic human urges. Individuals have urges or inclinations, but a value is something that a person thinks is worthwhile to pursue independent of any urge. I have an urge to gain knowledge, but I also think that the pursuit of knowledge is worthwhile. Basic values must also be distinguished from the conditions that make them possible. Intelligence is helpful to gain knowledge but is not a basic value. Basic values must be distinguished also from intermediate (or instrumental) ends that make the basic values achievable. Thus John Rawls' primary goods (liberty, opportunity, wealth and self-respect) are not basic values but intermediate ends that make the pursuit of the basic values possible. Liberty, one would think, is a primary good because without it we cannot pursue knowledge or the preservation of life, or for that matter any of the other basic values. Yet Finnis argued that liberty in itself is not a basic value in the sense of being an irreducible good, because liberty is a means to ends.

Finnis asserted that there are seven basic values that can be objectively established. They represent forms of 'human flourishing'. They are: (1) life, (2) knowledge, (3) play, (4) aesthetic experience, (5) sociability (friendship), (6) religion (in a broad sense), and (7) practical reasonableness. Why are these values basic? According to Finnis, they are basic and universal because: (a) they are self-evidently good; (b) they cannot analytically be reduced to being a part of some other value or to being instrumental to the pursuit of any other; and (c) each one, when we focus on it, may seem the most important (Finnis 1980, 92).

Self-evidence

The idea of self-evidence is central to Finnis' thesis, but is not easy to describe. What is self-evident must be evident to all reasonable people without the help of anything outside of itself. Hence, it is the intuitive grasp of the truth. We can say that we know something to be true although we cannot demonstrate that truth with independent evidence. However, Finnis made a strong effort to describe why certain values are self-evidently good. He began by stating that a value is not self-evident simply because: (a) one has a feeling of certitude about it; (b) great and intelligent persons think so; or (c) most people are inclined to participate in or desire that value (1980, 66–70).

What, then, is self-evidence? Finnis' explanation was heavily dependent on analogies drawn with the methodology of empirical science. Finnis pointed out that self-evidence is known to empirical science. In every empirical discipline there are principles or norms of sound judgment that are self-evident. Thus, we use deductive logic although its validity cannot be independently proved. Scientists trust the evidence of their senses. A proposition that is self-evident is indemonstrable. Any attempt to demonstrate it involves using the proposition. If I say knowledge is bad, I am professing some knowledge. What is self-evident is obvious to anyone who has experience of inquiry into matters of fact or of theoretical judgment, and to deny them is straightforwardly unreasonable.

Finnis asserted that there are self-evident notions in moral science. He focused most of his efforts on arguing that knowledge is self-evidently good. As mentioned before, knowledge cannot be denied without engaging in knowledge. Consider another example from Finnis' list of basic values – religion. Finnis used religion in the broadest possible sense to mean one's view of the cosmos and one's own place in the universal scheme of things. He was not suggesting by religion a theistic or creationist view of the universe. Even a scientist who denies God, has no belief in an after-life and understands the universe as a process governed by the laws of physics is engaging in religion in Finnis' sense. So is a person who believes that the universe is essentially chaotic. Consider the basic value 'play'. It is hard to imagine that this would be a self-evident value to an ascetic monk. Finnis' argument concerning the retorsive effect of any denial of a basic value is not altogether convincing. Equally, this is not the critical point about self-evidence. His most important argument is that when we seriously contemplate each basic value, we realise that it cannot be denied without being straightforwardly unreasonable.

Finnis pointed to anthropological evidence showing that all human societies value these basic goods (1980, 83). Empirical observations provide us with knowledge of the practical choices we have in determining what is good. The ultimate decision, though, rests with the individual's own intuitive grasp of the indemonstrable (Finnis 1980, 85).

Finnis maintained that the basic values cannot be reduced to a more fundamental value such as pleasure. He dismissed the utilitarian argument that pleasure is the ultimate criterion of good and bad, alleging that it makes nonsense of human history and anthropology and that it mislocates what is really worthwhile. Finnis made the Aristotelian argument that virtuous persons pursue the basic values not because they lead to pleasures, but because engaging in them is the highest form of pleasure (1980, 95–7). Utilitarians will say that we pursue friendship for the pleasure we get from it. Finnis' point was that although many people do seek friendship for pleasure, what makes friendship good is not the pleasure but its self-evident rightness. He distinguished the reasons why people happen to be good from the reason why something is good. Note, however, that there are other theories about how we gain our sense of good and bad, and the prevalence in all cultures of certain basic values and rules. Among them are evolutionary explanations (considered in Chapter 10).

Deriving moral rules from basic values: the requirement of common good

Finnis' basic values are not rules of behaviour. They are the values from which moral rules can be drawn. How do we proceed from basic values to moral rules? The first question is: why must we extend the benefit of the basic values to others? It is obvious that if values are not shared there can be no social rules. Social rules cannot arise without some notion of common good. If each person seeks to pursue the basic values in disregard of others, there will be no harmony, no cohabitation and no social rules. Finnis was not content to rest his theory of rules on pragmatism. He distinguished morality from mere prudence by the fact that it is based on generalised concern for others.

Finnis pointed out that friendship (sociability) is itself an objective good that leads to concern for others. It is good to have friends and one's life is impoverished without friendship. Having a friend is not simply a matter of enjoying someone's company or finding someone amusing. Friendship involves caring about the welfare of the other person for their own sake. Thus, friendship is an objective good that leads us beyond an exclusive concern with ourselves. The complete egoist who treats all other persons as resources or means to their own satisfaction will lead an impoverished life, as they are incapable of friendship. Friendship is therefore an essential part of the good life that can be attained only by our concern for the common good.

Finnis also said that practical reasonableness, which is a basic value, requires a person to have regard to the common good when determining their commitments, projects and actions. How did Finnis show that this is a self-evident requirement? To the utilitarian, the answer is simple. The common good is another name for the ultimate moral test, the greatest good of the greatest number when everything is considered. Finnis, predictably, rejected this notion of the common good. One of the charges levelled at consequentialist theory is that the individual is not intrinsically important in the *calculi* that determine the moral worth of an act or a rule.

Finnis' idea of the common good is defined by the principle of subsidiarity. This principle means that the group (whether it be the family, an association or a political community) exists to serve the needs of the individuals who comprise it, not that individuals exist to serve the group. As Finnis put it, 'the proper function of an association is to help the participants in the association to help themselves' (1980, 146). The inference from this principle is that the common good must be determined having regard to the purposes for which the group exists. A political community, according to Finnis, exists to facilitate the realisation by each individual in the community of their personal development. The common good of the political community is the securing of the ensemble of material and other conditions which tend to favour that object (Finnis 1980, 154). The principle of subsidiarity recognises the intrinsic worth of the individual. Finnis explained:

> Human good requires not only that one *receive* and *experience* benefits or desirable states; it requires that one *do* certain things; if one can obtain the desirable objects and experiences through one's own action, so much the better. Only in action (in the broad sense that includes the investigation and contemplation of truth) does one fully participate in human goods . . . one who is never more than a cog in big wheels turned by others is denied participation in one important aspect of human well-being. (1980, 147)

Deriving moral rules from basic values: practical reasonableness

The essential problem for Finnis remained: objective goods are abstract values, not moral rules. Even if objective goods (basic values) are everywhere and always the same, the moral rules differ from place to place and from time to time. According to Finnis, the basic values form the 'evaluative substratum of moral judgment' or the 'pre-moral principles of natural law'. The (moral) natural law is derived from these values by the observance of practical reasonableness, which, of itself, is a basic good (Finnis 1980, 103).

The importance of practical reasonableness lies in the facts that: (a) all basic values are worth pursuing; and (b) life is too short to enable us to pursue each and every value to the maximum extent. Hence we need to make choices concerning *commitments*, *projects* and *actions*. The requirements of practical reasonableness are: (1) a coherent plan of life; (2) absence of arbitrary preferences among values; (3) absence of arbitrary preferences among persons; (4) detachment; (5) commitment; (6) efficiency within reason; (7) respect for every basic value in every act; (8) requirements of the common good; and (9) following one's conscience. Few would quarrel with Finnis about the requirements themselves, but Finnis needs to meet the consequentialist alternative.

Practical reasonableness and consequentialism

Consequentialism (utilitarianism) offers a serious challenge to Finnis' statement of practical reasonableness. Consequentialists make utility the ultimate criterion of moral judgment, in direct contrast to the natural law criteria of immutable values. Finnis rejected the consequentialist philosophy and argued that one should have regard to efficiency only within reason. Consequentialists affirm, alternatively, that one should always choose:

(a)   the act that, so far as one can see, will yield the greatest net good for the whole (act utilitarianism), or

(b)   according to a principle or rule which will yield the greatest net good for the whole (rule utilitarianism).

Finnis made some of the well-known objections to consequentialist theory, based on its practical unworkability and theoretical unsoundness. Among his objections are the following. The methodological injunction to maximise good, he said, is senseless because human beings do not have a single, well-defined goal or function. What is good for one may be bad for another. There is also no common factor in all human goals, such as the 'satisfaction of desire'. The absence of common goals or a common factor in different goals makes it impossible to measure the greatest good of the greatest number. Finnis also argued that consequentialism leads to arbitrary preferences, as the satisfaction of desire is the sole criterion. He claimed that consequentialism does not enable us to criticise a person who maximises pleasure regardless of the welfare of others. Consequentialism, according to Finnis, does not yield a principle of distribution. There is no consequentialist reason why we should not, for example, promote the maximisation of goods regardless of equitable distribution. Thus, enslaving part of the population may be justified if it leads to an increase on overall net satisfaction (Finnis 1980, 111–18).

Finnis' seventh requirement – namely, having respect for every basic value in every act – raises certain moral dilemmas, such as those concerning abortion and euthanasia, both of which he vigorously opposed. According to Finnis, this requirement means that one should not choose to do any act which *of itself* does nothing but damage any one or more of the basic forms of good (1980, 118). It means that one should not damage a basic good even if the good consequences outweigh the damage. Finnis considered the example where a hostage taker demands that a named individual be killed in exchange for the release of the hostages, who otherwise would themselves be killed. He seemed to assume that in this situation, the consequentialist would say that killing the individual is justified as it saves many lives. Finnis called this a senseless argument, and surely it is. He contended that the release of the hostages is one consequence among a multitude of incommensurable consequences of the act of killing. Finnis said that the calculus 'one life versus many' is naively arbitrary (1980, 119). Finnis was caricaturing consequentialism here. No serious consequentialist would judge the issue according to that simple calculus. Rather, they would agree that the calculus should take account of a wide range of consequences. They would say that the consequentialist method may lead to Finnis' own conclusion: that the individual should not be killed. But their reasons would be based on utility as opposed to self-evidence.

What is law?

Finnis rightly pointed out that people use the term 'law' to mean different things in different contexts. The 'ordinary concept of law' is quite unfocused, hence very versatile. It enables us to understand lawyers when they talk about sophisticated legal systems, anthropologists when they talk about elementary legal systems, bandits when they talk about the customs of their syndicate and theologians and moralists when they talk about moral rules (Finnis 1980, 278). He said that each of these meanings is justified in its context. But in a much laboured definition, too long to repeat here, Finnis attempted to capture the 'focal meaning' of the term' law'. 'Focal meaning' refers to the central case of the law or the typical form the law takes in a complete (developed) community. In giving only the focal meaning he avoided excluding from the term 'law' things that fail to have all the characteristics of the central case.

Finnis' focal meaning definition traverses many aspects of the law and the legal system highlighted in definitions provided by other thinkers. It refers to rules made according to regulative legal rules (Kelsen, Hart) by a determinate and effective authority for a complete community (Austin). It refers to the fact that law is backed by sanctions (Austin, Kelsen, Hart). It emphasises that law typically exists where the conditions for the rule of law exist (Fuller). It identifies the law's central purpose as the resolution of the community's co-ordination problems, and points to the need for reciprocity between ruler and subject (Fuller) (Finnis 1980, 276–7).

Finnis admitted that his focal meaning definition allowed for the possibility of laws of an objectionable kind. So what sort of natural law theorist is he? He stated that the tradition of natural law theory is not concerned with the denial of the 'general sufficiency of positive sources as solvents of legal problems'. Rather, he said, the concern of the tradition has been to show that the act of 'positing the law . . . is an act which can and should be guided by "moral" principles and rules' (1980, 290).

Duty to obey the law

Even so, Finnis addressed the question that the theologians raised: is there an obligation to obey an unjust law? Finnis said that a person asking this question may conceivably be using the words 'obligation to obey the law' in any one of four different senses:

1. Empirical liability to sanction in the event of disobedience

In this case, the questioner is asking something like: 'Will I be jailed if I disobey this law?' This question is practically very important but, according to Finnis, theoretically banal. Finnis said that this is the least likely sense in which the question might be asked. Yet Austin understood the concept of law only in this sense (Finnis 1980, 355).

2. Legal obligation in the intra-systemic sense

Put simply, the question posed is: 'Is there a legal obligation in the legal sense?' But what does the question mean by 'legal sense'? It means the obligatoriness of the law derived from the fact that the law satisfies the formal criteria established in the legal system for recognising obligatory rules. This is the sense in which the lawyer poses this question in the ordinary course of practice. Lawyers tend to regard the legal system as internally complete, coherent and thus sealed off from the debate about what is just or unjust. The lawyer working within the system would regard the morality of the law as ordinarily irrelevant to its validity. Finnis did not dismiss the importance of the question when posed in this sense. He considered that the intra-systemic approach to the question reflects 'practically reasonable responses to the need for security and predictability, a need which is indeed a matter of justice and human right' (1980, 355–6). The separation of the issue of justice from the issue of validity promotes the certainty of the law, which is a necessary condition of the rule of law.

However, Finnis did not think that a total separation of law and morality was possible. He pointed out that even within a so-called sealed off legal system, there is room to make moral arguments. There are many open-ended principles of justice that admit moral reasoning. The golden rule in statutory interpretation permits a court to give an ambiguous statute a meaning that avoids absurdity or manifest injustice. The test of reasonableness is often a moral test. There are endless opportunities for moral reasoning in legal argument. Finnis conceded that if the highest court has rejected the moral argument and upheld the law, it is idle to deny the obligatoriness of that law in the intra-systemic sense, and agreed with Hart that such denial would not be conducive to clear thought.

3. Legal obligation in the moral sense

According to some positivists, once a law is obligatory in the intra-systemic sense, insofar as jurisprudence is concerned the argument is over. Any further inquiry must be conducted within some other discipline. Finnis disagreed. He argued that we may rightly inquire of a valid unjust law whether it is also obligatory in a further sense. We may ask the question: 'Given that legal obligation presumptively entails a moral obligation, and that the legal system is by and large just, does a particular unjust law impose upon me any moral obligation to conform to it?' (Finnis 1980, 357). Positivists would not have this question discussed within jurisprudence. Finnis said that they are wrong, for three reasons.

First, the proposed separation is artificial. The types of moral arguments that positivists expel from jurisprudence are in fact used in legal practice and often find favour with judges. Second, a jurisprudence that banishes such questions to another discipline will amount to no more than lexicography of a particular culture. At the most basic level of jurisprudential inquiry, one has to ask the question: what is to count as a law in a given society? The basic positivist answer will be true of some legal systems but not of others. An intra-systemic description of the law is valid only for the particular culture. Finnis says that jurisprudence is a social science which seeks to describe, analyse and explain the object that is called 'law'. The conceptions of law that different communities entertain and that they use to shape their conduct are quite varied. The subject matter of the jurisprudential theorist's description does not come neatly demarcated from other features of social life and practice of the relevant community (Finnis 1980,

3–4, 358). Third, Finnis accused those who propose to separate moral questions from their descriptions of law of failing to consistently observe what they propose. He said that the works of these theorists are replete with undiscussed moral assumptions. Following are examples:

(a)   The formal features of the legal order contribute to the practical reasonableness of the laws that are made and the practical reasonableness of obeying them.

(b)   The formal features have some connection with justice, such that lawyers are justified in regarding some principles of justice as principles of legality.

(c)   The fact that a rule is legally valid gives reason for treating it as morally obligatory.

Finnis said that none of these assumptions can be shown to be valid or even discussed without transgressing the proposed boundary between jurisprudence and moral or political philosophy (1980, 358–9).

Returning to the third meaning of the question, Finnis said that, for the purpose of assessing one's legal obligation in the moral sense, one is entitled to discount laws that are unjust. Thus, in the context of the third meaning, one may say *lex injusta non est lex*. In other words, for some purposes, an unjust enactment may be considered invalid although it may be 'obligatory' in the formal legal sense (Finnis 1980, 360–1).

4. Moral obligation deriving not from legality but from a collateral source

Even if the moralist finds that a law is not obligatory in the moral sense, there may still be a moral reason for obeying it. Where the constitution and the legal system are considered generally good or desirable, the disobedience of particular unjust laws may undermine public respect for the system, with probable harm to the common good. Hence a moral obligation may arise from this collateral source to obey a law that is not obligatory in the third sense.

The obligation in the fourth sense arises from the desirability of not rendering ineffective the just parts of the legal order. Following Aquinas, Finnis observed that in such a case there is no moral requirement to obey the law fully, but only to the degree that will avoid bringing the law as a whole into contempt (1980, 361).

The enduring legacy of natural law theory

Natural law theory, in its various forms, represents the moral dimension of the law. The natural law tradition draws its power from three sources. One is the need to constrain the abuse of the legislative powers by rulers. Unrestrained power leads inevitably to corruption and abuse. The notion of higher norms that rulers must not transgress has appeal in every age. A second source of strength is the universal human instinct for self-preservation. No rational person wishes to be deprived of their life, liberty and possessions. Hence, the idea of natural rights makes a compelling case for limiting the powers of rules. A third force is the universal aspiration to align the law with a community's moral notions, whether they are religious, utilitarian or rationalistic.

As we observed, the law of ancient communities was quite simply their moral law. The distinction between law and morality arises when rulers acquire political power to make law according to their will. The Greek philosophers looked to the cosmic laws that, in their teleological view, governed everything and directed each person and object to its proper end. The teleological view became the theological jurisprudence of St Augustine of Hippo and St Thomas Aquinas. The later Scholastic debates, the great discoveries and the Enlightenment ideas shaped a new secular natural law tradition based on the natural needs of the individual in society, which has grown in influence with the rise of constitutionalism and liberal democracy.

The idea of natural law is not without its dangers. As the utilitarian positivists demonstrated, the failure to separate the positive law from moral law can defeat the values of clarity, predictability and certainty of rules that are themselves morally worthy attributes of law. The fact that its central concerns have gained recognition in so many national constitutions and in international law is the highest testament to the power of the natural law idea. That these principles have become part of the positive law of countries and of the community of nations is a tribute to the force of the legal positivist argument.

6

Separation of Law and Morality

Jurisprudence was enlivened in the second half of the 20th century by new debates about law and morality. Two of these involved Herbert Hart, the major figure in British legal positivism. Hart argued that the connection between law and morality was not necessary but contingent. He acknowledged that law often gives effect to morality, as when it prohibits crimes and torts and demands the performance of contracts. However, he maintained that a law, however immoral, will be law if it is recognised as law according to the established rules of recognition. The sensible response to such acts, Hart argued, is not to deny that they are law but to correct their effects by other laws passed where necessary with retrospective effect. (See discussion of Hart's views in Chapter 2.)

Two American professors of law questioned this general theory, and argued that law cannot be separated from morality in the sense proposed by Hart and his positivist predecessors. The first was Lon Fuller, whose theory was inspired by the German legal philosopher Gustav Radbruch. The second was Ronald Dworkin, who was a student of Fuller at the Harvard Law School. Their arguments are related in some ways to the classical ideas of natural law discussed in the previous chapter, but they also introduced new dimensions to the debate about the relation of law and morality. Fuller and Dworkin approached the question from different directions, but I conclude that their theories are fundamentally similar. We cannot leave the subject of law and morality without discussing their philosophies.

Lon Fuller on the morality of law

Lon Louvois Fuller (1902–78) was Carter Professor of General Jurisprudence at the Harvard Law School. The significance of his work in legal philosophy is

161

insufficiently recognised outside the United States. He is best known for the debate with Hart on the connection between law and morality. Fuller was not a natural law theorist in the traditional sense, but in some respects his theory is more far reaching. Fuller's theory of the morality of law is best understood against the background of the post-war debate about the legality of crimes against humanity committed under positive law.

Historical roots of Fuller's theory: the closing period of the Nazi regime in Germany

The first of the great 20th century debates on law and morality arose in the aftermath of the Second World War, which witnessed human atrocities on an unimaginable scale in Europe and Asia. The victorious Allied powers (the United States, the United Kingdom, France and the Soviet Union) established international military tribunals in Nuremberg, Germany and in Tokyo, Japan to bring to justice officials of Nazi Germany and Imperial Japan accused of war crimes and crimes against humanity. The common defence of the accused persons was that they were acting under lawful orders and hence their actions were lawful. Any retrospective punishment of these acts, they argued, would contravene the basic rule of justice that a person should only be punished for crimes against the law (*nullum crimen, nulla poena sine lege*). The debate was precipitated by the conviction of Nazi officials by the Nuremberg Tribunal.

The National Socialist (Nazi) Party came to power through democratic elections under Germany's Weimar Constitution. The Constitution, though democratic in character, had certain fatal defects, including the president's power to suspend civil liberties in case of emergencies and the legislature's power to amend the constitution by two thirds majority. These defects allowed the Nazi Party to transform the Constitution from within. In the short period that it held power, the Nazi Party under Hitler converted the liberal-democratic German state into an unrecognisable abomination of tyranny. At the height of Hitler's powers, the German political system displayed the following features:[1]

- frequent retroactive laws punishing the guiltless or excusing atrocities
- enforcement of secret (unpublished) laws that denied citizens the guidance of the law
- uncontrolled discretions that identified the law with the momentary wishes of officials
- the fact that a verbal order by Hitler was regarded as sufficient authority to exterminate thousands of people

---

1 These facts are taken from the judgments in the Nuremberg trials, particularly from the judgment in *USA v Alstötter* (*The Justices Case*) 3 TWC 1 (1948); 6 LRTWC 1 (1948); 14 Ann Dig 278 (1948). They are also set out in detail in Lon Fuller's essay 'Positivism and fidelity to law: A reply to Professor Hart' (1958) 71(4) *Harvard Law Review*, 648–57.

- frequent lawlessness, seen in the practice of extra-judicial punishment by the state acting through 'the Party in the streets' – a euphemism for party thuggery
- unification of legislative, executive and judicial power in the person of Adolph Hitler (the Fuehrer principle)
- total intimidation of courts, which did the bidding of party officials. Judges were required to decide cases as the Fuehrer would.

The question that Fuller raised was whether in such conditions there can be a legal system capable of producing laws in a meaningful sense.

The Radbruch doctrine

Gustav Radbruch (1878–1949) was a professor of law at the University of Heidelberg and one of the leading German philosophers before the Second World War. A member of the Social Democratic Party, he was elected to the Reichstag (the lower house of parliament) and served as Germany's Minister of Justice from 1921 to 1924. He returned to Heidelberg in 1926 and taught until his removal by the Nazi government in 1933. After the war he resumed his academic life at Heidelberg, where he proposed the so-called 'Radbruch doctrine', which became influential in the post-war jurisprudence concerning crimes against humanity.

Radbruch's early views on the concept of law are found in *Legal Philosophy* (*Rechtsphilosophie* 1932). He sought to combine elements of German legal positivism with natural law thinking, but the finished theory placed him closer to the positivists than to the natural lawyers. The idea of law, according to Radbruch, has three aspects: (1) Law serves expediency – the various purposes of human co-existence. (2) It serves justice. (3) It promotes legal certainty. (Radbruch 1950 (1932), 118) These three aspects are of equal value. He wrote that 'the legal certainty that positive law affords may justify even the validity of unjust or inexpedient law', but argued that the demand of legal certainty has no absolute precedence over the demands of justice and expedience (1950, 118). Conflicts between these qualities are left to the resolution of individual conscience. Conscience will usually choose legal certainty over personal conviction 'but there may be "shameful laws" which conscience refuses to obey' (Radbruch 1950, 118). A judge's conscience may direct them to enforce an unjust law against a person who disobeys it because of their own conscience. Radbruch stated that in relation to such a person, 'the law may prove its power but can never demonstrate its validity' (1950, 119). What does this mean? The power of the law is different from the validity of the law. Validity in the case of an unjust law is a matter of subjective judgment according to one's conscience. An unjust law may be valid from a judge's point of view, but from the viewpoint of the person who violates it the law may be effective but invalid. This suggests that officials may in good conscience enforce even the most unjust laws.

The horror of the Nazi reign of terror led to much soul searching by German legal positivists. In 1946 Radbruch published the essay 'Statutory lawlessness and supra-statutory law', in which he revised his pre-war theory of law. Radbruch used as his context one of the so-called 'grudge informer' cases. Grudge informers were persons who betrayed critics of the Nazi regime to the authorities, with knowledge that the betrayed persons faced certain execution. The common defence of grudge informers was that they did not violate any law by informing on critics. The defence of the officials who ordered the executions was that they were simply obeying the law in putting to death the betrayed critics. Radbruch argued that post-war German courts were right to convict the informers in disregard of the Nazi law. He could not do this without revising his pre-war theory that left the resolution of conflicts between statutes and justice to the conscience of judges. Radbruch reformulated his theory in the following terms:

> The conflict between justice and legal certainty may well be resolved in this way: The positive law, secured by legislation and power, takes precedence even when its content is unjust and fails to benefit the people, unless the conflict between statute and justice reaches such an intolerable degree that the statute, 'as flawed law' must yield to justice. It is impossible to draw a sharper line between cases of statutory lawlessness and statutes that are valid despite their flaws. One line of distinction, however, can be drawn with utmost clarity: Where there is not even an attempt at justice, where equality, the core of justice, is deliberately betrayed in the issuance of positive law, then the statute is not merely 'flawed law', it lacks completely the very nature of law. For law, including positive law, cannot be otherwise defined than as a system and an institution whose very meaning is to serve justice. Measured by this standard, whole portions of National Socialist law never attained the dignity of valid law. (2006 (1946), 7)

Radbruch thus proposed a moral test that applies to all positive laws. His test is not a high hurdle to clear. It does not invalidate every unjust law, for what is unjust is a matter of legitimate debate. It nullifies only laws whose injustice is beyond rational doubt. The Radbruch doctrine proved influential in many post-war trials in German courts and in the Nuremberg trials.

Hart's criticism

In 1958, the *Harvard Law Review* carried articles by Professors Hart and Fuller presenting opposing views on the Radbruch doctrine and post-war trials of war criminals. In 'Positivism and the separation of law and morality' Hart defended his version of positivism and levelled two criticisms at the Radbruch doctrine. The first was that Radbruch had confused the distinction between legal duty and moral duty. According to Hart, one may be under a *legal* duty to obey an inhumane law but have an overriding *moral* duty to disobey it. (This was, in substance, Radbruch's pre-war position.) The grudge informers and Nazi officials should not have been punished, because they acted in breach of morality and not law. Hart's second criticism was that the Radbruch doctrine, by denying legal status to inhumane law, does more harm than good. He accused Radbruch of 'extraordinary naiveté' and of having 'only half-digested the spiritual message of liberalism' (Hart 1958, 617–18). Hart considered the case of a woman convicted by the post-war West German court of appeal of the offence of illegally depriving her husband of his freedom. The woman wanted to be rid of her husband and to this end reported him for criticising the Reich, knowing that he would be sentenced to death. He was sentenced but sent to the battlefront, where he survived against great odds. The woman argued that she did no wrong under the law. Hart's point was that in convicting her, the post-war German court violated a different cherished value – the fidelity to law. The case raised a moral dilemma. The woman had committed an outrageously immoral act. Hart argued that from the positivist standpoint there were two choices before the German state: to let her go free, or punish her under a new retrospective statute. The latter course 'would have made plain that in punishing the woman a choice had to be made between two evils, that of leaving her unpunished and that of sacrificing a very precious principle of morality endorsed by most legal systems' (Hart 1958, 619).

This raises another question. What difference does it make if the woman is punished by the court under the Radbruch doctrine or by the legislature under retrospective law? In either case the result is the same. Hart argued that the latter course has the value of clarity. Everyone can understand the idea that 'laws may be law but too immoral to obey', whereas the contrary opinion that an immoral law is not law is not widely held and 'raises a whole host of philosophical issues before it can be accepted' (1958, 620). This is a utilitarian argument. Why engage in difficult debates when a simple solution is at hand? Hart's argument, though, is not without its own problems.

First, Radbruch was not saying that all immoral laws are invalid, but only those of the most inhumane kind. Hart's confidence that the general public will regard as law even the most heinous statutes may be misplaced. Lawyers are familiar with the disbelief of clients when they are informed that some statute or precedent bars their claim. 'How can this be law?' they ask, and they are not referring to genocidal laws but to laws such as those taking property without compensation. Hart's claim that the public would have difficulty accepting the Radbruch formula is untested. In any event, the Radbruch doctrine is now implemented in substance by the *Rome Statute of the International Criminal Court*.

Second, the option of punishment by retrospective legislation is available only if the evil regime is ousted. The Allied powers and the West German state had this choice because the Nazi regime was defeated and replaced by an authority that could enact retrospective laws. If the odious regime continues in power, its inhumane laws will remain in force nationally. What happens when a foreign court is asked to apply these laws? In *Oppenheimer v Cattermole*, the House of Lords considered the effect of the 1941 Nazi decree that took away the German citizenship of Jews who left the country, and confiscated their property without compensation. Most Jews fled out of fear for their lives. Lord Cross of Chelsea declared: 'To my mind a law of this sort constitutes so grave an infringement of human rights that the courts of this country ought to refuse to recognise it as a law at all' ([1976] AC 249, 278). Lord Salmon agreed:

The Crown did not question the shocking nature of the 1941 decree, but argued quite rightly that there was no direct authority compelling our courts to refuse to recognise it. It was further argued that the authorities relating to penal or confiscatory legislation, although not directly in point, supported the view that our courts are bound by established legal principles to recognise the 1941 decree in spite of its nature. The lack of direct authority is hardly surprising. Whilst there are many examples in the books of penal or confiscatory legislation which according to our views is unjust, the barbarity of much of the Nazi legislation, of which this decree is but an example, is happily unique. I do not consider that any of the principles laid down in any of the existing authorities require our courts to recognise such a decree and I have no doubt that on the grounds of public policy they should refuse to do so. ([1976] AC 249, 281–2)

The point I make is that from time to time a court is confronted with a statute whose injustice cannot, in a practical sense, be rectified by retrospective statute. Lords Cross and Salmon held, as a matter of English law, that an English court will not recognise the heinous laws of a foreign country.

Third, the utilitarian reasoning that Hart adopted is no more conclusive than the natural law reasoning he rejected. There is reason to think that officials may be less willing to enforce evil law if they know that in the event of a regime change a court will not entertain the defence of lawful orders. The Radbruch doctrine, by utilitarian calculation, may do more good than harm, though we will never know for certain.

Fourth, Hart's argument conflicts with his own concept of law. In his book *The Concept of Law*, Hart criticised the command theory of law on the ground, among others, that it misunderstands the idea of a rule. A rule of law has an external and an internal aspect. The external aspect is objective and factual. (Parliament has enacted the law.) The internal aspect is mental and subjective. (I ought to obey the Act of Parliament for reasons A, B and C.) It is the internal aspect that distinguishes a law from the demand of a gunman. An armed robber forces the victim to hand over their wallet. In contrast, a citizen regards the law as obligatory, even without the threat of force. In Hart's own words, 'Law surely is not the gunman situation writ large, and legal order is surely not to be thus simply identified with compulsion' (1958, 603). This was precisely Radbruch's argument.

Fuller's response: the morality that makes law possible

Radbruch, having died in 1949, was not around to answer Hart's criticism. Harvard professor Lon Fuller, however, developed Radbruch's central ideas into a theory of the morality of law. The editors of the *Harvard Law Review* published Fuller's response right next to Hart's essay. Fuller argued that Hart's proposal to invalidate the inhumane Nazi laws by retrospective statutes (as against judicial annulment) does not advance the value of fidelity to the law. Whether the laws are set aside by court or legislature, the effect is the same – what was once law is declared not to have been law. The only question then is 'who should do the dirty work, the courts or the legislature' (Fuller 1958, 649). Fuller defended the post-war decisions, arguing that the German legal system under Nazi rule had degenerated to the point that it ceased to make law 'except in the Pickwickian sense in which a void contract can said to be one kind of contract' (Fuller 1969, 39). 'To me there is nothing shocking in saying that a dictatorship which clothes itself with a tinsel of legal form can so far depart from the morality of order, from the inner morality of law itself, that it ceases to be a legal system' (Fuller 1958, 660).

Fuller's own substantive theory of law maintains that law and morals cannot be separated because the very concept of law carries within it certain moral qualities. Fuller's thesis may be summarised as follows:

- Law's authority cannot be based on law, but on the moral attitudes of the community.
- Law is an ongoing purposive enterprise. We cannot fully understand the nature of law without considering its purpose.
- The purpose of law is to allow individuals to communicate and coordinate with each other.
- The purpose of the law requires reciprocity between the ruler and the citizens. Law is not a one-way projection of authority but a system of cooperation.
- Law's purpose cannot be achieved unless it displays certain qualities. These qualities represent the internal morality of the law.
- A legal system that wholly lacks one or more of these qualities fails to make law, except in the Pickwickian sense that a void contract is a type of contract.
- The internal morality of law involves both morality of duty and morality of aspiration. Morality of duty demands that law provides the basic rules that make social life possible. A community may aspire beyond this point to achieve the best possible laws. This is the morality of aspiration.
- The external and internal moralities of law have reciprocal influence. The decline of one leads inevitably to the decline of the other.

Moral basis of law: external and internal moralities of law

It is a ridiculous tautology to say: 'The law is valid because the law says it is'. Law's authority must ultimately rest on the moral attitudes of the people. The law earns fidelity by the general moral quality of its rules. Fuller called this the external morality of the law. The external morality of the law refers to the substantive content of legal rules. If this content is pervasively unjust the legal system will fail to command the respect of the community and must maintain itself by force. This is common sense. Hart agreed when he argued, in *The Concept of Law*, that a legal system must have a minimum content of natural law to be effective (1997, 193–200). Fuller argued that law also has an internal morality that arises from its very nature as a purposive human activity. The internal morality is not principally about the content of the law, but concerns the qualities that enactments must possess to become law at all. Fuller's project of demonstrating the morality of law started in his *Harvard Law Review* reply to Hart, continued in his Storrs Lectures at the Yale Law School and was completed in the two editions of his book *The Morality of Law*.

Law is a purposive, reciprocal and ongoing enterprise

Fuller regarded law as: (a) purposive, (b) reciprocal, and (c) an ongoing enterprise. This proposition goes to the heart of Fuller's theory and marks a point of sharp difference from legal positivism. He began with the insight that law cannot be understood without considering its purpose. If we describe to a child the various parts of a computer without explaining what it does or what purposes it serves, we give them a very limited idea of what a computer is. Similarly, if we describe the law, say to a Martian, only by its formal features (that it is made by parliament, is applied by courts, etc) without saying what purpose the law serves, we give an incomplete account of it. Fuller here is not talking about the specific purposes of particular laws (to raise revenue, to provide social security, to ban narcotics, etc) but the purpose of having law at all. The abstract purpose of law is to make it possible for individuals to communicate, to coordinate and to reach understanding with each other (Fuller 1969, 185–6). Law does this by subjecting human beings to the governance of rules (1969, 106).

Law's purpose reveals the second aspect of the enterprise – its reciprocal nature. The law cannot be conceived as whatever the ruler wills if its purpose is to facilitate human coordination. Fuller claimed that legal positivists wrongly conceive the law 'not as the product of an interplay of purposive orientations between the citizen and the government but as a one-way projection of authority, originating with government and imposing itself upon the citizen' (1969, 204). It is common knowledge that laws made by democratic legislatures do not always advance human coordination, and often impede it. Yet history shows that legal systems that consistently fail to serve law's human purpose degenerate into dictatorial command systems.

The third aspect is that law by nature is an ongoing enterprise. It is also an aspirational activity, in the sense that it aspires to an ideal of the law that can never be fully achieved. An analogy is helpful here. A motor car may be described by its structure, capacity, mechanical devices and its purpose, which is to carry passengers from one location to another. A brand new Rolls Royce may come close to a person's ideal motor car. At the other end we see a shell of what was once a car, with no wheels, seats or engine. It would be silly to call this a car. In between the Rolls Royce and the wreck, there are cars in various conditions of excellence and dilapidation. At some lower point on this spectrum it is no longer sensible to call the object a motor car. Different persons may draw the line at different points. Yet if the motor car is beyond repair and ceases to serve its purpose, most rational persons will agree that it is no longer a motor car, except in the special sense that a wrecked car is a kind of car. According to Fuller, it is the same story with legal systems: they achieve law to varying degrees, from excellence to abomination. At some point it is no longer sensible to call a law a law, for it fails law's purpose, which is facilitating social life. The question at this point is not whether the law is good or bad but whether there is a law at all. If the law, for example, is not publicised or requires the impossible, it cannot do its job – that of guiding people's conduct. Even a well-meant law can fail for these reasons. Just as a motor car needs continual maintenance, the legal system needs constant attention to what makes law possible.

Internal morality of law

Fuller explained the inner morality of law with the help of an allegory. Assume that a country is ruled by King Rex, who has unlimited law making power. He is utterly selfish, uncaring and incompetent. He does not lay down any rules but from time to time issues commands intended to punish those who disobey him and to reward those who obey him. However, because of his incompetence he makes no attempt to find out who has been obedient and who has been disobedient. Consequently, he frequently punishes obedience and rewards disobedience. Rex will not achieve his aim, as there is no meaningful connection between his commands and his actions. He fails to produce law. At other times, Rex's commands are so confused, ambiguous and inaudible that his subjects do not know what Rex wants them to do or not do. Sometimes he commands today that something must have been done yesterday. Again, he fails to make law capable of guiding conduct. Fuller used this analogy to demonstrate how the Nazi regime debased and destroyed the legal system through *ad hoc* commands, retroactive laws, *ad hominem* laws, secret enactments, punishment without trial, indemnities for state condoned crimes, official disregard for the law and the practice of thuggery.

Fuller proceeded to identify what he termed 'eight ways to fail to make law':

1.   failure to achieve rules at all, in the sense that every command of the ruler is *ad hoc* and lacks any degree of generality – if this is the case, the subjects have no guidance as to how they should behave
2.   failure to publicise the rules that people are expected to observe
3.   abuse of the practice of enacting retroactive laws – such laws not only fail to guide conduct but also undercut the integrity of prospective rules by placing them under constant threat of retrospective change
4.   failure to make rules comprehensible
5.   enactment of contradictory rules
6.   enactment of rules that require conduct beyond the powers of the affected persons
7.   frequently changing the rules such that the subjects cannot orient their actions by them
8.   lack of congruence between the rules as announced and their actual administration.

Fuller contended that the total failure in any one of these eight directions does not simply result in a bad system of law; it results in something that is not properly called a legal system at all except in the Pickwickian sense described above. Fuller wrote:

> Certainly there can be no rational ground for asserting that a man can have a moral obligation to obey a legal rule that does not exist, or is kept secret from him, or that came into existence only after he has acted, or was unintelligible, or was contradicted by another rule of the same system, commanded the impossible, or changed every minute. It may not be impossible for a man to obey a rule that is disregarded by those charged with its administration, but at some point, obedience becomes futile – as futile, in fact, as casting a vote that will never be counted. (1969, 39)

The eight failings are mitigated by the eight virtues of the internal morality of law. They are: (1) generality, (2) publicity, (3) prospectivity, (4) clarity, (5) consistency, (6) possibility of compliance, (7) constancy, and (8) faithful administration of law.

The internal morality of law is morality of duty and of aspiration

Fuller, following Kant, Adam Smith and other moral philosophers, distinguished morality of aspiration from morality of duty. If we imagine a vertical moral scale, the lower half will occupy the morality of duty and the upper half the morality of aspiration. Morality of duty relates to the fundamental and essential moral duties. These consist mainly of forbearances or negative injunctions such as 'Do not murder', 'Do not steal' and 'Do not break your contracts'. Morality of aspiration occupies the upper part of the scale. This is the morality of striving towards the highest achievements open to human beings. At some point on the scale what is a duty becomes an aspiration. 'Somewhere along this scale there is an invisible pointer where the pressure of duty leaves off and the challenge of excellence begins' (Fuller 1969, 10). This is a fluctuating pointer, hard to locate but vitally important. Social attitudes about rewards and punishments are important indicators of where the pointer rests. A person is usually condemned for violating morality of duty but not praised for observing it (Fuller 1969, 30). I will be condemned if I commit theft but will not be praised because I did not steal. In contrast, a person is usually praised for displaying morality of aspiration but not condemned for the lack of it. I will be praised for plunging into the raging torrents to save my neighbour's cat, but will not be condemned if I thought better of it.

A legal system is also measurable on the moral scale. A system that fails to provide a basic framework of rules that enable peaceful social life fails the morality of duty. This is Fuller's basic argument. We must note, though, that no legal system in history has fully met the requirements of the external and internal morality of law. No legal system ever will. Let me focus on the legal system that I know best – that of Australia. The Australian legal system is nowhere near perfect by Fuller's yardsticks. There are arbitrary discretions that allow officials to determine the law for the particular case. Some laws have retrospective effect, such as those that impose taxes or take property without compensation.

Some laws are so complex that ordinary citizens who must observe them have no idea what they are. Some obscure rules, regulations, orders and judicial precedents lie in the crevices of the legal system, undiscovered even by the best judges and lawyers. There are contradictions within laws that remain unresolved. Yet most rational observers will place the Australian legal system at the upper end of Fuller's moral scale, well above the pointer that separates the moralities of duty and aspiration. The reason is that the Australian legal system by and large serves the social purpose of law. This is mainly because the constitutional features of the system make it open to self-correction. In contrast, Fuller argued that the legal system and laws of the Nazi regime fell far below the pointer.

Fuller's overall position was that law may fail by some standard of aspirational morality but will still be law. A law that fails the morality of duty is not law at all except in the Pickwickian sense.

Hart's rejoinder

The first edition of *The Morality of Law* was published in 1964, and Hart lost no time in publishing a critical review of it. A major part of the review criticised Fuller's misunderstandings of positivist positions and identified technical deficiencies in Fuller's theory. One criticism, though, went to the heart of Fuller's thesis of the internal morality of law. Hart had earlier noted that the inner morality of law is 'compatible with very great iniquity' (1961, 202). Hart's point was that a legislature may comply with all the requirements of the inner morality of law and still produce unjust law. Hence, the requirements are ethically neutral. They can be put to good or bad use. In the book review, Hart argued that the eight requirements Fuller specified are not principles of morality but principles of good legal craftsmanship. In short, he accused Fuller of confusing morality with efficiency (Hart 1965, 1286).

Hart argued that Fuller's logic would mean that principles of efficacy in any purposive activity would represent the inner morality of that activity. This would lead to the absurd conclusion that even despicable activities have an internal morality. Hart took the example of a person who wishes to poison to death another person. Common sense tells the poisoner to choose a poison that is hard to detect and administer the poison without being observed. 'But to call the principles of the poisoner's art "the morality of poisoning" would simply blur the distinction between the notion of efficiency for a purpose and those final judgments about activities and purposes with which morality in its various forms is concerned' (Hart 1965, 1286). This is a grotesque misreading of Fuller's theory.

Fuller's counter

In the first edition of *The Morality of Law*, Fuller had already offered a defence against the charge that his internal morality is in fact ethically neutral. The demand that rules be known, general and observed in practice seems at first sight ethically neutral, but Fuller argued that without these qualities one cannot judge the morality of the law at all because one only sees patternless *ad hoc* commands. He said that an unlimited power expressing itself solely in unpredictable and patternless interventions could be said to be unjust only in the sense that it does not act by a known rule. It is hard to call it unjust in any more specific sense until one has discovered what hidden principle, if any, guided its interventions (Fuller 1969, 157–8). Generality also has ethical merit in mitigating discriminatory laws, such as those used in apartheid and segregation (Fuller 1969, 160).

Fuller's most important argument was that the internal morality arises from a particular view of human beings as responsible agents. Every departure from the principles of inner morality, he argued, is an affront to people's dignity as responsible agents. To judge a person's actions by unpublished or retroactive law, or to order a person to do an act that is impossible, is to convey to them your indifference to their powers of self-determination (Fuller 1969, 162).

In the revised edition of *The Morality of Law*, Fuller directly addressed Hart's claim that his internal morality was in fact efficiency. He compared two different types of social ordering: managerial direction and law. Five of the principles of internal morality are applicable to managerial activity. Managers who wish to ensure that subordinates work according to plan will announce their directions as clearly as possible and without contradictions. They would be silly to give impossible directions, and good managers will not change their instructions frequently. However, the qualities of generality, prospectivity and congruence of rules and actions have a special place in law that they do not have in management. Generality of directions is only a matter of convenience in management. Subordinates have no cause to complain if the manager directs them on occasions to depart from the general orders. There is also no compelling reason for a manager not to depart from announced rules. As for the principle of prospectivity, Fuller stated that the issue does not arise: no manager with a semblance of sanity would direct a subordinate today to do something yesterday (1969, 208–9).

Fuller argued that the inapplicability of these three requirements brings out the essential difference between managerial direction and law. Management represents a one-way projection of authority, and hence only requires principles of efficiency. On the contrary, a relatively stable reciprocity of expectations between the law giver and the subject is part of the very idea of a functioning legal order. Law, unlike management, is not simply about directing persons to perform tasks set by a superior, but is a matter of providing citizens with a sound and stable framework for their interactions with one another, the role of government being that of a guardian of the integrity of this framework. Fuller claimed that his positivist critics confused his principles of inner morality with requirements of efficacy because they regarded law essentially as a one-way projection of authority.

The connection of internal and external moralities

The external morality of law concerns the moral content of the rules. A law that authorises torture is bad and a law that bans torture is good. The internal morality is about the qualities that make the law serve the general social purpose of human coordination. It provides stable rules of the game. Fuller conceded that a law that complies with internal morality may yet be unjust. The law in the People's Republic of China that prohibits parents from having more than one child is general, prospective, promulgated clearly, and so forth. Yet it has been widely condemned as unjust. Inner morality is logically consistent with external injustice. This does not mean that the inner morality is not true morality.

Imagine two bad regimes, A and B. Regime A operates by clearly declared prospective and general rules that are consistently and scrupulously enforced, while regime B operates through *ad hoc* commands, retrospective laws, secret laws and extra-judicial punishment without charges or trial. Is there any moral difference between the regimes? Clearly there is. Regime A provides a degree of order that allows citizens to avoid official retribution and go about their lives even within the confines of harsh laws. In regime B nothing is certain and people are in constant jeopardy. History also demonstrates repeatedly that the internal and external moralities of law are symbiotic. One does not live long without the other. This is why the internal morality of law, under its other name 'the rule of law', is widely regarded as a moral imperative.

Ronald Dworkin and the integrity of law

Ronald Dworkin, like Lon Fuller, advanced a theory of law that asserted a necessary connection between law and morality. There are similarities between the legal philosophies of these two Americans, though Dworkin hardly mentioned Fuller's work. I will say something about these similarities in the course of this discussion. Dworkin is considered by many as the leading contemporary American legal philosopher. He succeeded Hart in the chair of jurisprudence at the University of Oxford in 1969 and later held the WN Hohfeld chair of jurisprudence at Yale University. He currently holds chairs at University College, London and New York University. Dworkin's philosophy was developed over two decades. Its most definitive statement is found in his book *Law's Empire*.

Dworkin, like many natural law theorists, posed this question: what justifies the use of force by the state against its citizens? In other words, what is the reason that makes it acceptable for the state to make and enforce laws even against persons who disapprove of them? Dworkin, like the natural lawyers and many modern legal positivists, rejected the notion that power alone justifies law. The duty of a citizen to submit to the authority of law is seen, then, as a moral duty (Dworkin 1998, 191).

Dworkin's legal philosophy makes the following intellectual claims regarding law:

1.   We can truly understand our law only if we consider it within the context of our own culture. Law can mean different things in different cultures.

2.   In the Anglo-American legal culture, law is not the command of whosoever has physical power to enforce it. The state's monopoly of power to coerce citizens – in other words, the power to make law – is founded not on physical force but on moral authority.

3.   This moral authority to make law is a feature of a special kind of community. Such a community is one that accepts integrity as a political virtue (1998, 188). It is the integrity of the law that creates the moral duty of citizens to obey the law. Integrity is not fairness or justice. People obey laws that they think are unfair or unjust provided that the law as a whole has integrity. There are two principles of political integrity:

    (a) *Legislative principle*: law makers should try to make the total set of laws morally coherent. Political integrity asks legislators to make law in keeping with the principles established within the legal system (1998, 176). This is essentially an argument about consistency. A statute that imposes strict liability on motor car manufacturers but not on makers of trucks fails the aim of integrity.

    (b) *Adjudicative principle*: judges should view the law as coherent in the same way as far as possible.

4.   The duty of the judges to maintain coherence means that the judges must interpret common law precedents and statutes in a manner that maintains coherence. The judicial task, therefore, is never mechanical and is always creative. (Dworkin compared a judge to a chain novelist whose duty is to continue an ongoing story by interpreting previous chapters while seeking to make the novel the best it can be.)

5.   Although there is no explicit claim that morality and law are inseparable, if integrity is a moral value the necessary connection of law and morality follows.

Beginning of Dworkin's legal philosophy: the rights thesis

Dworkin launched his initial assault on legal positivism's thesis of the separation of law and morality in his 1977 book, *Taking Rights Seriously*. The principal aim of this book was to contest one of Hart's central contentions. Hart claimed that in a 'hard case' the judge makes law. A hard case is one where existing statutes and judicial precedents do not provide a clear or conclusive answer to the legal question before the court. Hart argued that the rule of recognition in England authorises the judge to act as a deputy of Parliament and supply a rule to resolve the case. This argument was necessary for Hart to maintain that law and morality are separate. The judges in these hard cases will consult their own sense of justice. In other words, they will make a decision based on their own moral views. Hart argued that the decision of the judge is law, not because of its moral content but because it is made by an official (the judge) who is authorised by the rule of recognition to make law. Dworkin said that this cannot be right. A litigant has no right to a favourable decision, but has a right to a decision in accordance with law. A judge cannot say: 'There is no law, so I am going to make the law'. Dworkin argued that Hart's view is flawed by a serious misunderstanding about the concept of law.

Principles and policy

The law, according to Dworkin, comprises not only rules but also principles. When rules run out, judges look to the legal principles that are imbedded in the general body of the law. In Hart's view, a judge may decide a hard case on grounds of *policy*, whereas Dworkin argued that a judge must always decide according to *principle*. Legislators are entitled to make law on policy, but judges are not. So what is the difference between policy and principle? Policy does not require consistency, principle does. Parliament may decide to grant workers in the mining industry a statutory wage, while ignoring the claims of auto workers. Parliament may impose strict liability on some manufacturers but not on others. Judges cannot make these kinds of decisions without undermining public confidence in the judiciary. They have to give a judgment that is consistent with past non-recanted decisions. The political responsibility of judges is to make only decisions that they can justify within a theory that also justifies other decisions that they propose to make. The rights theory 'condemns the practice of making decisions that seem right in isolation, but cannot be brought within some comprehensive theory of general principles and policies that is consistent with other decisions also thought right' (Dworkin 1977, 87).

A principle, unlike a rule, does not provide an automatic answer to a legal question. A principle may be contradicted by a rule of law or by another principle. The legal principle 'No man may profit from his own wrong' is contradicted by some laws. A trespasser may get ownership of a piece of land if he occupies it long enough. An employee who leaves without notice to take a better paid job gets to keep the higher wage despite her breach of contract. This is because parliament's will or some other principle outweighs the principle against profiting from wrong. 'All that is meant when we say that a particular principle is a principle of our law is that the principle is one which officials must take into account, if it is relevant, as a consideration inclining in one direction or another' (Dworkin 1977, 26).

Dworkin's overall thesis in *Taking Rights Seriously* was that there is always a right answer to a legal dispute that a good judge like Hercules (Dworkin's fictional ideal judge) can derive from the rules and principles of the legal system. Judges, of course, make mistakes – unlike Hercules, they are fallible mortals. The fact that judges err does not mean that there is no right answer. A good legal system, through its institutional safeguards and juristic techniques, seeks to reduce the number of mistakes overall (Dworkin 1977, 130).

The rights thesis did not establish a *necessary* connection between law and morality. Judges who summon principles in aid of a decision import morality. It is not their personal morality but the morality of the legal system. However, a statute that is constitutionally valid may enact an immoral law and, where its meaning is free of doubt, the court will give effect to it. In *Law's Empire*, Dworkin reformulated his thesis in a way that makes the value of integrity indispensable to the concept of law. If true, it means that law and morality are inseparable.

Dworkin's concept of law

Dworkin did not attempt to define law. He rejected what he called semantic theories of law. Semantic theories are those that try to provide a universally true description of what is known as 'law'. He included the various theories of legal positivism and natural law in this category. Dworkin considered the semantic approach to be futile because different communities understand law in different ways. He therefore tried to understand what law meant in his own culture, the Anglo-American political culture. He identified the domain of law or legal practice that most theorists can accept with respect to that culture. He said that 'the most abstract and fundamental point' of legal practice is to guide and constrain the power of government in the following way:

> Law insists that force not be used or withheld, no matter how beneficial or noble these ends, except as licenced or required by individual rights and responsibilities flowing from past political decisions about when force is justified. The law of a community on this account is the scheme of rights and responsibilities that meet the complex standard: they licence coercion because they flow from past decisions of the right sort. (Dworkin 1998, 93)

It takes some effort to work out precisely what Dworkin was saying here. He made three points:

1. Law consists of rights and responsibilities of citizens.
2. Rights and responsibilities flow from past political decisions of the 'right sort'. These are primarily the constitution, legislation and judicial decisions.
3. Coercion by the state is justified only to enforce the rights and responsibilities established by past political acts.

Let us try to understand these propositions even more simply. Consider the following two typical legal cases. Parliament passes the *Minimum Wage Act* today. A year later, employee A complains to the court that her employer B has not paid her the minimum wage, and asks the court to order B to pay the shortfall. The court's decision to compel B to pay this sum is justified by the *Minimum Wage Act*. If the *Minimum Wage Act* did not exist, the court could not justify coercing B to pay the sum that A claims. Now consider the case of C, whose brand new motor car is damaged because its braking system failed. C sues the manufacturer of the motor car, D & Co, though he actually bought the car from a local dealer. The court's decision to award damages and enforce judgment against D & Co (with whom C has no contract) is justified by previous decisions of the court in similar cases. All this is plain to the legal practitioner and is uncontroversial.

There are, of course, other ways of understanding law. Dworkin looked at law primarily from the point of view of justifying the use of force by the state. It is worth remembering that law may exist without state intervention. It is true that a party may enlist the state's assistance to enforce its rights in the last resort by obtaining judgment in a court of law, but the state's coercive power plays no part in the vast majority of private transactions that make up social life. Let us stay, though, with Dworkin's concept of law.

Justification for the use of force

Dworkin first addressed the question of why coercion is justified only when it is applied in conformity with rights and responsibilities established by law. If courts disregard statutes and precedents and act as they please, the law obviously will become unpredictable and arbitrary. Dworkin stated that limiting state coercive power in this manner also 'secures a kind of equality among citizens that makes their community more genuine and improves its moral justification for exercising the political power it does' (1998, 97). Notice that Dworkin referred to a 'kind of equality'. This is the kind of equality that Fuller identified with generality, which is a moral attribute of law. The principle of generality does not require absolute equality, but only the like treatment of persons in like situations (Dworkin 1998, 165).

The problem for Dworkin was that past political acts (statutes and precedents) do not always secure equality. Even democratically elected legislatures discriminate between interest groups for political expediency. This led Dworkin to identify another essential quality of law – integrity. Fuller had argued previously that legislative power to discriminate must be contained if law is to maintain its moral authority. A legal system that continually disregards the moral demand of generality will lose its capacity to make law. Law becomes a jumble of *ad hoc* commands that provides no guidance for human conduct. Fuller also identified other factors that defeat the purpose of law: public ignorance of what the law demands, inconsistency (incoherence within the system of laws), lack of clarity, instability of the laws (frequent change), retrospectivity, impossibility of compliance and the disregard of the law by officials. Dworkin collapsed all these virtues into a quality that he termed 'integrity'.

Law as integrity

Dworkin's notion of integrity requires internal consistency of the system of rules and principles that make up the law. It has a close affinity to the principle of equal protection of the law entrenched in the Fourteenth Amendment of the US Constitution (Dworkin 1998, 183).

We say that a person has integrity when they are known to act always according to their principles. We respect such a person even if we do not agree with all of their principles. Dworkin argued that law is similar. People may disapprove of some laws as unfair or unjust, but overall people respect and observe the law because of its integrity. Law's integrity depends on legislators and judges. If they legislate or adjudicate arbitrarily the law loses its integrity and its moral authority.

Dworkin selected integrity as the chief virtue of law, in preference to justice or fairness. There are different notions of justice, but for Dworkin justice represents 'morally defensible outcomes' (1998, 165). Fairness in politics is about fair political procedures. These are the methods of electing officials and making their decisions responsive to the electorate (Dworkin 1998, 164). Some thinkers consider justice as fairness, but according to the way Dworkin understood these concepts they are different. A fair procedure may produce an unjust outcome, while an unfair process can yield a just result. In a democracy people do not always agree on what is just, and they tolerate many decisions that they find unjust. However, people expect integrity in their legal system. This means that statutes and judicial precedents must show consistency in the way they treat like cases.

Dworkin explained his notion of integrity by contrasting it with checkerboard solutions (1998, 178). The checkerboard approach leads to laws that treat groups of people differently when there is no rational difference between them. A law that imposes strict product liability on makers of washing machines but not refrigerators is a checkerboard response. So is a law that forbids racial discrimination on buses but not in restaurants. Integrity bars 'Solomonic justice' that calls for a dispute to be settled by compromise in disregard of right and principle (Dworkin 1998, 178–9). Dworkin acknowledged that sometimes circumstance may compel piecemeal solutions that are better than no solutions. Universal product liability law, for example, may be forestalled by the power of manufacturing lobbies, so legislatures go about it selectively (Dworkin 1998, 218).

Integrity and interpretation of statutes

The principle of legislative integrity, which calls on legislatures to treat like matters alike, is generally accepted in liberal democracies as an article of political morality. However, Dworkin proceeded from this point of consensus to the most controversial aspect of his thesis. Dworkin argued that 'The integrity of a community's conception of fairness requires that the principles necessary to justify the legislature's assumed authority be given full effect in deciding what a statute it has enacted means' (1998, 166). In simpler English, what he said is that the courts have the power and the duty to interpret statutes in a way that maintains the integrity of law. This can be done only if courts interpret each statute to ensure as far as possible its consistency with other statutes and the system as a whole. This argument marks the sharpest point of difference between Hart and Dworkin.

The problem arises in this way. The legislature of a state does not always respect the principle of integrity in making statutes. In some countries, constitutional provisions (such as the US Fourteenth Amendment) will limit the power of legislatures to enact checkerboard statutes. Constitutional checks, though, inhibit only the more outrageous acts of discrimination. The US Congress is notorious for pork barrelling, the practice of granting benefits to the constituents of a legislator in return for their vote in Congress. Australians, Britons and others living in Westminster systems are familiar with legislation that shamelessly favours critical voting blocs in marginal electorates. According to orthodox doctrine, courts must enforce these statutes, provided that they pass the constitutional tests. There are juristic techniques for limiting the mischievous effects of statutes. If the language is not clear and is open to different interpretations, the court will adopt an interpretation that is constitutional in preference to one that is not. There are also many presumptions in the common law that promote integrity in statute law. The courts will presume (in the absence of clear words to the contrary) that an act is not intended to have retrospective penal effect, or to take property without compensation, or to deny the safeguards of natural justice and procedural fairness, or to take away vested rights. Courts also presume that parliament does not authorise officials to abuse their power. There are many more presumptions that are well known to legal practitioners. If this was all that Dworkin meant by judicial interpretation, there is no dispute between him and Hart, but Dworkin claimed much more.

Hart argued that where the meaning of a statute and its constitutional validity are not in doubt, the court's duty is simply to apply its provisions. It is then a case of application rather than interpretation. When the meaning is not clear and past judicial decisions are unhelpful, a judge, according to Hart, acts as a deputy of the legislature to determine the effect of the statute. Dworkin disagreed.

As observed previously, in *Taking Rights Seriously*, Dworkin argued that judges in hard cases do not legislate but draw on the principles of the law to make the right decision. In *Law's Empire* Dworkin went further, claiming that judges are involved in creative interpretation in every case – even in relation to the clearest statute. The duty to interpret arises from the demand of integrity that the law show consistency. Dworkin said that the aim of creative interpretation is not merely to *discover* the purpose intended by the law maker but to *impose* purpose over the text (1998, 228). This is not the kind of statutory interpretation that students learn in law school or judges profess in their written opinions. Dworkin identified three stages in the process of interpretation.

Pre-interpretive stage

In this stage, the interpreter identifies the rules and standards of the tentative content of relevant materials. In the typical legal case these would be the relevant statutory provisions and case law. Some degree of interpretation, Dworkin said, is involved in locating this material (1998, 66).

Interpretive stage

The interpreter at this stage 'settles on some general justification of the main elements of the practice identified in the pre-interpretive stage' (Dworkin 1998, 66). Translated into plain English, this means that the interpreter must determine the reason for treating the legal document as relevant to the case. The *Crimes Act* should be considered in a murder case because it is an Act of Parliament on the subject and the Constitution requires courts to give effect to Acts of Parliament.

Post-interpretive stage

This is a 'reforming stage at which [the interpreter] adjusts his sense of what the practice "really" requires so as better to serve the justification he accepts at the interpretive stage' (Dworkin 1998, 66). In plain English, there is a moral justification to regard Acts of Parliament as binding, or for that matter to consider the Constitution to be binding. The justification is that the system as a whole promotes integrity of the law. Hence, the initial interpretation must be adjusted or 'reformed' to ensure that the integrity is not undermined. This means that the court should creatively interpret the statute so that it is consistent with other laws and principles of the legal system.

Dworkin said that this is what judges and lawyers actually do in legal practice, though their legal rhetoric suggests otherwise. More critically, he claimed that in the post-interpretive stage judges are not making law but enforcing the law, as law's legitimacy depends on its integrity. Hart, of course, took the opposite view: in difficult cases the legal rhetoric belies the fact that judges in fact are making law.

Law as a chain novel

Dworkin compared the law to a chain novel and the role of the judge to that of a chain novelist. A chain novel is a work of fiction that is written by successive authors. It is similar to the soap operas familiar to television watchers. Different script writers, and even different actors and directors, take charge of the production over time. The readers of the chain novel and the viewers of the soap opera expect the story to unfold in a coherent manner. The characters usually retain their character and the history and the geography are not rewritten. Dworkin saw law as a similar phenomenon:

> In this enterprise a group of novelists writes a novel *seriatim*; each novelist in the chain interprets the chapters he has been given in order to write a new chapter, which is then added to what the next novelist receives and so on. Each has the job of writing his chapter so as to make the novel being constructed the best it can be, and the complexity of this task models the complexity of deciding a hard case under law as integrity. (1998, 229)

Dworkin's point is this: just as a discordant chain novel may turn away readers, a discordant legal system will lose the faith of the community. The difference is that we can pick up another novel to read or another television drama to watch, but most of us cannot change the legal system under which we live.

Law and morality in Dworkin

Dworkin's account of law is specific to his own legal culture, which is the Anglo-American culture. The use of force on citizens by the government is justified in this culture by the facts: (a) force is used according to established legal rights and duties of citizens; and (b) the laws that determine rights and duties have the quality of integrity. The process of interpretation, by which judges try to make the law the best it can be, introduces a moral dimension to Anglo-American law. What about other legal cultures that justify the use of force on other grounds? Did Nazi Germany have law? According to Dworkin, the answer depends on what conception of law we adopt to address this question. In one sense Nazi law was law, and in another sense it was not:

> We need not deny that the Nazi system was an example of law, no matter which interpretation we favour of our own law, because there is an available sense in which it plainly was law. But we have no difficulty in understanding someone who does say that Nazi law was not really law, or was law in a degenerate sense, or was less than fully law. (Dworkin 1998, 104)

Nazi law, according to Dworkin, was law in the pre-interpretive sense, because German courts of the era did not engage in the kind of moral interpretive exercise that our courts undertake. Hart argued that this concession strengthens the positivist argument (1997, 271). The real difference between Dworkin and positivists like Hart turns out to be as follows.

The positivists offer descriptive theories of law – the kind of theory that Dworkin calls semantic. According to these theories, immoral law can be law in a descriptive sense. Dworkin agreed that, according to a particular semantic theory such as legal positivism, even the most unjust laws may be regarded as law. Dworkin, though, rejected semantic theories in favour of a justificatory theory of law that recognises creative interpretation as a feature of Anglo-American law. Nevertheless, Dworkin said that a community's law is different from its popular morality.

Dworkin understood popular morality as 'the set of opinions about justice and other political and personal virtues that are held as matters of conviction by most members of a community, or perhaps of some moral elite within it' (1998, 97). Law in the Anglo-American culture consists of rights and duties that flow from past decisions as those decisions are interpreted by judges. These past decisions may not always reflect popular morality. The judge's duty is not to align the law with public morality but to give an interpretation that maintains the integrity of the law. Thus, law may fail popular morality while retaining its integrity. This is true of the Anglo-American legal culture. A different community's legal culture may contain an additional requirement that judges must consider popular morality in addition to past decisions, but this is not a feature of all legal systems.

So, in what sense, if any, does Dworkin's theory challenge the positivists' contention that law has no *necessary* connection with morality? Dworkin said that legal practice in Anglo-American political culture demands the integrity of law. Integrity is a moral virtue of the law irrespective of outcomes. This is very similar to Fuller's theory of the internal morality of law. Fuller argued that we can recognise the internal morality of law even when we disapprove of its moral outcomes. Dworkin argued that there is moral value in the integrity of law even when its results are unwelcome.

PART 3
SOCIAL DIMENSIONS OF LAW

7

Sociological Jurisprudence and Sociology of Law

Sociological jurisprudence and its related field sociology of law together constitute an immense field of study, embracing all aspects of the relations and interactions between law and society. Legal positivism and natural law theory are focused on a central question in legal theory. In the case of legal positivism it concerns the formal tests for identifying a law. Natural law theory is mainly about the relation between law and morality. The methodology of legal positivism is empiricism and logical reasoning and, in the case of Kelsen, transcendental idealism and logical reasoning. The methodology of natural law is mainly practical reason. Thus, legal positivism and natural law theory are limited by both their aims and their methodology

American legal realism threw open the door of jurisprudence to admit facts about the way the legal system actually operates in society. The rule sceptics focused on the differences between the law as written down and the law as applied in particular cases by the appellate courts. The fact sceptics studied the uncertainties that attend the trial process. The rule sceptics argued that if judges are the real law makers, they might as well take that role seriously and do it more openly and competently by taking explicit account of the social consequences of their decisions. Legal realism of the American kind broadened the scope of jurisprudence by connecting what lawyers and judges actually do with the society that they are asked to serve through the processes of the law. Even so, the American realists were preoccupied with official law – the law of the courts and of the legislatures as interpreted by the courts.

Sociological jurisprudence, with the help of sociology of law, expanded the boundaries of jurisprudence much further – so much so that the field is difficult to demarcate. There are innumerable connections between law and society: every branch of human learning, from physics, chemistry and medicine to philosophy, religion and psychology, produces knowledge about law and society. Sociology borrows from all these fields, and sociological jurisprudence borrows from sociology. It would take a sizeable volume to give even a reasonable account of this field. This chapter offers an explanation of the tradition of sociology of law and sociological jurisprudence through the work of its founders.

The ideas of the thinkers considered in this chapter, apart from those of Karl Marx, fall within the liberal legal tradition. The later part of the 20th century saw a new wave of theories about the role of law and its impact on society from angles that questioned the liberal interpretations of this relationship. They include the theories of the critical legal studies movement, postmodernist jurisprudence and feminist jurisprudence. Although much of this later work is properly classified as sociological jurisprudence or sociology of law, it is also unified by another common element – the rejection of some of the central assumptions of liberal legal ideology. Hence, there is good reason to consider these three approaches separately, as I do in the next chapter.

Sociology, sociology of law and sociological jurisprudence

Roscoe Pound (1870–1964) was the first jurist to make the social dimensions of law a central concern of Anglo-American jurisprudence. He was by no means the originator of the sociological tradition in law, which in fact commenced in Germany and France. Pound's achievement was to combine thoroughgoing technical study of the law in all its aspects with the insights and methods developed by sociologists of law. He called this branch of study sociological jurisprudence, to distinguish it from sociology of law. However, sociological jurisprudence – as the name suggests – draws inspiration, ideas and methods from sociology of law.

Sociology

The study of society is as old as philosophy. Political theory, moral philosophy, and even religion are concerned with society in one way or another. Sociology as a distinct discipline has a more recent origin, in the work of the French philosopher Auguste Comte (1798–1857). Sociology seeks to understand the workings of society in a scientific way. There are two main sociological schools: positivist sociology and interpretive (antipositivist) sociology.

Positivist sociology

Positivist sociology is based on empiricism and scientific method. Empiricism is the belief that the only true knowledge is knowledge gathered from observed facts. It is the philosophical foundation of science. Physical science consists of theories about the behaviour of non-living things, ranging from celestial bodies to sub-atomic particles. Biological science studies living organisms, from the largest animals and plants to the smallest micro-organisms. Social science tries to do something similar with societies. Positivist sociology is a branch of social science that applies the objective methods of empirical science to the study of society. Its method typically involves the collection and analysis of empirical data and the construction and testing of theories. If crime rates are consistently higher in poorer neighbourhoods than in prosperous ones, a positivist sociologist may construct the hypothesis that poverty is a cause of crime and then test this against further evidence. Positivist sociologists have produced specific theories on subjects such as crime, family breakdown and race relations, as well as general theories about society and social change. The object of positivist sociology is to make knowledge about society less speculative and more evidence based.

Interpretive sociology

Interpretive sociologists maintain that the social world is very different from the natural world; hence, it cannot be studied by the methods of natural science. Society is not governed solely by the laws of nature. Society consists not of robots but of thinking individuals, who are guided by norms, symbols, values, beliefs, ideals, ideologies and many other cultural factors. There are psychological and spiritual dimensions of society that cannot be understood or measured by external observation alone.

Georges Gurvitch explained that social reality consists of different layers. There is an outer layer that we can perceive by our senses, such as the demography, geography and technology of the society. What is the population of the society? What languages do people speak and what are their faiths? Does the society live in the Stone Age, Bronze Age, feudal age, industrial age, or in the post-industrial age? What do people eat and drink? Beneath this lie the organisational layer (governments, laws, courts etc), the layer of unorganised social patterns (traditions, fashions etc) and several more. Gurvitch identified eight such layers, with the lowermost representing the spiritual values of people (1947, 25–37). The scientific method is only capable of penetrating the outer, perceptible layers. Hence, the sociologist must take a more holistic approach and enlist other kinds of knowledge, such as history, philosophy and psychology.

Leading sociologists of law, including Émile Durkheim, Max Weber and Eugen Ehrlich, adopted the interpretive approach. The interpretive method has been more influential in the sociology of law, although the positivist method is alive and well in the modern socio-legal research programs in universities, particularly in the United States. I propose to focus on interpretive sociology in this chapter.

Sociology of law

The law, being a fundamental feature of society, has always been a fertile field of inquiry for sociologists. Sociology of law is that part of sociology that seeks to understand the 'social reality' of law in all its dimensions (Gurvitch 1947, 48). Sociologists, though, have a different concept of law from that commonly held by lawyers. Lawyers limit the term 'law' to the formal law of the state, comprising statutes, official commands, judicial precedents and such like. Sociologists have a much broader view of the law. Law in this wider sense encompasses all forms of social controls, including customs, moral codes and internal rules of groups and associations such as tribes, clubs, churches and corporations. In this context, lawyers' law is only a highly specialised form of social control involving specialised agencies like legislatures and courts.

Intelligent lawyers know that social order is maintained not only by the formal law, but also by many social rules, standards and practices not found in law books. The academic and social life in my university is governed by a large number of statutory provisions, including the *University of Queensland Act* and the statutes and rules made by the university senate. However, the civility and order among students and staff and the success of the university enterprise owe a great deal to many other informal norms that prevail within the community. People invariably stand in a queue to be served at the campus bookstores and restaurants. Students largely respect each other's privacy. Foreign students from diverse cultures are made welcome. There is a high degree of self-discipline within the classroom. Students form private associations for scholarly or recreational pursuits. There is a general culture of mutual respect and cooperation that helps the university to carry out its functions. What is true of my university campus is true of all harmonious and successful societies. However, the lawyer sharply distinguishes these informal norms from the formal rules that a court will enforce. The distinction is not so clear to the sociologist. As Pound put it, 'what seems to the jurist as a deep cleavage seems to the sociologist as no more than a scratch' (1943, 4).

The laws of an association, according to lawyers, exist because of the validity that state law confers upon them. Customary laws are law because a state organ such as a court or parliament has recognised them as law. Moral rules and rules of social etiquette are not laws in the lawyer's sense. The sociologist of law, in contrast, treats all these rules as part of the 'social reality' that is law.

Sociological jurisprudence

Sociological jurisprudence is a method of studying law that combines the lawyer's view of the law, technical knowledge of the law and insights produced by the sociology of law. The term 'sociological jurisprudence' was coined by its most famous proponent, Roscoe Pound, who is also known as Dean Pound because of his extraordinarily long tenure as the Dean of the Harvard Law School. The sociologist of law approaches law from the viewpoint of society and its diverse forms of social control. These inquiries lead to the discovery of the specialised and organised form of social control which is the lawyer's law. The sociological jurist starts from the opposite end, the organised form of control that is the lawyer's law, and moves towards sociology in search of ways to improve the capacity of law to serve the ends of society. The meeting point according to the sociologist is the sociology of law, but according to Pound it is sociological jurisprudence. Pound explains the role of the sociological jurist:

> He holds that legal institutions and doctrines are instruments of a specialised form of social control, capable of being improved with reference to their ends by conscious, intelligent effort. He thinks of a process of social engineering, which in one way or another is a problem of all the social sciences. In sociological jurisprudence it is a special problem of achieving this engineering task by means of the legal order ... It is treated as a problem of jurisprudence, and yet in its larger aspects as not merely a problem of that science. Law in all its senses is studied as a specialized phase of what in a larger view is a science of society. (1943, 20)

The distinction that Pound draws between the sociology of law and sociological jurisprudence is not so clear in historical and contemporary scholarship. In fact, among some of the most prominent early sociologists of law, such as Leon Duguit, Emmanuel Levy, Eugen Ehrlich and Maurice Hauriou, were jurists who went to sociology from law. Sociology itself emerged in the late 19th and early 20th centuries through a burst of intellectual activity in Europe, at the centre of which were Émile Durkheim, Max Weber and Eugen Ehrlich. However, Karl Marx and Herbert Spencer had previously published their work, interpreting the history of human society as a process of evolutionary progression. I will begin the story of the sociology of law with Marx's influential thinking.

Society and class struggle: the sociology of Karl Marx

Karl Heinrich Marx (1818–83) was born to a Jewish family in Trier, Prussia. His revolutionary views led him into exile – first in Paris, thence to Brussels and finally to the most tolerant European nation of the day, England, where he worked until his death. Marx's theory of society has been regarded as a forerunner of sociology, but it is now considered as sociology in the strict sense. Many of Marx's writings were undertaken in collaboration with his friend and fellow German philosopher, Friedrich Engels (1820–95). Marx's philosophy of human beings and society was first formulated in his work *The German Ideology*, written in 1845 but not published until 1932.

Marx rejected religion and metaphysics and produced a materialistic interpretation of human existence and history. Human beings are a species of animal. What distinguishes human beings from other animals is the fact that they are able to produce their means of existence. Other animals simply consume what nature offers. Lions and tigers do not breed their prey; they simply hunt them down and eat them. In other words, non-human animals do not engage in agriculture or industry. At some stage of their history human beings began to produce their own means of livelihood by growing things and making objects such as hunting weapons. This is when human beings began to distinguish themselves from other animals (Marx & Engels 1973 (1845), 42). Marx said that this form of production is possible only with the increase of the human population and intercourse among individuals (1973, 42). (More likely, increases in human populations followed agriculture, but this is only a minor oversight when compared to other failings of Marxism.)

Marx produced an elaborate theory of how society progresses, from its ancient tribal roots to feudal society and then to industrial and commercial society. The means of producing livelihood determines the nature of society. In the ancient tribal group people live by hunting and gathering on tribal lands. There is no concept of private property and the laws are determined by the conditions of primitive existence. A feudal form of society emerges as the means of production becomes agricultural. Land is held by feudal landlords and worked by tenants, who are attached to the land. In the towns, where the population is cosmopolitan, the lands are held by the state, with townsfolk having the right of possession. True private property, according to Marx, arises only in the industrial age, with the rise of the capitalist class. The changes in the means of production are accompanied by increasing division of labour. As society gets larger and more complex different people specialise in doing different things – an observation that Adam Smith made before Marx. Consider the loaf of bread on your table. The wheat is grown by a farmer, converted to flour by a miller, transported by a trucker, baked by a baker and sold by a supermarket. Marx wrote:

> The division of labour inside a nation leads at first to the separation of industrial and commercial from agricultural labour, and hence to the separation of town and country and to the conflict of their interests. Its further development leads to the separation of commercial from industrial labour. At the same time through the division of labour inside these various branches there develop various divisions among the individuals co-operating in definite kinds of labour. The relative position of these individual groups is determined by the methods employed in agriculture, industry and commerce (patriarchalism, slavery, estates, classes). These same conditions are to be seen (given a more developed intercourse) in the relations of different nations to one another.
>
> The various stages of development in the division of labour are just so many different forms of ownership, i.e. the existing stage in the division of labour determines also the relations of individuals to one another with reference to the material, instrument, and product of labour. (Marx & Engels 1973, 43)

In market theory, specialisation and division of labour is an unambiguous good as it leads to greater efficiency, and hence to the production of more goods that are better and cheaper. Marx acknowledged this advantage, but argued that the division of labour inevitably leads to the exploitation of some groups by others. He thought that the process would lead to the concentration of property and capital in an ever smaller group, at the expense of an ever larger population of propertyless and exploited workers whom Marx called the proletariat.

This would lead to 'alienation' of the latter group and to class conflict (Marx & Engels 1973, 56).

The law of a society, Marx rightly observed, changes to reflect the ways in which people produce the means of their livelihood. Every social system has a base and a superstructure. The economic relations constitute the base of the society. Law, state and the popular consciousness (understanding) of the base constitute the superstructure. The base and superstructure are inter-dependent. The base gives rise to the superstructure and the superstructure protects and rein-forces the base. The superstructure changes to reflect the changes in the base. The organisation, law and beliefs of ancient tribes (their superstructure) reflected the ways of the hunter gatherer existence (the base). Agriculture brought about a form of feudal kingship and feudal law. The main features of feudal law were the division of society into estates consisting of the monarchy, landholding aris-tocracy and tenants, who owed reciprocal rights and duties. The emergence of industrial and commercial modes of production brings about further dramatic changes in the law, state and beliefs. The whole system of law, including contract and property law and labour law, is adapted to facilitate commerce and indus-try (Marx & Engels 1973, 81). The estates are abolished, and instead society becomes divided into classes – owners of capital, industrial workers, commercial workers, and so forth. The superstructure consists not only of the law but also of the state and its ideology. The state and law, as superstructure, guarantee the conditions under which capital is accumulated and commerce and industry are conducted. In short, the state becomes the protector of the capitalist class and the instrument of oppression of the working classes.

Marx was not only an interpreter of the past but also a prognosticator of the future. The emergence of industrial society and capitalism is inevitable in Marx's theory of history. Equally, the end of capitalist society is also inevitable if Marx was right. Marx predicted that the concentration of capital in an ever diminishing class would worsen the condition of the proletariat to the point at which they would naturally rise in revolt, overthrow the capitalist state and establish a dictatorship of the workers (1973, 94–5). The dictatorship would be only a transitory phase, a means to an end. It would abolish capitalism and class divisions, and bring about a communist society in which the means of production and distribution would be commonly owned. Since there would be no classes or class conflict, and no private property to protect, the state would lose its relevance and wither away.

Findings in social anthropology contradict Marx's linear view of human history at many points. Studies of tribal societies reveal forms of private property, con-tract and trade. (See, for example, Gluckman 1967; Malinowski 1922; Pospisil 1958.) Marx's top-down 'law as domination' view hardly fits modern democracy, where law making is a messy process with outcomes determined by the interplay of interest group politics, often against the interests of ruling elites. In conceiv-ing the role of law purely in terms of the enforcement of capitalist economic relations, Marx overlooked the law's value in facilitating cooperation within and across classes. Sociologist Paul Rock's observation on deviancy theory in Marxist criminology applies with equal force here:

> The perspective offers no understanding of law as a complex and variegated rule-system whose origins are frequently as mysterious to elites as to the governed. It offers no vision of a legal system as a series of constraints upon law-giver and ruled alike. It does not refer to legitimacy and authority other than in the context of manipulation and mystification. It does not provide for the elaborate patterns of accommodation that characterise many social situations of social control. (1974, 144)

The histories of societies did not follow the path that Marx mapped. The first Marx-inspired workers' revolution occurred in a feudal empire (Russia) and not in an industrial capitalist society. The alienation of the proletariat did not occur in the industrialised democracies, since workers became property owners and shareholders and the welfare state taxed capital and profits and distributed wealth. The state intervened in the markets in times of serious instability. Changes in technology created new forms of work and working conditions generally improved. Class divisions, to the extent that they existed, dissipated. Most tellingly, the dictatorships established in the name of workers' revolutions proved not to be transitory. Many of these states were overthrown by counter-revolutions that established market economies and democratic governments. The collective mode of production was abandoned by one country after another that had embraced it.

Max Weber and the rationalisation of the law

Maximilian Weber (1864–1920), the German economist and sociologist, was one of the most influential writers in the fields of sociology, political economy and public administration. He taught at the universities of Berlin, Freiburg, Heidelberg, Munich and Vienna, and held a number of official positions. Max Weber was a man of enormous learning whose knowledge encompassed the cultures, philosophies and juristic thought of European, Sinic, Indian and African civilisations.

Weber, like Marx, was a student of society from its ancient tribal roots to its modern capitalist-industrial form. Like Marx, he was keenly aware that a society's legal system reflects its prevalent social relations. However, Weber differed from Marx in several ways. Unlike Marx, he did not identify social relations exclusively with the means of production. He also did not prophesy the end of capitalism and the birth of a stateless society. As a sociologist, his approach was more detached. Weber developed a theory about the progression of law from its ancient roots in tradition and magic to its current rational form. He identified the causes of the rationalisation of law with the needs of the capitalist economy and of the bureaucratic state. Weber's sociology of law appears in different parts of the three volumes that comprise his monumental work, *Economy and Society*. His sustained analysis of the history of law is found in the book-length chapter VIII of the second volume, entitled 'Economy and the law (sociology of law)'. Weber's main focus is the process of legal change in different stages of human history.

Spontaneous emergence of norms

Weber started with the question of how law emerges in primitive societies before there are law makers. Law formation begins with individual actions and plain habits. When these habits become diffused among a group of individuals, they become 'incorporated as "consensus" into people's semi-conscious or wholly conscious "expectations" as to the meaningful corresponding conduct of others' (Weber 1968, 754). In simpler terms, when people begin to behave similarly in similar conditions, social habits are formed as if by unconscious agreement and individuals count on these habits in going about their lives. If people in a society usually keep their promises they will begin to rely on the practice and, for example, engage in trade. These consensual understandings eventually acquire the guarantee of coercive enforcement, distinguishing them from mere 'conventions'. Weber made the critical observation that this kind of unconscious law emergence happens at all times, even in our own age of formal law making (1968, 754). If this seems improbable, think of how the rules of the internet came about before any regulator or national parliament thought of them.

How does legal change happen in a primitive society that lacks formal machinery for law making? The way laws emerge is also the way laws change. Changes in external conditions bring about changes in the conduct of individuals, leading to new patterns of behaviour and new consensual understandings (unconsciously or sub-consciously) about correct conduct (Weber 1968, 755). This is a process of adaptation to the changing environment – a kind of natural selection of rules. New content may also enter the law 'as a result of individual invention and its subsequent spread through imitation and selection' (Weber 1968, 755). Weber's hypothesis about the spontaneous emergence of legal norms is reminiscent of the evolutionary jurisprudence of the 18th century Scottish philosophers David Hume, Adam Smith and Adam Ferguson that I discuss in Chapter 10.

From irrational adjudication to judge-made law

The existence of legal norms does not automatically mean that there is rational adjudication according to the norms. Norms guide the behaviour of individuals in daily life, but when disputes arise there is no reliable way to determine the prevalent norm and the relevant facts. The primitive judge is usually a charismatic figure who will draw on magical inspiration to decide the case. Norm and fact are not distinguished but the case is heard as a whole. There is no understanding that the judge represents the law and must decide according to law. The judge makes an inspired decision about which party is right. However, judges cannot retain the confidence of their community without achieving some consistency in the way they decide cases. There is pressure to decide like cases alike. This leads to the formation of precedents and judge-made law (Weber 1968, 759).

Legal change in primitive society occurs mainly through the case law method. Legislation is unknown and the idea that a human agent can make or change the law does not occur to the primitive mind. The law had to be correctly known and interpreted, but not created. 'Their interpretation was the task of those who had known them the longest, i.e. the physically oldest persons or the elders of the kinship group, quite frequently the magicians and priests, who, as a result of their specialised knowledge of the magical forces, knew the techniques of intercourse with the supernatural powers' (Weber 1968, 760). When in doubt, the elders turned to charismatic revelation. When a new rule was needed to cope with the changing needs of the community, the elders looked to revelation to obtain a rule using magical devices. In practice, it was the opinion of the magic men that became the law. This was the origin of legislative power.

One of the important side effects of the appeal to magic was the formalism that attended the judicial process. The question (whether it was about disputed facts or about a norm generally) had to be precisely formulated, and presented according to the right ritual, in order to get the correct answer from the supernatural entity. This is the reason that all ancient legal processes were laden with rigid formalities. Traces of these magical elements are found in the Roman law and the English law. Even a simple contract for delivery of goods in Rome required the ceremony of *mancipatio* involving five witnesses, a person holding a pair of scales and a ritual utterance. A claim before a *praetor* (magistrate) failed in Roman law if it was not made and proved according to a strict formula. A similar formulary system was introduced to England by Henry II in the 12th century to replace the supernatural modes of trial such as ordeal and oath counting. It was fully abolished only in 1852 by the *Common Law Procedure Act*. Under the formulary system, a litigant had to make a claim in one of the court-approved written forms called a *writ*. If I wished to institute an action against a person who had assaulted me or physically restrained me, I had to present a *writ of trespass*. Against a person who invaded my land, I had to seek a *writ of trespass on the case*. Against a person who dishonoured a contract, I had to ask for the *writ of assumpsit*. The language of each writ was fixed and only the details of the relevant transaction had to be supplied – much like electronic form filling today. The litigant had to choose a particular writ and stand or fall by that choice. This rigidity caused injustice in particular cases. The equitable jurisdiction of the Roman praetor and the English Court of Chancery grew out of demands for the correction of the injustices that excessive formalism had created.

Emergence of legislation

Conscious law making first appeared in the form of compacts among heads of kinship groups or chieftains gathered as assemblies. Apart from attending to administrative matters, they assumed the role of providing authoritative interpretations of magically sanctioned norms. What began as interpretation led to the making of new norms (Weber 1968, 766). Germanic assemblies (and, indeed, the English Parliament) at first did not distinguish between statutory enactment and judicial decision. They switched from one form to the other depending on the case at hand (Weber 1968, 766).

Arrival of lawyers

The formation of a class of professional legal experts is an important development in the rationalisation of the law. It also signals the arrival of the capitalist era, with its demand for legal certainty and the guarantee of property and contractual rights. An established legal profession is practically necessary to consummate the rationalisation of law. In the charismatic stage law prophets advised courts. They were replaced over time by legal *honoratiores*, who were not quite professional legal experts but were persons acknowledged as repositories of legal knowledge because of their prestige and influence in society. The growth of commerce and increasing complexity of society created a demand for systematically trained legal professionals (Weber 1968, 775). In England, the training of barristers was provided through a guild system (the Inns of Court), where lawyers trained would-be lawyers. Solicitors were trained on the job by other solicitors. In Germany and France legal education was provided by universities, with admission to the profession controlled by government.

Legal training within the guild system produced 'craftlike specialisation' in law (Weber 1968, 787). Lawyers learnt not only to litigate but also to avoid litigation by drawing up appropriate contracts and other instruments. Weber thought, wrongly, that this kind of 'cautelary' jurisprudence could not produce a rational legal system (1968, 787). On the contrary, by ordering the affairs of people according to previously established law, lawyers brought greater rationality to the law.

Tension between formal rationalisation and substantive rationalisation

Weber identified two kinds of rationalisation – formal and substantive. Formal rationalisation eliminates the magical or charismatic element from the processes of law finding and adjudication. The law becomes the subject of professional study, with the result that it becomes a body of reasonably ascertainable and predictable rules. Formal rationalisation of the law demands that cases are decided according to established law, thus reducing the capacity of judges to adjudicate according to their subjective sense of justice or even to the popular view of what is just. Substantive rationalisation seeks to make the law more pliant, to produce what is thought to be expedient or just outcomes. Formal rationalisation promotes formal justice and substantive rationalisation seeks substantive justice.

One of Weber's most important insights about the law concerns the eternal tension between the demands of formal rationalisation and substantive

rationalisation, and between formal justice and substantive justice. Formal rationalisation enables people to know in advance the 'rules of the game'. This is a
necessary condition of individual freedom. It is much easier for me to stay out of
trouble and to do what is right for me and my family if I know beforehand what
I am allowed and not allowed to do. However, from time immemorial there has
been a different view: that the general rule should not obstruct the achievement
of moral or political goals.

Take the case of a trader who delivers certain goods to a buyer, expecting
the buyer to pay the agreed price. The trader enters this transaction because he
expects that the agreed price will be paid and that in the last resort a court will
compel the buyer to pay the price. Suppose that the buyer pays only half the
price because the quality of the goods did not match what she expected, or she
finds that she could have obtained the goods cheaper from a different trader. In a
formally rational system of law this would make no difference, and the court will
hold the buyer to the agreement and order that she pay the remainder. Formal
justice will be done, even at the expense of substantive justice. Hence, some legal
systems subordinate the general rule to judicial or administrative discretion,
which can be used to do what is thought to be right in the particular case. Laws
on price and wage fixing and fair trading typically allow tribunals to disregard
contracts. Weber wrote:

> Formal justice guarantees the maximum freedom for the interested parties to represent
> their formal legal interests. But because of the unequal distribution of economic power,
> which the system of formal justice legalises, this very freedom must time and again
> produce consequences which are contrary to the substantive postulates of religious
> ethics or of political expediency. Formal justice is repugnant to all authoritarian powers,
> theocratic as well as patriarchic, because it diminishes the dependency of the individual
> upon the grace and power of authorities. (1968, 12)

It is not only theocratic and autocratic rulers who dislike the freedom that formal
rationalisation of the law offers. As Weber observed, even democratic majorities
may resent the limits that formal justice places on their powers (1968, 813).
Democratically elected governments often find that they cannot deliver what
they have promised to various voting groups, or pursue their ideological objec-
tives, within the confines of formal justice. The demands for gender equality,
fair wages, consumer protection, for example, can be met only by legislation
that grants officials wide discretion to alter legal relations, in derogation of the
freedoms that exist under general and abstract laws. In other words, the pursuit
of substantive justice usually entails departures from the formal rationality of the
law. The opponents of substantive or social justice believe that such departures
lead to arbitrariness and authoritarian control.

Law and economics

Weber, unlike Marx, did not reduce all social relations to economic relations.
Law protects not only economic interests, but also personal security and purely

ideal goods such as personal honour or the honour of divine entities. Law also guarantees political, ecclesiastical and family structures, and as well as 'positions of social pre-eminence' that are 'neither economic in themselves nor sought for preponderantly economic ends' (Weber 1968, 333). However, economic interests are the predominant concern of the law and they are among the strongest factors that influence the creation of law (Weber 1968, 334).

Weber observed that, in theory, an economy may operate without state guaranteed enforcement of the law. Rights may be protected by mutual aid systems such as kinship groups (or, we might add, private security agencies). Money in all its forms has existed independently of the state. Debtors in the past may have feared excommunication more than state coercion (Weber 1968, 336). In modern times, credit rating by creditors' associations has proved to be an effective way of enforcing loan repayments. However, Weber argued that a modern economic system cannot exist in practice without a public legal order. This requires a state with monopoly power to coercively enforce the law. With the disintegration of tradition and the divergence of class interests, customary and conventional means of law enforcement have broken down. Weber explained:

> The tempo of modern business communication requires a promptly and predictably functioning legal system, i.e. one which is guaranteed by the strongest coercive power. Finally, modern economic life by its very nature has destroyed those other associations which used to be the bearers of law and thus of legal guarantees. This has been the result of the development of the market. The universal predominance of the market consociation requires on the one hand a legal system the functioning of which is calculable in accordance with rational rules. On the other hand, the constant expansion of the market . . . has favoured the monopolisation of all 'legitimate' coercive power by one universalist coercive institution through the disintegration of all particularist status-determined and other coercive structures which have been resting mainly on economic monopolies. (1968, 337)

Marx argued that the modern state and its laws exist to protect capitalist interests and modes of production. Weber did not say that the only purpose of the state is to serve the market, but he saw the expanding market as a driving force for the creation of a state monopoly of coercive powers.

Law and social solidarity: Émile Durkheim's legal sociology

Émile Durkheim (1858–1917) is considered to be one of the founders of sociology, together with Weber. He established the first sociology department in France, at the University of Bordeaux. Durkheim set out his sociology of law in the book *The Division of Labour in Society*, which was first published in 1893.

Division of labour as the cause of social solidarity

Durkheim regarded society not as an aggregate of individuals but as a system that has an independent existence. The whole that is society is greater than the sum of its parts. This is true even from a commonsense viewpoint, and was well known to earlier thinkers. A collection of individuals is not a society simply because they happen to be in close proximity to each other. They may have gathered to fight on a battlefield, or to watch a football match, or to catch planes to different destinations around the world. A society exists because of interdependence and bonding among a group of individuals. Durkheim called this 'solidarity'.

How does social solidarity come about? Durkheim argued that the principal cause of solidarity is the division of labour. Marx viewed the division of labour in industrial capitalist society as a cause of class division and class conflict. Some people were owners and managers, while others were industrial and agricultural workers. Specialisation within sectors, Marx argued, produces further divisions. The result is class conflict. In sharp contrast, Durkheim viewed specialisation and the division of labour as a powerful force for social solidarity. The division of labour is usually associated with economic efficiency. A system under which the blacksmith makes the plough and the farmer uses it to till the land is far more efficient than a system under which farmers have to make their own tools. The computer on which I write these words is the product of the efforts of many groups of specialists. Some have made the microchips, others have made its mechanical devices and yet others have written the programs that make it carry out my commands. People in all parts of the world benefit from the economic efficiency that the division of labour produces.

Durkheim acknowledged the economic advantage of the division of labour. However, he argued that the division of labour has a more important (moral) function – that of bringing people together in a diverse society. The division of labour not only creates a technologically advanced society but also maintains its social cohesion by making people depend on each other's functions. What can I gain by robbing my butcher or my greengrocer? I will have to grow my own food. I want the butcher and greengrocer to prosper so that I can get a convenient supply of food. Traders want their customers to prosper so that they can remain in business. This, then, is the bond or solidarity between producers and consumers. Durkheim wrote:

> We are thus led to consider the division of labour in a new light. In this instance, the economic services that it can render are picayune compared to the moral effect that it produces, and its true function is to create in two or more persons a feeling of solidarity. In whatever manner the result is obtained, its aim is to cause coherence among friends and to stamp them with its seal. (1964, 56)

The division of labour tends to be less pronounced in primitive societies, in which individuals are very similar to each other. They hunt and gather food in the same manner, jointly defend their territories and live their lives in the same way. Durkheim claimed, somewhat dubiously, that even the roles of men and women are not strongly differentiated in primitive society. Hence, the division of labour in marriage is negligible and marital solidarity tenuous (Durkheim 1964, 58–9). However, modernity brings dissimilarity through specialisation, and specialisation brings about the division of labour and a new form of solidarity based on mutual need.

Durkheim observed that solidarity, as a moral (mental) phenomenon, cannot be accurately measured. Hence, we need to observe and measure the facts that represent or symbolise solidarity. Consider the relationship between two friends. We cannot measure their mental feelings towards each other as we cannot get into their minds. Yet we can gain some measure of their friendship by observing the patterns of their actions. They always help each other and never harm each other. (They may even remember each other's birthdays and wedding anniversaries!) Likewise, we cannot directly measure social solidarity, but we can measure the evidence or the visible symbols of it. Durkheim thought that the visible evidence of social solidarity is found in the law of the society (1964, 64). He acknowledged that the law will not provide full evidence of social solidarity. There are customs that people observe which are not recognised by authorities as law, or in fact are contrary to law. Normally custom is not opposed to law but is the basis of law. A custom arises in opposition to law only in exceptional circumstance. This is when the law no longer corresponds to the state of existing society (Durkheim 1964, 65). It is not altogether clear why he did not simply regard custom as law in the sociological sense, as opposed to the lawyer's sense. Durkheim's key sociological insight was that the contours of society are reflected in its laws. We can find the nature of the social life of a society by findings its laws. Law, in other words, mirrors society. Durkheim asserted that 'Since the law reproduces the principal forms of solidarity, we have only to classify the different types of law to find therefrom the different types of social solidarity which correspond to it' (1964, 68).

Durkheim's view of law as the symbol of social relations is different from Marx's view of law as the superstructure of society. First, in Marx's theory law as superstructure interacts with the economic relations that represent the base of society. The law not only reflects the base but also consolidates the economic relations and class divisions that form the base. According to Durkheim, law as symbol is evidence of the social accommodations that bring about solidarity. Second, for Marx law is an instrument of oppression, in the sense that it maintains the exploitative means of production that characterises capitalist industrial society. Durkheim regarded law not as oppression but as facilitation of social cooperation.

Law in the sociological sense

If we have to find the law in order to find the form of solidarity prevailing in a society, we must know what law means. Durkheim started with the broad view of law as a 'rule of sanctioned conduct' (1964, 68–9). Sanctions change according to the importance of the rule within the community – the place the rule holds in the public consciousness. Laws can be classified according to the nature of the sanctions. There are two types of sanctions: repressive and restitutive (Durkheim 1964, 69). Repressive sanctions take the form of punishments. They relate typically to crimes. Restitutive sanctions are meant not to inflict suffering but to restore the parties to the position that they were in before the unlawful act was committed. Restitutive sanctions are characteristic of civil law, including commercial law, procedural law, administrative law and constitutional law (Durkheim 1964, 69). The *Criminal Code* prohibits theft and imposes the punishment of imprisonment on a convicted thief. This is a repressive sanction. A motorist drives a car negligently and causes damage to another car. The law requires the motorist to compensate the victim to the extent of the cost of repairing the car. This is a restitutive sanction.

The position, then, is this. The type of law in a society is the indicator of the type of social solidarity. The type of sanction is the indicator of the type of law.

Mechanical and organic solidarity

Durkheim thought that the two kinds of law represent two kinds of solidarity. Repressive law indicates a mechanical form of solidarity and restitutive law is the reflection of an organic form of solidarity. Every society today has both forms of law. Hence, it must follow that every society has both mechanical and organic solidarity. Durkheim argued, though, that restitutive law – and hence organic solidarity – is predominant in societies that have a high degree of specialisation and division of labour. Conversely, societies made up of like individuals and little division of labour will have mainly repressive law, indicative of mechanical solidarity.

Mechanical solidarity

Criminal law is the classic repressive law, in Durkheim's definition. According to Durkheim, 'an act is criminal when it offends strong and defined states of the collective conscience' (1964, 80). An act is not a crime, in the sociological sense, because it is highly immoral. Many people consider incest even between adults and adultery to be highly immoral, but they are not etched in the collective conscience as crimes worthy of punishment. So what is collective conscience? Durkheim wrote:

> The collective sentiments to which crime corresponds must, therefore, singularise themselves from others by some distinctive property; they must have a certain average intensity. Not only are they engraven in all consciences, but they are strongly engraven. (1964, 77)

Durkheim observed, correctly, that of all the branches of the law, criminal law changes the least. This is because it is so strongly ingrained in the collective conscience. Durkheim, of course, was not using the term 'crime' to include all the acts that the modern law punishes. The statute laws of the modern state impose punishments on all sorts of acts that are hardly etched in popular conscience. Consider the offence of driving after drinking even moderate amounts of alcohol, or of driving above ultra-cautious speed limits on country roads, or of failing to lodge a tax return on time. These are the sorts of crimes that are known in classical terminology as *mala prohibita* (wrongs by prohibition). The criminalisation of these acts has little to do with popular conscience. Durkheim was referring to the well-known categories of universally condemned acts known as *mala in se* (wrongs by their nature). These are the crimes that are found in the standard criminal code of a country. Durkheim attempted a rough tabulation of these acts (1964, 155–6).

Organic solidarity

Restitutive law corresponds to organic solidarity. Whereas repressive law arises from the core of the collective conscience, restitutive law lies at its periphery or outside it (Durkheim 1964, 112–13). Restitutive law governs relations between persons and things, as in real property, and between person and person, as in contract. Restitutive law does not impose punishments but repairs relations to where they stood before a breach of the law occurred. Thus, the plaintiff is given compensation for damages caused by the negligent defendant, and in contract the buyer is compelled to pay the seller the purchase price.

Restitutive law arises from the division of labour. I have certain competencies that enable me to perform services to others. I also depend on the services of many others. I buy my food from the supermarket and the grocer, my clothes from clothes shops and gasoline from the gas station, and get my hair cut by the barber. These people themselves depend on others for functions that they either cannot perform or perform inefficiently. Civilised life, therefore, is based on countless dealings among thousands and millions of persons, most of whom are strangers. Restitutive law grows out of the nature of these relationships. Durkheim explained:

> The relations which are formed among these functions cannot fail to partake of the same degree of fixity and regularity. There are certain ways of mutual reaction which, finding themselves very comfortable to the nature of things, are repeated very often and become habits. Then these habits, becoming forceful, are transformed into rules of conduct. The past determines the future. In other words, there is a certain sorting of rights and duties which is established by usage and becomes obligatory. The rule does not, then, create the state of mutual dependence in which the solidary organs find themselves, but only expresses in a clear cut fashion the result of a given situation. (1964, 366)

This is essentially the evolutionary theory of the insensible growth of law through mutual convenience, first formulated by 18th century evolutionist thinkers such as Bernard Mandeville, David Hume, and Adam Smith. I discuss this theory in Chapter 10.

Although restitutive law concerns relations between individuals, society is not completely out of the picture. When the law needs to be enforced, the individual must seek the collective power of the society. The society, according to Durkheim, is not just a third party arbitrator in such instances: 'The law is, above all, a social thing and has a totally different object than the interest of the pleaders' (1964, 113). The society has an independent interest in upholding the law.

Anomic division of labour

The division of labour sometimes leads to conflict and defeats solidarity. Durkheim called this kind of dysfunctionality 'anomic' division of labour. Industrial and market collapses, recessions and labour disputes are some of the dislocations that can happen when the division of labour intensifies. Information asymmetry can cause too much or too little to be produced, leading to economic disruptions and conflict. Marx and his followers believed that the division of labour inevitably leads to conflict among classes. Durkheim thought otherwise.

He argued that 'if in certain cases organic solidarity is not all it should be it is . . . because all the conditions for the existence of organic solidarity have not been realised' (1964, 365). The state of anomie, Durkheim thought, is theoretically impossible 'wherever solidary organs are sufficiently in contact or sufficiently prolonged' (1964, 368). The reason is that such close contact will reveal mutual dependence, and breakdowns in relations can be quickly identified and repaired. It is the breakdown of communication that disrupts the mutually adjusting process of social order. Durkheim anticipated, and feared, that globalisation of markets would lead to more conflict because of the disconnection between different producers and consumers. He, of course, had no way of foreseeing the astonishing means of instant communications that have become a hallmark of global trade.

An evaluation of Durkheim's sociology of law

Durkheim's views of the evolution of restitutive law through mutual convenience and the division of labour closely follow the insights established by Adam Smith and other evolutionary thinkers of the 18th century. The value of his work lies in his explicit application of these insights to the law in a more technical way. Durkheim's treatment of repressive law, though, is deeply flawed.

Durkheim identified repressive law with penal law. Repressive law punishes acts that shock the collective conscience. He contrasted repressive law with restitutive law, which is at the periphery of collective conscience or outside it. It is historically indisputable that many of the wrongs against person, property and honour that are now considered crimes were initially simply private wrongs settled between wrongdoers and victims or their families. The remedy was initially personal vengeance, and later compensation. Even today these crimes give rise to both penal sanctions and civil remedies. The attachment of penal sanctions to these acts was a later development. (For an illuminating economic history of criminal law, see Benson 1990.) The point I make is that many of the repressive laws that Durkheim identified were restitutive in nature, and became repressive only because the state at a certain stage of history decided to make the acts in question punishable by the state. If these acts are repulsive to the collective conscience, they would have been repulsive even before their criminalisation by statute.

There are crimes against the state (treason, sedition etc) and against religion (blasphemy etc) and public order (rioting etc) that are not private in nature. These fit better into Durkheim's category of repressive laws. Even in such cases, their recognition as crimes has more to do with the threat they pose to public safety and the legal process than to some notion of collective conscience.

The living law: the legal sociology of Eugen Ehrlich

The predominant view of law today is that it consists of the norms that a court would use to decide a case. Legislation enacted by parliaments and precedents set by past judicial decisions are considered now to be the primary sources of the norms used by courts. However, most people go about their lives in complete ignorance of the technical law that the courts apply in the cases that come before them. If I ask 1000 people on the street for the definition of the crime of theft or the requirements of a valid contract, most of them will give me a wrong answer. Yet most of them would be law abiding citizens who in all probability will never see the inside of a court. What does this tell us? It tells us that social order rests on rules that most people observe without knowing their legal meanings. Average citizens do not commit theft or any other crime, not because of the risk of punishment by a court but because they think that it is the law that they live by.

Eugen Ehrlich, the Austrian jurist and sociologist, tried to summarise his book *Fundamental Principles of the Sociology of Law* in one sentence. In the preface he wrote: 'At the present as well as at any other time, the centre of gravity of legal development lies not in legislation, nor in juristic science, nor in judicial decision, but in society itself'. Ehrlich (1862–1922) was born in Chernivtsi in Ukraine, which at the time was part of the Bukovina province of the Austro-Hungarian Empire. He studied and practised law in Vienna before returning to Chernivtsi to teach law. Ehrlich is most famous for developing the idea of living law.

Society as an association of associations

Ehrlich took an evolutionary view of the emergence and growth of society and its laws. The human race became social beings through the process of natural selection. Those who learned to associate with others gained a survival advantage over those who did not. The earliest associations were 'genetic' in nature – by which Ehrlich meant family groups and clans. As society advanced there came into being many other associations, such as the commune, the state, guilds, social clubs and agricultural and industrial associations. A person usually belonged to several of these associations. Overall society was made up of the interaction of these associations (Ehrlich 1936, 27–8). Each association had its internal order, and at first there was no general law of the land but only the rules of the internal orders of associations, which were their legal norms. Eventually European societies reached the feudal age. Then too, what passed for law were the agreements between king, the lords and different classes of serfs. To know the law, one must know the terms of these agreements (Ehrlich 1936, 32–3). The first true laws were found within city walls, where a number of different associations (of merchants, craftsmen etc) interacted, forming broader associations. The laws of real property, of pledge, of contract and inheritance were first established in these cities.

Ehrlich identified the main associations of human society as the following: 'the state with its courts and magistracies; the family, and other bodies, associations, and communities with or without juristic personality; associations created by means of contract and inheritance, and, in particular, national and world-wide economic systems' (1936, 54). Thus he foresaw the convergence of national economies and the formation of international associations of various sorts that we see today.

Legal norm and legal proposition

Ehrlich distinguished a legal norm from what he called a legal proposition. A legal norm is a rule found in the form of actual practice. It is the rule of the inner order of an association. A legal proposition is 'is the precise, universally binding formulation of a precept in a book of statutes or in a law book' (Ehrlich 1936, 38). The actual practices of making and observing contracts for the sale of goods among persons constitute legal norms. The *Sale of Goods Act*, which formally states the law relating to the sale of goods, contains legal propositions. This distinction is critical in Ehrlich's theory. The crucial point is this: the legal norms of the sale of goods contracting and the legal propositions are not the same. The legal norms in the form of social practice exist even without the legal propositions. The state existed before the constitution, there were contracts before the law of contracts and there were testaments before the *Wills Act* (Ehrlich 1936, 35–6). The legal norms, the rules of inner order, represent the living law, and legal propositions comprise the law in the books. The living law gives content to the law in the books. Ehrlich wrote:

> The inner order of the associations of human beings is not only the original, but also, down to the present time, the basic form of law. The legal proposition not only comes into being at a much later time, but is largely derived from the inner order of associations. (1936, 37)

Legal norm and norm for decision

There are times when the inner order of an association is disrupted by a breach of its legal norms. A used car dealer may claim that the car sold was a serviceable vehicle. The buyer may claim that it was unserviceable without costly repairs. The inner order is disrupted. Most of these disruptions are resolved without the aid of a court. Negotiation, private arbitration and even market pressure may solve the problem. Even in the modern age, the proportion of legal disputes that end in court cases is minuscule. However, some disputes will need judicial resolution. When this happens, the legal norms of association will not be a sufficient guide to decision.

A legal norm, in Ehrlich's definition, is a rule that members of an association observe without compulsion. It is the rule that prevails in times of peace but not in times of war. If the living law is broken, the judge cannot restore it to life but must offer a remedy. The judge deals with a new situation. The inner order of the family works well when the couple have harmonious relations. They do not need the assistance of a court or of remedial law. If the relations break down, the association is at an end and so is its inner order. If the dispute goes to the court, the judge will have to make orders for the division of property, custody of children, maintenance, and so forth. The judge will apply legal propositions (law in the books) as well as moral and policy considerations in the exercise of judicial discretion. Ehrlich called these the norms for decision (1936, 126–7). These include the law of damages and restitution, standards and burden of proof, injunctions and so forth (Ehrlich 1936, 127).

Judicial discretion is not unbounded. A norm for decision used in a particular type of case ought to be applied in similar cases. Ehrlich calls this the law of the stability of norms. This not only saves intellectual labour but also serves the social need for stable norms for decision, which provides a measure of predictability of judicial action that allows people to arrange their lives accordingly.

State and state law

State law is law created by the state. State law is possible only where there is a state and the state possesses sufficient military and police power. Although state law is pervasive today, it was rare in the past except in city states and the more powerful kingdoms and empires. Unlike today, state law was mainly concerned with the organisation of the state organs and the declaration of existing law. The original courts were not state courts but private bodies created by associations.

Ehrlich considered the state to be one of the associations (in fact the largest) that make up society. It is a product of social need, of the growing complexity of relations among the intertwined and interdependent associations. Ehrlich wrote:

> We must think of it as an organ of society. The cause of it is the steadily progressing uni-
> fication of society; the quickened consciousness that the lesser associations in society,

which in part include one another, in part intersect one another, in part are interlaced with one another, are merely the building stones of a greater association of which it is composed. (1936, 150)

The interdependence of the associations creates the overall order of society. It is still possible in modern society to have associations with their own rules of behaviour. Members of the Old Amish community of Lancaster County, Pennsylvania, live by their own special rules. There are various communes of religious sects and counter-cultural groups living by special rules in most free societies. These are exceptions that confirm the general rule that associations through interactions form larger associations, leading eventually to national and global associations.

Society (the grand association of associations) uses the state as its organ to impose its order upon the associations that belong to it. This means that 'state law in all its essentials merely follows the social development' (Ehrlich 1936, 154). The earliest statutes were in the form of agreements among those affected by the instrument. The Roman *leges sacratae* and the German *Landfreiden* were agreements. The enacting recital of British Acts of Parliament commences with the words: 'Be it enacted by The Queen's most Excellent Majesty, by and with the advice and consent of the Lords Spiritual and Temporal, and Commons, in this present Parliament assembled and by the authority of the same'. In theory, British statutes are agreements between the people, the lords and the Crown. The reality, of course, is different in today's world. Rulers, elected and unelected, make law by unilateral will.

Ehrlich argued that there is a limit to the kind of unilateral law that the rulers can impose upon society (1936, 373). In other words, rulers, even those whose powers are not constitutionally limited, cannot make law as they please – not in the longer term, anyway. Legislation does not operate in a social vacuum. It must overcome social forces that operate independently of the state. Military power is not a match for these social forces in the long term. It may defeat foreign enemies but is ill-equipped to impose permanent ways of life on the population. There is no better example of this than the efforts of the dictatorship in the old Soviet Union to recreate society according to the socialist ideal. The state laws enacted by the regime attempted to abolish private ownership of the means of production, outlaw institutionalised religion, control the freedom of communication, movement and association, eliminate political opposition and equalise incomes. The regime failed to achieve any of this, and the whole system collapsed within 70 years. The principle is evident even in modern democratic societies. Price controls are notoriously ineffective, and so is excessive censorship. There is widespread tax evasion. People in business and industry migrate from the official legal system to their own, through contractual arrangements that establish rules of conduct, and private forums for resolving disputes through associations such as the International Chamber of Commerce (ICC).

Ehrlich's contribution to the sociology of law

Ehrlich demonstrated, better than any other sociologist of law, the difference between the law in the books and the living law. However, he underestimated the effect of the norms for decision and state law in shaping the living law. This is not entirely surprising, because Ehrlich was writing before the era of extensive legislation and government intervention in the economic and social life of communities. The force that the state applies through its laws is a factor that individuals and associations of individuals take into account in ordering their lives. State law has social consequences and some of these are unintended. State laws of any significance will create a series of behavioural adjustments in social relations, much like ripples in a pond. As individuals adapt to a new law, they cause changes in the inner order of the various associations in which they participate.

Ehrlich also underestimated the capacity of the state to develop interests that are hostile to the interests of the associations that it is meant to serve. The modern state, with its immense bureaucracy and multiple power centres, has acquired a life of its own. He also did not pay enough attention to the competition among associations, particularly in democracies, to bend the state law in their favour at the expense of other associations. I am here referring to the intense interest group politics that are a feature of majoritarian democracies. State law is often born out of these distributional struggles. Ehrlich was historically correct when he pointed out that in the longer term rulers cannot sustain systems of laws far removed from the living law of the people. In the shorter term, though, people put up with much that they dislike.

Roscoe Pound and law as social engineering

Nathan Roscoe Pound (1870–1964) was the most prominent American sociological jurist. He differed from the previously considered theorists in an important way. Whereas the others were concerned with the law in the broader social sense, Pound was mainly focused on the lawyer's law – the law that legislators, judges and other authorised officials make. He was not unmindful that the term 'law' has wider connotations, but the task he set himself was the discovery of the ways in which the formal legal order serves its social purpose. The legal order is not simply the set of legal rules but the whole legal system, comprising its institutions, doctrines, rules and techniques.

Task of the legal order

What is the task of the formal legal order? According to Pound, it has changed over time. In primitive societies, 'the law aimed at nothing more than keeping the peace ... putting an end to revenge and private war as the means of redressing injuries' (Pound 1940, 68). The law was not an instrument for social change. The role of the legal system in the Greek city states was the orderly maintenance of the status quo. As the reader will recall from the discussion in Chapter 5, the Greek teleological view assigned individuals to specific roles according to a cosmic plan. The law served to keep society in harmony with this universal scheme of things. This theory persisted through the Roman law and the Middle Ages, until after the Reformation. The Reformation introduced the idea of individual freedom, and the law's primary role was seen in the 17th and 18th centuries as the provision of maximum individual liberty consistent with the similar liberty of others. This idea of the law's task later merged with the aim of 'bringing about and maintaining a maximum strength and efficiency in organised society, identifying the political organisation of society with civilisation' (Pound 1940, 69). It is fair to say that the notion of the law's role has been further transformed since Pound wrote these words.

Pound's view of the law's role is practical and modest: law's task is to recognise and adjust competing interests with a minimum of friction and waste (1940, 80–1). He identified legal and judicial activity as a form of social engineering. Pound did not use the term 'social engineering' in the modern sense of deliberate attempts to restructure society or rearrange social relations. Rather, it was a comparison of the legal task to that of a problem-solving design engineer who tries to make the machine run more efficiently and smoothly. Pound thought that the adjustment of competing interests with minimum friction and waste had a philosophical value, but did not elaborate on the question (1940, 80).

What are interests?

Interests are claims that persons make of the legal system. Some of these claims are already recognised by law, but there are others that are not so recognised. My claim not to be subject to physical violence is recognised by the criminal law. A terminally ill and long suffering person's claim to be assisted in terminating their life (euthanasia) is not recognised by Australian law. Trade unions make many claims on behalf of workers. Some are granted by the legal system and others are not. Pound identified three kinds of interests: individual interests, public interests and social interests. Individual interests relate to person, property and personal relations such as marriage. Public interests relate to the dignity of the state as a juristic entity. In the past the government claimed immunity from actions in tort; even now there are surviving Crown prerogatives. This is a dwindling category. Social interests include the interest in public safety, peace and order, and public health. These interests overlap with individual interests. There are also social interests in the security of social, domestic, religious and economic affairs (Pound 1940, 66). These interests are frequently in conflict. Labour claims for minimum wages conflict with claims for contractual freedom. A factory owner's claim to operate machinery may conflict with a neighbour's claim against noise. Claim of parliamentary privilege may conflict with a claim of damages for defamation in parliament. Pound's simple point is that there are incessant efforts by individuals and groups to gain recognition of new rights and to defend established rights. The resulting conflicts have to be resolved by the legislature and, in the absence of legislation, by the courts.

The principle or measure of valuing and adjusting competing interests

How should the different competing interests be valued? Pound saw no grand theory to deal with this question. Legislatures resolve them according to political convenience, but how should courts go about it? Pound offered only the most practical commonsense advice: namely, that courts should secure as much as possible of the scheme of interests as a whole with the least friction and waste. Pound claimed that this is what the courts, lawyers and judges have been doing since the Roman jurisconsults of the first century: 'No matter what theories of the end of law have prevailed, this is what the legal order has been doing, and as we look back we see has been doing remarkably well' (1940, 76). In short, there is no theory available to judges other than the judicial pragmatism that has served society well. Thus, in Pound's view the aim of the legal order is also its principal method.

Pound's worth

Pound's main point was that, whatever theory of adjudication we use, we cannot get away from the problem of reconciling and balancing competing interests. He wrote: 'For the purpose of understanding the law of today I am content with a picture of satisfying as much of the whole body of human wants as we may with least sacrifice' (1954, 47). However, we can derive certain principles imbedded in his proposition.

The first is that the courts should try to satisfy as many interests as possible *with the least sacrifice*. This means that certain claims may not be admissible because they call for too much sacrifice. The law bans narcotics, child pornography, under-age alcohol consumption, because of their social costs and danger to vulnerable groups. There is another kind of cost that excludes certain types of claims being entertained by the courts, though they may be granted by a legislature. Take the hypothetical claim of a trader to sell a product above the price set by an Act of Parliament. The court may uphold the claim only at the sacrifice of a weightier claim, the supremacy of Parliament's law. The second is that a court cannot be arbitrary in adjusting competing claims. This means that similar conflicts should be similarly resolved. This cannot be a hard and fast rule, but without a reasonable degree of decisional consistency the court will lose its reputation as an impartial adjudicator and eventually its power to command. That is a price too high to pay. Third, a court must have a rational basis to recognise a new right or to diminish an existing right, and must explain the reasons for its decision. A departure from the existing law is usually rationalised on the ground that the new case is materially different from the past decided cases, or the past decisions were clearly mistaken or, more rarely, that there are compelling policy reasons for not following a precedent. The court's decision may not stand the test of logic, but that is less important than the public perception that the court is not acting capriciously. In other words, a court cannot be seen to make new law openly without losing public confidence. The element of logical pretence, to the extent that it is present in judgments, is critical to the functioning of the courts. A court that reveals to society that it is open to any sort of claim and all kinds of arguments will be short lived. What all this means is that judicial discretion, in practice, is confined to what are known as hard cases – or, as Hart called them, cases of the penumbra.

A major problem with Pound's theory concerns his failure to separate the aim of the legal order as a whole from the methods available to the courts. Even if we accept his formulation of the end of the legal order, there is much left to be said about the judicial role in serving that end.

Pound's major sociological contribution is his explanation (incomplete as it is) of the way interests that form outside the legal order are transformed into enforceable rights within the legal order. His sociological message was most clearly stated in the following observation from his essay 'The next feudal system':

> We shall achieve nothing by an obstinate rearguard action against the adapting of legal institutions and legal doctrine to the society they govern. In the end they will conform to the needs of the economic and social order, not the economic or social order to their logical or dogmatic demands. (Pound 1930, 397)

The achievements of the sociological tradition

The sociologists of law and sociological jurists enriched jurisprudence and expanded its frontiers in a number of ways. First, they demonstrated the inseparability of the legal order from the order of society. There is no society without law and no law without social order. Second, they showed that the lawyer's law or the law in the books is not the only law by which people live, and not the only law that determines the structure of society. This is the case for two reasons. One is that there are many more social rules that people observe than are recognised or enforced by the official legal system, and yet without them social order is unsustainable. A second reason is that many of the rules in the law books would be ineffectual but for the fact that they are already observed as social rules. The law of contract would be meaningless if people routinely broke their promises. Criminal law is effective not because of super-efficient crime prevention and crime punishment but because most people live by its rules most of the time anyway. Third, the sociologists and sociological jurists demonstrated the dynamic and adaptive nature of the legal order. The legal order, being part of the social order, changes with it. Tribal law, feudal law and the liberal law of industrial societies each reflect a stage of social development. Fourth, they demonstrated that the law as a social phenomenon has a life of its own and that the path of the law is not entirely, or even mainly, determined by legislators. Fifth, by all this they demonstrated the poverty of jurisprudence that limits itself to the study of the law in the books.

8

Radical Jurisprudence: Challenges to Liberal Legal Theory

The jurisprudential theories discussed in previous chapters, with the notable exception of the theory of Karl Marx, are cast within the intellectual tradition of political liberalism. There are significant differences among these theories, but they are ultimately grounded in liberal views of law and society. This chapter discusses the challenges to the fundamental assumptions of liberal legal theory that came to prominence during the later decades of the 20th century. It will focus in particular on the ideas of the critical legal studies (CLS) movement, postmodernist legal theory and feminist theory. It is not possible to understand criticism without knowing what is being criticised. Hence, I start with a brief discussion of liberalism and liberal legal theory.

Liberalism and liberal legal theory

Liberalism is a tradition in political and legal theory that gives primacy to individual liberty in the political and legal arrangements of a society. 'Liberalism' is a term of recent origin. Originators of the liberal philosophy such as Hobbes, Locke, Hume, Smith and Montesquieu did not use the word. In fact, 'liberal' in early English usage was a term of ridicule meaning a libertine. The term gained respect and influence during the 19th and 20th centuries and (in its various forms) has become the dominant political ideology of the Western world. There are many kinds of liberal theory, and important differences among them. The following questions draw different responses from liberal thinkers.

1.   Why is individual liberty the pre-eminent political value?
2.   What does individual liberty mean and what are its bounds and require-
      ments?
3.   How can individual liberty be achieved and protected; what kinds of insti-
      tutional arrangements serve individual liberty?

Kinds of liberalism

There are two main liberal schools of thought about the pre-eminence of individual freedom. The natural rights theorists such as Hobbes, Locke, Grotius and
Rousseau argued that liberty was inherent in personhood. Self-ownership, property acquired by one's labour and capacity to pursue one's chosen life ends were
considered essential to existence *as a person*, as opposed to being another's property. Utilitarian thinkers such as Bentham and Mill, and evolutionary theorists
such as Hume and Smith, believed in the intrinsic worth of individual liberty but
made further arguments on grounds of efficiency. Societies that allow greater
freedom for individuals have achieved greater prosperity than those that suppress
liberty. This is also the message of modern economics based on methodological
individualism.

Modern liberals divide into two broad categories on the question of what
liberty means. Classical liberals regard liberty as freedom from legal or illegal
restraint. They generally adopt John Stuart Mill's 'harm principle' as their guide
on this question. In his essay *On liberty*, Mill argued:

> . . . the sole end for which mankind are warranted, individually or collectively, in
> interfering with the liberty of action of any of their number, is self-protection. That
> the only purpose for which power can be rightfully exercised over any member of a
> civilised community, against his will, is to prevent harm to others. His own good, either
> physical or moral, is not sufficient warrant. (2002 (1869), 8)

Welfare-state liberals have a different view of liberty. (Welfare-state liberals are
known simply as liberals in North America, and elsewhere they are better known
as social democrats.) They believe that in addition to legal freedom, people must
be freed from want so they can better enjoy their legal liberty. What good is
the freedom of movement, they might ask, to a person who has no money to
travel? Many welfare liberals believe that poverty has social causes. They argue
that markets that result from individual liberty do not ensure fair distribution of
wealth. Classical liberals reply that the market process is the most efficient way
of increasing everyone's wealth. They argue that the quest for just distribution
is doomed because it is impossible to find the just distribution, and it can be
pursued only by limiting individual liberty and causing greater poverty. Usually
some sort of compromise between these two views prevails in the real politics of
present-day liberal democratic societies. The important point here is that classical

liberals and welfare liberals in their different ways regard individual liberty as the pre-eminent political value.

Liberal legal theory

The jurisprudential theories so far considered, with the exception of the Marxist doctrine, share a broadly liberal view of the relation between law and society. This is the case despite their widely differing views about the scope and means of attaining liberty. Liberal legal theorists generally agree on four propositions about law and society.

1. Law is a public good

Law serves the public interest by providing a framework of rules that allows individuals to coordinate and harmonise their actions. The idea of a lawless society is a self-contradiction. Liberal legal theorists admit that law is used by rulers in their own interests, but they reject the notion that law by nature is an instrument of oppression. Law emerged in response to the coordination needs of the community and is not *in itself* a source of conflict. This is the message of the pioneers in the sociology of law: Weber, Durkheim, Ehrlich and Pound.

2. The rule of law is necessary for liberty

Liberalism in all its forms is formally committed to the ideal of the rule of law as the means of securing liberty. The rule of law has many meanings, but in this context it means subjection of both public and private actions to the governance of knowable and reasonably certain law. The rule of law serves individual liberty by curbing arbitrary actions of officials and making the law more certain and predictable. As Fuller vividly illustrated, if the law is whatever the ruler commands at any given moment, if the law lacks the semblance of generality and if the law is not consistently observed by officials, the citizen will find it hard to know what is right and wrong according to the law. Life becomes less predictable and an essential condition of liberty is lost (Fuller 1969, 39).

Legal positivism, it is said, is consistent with the most arbitrary forms of law, and this is true. Hart refused to deny the name 'law' to the utterly capricious and inhumane dictates of the Nazi regime during its final years. Kelsen's theory led to the same conclusion. However, the ideological reasoning behind legal positivism is quite the opposite. Hobbes, Bentham and Austin identified the law with the commands of a sovereign, chiefly for the utilitarian reason that it makes the law more certain and more knowable. Hart thought that nothing was gained by denying the legal effect of Nazi laws. The positivist position is that if we admit the formal validity of evil enactments, in other words that they are laws, we can do something about them. If we deny that they are law, we commence a needless and endless philosophical debate that only makes the law harder to know and reform.

3. The rule of law is possible

There are three essential conditions for the rule of law: (a) the law must be knowable and reasonably stable; (b) facts must be ascertainable to a generally acceptable standard; and (c) the making of the law and the application of the law must be distinguishable to an appreciable degree.

(a) Law must be knowable

The law is not effective unless most people to whom it is directed understand it in the same way. Take the rule 'Parties to a contract must observe the terms of the contract'. Most people understand this simple rule even if they cannot give technical definitions of the words 'contract', 'parties', 'observe' and 'terms'. If people have wildly differing notions about these words, the law will be ineffectual. There is, of course, much law that a lay person will not understand because of its complexity and technicality. (The Australian income tax legislation is known to defeat even able legal minds.) The point is that the law will be meaningless if people have no shared sense of what it requires or permits. Liberal legal theorists believe that law in the normal case is comprehensible, often without, but sometimes with, the help of trained lawyers. It is true that the American realists question the belief that the law can be reliably gathered from law books. They are not saying that the law is unascertainable, but that the law can be found only by close study of judicial decisions of appellate courts. Legal positivists such as Hart conceded that the open texture of language left uncertainty at the margins. A law that prohibits vehicles from a public park clearly forbids cars, trucks and motorcycles, but a penumbra of uncertainty exists as regards bicycles, roller blades and skateboards. The uncertainty will be progressively reduced through judicial interpretation, but not eliminated.

(b) Facts must be ascertainable

The law has no meaning except in relation to persons, things and events – in other words, facts. Therefore, the rule of law is not possible unless relevant facts can be ascertained. Take the case of a man who shoots another man in a public place in full view of many bystanders. The fact of the shooting can be easily established in a court of law by witness testimony. This is because people usually trust the evidence of their senses and usually perceive facts the same way. They all see the object that the man points at the victim and recognise it as a gun. Not every case will be as simple as this. Sometimes the judge (or jury) will come to the wrong decision for a variety of reasons, including false testimony, impaired observation or faded memory of witnesses and the sheer lack of reliable evidence. The 'fact sceptics' within the American realist tradition (discussed in Chapter 4) are preoccupied with the factual dimension of the law. However, they do not question the possibility of finding facts, but only the way that courts go about finding facts. Thus, liberal legal theorists generally agree that both law and facts can be determined – not perfectly, but to the degree that enables the law to serve its social function of securing liberty and facilitating peaceful and productive social intercourse.

(c) The making of law must be separated from the application of law

The orthodox legal view is that courts decide cases according to pre-existing law, at least in the vast majority of cases. Liberal legal theorists know that courts, particularly the appellate courts, play a creative role in the course of deciding novel cases (Hart's cases of the penumbra). However, they believe that the courts have very limited legislative scope overall. Dworkin argued that the courts in the Anglo-American common law system generally maintain the law's integrity in administering justice.

If judges and other officials responsible for law enforcement are not guided by law but are free to make law for the individual case, the rule of law is displaced by the rule of particular men and women. This would be the case if judges enforced contracts or awarded damages in negligence cases, not according to established rules but on their own views of what is just. Liberal legal theorists believe that the discretions involved in judicial decisions do not, on the whole, destabilise the rule of law.

4. The political institutions of liberalism protect liberty and the rule of law

Liberals count on constitutional devices such as the separation of powers (with independent courts), due process, representative democracy and the constitutional guarantees of basic rights to promote the rule of law and secure individual liberty. Representative democracy plays a central role in these systems by electing and removing governments and by electing and removing legislators, who in theory represent people's views.

There is a school of anarcho-liberals who reject the idea of the state altogether as an inherently oppressive organisation. They call themselves libertarians, to distinguish themselves from classical liberals. The anarcho-liberals argue that all the services that the state provides, including defence and the security of person and property, can be arranged by contractual arrangements among free individuals. Murray Rothbard was the most influential theorist of this movement (Rothbard 1985).

Classical liberals, on the contrary, believe that the state is inevitable but should be retrained. They generally embrace the concept of the minimal or 'night-watchman state' that Robert Nozick illustrated in his *Anarchy, State and Utopia* (Nozick 1974). Classical liberals argue that laws must be general and abstract, and discretionary powers of government should be strictly limited, to secure liberty. Hence, they oppose over-regulation of economic and social life, particularly through arbitrary methods such as licensing schemes, price and wage fixing, tax-subsidy schemes, and affirmative action. Welfare liberals grant the state a more interventionist role, consistent with their commitment to provide material assistance to those whose enjoyment of legal liberty is diminished by poverty or disadvantage. In practice, the modern liberal democracies tend to oscillate between the classical liberal and welfare liberal conceptions of the state. Liberals accept this as an inevitable consequence of political liberty.

Liberals of all types believe that the institutions of the liberal-democratic state offer the best means of preventing oppression of individuals and groups. They admit that much injustice occurs under liberal legal regimes, but argue that there is no better political system available to us. Liberal legal theorists believe that liberal political systems are self-correcting. Abolition of slavery and the enfranchisement of women are two early examples of the corrective power of liberal democracy.

Challenge of the critical legal studies (CLS) movement

'Like a meteor the Crits appeared, shone brightly for a short time and have gone' (Freeman 2001, 1055). The CLS movement had its roots in the anti-capitalist and anti-liberal intellectual revolt that swept the Western world in the late 1960s and early 1970s. It flourished in the late 1970s to mid-1980s, mainly in the United States, but was a spent force in jurisprudence by the end of the 20th century. It failed to dent the edifice of orthodox legal doctrine and culture, and within the intellectual left it was eclipsed by the more radical postmodernist movement. So why discuss CLS? Like the Marxists and American realists before them, CLS scholars challenged prevailing comfortable assumptions about the law and compelled liberal legal theorists to re-examine, revise and refine their views. Although CLS has declined as a movement, its ideas continue to energise left critiques of liberal law and CLS scholars continue to produce some of the most challenging literature on legal theory

The central charge that CLS levels is that law as developed in liberal societies is oppressive. Law papers over contradictions and conflicts within society that the law itself has created. Law formalises oppression, makes it respectable and indoctrinates people to accept it. CLS, like Marxism, argues that law, at least in the way it has historically developed, is a system of domination. However, unlike Marxism, CLS does not break down society into the simple division between capitalist and working classes. The law, according to CLS, splinters society in all sorts of ways – between traders and consumers, employers and employees, landlords and tenants, men and women, straight and gay, white and black, locals and foreigners, skilled and unskilled, and so forth. Unlike Marxism, CLS does not offer a clear political program to address the problems that afflict society, though thinkers such as RM Unger have proposed new kinds of social cooperation. CLS allegations against liberal notions of law are too serious to ignore, and must be explained and examined.

CLS spawned a large volume of critical literature that cannot be fully surveyed in this chapter. I will discuss four main aspects of this body of theory:

1. fundamental contradiction within society
2. alienation by categorisation and reification
3. denial of the value neutrality of law
4. alternative legal world of CLS.

Fundamental contradiction

CLS scholars share the view that society has a fundamental contradiction, or paradox. The contradiction is that individuals cannot do without others, but also need to be free of others. In other words, we want society as well as autonomy. We depend in life on the support of our family, friends, community and state – what CLS calls 'the collective'. At the same time, we need to be free from the violence of others. We need our own space to live freely and well, but we cannot find this security except with the help of others. This is not a new insight. As John Donne memorably wrote, 'no man is an island, entire of itself' (*Meditations*, XVII). Our personhood is defined not only by our individual characteristics but also by our relations with others. Everybody knows it, and liberal legal theorists worked on this premise. CLS sees a further problem. Duncan Kennedy stated it this way:

> But at the same time that it forms and protects us, the universe of others (family, friendship, bureaucracy, culture, the state) threatens us with annihilation and urges upon us forms of fusion that are quite plainly bad rather than good. Numberless conformities, large and small abandonments of self to others, are the price of what freedom we experience in society. And the price is a high one. (1978, 212)

Kennedy argued that until recently (that is until CLS revealed it), Western legal thinkers have not acknowledged this contradiction (1978, 213). This is simply untrue. Republicans and liberals have always feared the power of the collective to do more bad than good. They are acutely aware that the governments people erect for their own protection and advancement tend to gain lives of their own and threaten individual freedom unless they are contained by checks and balances. Kennedy, though, insisted that liberal legal thinking has produced elaborate mechanisms of denying the contradiction. He said that one form of denial is to present this contradiction as a case of 'tension between conflicting values that we must balance rationally' (1978, 214). This, to him, is so clearly false that the person who asserts it is probably trying to 'minimise or conceal the element of paradox, stalemate and desperation that we experience when we try to decide what kind of collective coercion is legitimate and what illegitimate' (1978, 214).

'Contradiction', 'paradox' and 'conflict' are distinct concepts. A contradiction, in the logical sense, cannot be resolved. Socrates lives or he does not live. He cannot do both. Unicorns exist or they don't. A paradox occurs when one makes a statement that leads logically to its converse. A famous paradox is that of the Cretan 'C' saying that all Cretans are liars. The statement is false if 'C' is saying the truth, because 'C' is a Cretan. Another is Heraclitus' assertion that 'Knowledge is impossible'. How does Heraclitus know this except with knowledge? Kennedy did not use 'contradiction' and 'paradox' in these senses. So what exactly did he mean, and how is it different from the liberal view of the eternal tension between the need for collective action and the need for protection from collective power? Kennedy did not provide a clear answer. The fact that the state (or collective) is both useful and dangerous is not a contradiction or paradox in the logical sense. It is not logically or pragmatically impossible to contain power and channel it to useful social ends. Hence, liberal legal scholars are right in treating it as a case of conflicting needs that have to be practically reconciled. Life is full of these conflicts and living involves ceaseless pragmatic compromises at all levels. I love chocolate ice cream, but eating too much of it is not healthy and so I must strike a balance. We make compromises within family about spending. At the social level the police must be given power to protect us, but we have to protect ourselves from the police. None of this involves denial. It is simply a matter of managing conflict as best as we can.

Liberals identify what they consider to be the proper, and hence legitimate, functions of the state – such as defence, responsibility for major infrastructure, supporting the judicature and, in modern times, the provision of social security to varying degrees. This, according to Kennedy, is a denial of the contradiction. His reasoning, again, is not clear. The fact that in a democracy the proper role of the 'collective' is continually debated, and the state's boundaries are constantly redrawn, is evidence not of denial but of recognition of the need to reach practical compromises.

Other CLS writers have seen different contradictions in liberal theory. M Kelman claimed that the positivist method of the liberals leads to the identification of the social good with the aggregate of personal preferences ascertained through markets and voting systems. Values, he said, are not merely matters of preference or taste but universal maxims (Kelman 1987, 68). This is another instance of CLS attacking the straw man of liberalism. There are many natural law theorists within the liberal ranks who explicitly embrace universal values. It is also grossly incorrect to say that positivists regard values solely as a matter of preference. Their position is that mixing legality and morality of law does not help clear thinking, and if we mix the two we diminish our chances of making the law better reflect values. Liberal economists are also aware that markets cannot operate in a valueless environment. The moral rules that secure person and property, sanctity of contract and trust are the foundations of trading systems. Neither do democratic systems function without supporting values such as the toleration of opposing views and fair conduct in seeking office.

Alienation by categorisation and reification

Life consists of a series of moments lived. However, to make sense of the world – and indeed to survive in the world – we have to think and talk in categories.

Take the case of the category 'human being'. One way of speaking of human beings is to describe each and every human being. Since no two persons are identical we end up having to refer by description to billions of individuals. This is impossible. In any case, a description of a single human is not possible without the use of other categories such as 'tall', 'short', 'fat', 'slim', 'heart', 'lung' and so forth. Therefore we have an abstract category called 'human being'. When a person refers to a 'human being' other people get the same rough idea. In short, we can only communicate by resort to categories such as 'human being', 'man', 'woman', 'child', 'sister', 'brother', 'dog', 'cat', 'parliament', 'aeroplane', 'football match', 'red wine' and so on.

These categories are abstractions. They are not real things but ideas that group things and events for convenient reference. Legal language is made up of categories. CLS scholars regard the law as 'reifying' these abstractions – treating them as real things. The categories stereotype or pigeonhole individuals into particular roles and destroy their sense of personhood and interconnectedness. CLS calls this alienation. P Gable wrote: 'One is never, or almost never, a person; instead one is successively a "husband", "bus passenger", "small businessman", "consumer", and so on' (1980, 28).

This kind of argument cannot be denied. Citizen X might say that, despite all the different roles he plays in daily life, he feels like a person and feels connected to his fellow beings in many ways. CLS would reply: 'Ah, but your view doesn't count because you have been indoctrinated and conditioned to think that way – you are an alienated being'. X might protest that he is not conditioned and that he is quite capable of forming an independent judgment. CLS would answer: 'That only proves that you have been thoroughly conditioned to think so'. It is very much like saying you don't believe in fairies. The believer in fairies will say, 'You can't possibly know. You have been conditioned to deny that fairies exist because in your community anyone who believes in fairies is regarded as a lunatic'.

The alienation is blamed on liberalism and capitalism. Gable wrote:

> The source of this absence of interconnectedness is the passivity, impotence, and isolation generated by the structure of groups, as those groups are themselves organized by the movement of capital. Within these groups no one is normally aware of his or her sense of unconnectedness, passivity, impotence, and isolation, because this felt reality is *denied* by the socially communicated reality. Each person denies to the other that he or she is suffering, because this collective denial has been made a condition of what social connection there is. (1980, 28)

This means that either we do not feel our suffering, or we cannot admit it because of social conditioning. If we do not *feel* suffering we are not suffering. If the suffering was real and widespread, one has to doubt whether social pressure could prevent its expression. As Marx said, alienation will eventually lead to revolt. Social pressures are formed by the convergence of individual feelings. If most people shared this sense of alienation it should create new social pressures in reaction.

Denial of the value neutrality of law

CLS is on much firmer ground in denying that law in liberal legal systems is value neutral. What is meant by the law's value neutrality? The reference here is not to particular laws, but to the abstract concept of law. No one claims that particular laws are value neutral. The criminal laws concerning murder, theft, robbery and rape are far from value neutral – they enforce moral standards. The law of contract that asks people to perform their contracts and the law of tort that holds people responsible for their negligent acts are value laden. So are the laws that redistribute wealth from some groups to others.

CLS says that liberals believe in the neutrality of law in a deeper and more abstract sense. Law is neutral in nature because it can serve different social values and aims. The *form* of the law retains its neutrality while its *content* is politically changed. In Australia, the law once criminalised adultery and adult homosexuality, but no longer does so. Slavery is prohibited today, though the law permitted it in the past. The law, as generally understood, is neutral as regards the uses to which it is put.

CLS scholars disagree. There are two kinds of law: one consisting of rules, and the other of standards. At one end of the spectrum there are rules that can be mechanically applied – rules that Kennedy called 'formally realisable' rules (1976, 1687–8). A good example is the legal rule that a person must be at least 18 years old to be eligible to vote at parliamentary elections. At the other end of the spectrum there are what Kennedy called 'standards', such as the notions of 'good faith, due care, unconscionability, unjust enrichment and reasonableness' (1976, 1687–8). Kennedy argued, correctly, that rules are more compatible with individualism. They may appear superficially neutral, but at the deeper level they are consistent with the liberal conception of law. A rule informs the individual in advance of the permitted range of actions. Traders know that they cannot sell liquor to minors. Pharmacists know that they cannot sell a drug without a prescription. Motorists know that they cannot drive faster than 100 kph on the freeway. Landowners know that they cannot cut down protected trees. Each has prior knowledge because of rules. The rules limit their freedom, but at least they know what the limits are so that the freedom they have is secure. Rules, however, can work unjustly in the individual case. A patient may need a drug before she can get to a doctor. A minor may be mature enough to drink responsibly. A motorist may have to exceed speed limits to pick up his child from school. Rules, in short, do not cater to each individual situation. Rules, in this sense, are impersonal.

In contrast, standards allow decision makers to tailor the law to what they think is the right outcome considering the situations of the parties and of society generally. Kennedy argued that impersonal rules favour individualism, whereas standards are more conducive to 'altruism' (1976, 1712). An employer, under the impersonal rules of contract law, has only to pay the employee the wage fixed by contract, regardless of the employee's needs. Such law is individualistic. In contrast, Australian labour law for most of its history has authorised tribunals to fix wages according to an employee's need, regardless of contract. In Kennedy's lexicon, this is altruistic law. Standards, Kennedy argued, are also not value neutral. What is 'reasonable' or 'unconscionable' or 'good faith' is a matter of moral or political judgment. What seems reasonable to a man may be unreasonable from a woman's standpoint. The law may impose the standard of the reasonable *man* to the exclusion of the reasonable *woman*. What is a reasonable wage, or a reasonable standard of diligence, is by its nature a political question.

CLS scholars are right to question the value neutrality of law. The very idea of predictable law and the rule of law is value laden. It privileges individual autonomy over collectivism. However, the laws of liberal societies are not ideologically clear cut. There is a continuous political tug-of-war between the ideals of impersonal abstract rules and discretionary power to determine rights and duties. It is, nevertheless, a battle of political values.

Alternative legal world of CLS

Assuming that people suffer oppression and alienation under liberal legal systems and they are in denial about their condition, what remedy do CLS scholars offer? CLS rejects Marxist-type revolution and dictatorship as an oppressive alternative. Kennedy had a modest and honest view of what could be done. He believed that the contradiction within society cannot be eliminated because it is society that has created and sustains it. 'The enterprise thus appears twice defeated before it is begun: we cannot resolve the contradiction within legal theory, and even if we could, the accomplishment would be of limited practical importance' (Kennedy 1978, 221). However, he argued that it is a worthy undertaking, because in its absence we intensify the contradiction by regarding it as part of the nature of things.

Gable proposed the radical solution of getting rid of law, which he regarded as 'an imaginary form of social cohesion'. He recommended the 'delegitimation of the law altogether, which is to say the delegitimation of the notion that social life is created and enforced by imaginary ideas' (Gable 1980, 46). How this can be done is left unexplained. Unger, one of the iconic figures in the CLS movement, had a more ambitious plan of social construction. It involved multiplying the branches of government and subjecting them to popular sovereignty in different ways (Unger 1983, 31–2). The scheme called for the overhaul of the market based economy as we know it. Unger stated that 'the central economic principle would be the establishment of a rotating capital fund', from which capital would be 'made temporarily available to teams of workers and technicians under certain general conditions fixed by central agencies of government' (1983, 35). These conditions would be designed to limit income disparities and 'imperial expansion' of the organisations (Unger 1983, 35). The citizen would have four types of rights: *immunity rights* (security against others); *destabilisation rights* (right to challenge established institutions and social practices); *market rights* (provisional claims to portions of social capital); and *solidarity rights* (legal entitlements of community life representing standards of good faith, loyalty and responsibility). Unger called this political theory 'superliberalism'.

What CLS achieved

Unger claimed that the result of the CLS attacks on formalism and objectivism (characteristics he attributed to the law) 'is to discredit, once and for all, the conception of a system of social types with a built in institutional structure' (1983, 8). Despite such self-laudatory statements CLS has not had great traction in jurisprudence or social theory. A key problem for the CLS scholars has been the fact that few outside their own circle perceive the world the way they do. The same sets of facts and circumstances are felt and interpreted differently by different people. What is seen as alienation by some may be seen as liberation by others. CLS tries to make people conscious of the alienation and oppression claimed to be imposed by the categories and modes of reasoning of liberal law and institutions. This consciousness raising is required because of the power of the law to condition people's thinking. Perhaps CLS has over-estimated the law's power over people and undervalued the people's power over law in liberal societies.

Unger's superliberal society at a glance seems unfeasible. Its economy needs a government to manage the allocation of resources for producing the means of existence. This is a return to socialist command and control that has been tried unsuccessfully. Unger's society also needs a government, however decentralised and fragmented, to define and enforce the four types of rights that he commended. How are these bodies constituted? If they are elected, how can we be sure that noble critical legal scholars are elected? How can elections be kept free of pressure group politics? How stable would such a political system be? Designing utopian systems is easy, but achieving them in the world of real people is hard.

Postmodernist challenge

The term 'postmodern' has its origins in the architectural movement that started in the 1950s as a breakaway from modern architecture. Whereas modern architecture sought perfection of form and detail, postmodern architecture shed the restrictions of form to embrace adventurous and unconventional design ideas.[1] The postmodern attitude of irreverence to tradition, freedom from form and creativity spread to art, music and literature and thence to philosophy and jurisprudence.

---

1 The modernist Seagram Building in New York and the postmodernist San Antonio Public Library in Texas, found easily on the internet, are excellent examples of the two styles.

Roots of postmodernist philosophy

Postmodernism did not start a new movement in philosophy but re-ignited an ancient debate under a new name – a debate that stretches back to the quarrels between Plato and the Sophists in the 5th century BC (see discussion in Chapter 5). The debate, at its core, is about the possibility of objective knowledge of the world and about right and wrong. The postmodernist attack aims at the heart of all science, including legal science, that is based on empirical observation and logical reasoning. If knowledge of the law and of facts is subjective, the rule of law is impossible. The Sophists rejected Plato's view that everything had an ideal form, and generally denied the possibility of objective knowledge. Our knowledge of the Sophist arguments comes mainly from the reports of their opponents, Plato and Aristotle. In the first book of Plato's *The Republic* Thrasymachus argues that there is no objective standard of justice, stating that 'right is the same thing in all states, namely the interest of the established government' (Plato 1974 (360 BC), 78). Gorgias of Leontini maintained that whatever exists cannot be known, and if it is known to one man he cannot communicate it to another (Russell 1962, 95).

The more recent inspiration for postmodernism in philosophy is found in the thinking of the German philosophers Friedrich Nietzsche (1844–1900) and Martin Heidegger (1889–1976). The way ordinary people observe the world around them has two aspects. One is the observer, the individual who observes. The other is the thing that is observed. The thing observed is assumed to have an existence that is real and independent of the observer. Thus, when I say that 'I see that table', I assume that I see a true table existing apart from myself. Nietzsche argued that the notion of a true world outside our perception of it is a useless and superfluous idea (1954, 485–6). In fact, the self too has no real existence. What I call 'I' is simply a social construct arising from the moral imperative of society to attribute responsibility for my actions (1954, 482–3). Heidegger's importance to postmodernism lies in the question that he posed in his famous book *Being and Time* (*Sein und Zeit*), published in 1927. Heidegger's language is unnecessarily convoluted, but the central question is easily understood. Knowledge is knowledge about what exists: things, persons, animals, events, the world, the universe, technology, science, and so on. Heidegger used the name 'beings' to cover all these. Knowledge is about 'beings'. Heidegger pointed out that although philosophers from Plato onwards have discussed the nature of 'beings', no one has inquired about what it really means for something to 'be' or exist. Rocks, motor cars and bacteria are beings, but they cannot think and hence cannot ask questions about the meaning of their existence (being). Human beings are different because they can ask such questions. Heidegger gave such an inquiring being the special name '*Dasein*', which in German means 'the Being'. Heidegger did not answer the question of what being means, except to say that being is in time (temporality). He did not use time in the ordinary sense of years, months and days, but in the sense that we are constituted partly by what we have been

(Heidegger 1993, 62–4). We are creatures of our past. Our birth, upbringing, education, environment, and all our life experiences make us what we are. Although Heidegger provided no answer, the question he posed inspired postmodernist theorists to challenge the very idea of an individual that is at the core of liberal theory.

The most radical of postmodernist scholarship is deconstruction theory. Deconstructionism, out of all postmodern views, is the most subversive of the liberal concept of law and of liberal political institutions. Hence, the following discussion will have a special focus on that school of thinking.

The nature of the problem

Lawyers are not alone in thinking that there is a real world out there. Most people go about their lives without questioning the realness of the world that they perceive with the help of their senses and their minds. When I see my neighbour's dog I think that there is a real dog. However, scientists know only too well that the way we see a dog is not the way the dog really is. To begin with, what we sense is mediated by the nature of our sense organs. We live in a world of perception. Although we may have reason to think that the perceptual world is affected by, and hence bears some correspondence to, the physical world, the two are very different. In microbiological terms the dog is a collection of cells with lives of their own. In the world of the particle physicist, it is a collection of interacting quanta. The world of our daily life is very different from the world of the scientist.

As already mentioned, philosophers at least from the time of the Sophists have identified an even deeper problem concerning our belief in a real world. The world of the scientist, though different from the world of mere lawyers, is nonetheless built on perceptions or mental pictures of things that are assumed to exist outside the mind. Hence, science presupposes the presence of a physical world. However, no scientist or philosopher has shown conclusively that the perceptions of our mind have anything to do with an external reality, although no one has established the contrary either. There are, in fact, two problems here. First, we cannot show that a world outside the mind exists without using our minds. Every perception of a thing is mediated by the mind. If we get rid of our minds we cannot perceive anything, and hence cannot demonstrate anything. Second, even if there are things out there, we cannot be sure that our perceptions represent things as they are. In other words, no one has seen the bridges that connect things to our minds. As Hume wrote, 'nothing is ever present to the mind but its perceptions, impressions and ideas' (1978 (1739–40), 67).

Philosophers have responded differently to these problems. Some maintain that there is a real world outside the mind. They are called 'realists'. Some realists think that the mind itself is a physical phenomenon, the result of the operations of our neurons. Then there are 'idealists' who maintain that all we know are products of the mind. The idealists Berkeley and Mach denied the existence of a material world. 'Transcendental idealists', notably Immanuel Kant, theorised that there are two worlds: (1) the world of *phenomena*, which consists of perceptions; and (2) the world of *noumena*, or things in themselves, which exist outside our minds. According to Kant, we can only know the phenomenal world. The *noumena* of the outer world cause sensations in us, but these sensations are ordered by our own mental apparatus into the things that we perceive. Believers in this theory are also called phenomenologists. (See discussion in Chapter 3.)

Idealism raises a fundamental question concerning human knowledge: if all that we know are products of our own minds, is it possible that the objects we perceive are our own creations? It suggests that consciousness is not simply a passive receptacle or, as Locke envisaged, a white paper upon which the external world inscribes itself, but in fact is constitutive. If so, it may be argued, as some postmodernists do, that truth is a matter of the coherence of one's subjective beliefs or, at best, a question of conformity with the conventions of the epistemic community to which one belongs. It is not hard to see that such a conclusion is completely at odds with the way knowledge is regarded in society. It is generally thought that on most questions there is a right view, or at least an objectively preferable view. There are frequent disagreements among reasonable persons as to the truth, but there is a general consensus concerning the criteria by which the better view can be determined.

Postmodernism, on the contrary, represents a revolt against rationality and a rejection of objective reality. The adage 'knowledge is power' takes on a new meaning in postmodern thinking. In the past, this meant that knowledge was helpful in an instrumental sense. Knowing something that your opponents did not know (e.g. knowledge of the battlefield or of the state of the coffee crop in Brazil) gave you an advantage over them. According to postmodernists, knowledge is power in a deeper and more oppressive way. Since there is no objective knowledge, what passes for knowledge is simply claims of truth legitimated by convention or by some 'epistemic authority' that determines the criteria by which truth is established. What is scientifically true is determined by the norms set by the scientific community, and what is legally correct is determined by the modes of reasoning of the legal fraternity. Thus, knowledge is seen as a form of power. What are presented as examples of rational and objective knowledge in the Western intellectual tradition are subjective views. The rational subject, while holding essentially subjective views, 'constitutes itself as an authorised knower of that world while excluding other forms of subjectivity from having a similar, representational voice [and] these other forms of subjectivity, for example certain feminist and non-Western types, are invalidated or marginalised to greater or lesser degrees' (Poster 1989, 159). Rationality is seen as an indeterminate process involving standards that are 'historically contingent matters of convention, interpretation, or the imposition of power' (Smith 1988, 149).

The challenge to liberal legality

The certainty of the law depends to a large measure on people being able to agree on its meaning. This is impossible if all knowledge is subjective. The commonsense view is that law, whether it consists of custom, judicial precedent or express enactment, is objectively knowable, as are the facts to which the law is applied. The postmodern thesis that all knowledge is subjective, conventional or dictated by authority radically undermines this notion. We have to make two very important distinctions here between conventional theory and postmodernism.

First, according to mainstream theory, there is a difference between the statement that the law is conventional or authoritarian and the statement that *knowledge* is conventional or authoritarian. Traditional jurisprudence readily accepts that law is often a matter of convention (custom) or the result of authoritarian rule (as in the case of the commands of a sovereign). However, lawyers believe that the law, once established, is a matter of objective knowledge. If the postmodernist thesis is true, nothing is objectively knowable and hence there can be no correct or privileged interpretation of the law. Every statement of knowledge, whether it concerns law or science, is an act of legislation in the most fundamental sense (Lyotard 1984, 8). Second, traditional legal theory admits that there can be equally persuasive alternative interpretations of the law. Indeed, disagreements concerning the law and its application to particular facts are the very stuff of legal practice. However, lawyers generally agree on the modes of reasoning that are relevant to the understanding and application of statutes and precedents. There are always hard cases, but that is because of the inadequacy of existing rules or the lack of decisive factual evidence either way. In contrast, the postmodern denial of the possibility of a right answer is radical. No amount of information can help us overcome this problem, for information itself is subjective. Hence, a claim of the right view can be justified only by convention or authority.

Deconstruction and the law

Jacques Derrida (1930–2004), the Algerian-born French thinker, is one of the most influential figures in modern European philosophy. His theory of deconstruction poses the most profound challenge to liberal theories of law and hence deserves close attention. Derrida was not a jurist but a philosopher of language. The quality of his writing is appalling and some of his work is near impenetrable. Yet he is important enough for us to make the effort to understand his work.

It is not easy to understand post-structuralism without understanding structuralism. Ferdinand Saussure (1857–1913), the Swiss linguist, is widely regarded as the founder of the structuralist tradition. Structuralists were a group of thinkers who were interested in the deep structure of the different systems that make up our world. Saussure understood language in the broadest possible sense. Language includes writing, speech, signs, and even mental images of sounds and signs (Saussure 1989, 15). He explained that language can be meaningfully studied only by giving the linguistic structure pride of place (1989, 10). There are several problems in understanding language.

In speech there are 'signifiers' and the 'signified'. The word 'cat' is a signifier. The object it signifies is the cat. However, there is no real or logical connection between the word 'cat' and the animal. If we simply utter the word 'cat' it is just a meaningless sound. There are two lessons from this observation. One is that a word has meaning only when it is delimited or separated from other words in a sequence. If I say that 'the cat is on the roof', the sound 'cat' begins to have some meaning.

> To summarise, a language does not present itself to us as a set of signs already delimited, requiring us merely to study their meanings and organisation. It is an indistinct mass, in which attention and habit alone enable us to distinguish particular elements. The unit has no special character, and the only definition it can be given is the following: *a segment of sound which is, as distinct from what precedes and what follows in the spoken sequence, the signal of a certain concept.* (Saussure 1989, 102)

A second lesson is that we cannot just string together words. The sequence 'roof the on is cat the' has no meaning. Hence, one can communicate in language only by making up sequences of words according to certain conventions or rules established in the community within which the language has grown (Saussure 1989, 11). These conventions represent the structure of the language.

Western philosophy is founded on the belief in the possibility of knowledge of the world around us. Although we may not be able to know directly and accurately the things that are outside our minds, we have perceptions about them and reliable knowledge can be gained from perceptions. Saussure argued that thought is possible only through language, hence there is nothing, even perceptions, before language (1989, 110). This means that a deaf and blind person such as the famous author and intellectual Helen Keller had some form of mental language before her teacher Annie Sullivan taught her to speak. (Presently, I argue the contrary, that language is a form of perception.)

Derrida, following Saussure, argued that there is no such thing as a perception that is independent of language:

> Perception is precisely a concept, a concept of an intuition or of a given originating from the thing itself, present itself in its meaning, independently from language, from the system of reference. And I believe that perception is interdependent with the concept of origin and of center and consequently whatever strikes at the metaphysics of which I have spoken strikes also at the very concept of perception. I don't believe that there is any perception. (1972, 272)

Derrida's point was that the idea of perception suggests that there is something that exists independent of language and prior to language. This is impossible, in Derrida's view, because there is nothing outside texts (*il n'y a pas de hors-texte*) (Derrida 1976, 163). People use words thinking that they represent real categories such as 'man', 'woman', 'child' and 'dog'. Derrida called this kind of false category 'logos' and the belief in such categories 'logocentrism'. In Derrida's own difficult language: 'The system of language associated with phonetic-alphabetic writing is that within which logocentric metaphysics, determining the sense of being as presence, has been produced' (1976, 53).

Derrida was convinced that there is nothing outside texts, not even perceptions. This belief is fundamental to the deconstruction project. If there are no real objects to which words can refer, words can only refer to other words. Saussure said this before Derrida. However, in Saussure's view words have relatively stable meanings derived from their differences from other words. The aim of deconstruction is to show that words have no stable meanings at all. Hence, Derrida needed to destroy Saussure's structural theory to make deconstruction possible. In Saussure's theory of differences, words have a centre or core meaning that allows them to be differentiated from other words. Derrida argued that a centre imports the idea of a transcendental signified or a real thing outside language. Such a centre, he said, is impossible because there are only differences in a state of infinite play. He stated:

> [I]n the absence of a centre or origin, everything became discourse . . . that is to say, a system in which the central signified, the original or transcendental signified, is never absolutely present outside a system of differences. The absence of the transcendental signified extends the domain and the play of signification infinitely. (Derrida 1981, 280)

Why infinitely? It is common sense that you cannot know what a dog is without also knowing something of what a dog is not. Included in the notion of a dog are traces of the non-dog. However, Derrida's point is: all that a dog is not cannot be determined, now or ever. There is a spatial as well as a temporal aspect to this problem. Spatially, we cannot determine what 'non-dog' is because words representing instances of 'non-dog', such as 'octopus' or 'elephant', themselves derive their meanings from differences from other words, and so on forever. The temporal dimension arises from the fact that 'all that is not dog' depends not only on what is 'not dog' now, but what will be 'not dog' in the future. Since the future is infinite, the possibilities of 'not dog' are also infinite Hence, the meaning of 'dog' is never present, but is ever deferred. To indicate this temporal dimension, and to distinguish his idea from that of Saussure, Derrida employed a new word of his own making: *différance*. This infinite dissemination of meaning, and the fact that a word contains within itself its 'Other', makes language 'undecidable'. It is impossible to separate what is inside from what is outside. Every inquiry concerning meaning ends in an abyss, or '*aporia*'.

What are the consequences of deconstruction for law and justice? Derrida explained his view of justice at a symposium on 'Deconstruction and the possibility of justice' held in New York in 1989. His speech is published in a book bearing that name, in a chapter titled 'Force of law: the "mystical foundation of authority"' (Derrida 1992). The gist of Derrida's argument is as follows. Derrida said that no judicial decision can be just unless it is a 'fresh judgment'. To be just, a decision must 'be both regulated and without regulation: it must conserve the law and also destroy it or suspend it long enough to have to reinvent it in each case, rejustify it, at least reinvent it in the affirmation and the new and free confirmation of its principle' (Derrida 1992, 23). The need for this reinvention or reaffirmation arises from the fact that every case is unique, and hence calls for an 'absolutely unique interpretation, which no existing, coded rule can or ought to guarantee absolutely' (Derrida 1992, 23). Most common law judges would agree with this view, notwithstanding the radical terms in which it is presented. Every case is undoubtedly unique, though many of them may look very similar. In applying a rule to a case, the judge is actually saying that the rule is such that it extends to the case at hand. Where a case is clearly within a rule or precedent, it may appear that the judge is making a mechanical decision. This is not so, as the judge must contemplate the meaning of the rule and the nature of the case, however simple the exercise may seem. Now, you may call this process the application of the law to each new case, or you may call it reaffirming the law in each case. Either way, you are describing the same process. Thus far, then, Derrida did not subvert the traditional notion of justice.

However, Derrida was committed to the notion of the undecidability of language. He said that the judge must take account of rules but in the end is confronted by the 'always heterogeneous and unique singularity of the unsubsumable example' (1992, 24). In simple words, Derrida was saying that, in the ultimate analysis, it is impossible to do justice by applying rules because each case is unique. It is critical to understand this point in order to realise the extent to which Derrida departed from the liberal notions of law and justice. We mortals think that sometimes a collection of individual things may differ from each other in various respects but may nevertheless have certain common characteristics that enable all of them to be grouped within one class or rule. A child who opens a bag of marbles may find that each item of this treasure is different from the others in colour and size. Yet, after examining them, the child may conclude that they are all marbles. Every act of killing a human being is unique in innumerable ways. Yet we think that the presence of certain qualities – such as the causing of death, the causal connection to the accused, and a defined state of mind – together with the absence of exculpatory circumstances, enables us to classify some of these acts as murder. No one has ever said that murder can be conclusively proved, only that it may be sometimes proved beyond the reasonable doubts of 12 jurors. We are able to make these classifications because we act as if there are real things out there and we believe that words can refer to these things. We can distinguish a marble from a dice because we think that both exist and that the word 'marble' refers to the spherical item and the word 'dice' to the cube-shaped item. In Derrida's world there are no objects, but only words without centres whose meanings are in constant flux as they interplay with other words. The trace of the dice is found in the marble and neither word has a core meaning that enables it to be differentiated from the other in a permanent way. Hence classifications and rules are impossible. What is outside is inseparable from what is inside. So, in the end, the judge must be guided and also not be guided by a rule. This is the 'ordeal of the undecidable', which alone can produce justice. According to Derrida, as the just decision is made beyond rules, it is an act of madness:

> The instant of decision is a madness, says Kierkegaard. This is particularly true of the instant of the just decision that must rend time and defy dialectics. It is madness. Even if time and prudence, the patience of knowledge and the mastery of conditions were hypothetically unlimited, the decision would be structurally finite, however late it came, a decision of urgency and precipitation, acting in the night of non-knowledge and non-rule. Not of the absence of rules and knowledge but of a reinstitution of rules which by definition is not preceded by any knowledge or by any guarantee as such. (1992, 26)

If language is inherently undecidable, it is difficult to see how there can be any rules at all. In any case, Derrida was maintaining that the ultimate decision is uninformed by any rule. At the moment of judgment, judges are unfettered by law. What guides them at the moment of reckoning? According to Derrida, it is 'another sort of mystique' (1992, 25). Fortunately for those who cherish the rule of law, judges decide cases in a reasonably predictable way.

Could Derrida be wrong?

Derrida denied the existence of physical objects to which words could refer. If there are things outside texts, then words could refer to them and have relatively stable meanings. Derrida also denied that there is anything like perceptions. He equated perceptions to concepts. A mental world of concepts that exist outside language also makes deconstruction impossible. In such a world, concepts take the place of things and words could have determinate meanings by reference to the concepts. It does not matter whether a 'dog' is a physical entity or a mental entity. If such an entity exists outside language the word 'dog' can have a meaning anchored in that entity, so that the word will not 'disseminate' into Derridean indeterminacy. In other words, if there is such a mental dog, the claim that the word 'dog' has only momentary meanings resulting from interplay with other words loses its force.

Let us first look at Hume's idea of perception, as a convenient way to assess Derrida's thesis. Hume believed that only perceptions are immediately present to the mind. He distinguished two types of perceptions: (1) impressions, and (2) thoughts or ideas. Impressions are the more lively perceptions, such as those that we gain when we hear, see, feel, love, hate, desire or will (Hume 1978 (1739–40), 67). These are single mental experiences associated with sense data and emotions. Ideas are less forceful, as they are inferences formed out of impressions that are remembered. Single impressions are recalled as simple ideas and then linked together as compound ideas. I see an orange colour, feel a shape and texture, and smell a fragrance and I conclude that there is an orange in my hand. We link impressions and ideas according to the principle of cause and effect. We observe that certain objects are 'constantly conjoined with each other'. Where there is fire, heat is felt, from which fact people conclude that fire causes heat. We expect cause and effect, not because of some 'inseparable and inviolable connection' between impressions but because of past experience (Hume 1978, 157). In the final analysis, human knowledge is experience or customary knowledge. Hume wrote: 'Without the influence of custom we should be entirely ignorant of every matter of fact beyond what is immediately present to the memory and senses . . . There would be an end at once of all action as well as of the chief part of speculation' (1975 (1748), 465).

Unlike Hume, Derrida denied that any kind of perception exists, and insisted that all we have are texts. Here, Derrida walked into his own trap. How do we know that there are texts? We know this only because we have perceptions or impressions of them. We see them, feel them, and hear them (Derrida's texts included speech). Saussure and Derrida thought that text even included mental images of words, but how do we have mental images of sounds or signs without perceiving them? Without perceptions or impressions there are no texts, however we define text. Without perception there are no texts, no authors, no Derrida – in short, nothing to deconstruct. If we admit that we perceive texts, we have no grounds to deny other perceptions. Derrida ignored this problem. His pronouncement '*Il n'y a pas de hors-texte*' is an *ex cathedra* pronouncement made without argument. As MH Abrahams stated, 'it functions as an announcement of where Derrida takes his stand – namely within the workings of language itself' (Abrahams 1989, 35). It is the metaphysical foundation of Derrida's philosophy. Take it away, and the edifice of deconstruction theory collapses.

Law and language game theory

All postmodernists share Derrida's disbelief in the possibility of objective knowledge, but not all of them treat knowledge purely as a matter of momentary personal taste. Language game theorists treat knowledge as something that is legitimated by the conventions of the relevant speech community. According to them, knowledge questions are not 'undecidable'. On this question Richard Rorty, a postmodern champion of rhetoric against philosophy, accused Derrida of succumbing 'to nostalgia, to the lure of philosophical system building, and specifically that of constructing yet another transcendental idealism' (1982, 89). According to language game theorists, knowledge, though lacking a transcendent foundation, is not a matter of unbridled subjectivism. These theorists:

> . . . try to show that the standards we develop for such matters as justice and truth are the products of specific language games, conventions, shared normative understandings or community practices, due to change when new contingencies arise from whatever source, including pure happenstance (Wolfe 1992, 361; compare Fish 1989, 23).

According to language game theory, knowledge is anchored in a contingent 'reality'. However, this 'reality' consists not of unsubsumable singularities, as Derrida alleged, but of understandings that are in harmony with the conventions of the relevant community. As François Lyotard saw it, truth is that which conforms to the 'relevant criteria . . . accepted in the social circle of the "knower's" interlocutors' (1984, 19). According to Stanley Fish, this makes the individual a 'situated subject . . . who is always constrained by the local or community standards and criteria of which his judgment is an extension' (1989, 323). Language game theory's concession to a relatively stable, though contingent, form of communal knowledge appears to accommodate the rule of law to a much greater extent than does deconstruction. It means that rules can have stable meanings such that they are capable of guiding human action in the context of a given community.

Feminist jurisprudence

Feminist jurisprudence posed the third major challenge to liberal legal theory in the late 20th century. It owes much to the previously discussed CLS and postmodernist attacks on liberal legal theory, but has developed its own independent lines of reasoning. Unlike the CLS and postmodernist movements, feminism is grounded in a powerful moral case acknowledged by most liberal thinkers. It is the case for equal treatment of women and the elimination of all forms of oppression, whether direct or systemic.

Feminist jurisprudence must be distinguished from the much older political movement for equal rights and justice for women. The latter struggle began, and continues to be conducted, within the framework of the rules of liberal democracy. Feminist jurisprudence, on the contrary, finds liberal legal theory and methods of reasoning to be largely responsible for the oppressed condition of women. In particular, feminist jurists think that the liberal notion of objective legality is founded on abstract categories that do not recognise the circumstances and experience of women. Hence, this brand of feminist jurisprudence belongs to the genre of radical anti-liberalism.

Women are subjected to unspeakable oppression and cruelty in different parts of the world. In some Islamic societies women are punished for not covering their faces in public or even for being seen in public in the company of a male who is not a relative. Women in many societies are forced to marry against their wishes. Some are genitally mutilated. Women who cohabit without paternal approval are murdered in the name of family honour. The litany is endless. This kind of treatment is unlawful in liberal societies and feminists also condemn it. However, the main focus of feminist jurisprudence is not on the atrocities that women endure in illiberal societies but on the condition of women in liberal societies, under liberal law.

Feminist jurisprudence has generated a vast volume of literature and there are numerous overlapping strands of feminist legal theory. In an important essay, Patricia Cain identified four schools of feminist legal theory: (1) liberal feminism, (2) radical feminism, (3) cultural feminism, and (4) postmodern feminism (1990, 829–47). I propose to consider these in turn, but first will say something of the status of women in liberal theory.

Liberalism and women

Liberalism, by definition, rejects discrimination and oppression of individuals or groups. Its commitment to the liberty of individuals from unjustified governmental or private interference is unqualified. The first political philosopher to state the case for the equality of men and women was John Stuart Mill, an iconic thinker of the liberal tradition. His essay *The Subjection of Women* remains to date the definitive liberal statement of the equality of men and women.

> The object of this Essay is to explain as clearly as I am able grounds of an opinion which I have held from the very earliest period when I had formed any opinions at all on social political matters, and which, instead of being weakened or modified, has been constantly growing stronger by the progress of reflection and the experience of life. That the principle which regulates the existing social relations between the two sexes – the legal subordination of one sex to the other – is wrong itself, and now one of the chief hindrances to human improvement; and that it ought to be replaced by a principle of perfect equality, admitting no power or privilege on the one side, nor disability on the other. (Mill 1997 (1869), 1)

Mill regarded discrimination on grounds of gender as offensive to the most fundamental value of liberalism, which is the liberty of the individual. Mill's political theory was utilitarian. Like Bentham, he thought that the only irrefutable criterion of moral judgment was utility or advantage, not just for the individual but for society as a whole. All of humanity gains by eliminating discrimination and oppression of women, who constitute half its number. Mill feared that his message of women's liberation would not prevail against the popular opinions and feelings of his time. Yet in the century and a half since he wrote the essay, women in liberal democracies have made impressive gains through political action. They have won equal voting rights, marital rights, property rights and access to education, professions and most occupations. They have increased their representation in the branches of government and corporate boardrooms. Liberalism in theory rejects all formal and informal barriers to entry into professions, occupations and public offices.

Most liberal democracies have constitutional or statutory prohibitions against discrimination on grounds of gender. Liberal views on gender equality were the prime movers for the preparation and adoption in 1981 of the United Nations *Convention·on the Elimination of All Forms of Discrimination*. It has been ratified by all liberal democratic nations. The treaty has been operationalised in these countries in a variety of ways, including constitutional entrenchment, special legislation and judicial application.

Liberal feminist jurisprudence

Liberal feminism is based on the belief that women are rational autonomous individuals who are entitled to the same rights as men. Women are capable of making rational decisions about their own interests and should be treated equally under the law and have equal opportunities with men. Liberal feminist jurists uphold the basic principles and institutions of liberal society and seek to use them to better the conditions of women. Their object is to make liberal laws more truly liberal in relation to women.

Liberal feminists realised that despite formal legal assurances of equality they were not always equally treated by the law. Equality, as understood in liberal jurisprudence, is the equal treatment of persons in similar conditions. Equality does not require that children and adults receive the same punishment for a crime, or that the poor and the rich pay income tax at the same rate, or that infants should have voting rights at the general election, or that clergymen and women should perform military service like everybody else. Different treatment of persons similarly placed defeats the aim of equality. So does the similar treatment of differently placed persons.

Liberal feminists argue that the law sometimes treats men and women differently when it should treat them the same way, and treats them the same way when it should treat them differently. The Idaho statute struck down by the US Supreme Court in *Reed v Reed* 404 US 71 (1971) gave preference to males over females in the appointment of administrators to administer the estates of deceased persons. The Supreme Court could not see any material difference between men and women that allowed the state law to treat them differently. This success was the culmination of sustained legal research and advocacy by liberal jurists such as Ruth Bader Ginsburg, a professor of law at Rutgers and Columbia universities who is now a justice of the United States Supreme Court. At the other end we find laws that do not recognise material differences. Some rules and doctrines of criminal law and tort law seem not to acknowledge special circumstances that differentiate the condition of men and women. Criminal law in the past did not accept that women who are subject to continual domestic violence and abuse ('battered women') could plead diminished responsibility for killing their spouses or partners unless it was done in self-defence. Common law courts now admit evidence of the mental condition of battered wives in determining the defence of provocation: see, for example, *R v Ahluwalia* (1992) 4 All ER 889; *R v Thornton (No. 2)* (1996) 2 All ER 1023; *R v Charlton* (2003) EWCA Crim 415; *The Queen v Epifania Suluape* (2002) NZCA 6.

The defence of provocation reduces liability from murder to manslaughter where the killing results from a loss of self-control in response to provocation, in circumstances where an ordinary person could also have lost self-control. The 'ordinary person' tended to be identified with the 'ordinary male person'. The ordinary male person has no experience of being a battered spouse. Hence, the category did not accommodate the special condition of women. The efforts of the lawyers in the cases mentioned resulted in the reformulation of the category. Liberal feminist litigation seeks to break down male-oriented categories and thereby attune the law to women's experiences. This is entirely consistent with classical liberal thinking.

An important debate within feminism concerns the sameness of men and women and the difference between them. Should the law treat men and women as formally equal, or should it recognise women's special circumstances and needs? Formal equality requires that the law does not acknowledge sex-based distinctions. Liberal feminists tend to favour the sameness thesis. They say that differences between men and women have been used to discriminate against women. Women, for example, were barred from many kinds of employment on grounds that they were physically or psychologically unsuited for the work involved. Sameness feminists argue that the emphasis on differences weakens women's abilities to gain equal rights. Women do not have to deny their differences from men, but they can gain more by discrediting false differences that are used to deny them opportunities open to men. Wendy Williams expressed the equality argument this way:

> We who are different share in this particular context at this particular time a quality, trait, need or value that locates us on the same platform for this particular purpose. We see a connection in a particular respect that we who are different think entitles us to partake in the same meal, drink at the same trough, or march to the same drummer – at least in this particular parade. (1989, 104)

Cultural feminism

Cultural feminists emphasise differences between men and women. Liberal notions of law, legality and legal process, they believe, are shaped by masculine values and views of the world. Men think of themselves as individuals disconnected from each other, whereas women think of themselves as connected to others. The difference is illustrated by Carol Gilligan's hypothetical dilemma posed to sixth graders Jake and Amy. They are told that Heinz's wife will die without a certain drug that Heinz has no money to buy. Should he steal the drug? Jake opts for stealing, giving priority to saving life over being honest. Amy, on the contrary, says that 'they should talk it out and find some other way to make the money'. Gilligan concluded: 'Amy's judgments contain the insights central to the ethic of care, just as Jake's judgments reflect the logic of the justice approach' (1982, 30). Gilligan accepted that this was not a scientific study, but presented it as an illustration of what she believed is an important difference in the way men and women develop psychologically. Cultural feminism has been greatly influenced by Gilligan's work on gender difference.

Robin West argued that virtually all modern legal theories explicitly or implicitly embrace what she called the separation thesis about what it means to be a human being. This is the view that a human being is physically separated from every other human being. West gave the following statement by political philosopher Michael Sandel as the definitive statement of the separation thesis:

> [w]hat separates us is in some important sense prior to what connects us – epistemologically prior as well as morally prior. We are distinct individuals first, and *then* we form relationships and engage in co-operative arrangements with others; hence the priority of plurality over unity. (Sandel 1982, 133; West 1988, 1–2)

West argued that even CLS theory is based on the separation thesis. Liberals celebrate the separateness and fear its destruction, whereas CLS theorists lament the separation and long for association (West 1988, 5).

West presented the 'connection thesis' as the central insight of feminist legal theory. According to this thesis, 'women are "essentially connected," not "essentially separated" from the rest of human life, both materially, through pregnancy, intercourse, and breast-feeding, and existentially, through the moral and practical life' (West 1988, 3). West claimed that women are 'more nurturant, caring, loving and responsible to others than are men'. She said: 'Women think in terms of the needs of others rather than the rights of others because women materially, and then physically, and then psychically, provide for the needs of others' (1988, 21). West and Gilligan have been accused by other feminists of essentialism. Essentialism is the belief that an entity (such as, say, 'woman') invariably displays certain essential characteristics – a charge that they have denied. Obviously there are women who do not fit West's stereotype. Many women 'attain atomistic liberal individuality' but, West said, 'just as obviously most women don't' (1988, 71).

The legal system, from the cultural feminist standpoint, fails to reflect the way women live their lives and think about life. It is too focused on rights and individuality that reflect the male nature. Yet men and women live in a common space in society. Cultural feminists imagine a utopian world where the legal system 'will protect against harms sustained by all forms of life' (West 1988, 72).

Radical feminism

Radical feminists agree with cultural feminists that women are different from men. Unlike cultural feminists, they believe that these differences are constructed through male domination. Men have defined women. The main difference between men and women is power. Men have power and women are subject to power. A leading feminist radical, Catharine MacKinnon, argued that feminists are mistaken in fighting for equality, which is a liberal ideal. Equality means sameness, and men and women are different. MacKinnon wrote:

> Put another way, gender is socially constructed as difference epistemologically; sex discrimination law bounds gender equality by difference doctrinally. A built-in tension exists between this concept of equality, which presupposes sameness, and this concept

of sex, which presupposes difference. Sex equality thus becomes a contradiction in terms, something of an oxymoron, which may suggest why we are having such a difficult time getting it. (1987, 32–3)

MacKinnon's point is that to gain equality women have to be the same as or similar to men. This confirms domination. MacKinnon urged feminists to abandon the male ideal of equality and shift their attention to the real but neglected issue of subjection of women. She called this approach the dominance approach. The dominance approach calls on feminists to focus on rape, sexual assault of children, which is endemic in the patriarchal family, the battery of women in a quarter to a third of homes, prostitution and pornography, which exploit women for profit.

How radical is MacKinnon's feminism? Liberal jurists agree wholeheartedly with MacKinnon about the subjection of women in these ways. They would also like to see this subjection eliminated. On pornography they differ, because censorship gives the state the power to define what acceptable sex is for women. Lucinda Finley pointed out that not all women share MacKinnon's view of acceptable sex (1988, 382). MacKinnon treated women as a class, neglecting differences among women themselves. Problems such as domestic violence and child abuse, which usually happen in homes, cannot be fought with law enforcement alone. Feminists are surely right in pointing out that nothing short of a cultural and moral transformation of male dominance (to the extent that it exists) will be sufficient to address these problems.

Postmodern feminism

The reader would not have failed to notice the influence of CLS and postmodernism on feminist jurisprudence. Postmodernism informs feminist theory in two ways. First, it challenges the rationalism on which mainstream Western philosophy and science are based. Postmodernists deny that knowledge can be objectively established, and hold that all truths are contingent on subjective experience. Thus, what is true from the male point of view may not be true from the female point of view. Second, postmodernists say that the categories that we use in speech, such as 'man' and 'woman', have no privileged meanings, but only meanings that are given to them by the language community or by the community's 'epistemic authority' or the 'authorised knowers'. In one way or another, these categories are 'socially constructed' and have no independent validity. Feminists conclude from this proposition that these categories have been established by men according to the masculine point of view.

If these categories are socially constructed, it must be possible to socially reconstruct them, provided that the social forces that created the categories in the first place are tamed or reformed. This is what most feminist theories try to promote, through intellectual discourse and political action. One form of postmodernist thinking, namely deconstruction theory, poses a problem for feminist goals. Deconstructionist theory, like other postmodern views, exposes the lack of a transcendental reality and denies the possibility of objective knowledge. It provides a powerful analytical tool for deconstructing established categories and knowledge claims in society. Yet it turns out to be too powerful for feminist purposes. According to deconstruction, the very idea of a category is nonsensical. Every category disseminates into the hopeless indeterminacy that Derrida called *aporia*.

Feminists such as Drucilla Cornell who have embraced deconstruction theory use it to deconstruct male-oriented categories, but they also refuse to construct female categories in their place, since they deny the very possibility of categories. The problem for feminist action is obvious. As Cain pointed out, any theory requires some degree of abstraction, and if women are considered to be situated in their individual realities, as deconstructionist philosophy suggests, it is not possible to develop a theory or strategy to combat the injustices they face. According to deconstruction theory we create our worlds through myth and allegory. Cornell's answer is that women should create their own allegories and myths to counter those that are used to suppress them. This would involve collective imagining on the part of women. In other words, women should write their own story and create their own 'reality in which they achieve a superior way that is valued' (Cornell 1990, 699).

Challenges to liberal jurisprudence: concluding thoughts

The radical jurisprudence discussed in this chapter has raised new questions and contested long standing assumptions about the law. This is an unambiguous good. These theories have proved useful in providing analytical tools to break down stereotypes and to expose the artificialities of concepts assumed to be natural in law and society. In many ways, these theories have added new dimensions to the sociology and psychology of law. They have brought to centre stage the issue of social construction of legal language and the structural injustices that flow from the law's insensitivity to the experiences and circumstances of different groups. They have generated new awareness among liberal jurists and, to use Kant's words, awoken some of them from their dogmatic slumber.

The common theme among CLS scholars, postmodernists and feminists is the insight that concepts, categories and methods of law are socially constructed. The term 'construction' suggests deliberate designing on the part of someone or some group. Society as a whole cannot construct anything in this sense. Society is not a person with an independent mind, but a community of interacting individuals. Social construction, therefore, must mean construction in the following ways. First, certain persons or bodies, such as rulers, parliaments and their delegates, claim to represent the will of the society and to have the authority to make law for society. A great deal of law has been constructed in this manner in liberal societies. One needs only to look at the thousands of volumes of statutes, subordinate legislation and law reports in law libraries. Second, there is a great deal of law that has not been deliberately designed in this way. I include within this body of law the common law and all the informal social rules such as customs, traditions, etiquette, and even superstitions. They all affect the way social relations are formed and changed. In what sense have these rules and the categories that they create been socially constructed? As discussed in Chapter 10, these rules arise spontaneously from the interactions of members of society.

Spontaneous emergence does not mean that particular individuals or groups have not had superior or dominant influence on the law's growth. It is certain from what we know of the natural history of the human race that men from the beginnings of society would have had greater influence than women in the way social rules developed. Common law judges have historically been males from the upper ranks of society, and their worldview would have certainly influenced the development of the law. What spontaneous order means is that countless factors – including ecology, biology, psychology, economics of survival and, as Lyotard pointed out, sheer happenstance – are involved in the emergence of the complex order that we call society. The males of the human species, brutes as they are, cannot claim the honour of sole responsibility for the way civilisation has turned out. If we do not recognise the complexity of our condition we diminish our capacity to make our condition better.

CLS theorists, postmodernists and feminists wish to transform society to one extent or another. Unlike the political revolutionaries of the past, they do not propose violent change. Quite rightly, they do not trust violent revolution to produce the kind of society they envision. In any case, liberal societies have proved resilient against revolutions of the violent type. Liberal social and legal structures have remained largely intact, and in some respects have become stronger. The strengthening of international trade and commerce and the democratisation of many previously authoritarian nations provide the strongest, but not the only, evidence of this trend. Radical legal theorists aim to change the legal order by changing the minds and hearts of people through intellectual persuasion. Significant changes have occurred in the past four decades, and radical theorists deserve a generous share of credit. However, in the field of women's advancement I think the greatest credit goes to the liberal feminists, who tirelessly and unrelentingly pursued the cause of law reform through the institutions of the liberal state.

Radical legal theorists of every kind should ask the following questions and answer them honestly. Will their cause be served better by tearing down the liberal state and the liberal legal system? What kind of society and power structures will emerge if their theories overturn democratic liberalism? Will they be stable or will they fall prey to sectarian interests? How can utopian conditions be maintained without force? If force is granted to authorities, how can it be contained and directed solely to its proper end? Liberal society and liberal law are imperfect, and liberal thinkers know it. Yet liberal societies have proved stable and workable. The idea that liberal law is pervasively oppressive has proved difficult to sell among the general public. There might be a lesson in this. Radicals need to ask whether they could be wrong after all. The gains that have been made by disadvantaged groups have been through the political institutions of liberalism. Alternative imaginings and utopian speculation are useful as tools of analysis and criticism. It is mainly in this sense that they have served the causes of the disadvantaged in society.

9

Economic Analysis of Law

What has law got to do with *economics*? Most lawyers will probably say 'nothing' or 'not much'. However, if the question posed is 'What has law got to do with the *economy*?', most lawyers are bound to answer, 'quite a lot'. The laws of property and contract allow people to trade in goods and services. Consumer protection laws place restrictions on how traders may conduct trade. Labour laws regulate the labour market. Competition law aims to increase competition and prevent monopolies. Tort law gives protection to person and property from wilful or negligent harm, without which trade and commerce would be seriously restricted. How can farmers grow wheat and sell their crops if their land is not secure from trespass and their crops not protected from theft? How can General Motors or Ford make and sell cars if they have no ownership of the cars that they produce? International trade and investment law promotes trade and investment among nations. There will be little foreign trade or investment if states do not recognise the rights of citizens of other states. Even laws concerned with private morality have economic effects. Prohibition of alcohol consumption in the United States gave rise to a new industry known as bootlegging. Most lawyers accept that laws affect the economy, directly or indirectly.

Lawyers also have no difficulty in recognising that economic factors have quite a lot to do with legislation passed by parliaments. Governments, depending on their philosophies, react to economic forces in different ways. They may promote or suppress competition. They may enact laws to counter what they think is inequitable wealth distribution caused by markets. They may seek to limit rising costs of products through price controls, or try to support producers by subsidies. They fight inflation and deflation using whatever legislative devices they can find. So, what can economic science teach lawyers about law that lawyers do not already know? It turns out to be quite a lot. This chapter examines the contributions that economic science has made to the understanding of law.

The large body of theory and empirical studies produced by economic analyses of law and legal institutions is commonly known as law and economics (L & E). There are, in fact, three major branches of law and economics. They are:

1. *Transaction costs economics*, which evaluates the efficiency of legal rules with a primary focus on private law. The term 'law and economics' usually refers to this branch of learning.

2. *New institutional economics* (NIE), which develops economic explanations of the emergence and change of institutions. 'Institutions' in this context does not mean organisations like firms, government departments and central banks. It means all the constraints on human action, including formal legal rules as well as the more informal customs, traditions and social rules. (The term derives from the Latin *institutiones*, which refers to established rules.) The field includes game theory as applied to the study of institutional evolution.

3. *Public choice theory*, which is concerned with the study of democratic decision-making processes using the insights and methods of micro-economics. Public choice theorists typically study how majority voter coalitions are formed and votes are traded in legislative assemblies and the electorate, and the phenomenon of rent seeking.

New institutional economics is discussed in some detail in Chapter 10. This chapter mainly discusses transaction costs economics, but it includes a short discussion of the central ideas of public choice theory. The discussions in this chapter begin with a brief introduction to some basic concepts in economics that are central to understanding economic analyses of law. This is followed by an examination of the problem of transaction costs and its bearing on the formation of legal rules. The hypothesis that the common law system by nature tends to produce efficient rules is critically examined. The chapter proceeds to a brief discussion of the economics of legislation as revealed by public choice theory, and closes by considering some of the moral objections to the economic approach to law.

Background and basic concepts

The branch of economic analysis of law generally known as law and economics arose out of the work of American lawyer-economists Ronald Coase, Guido Calabresi and Henry Manne on the efficiency of common law rules concerning property and nuisance. The studies expanded into other areas of law as the field attracted a growing number of scholars in the United States and Europe, in law schools and economics departments of universities. One of the most prolific and influential current writers is Richard Posner, Chief Judge of the United States Court of Appeals for the Seventh Circuit.

Law and economics, in its 'pure' sense, is positive as opposed to normative. It is about the world as it is rather than as it ought to be. It is about the economic cost (or social cost) of different rules, and not about the morality or justness of rules. It does not tell judges and legislators what rules to make, but tries to inform them of the relative costs of alternative rules. Consider, for example, the ongoing efforts of governments in industrialised nations to reduce carbon dioxide emissions to address the global warming problem. Economists may show that legalising nuclear power plants is an efficient way to reduce emissions, and they may well be right. Although a government may rule out nuclear power for moral or emotional reasons, at least it will know the economic cost of its moral decision.

It is always possible to draw normative conclusions from positive science, and many writers of law and economics move back and forth between positive and normative theorising. The normative conclusions from L & E studies have tended to favour free markets and limited government regulation of property and contract. It is not surprising that law and economics have many strident critics. Some of the attacks do not distinguish between the positive and normative aspects of L & E theory, leading to much confusion in scholarly debate.

Positive L & E has narrower and broader versions. The narrower version concentrates on calculating the economic efficiency of particular rules and their possible alternatives. The broader version also does this, but goes further to claim that the common law system by its nature gravitates towards efficient rules. This is known as the 'efficiency of the common law hypothesis'. It is logical to proceed from the narrower to the broader version. However, we must start with some basic concepts in economics without which L & E cannot be understood.

Cost, price, value, utility

It is important distinguish these four concepts to get anywhere in this field. Imagine the following case. A is a carpenter. He makes a writing table with wood that he buys from a timber yard and with tools that he has bought from the hardware store. He spends three days making the table, and afterwards offers it for sale at his showroom with a price tag indicating that he is willing to sell it for $100. Many people inspect the table but do not buy it. Eventually B, a wealthy customer, offers $80 for it. C, who is a student on a subsistence income, would pay up to $110 for the table but has only $50 to spare. A sells the table to B. All the expenses that A incurred in making the table and the value of the time he spent making it constitute A's *costs*. The amount of $100 stated on the price tag is the *price*. The amount that B is willing to pay, namely $80, is the *value* of the table for B. C's need for the table is greater than B's need and the $110 that C is willing to pay may represent the *utility* of the table to C.

Value and utility are distinct ideas in economics. Value is what a person is willing to pay for a good or service. Utility is the subjective worth of the good or service to an individual. Utilitarians such as Bentham regarded the utility of a thing in terms of the pleasure it brought to an individual. Utility is difficult to measure, as it is subjective. Value is simply a fact. Hence, economic calculation is usually based on value. The disregard of utility makes economics distasteful to some people. Cost and price are also distinct. A might have incurred only $50 in costs to make the table. The price of $100 is what he thinks someone will be prepared to pay. The profit of $50 may seem very large and unreasonable, but that is again a subjective judgment. A is in the business to make an income so that he can pay his mortgage and household bills, send his children to school and do the kinds of things that most people like to do in life. Of course, he might find that no one is prepared to pay $100 for the table, so that he may have to keep reducing the price to the point at which it sells. If he is forced to sell products below cost, he will close his business and do something else. We assume that B buys the table for $80, which is the eventual price. However, B's cost of buying the table is more than the price, as B had to find the table, bargain with A and then transport the table home. The cost to B is the price plus all the other expenses and the time spent.

The concept of price has enormous significance. The price at which A finally sells the table ($80) conveys a large amount of information about what is going on in society. It tells us that $80 is likely to be the highest value that people attach to the table. At $81 B will find something better to do with the money. It tells us that people think that the extra $1 is not worth spending on the table. We are talking about just one product here. Since this is the case with all transactions, the mechanism of price is critical in the efficient allocation of resources to those who value them most, though not necessarily to those who need them or deserve them most.

Economic efficiency

Efficiency is achieved when more output is gained from the same resources. A car that runs 15 kilometres on a litre of petrol is more fuel efficient than a similar car that runs only 10 kilometres on a litre. When all the mathematics, tables, graphs, models and regressions are peeled away, economics is revealed as common sense (Gwartney *et al.* 2005). Most of us make economic calculations in living our lives, though we may have never taken a course in economics. We try to make efficient use of our resources. Apples are expensive to day, so should I buy some other fruit? Should I pay more for a stylish jacket or buy a cheaper one that keeps me warmer? Should I go to the movies tonight or stay at home and study for my exam? Should I join a law firm where I will earn more money, or work for Legal Aid and gain more personal satisfaction? Should I give to Charity A or Charity B? How should I invest my savings? Sometimes we sacrifice our short-term interest to achieve long-term goals. Families avoid luxuries for a few years so they can collect a deposit to buy a house with a bank loan. In short, we try to work out our preferences, value them and make the best choice. If we normally try to make efficient decisions in our personal lives, we would expect the same of our governments and law makers. So, what is efficiency in economic calculation?

There are many ideas about economic efficiency. The one used most widely by law and economics scholars is 'Kaldor-Hicks efficiency', named after the economists who formulated the concept – Nicholas Kaldor and John Hicks. The Kaldor-Hicks concept is a refinement of 'Pareto efficiency', named after the Italian economist Vilfredo Pareto. Let us start with Pareto efficiency.

According to Pareto efficiency, an outcome is more efficient if at least one person is made better off and nobody is made worse off. Let us say that A wishes to sell a painting that she values at $1000. B likes it so much that he is happy to pay $2000. However, he offers $1500, which A accepts. Both parties are better off and neither is worse off. The transaction is Pareto efficient. If a law reduces the tax on petrol (gasoline) and the reduced revenue has no impact on any of the services provided by the state, the law will be Pareto efficient. Pareto *optimality* (the level of greatest efficiency) is reached when no further improvement can be made without making a single person worse off.

The problem is that, in the real world, an action that affects a large number of persons will hardly ever be Pareto efficient. A reduction in income tax will benefit most taxpayers, but the resulting loss of revenue is likely to be felt elsewhere by others who rely on social services or state employment. A reduction in import tariff will make consumers better off but local producers worse off. A noisy textile factory will benefit the community generally but will cause nuisance to those living nearby. Any major change is likely to make at least one person worse off. Kaldor and Hicks proposed a new definition of efficiency, taking account of this reality. A measure is Kaldor-Hicks efficient if *in theory*, those who are made better off can compensate all those who are worse off. Kaldor-Hicks efficiency does not require that every person adversely affected *must be compensated*, only that the gains made by the winners should be sufficient to compensate the losers. Australia had a state-owned telecommunications monopoly over a long period, until it was ended in 1997. Some employees lost their jobs and the government lost revenue. However, the value of the benefits that consumers gained by the entry of new companies far outweighed the losses. The important point to remember is that Kaldor-Hicks efficiency can and does leave some people worse off. This is the nature of the real world. The Kaldor-Hicks formula remains the economic principle underlying cost and benefits analysis of laws and policy.

Wealth and wealth maximisation

A basic premise of law and economics, and one closely related to efficiency, is wealth maximisation. Wealth maximisation, in its technical sense, is not the maximisation of individual wealth but the increase in the wealth of society as a whole. Robbers increase their wealth by robbing banks, but decrease the wealth of the banks and their customers. The effects of the robberies flow on to the community at large, as the banks spend more on security and pass on the costs to consumers. What is society's wealth, and how can it be measured?

Wealth is not utility, and wealth maximisation is not utility maximisation. Utility refers to the happiness a person gets out of having something. Happiness is impossible to measure. Hermits may be happy with bare sustenance, while millionaires may be unhappy with all their riches. What can be measured even roughly is what a person is prepared to pay for a thing. In technical language, this is the value of a thing to a person. Hence, wealth is measured by the value that persons place on goods and services. Value, as we have seen, is not the same as the price of a thing. A customer might be prepared to pay $100 for the table in our example, but it has already been sold for $80. Wealth, then, is the aggregate of the values that people attach to things from their point of view and in their personal circumstances. The quest for measuring social utility is abandoned in favour of social wealth.

Economic analysis of law takes as its guiding principle the maximisation of wealth, not of the individual but of society. The moral objections to this approach are considered at the end of this chapter.

Transaction costs and the law

If economic efficiency requires the comparison of costs and benefits, it is important to identify all the costs. One type of cost that remained unnoticed for a long time is transaction cost. Classical economic theory did not consider transaction costs in a serious way until the arrival of L & E. Transaction costs include all the costs incurred in completing a transaction.

Here is a common scenario. Driving through farm country you notice that farmers are selling apples at $2 per kilo, but you find that your local greengrocer sells apples of the same kind and quality for $3 per kilo. You might think that the greengrocer is making a big profit, but that is because you are taking no account of her transaction costs. Clearly the greengrocer (if she has bought at $2 per kilo) is making a profit of somewhere between $0 and $1 per kilo. She incurs all manner of transaction costs to bring the apples to the point of sale. She must find reliable suppliers, strike bargains regarding price, quality and quantity of the fruit and pay for the transport of the fruit to the store. If the fruit is found to be substandard, she has to find a way of recovering the loss, as a last resort by court action. The major part of transaction costs relates to finding trading partners and goods (information costs), bargaining with them (bargaining costs) and enforcing contracts (enforcement costs). The greengrocer must take account of all her transaction costs in fixing the price of her apples.

The modern L & E movement, with its emphasis on transaction costs, is widely thought to have started with Coase's ground-breaking article, 'The problem of social cost', published in 1960. Coase (b. 1910) is an English economist, a product of the London School of Economics, who migrated to the

United States in 1951. He taught at the University of Buffalo and the University of Virginia (where he wrote 'The problem of social cost') before commencing tenure at the Chicago Law School. He was awarded the Nobel Prize in Economic Science in 1991. Coase revealed the basic insight behind L & E, namely the existence of transaction costs, decades earlier in his article 'The nature of the firm', published in 1937 when he was still at the LSE (Coase 1937).

Firms produce a great proportion of the goods and services in a modern industrialised society. Firms include incorporated companies and partnerships. The publisher of this book is a firm. The university that employs me is a firm. My superannuation is managed by a firm. My local supermarket is a firm. My lawyer is a partner in a firm. Life in commercial society is full of dealings with firms. Coase asked why firms emerge at all in a market economy, where individuals can simply make contracts with others to obtain what they want (Coase 1937, 390). The reason, Coase argued, is transaction costs.

Consider the case of Bev the builder, who makes a living out of building houses for others. She needs to hire architects, concreters, carpenters, bricklayers, electricians, plumbers, accountants, cleaners and scores of other technicians. One way of obtaining these services in the open market is by making contracts with individual craftsmen. Bev might hire A to build the walls, B to tile the roof, C to do the plumbing, D to do the electrical wiring, and so forth. Bev finds this terribly frustrating because of the difficulty in finding reliable tradespeople and in negotiating contracts for specific jobs and suing the tradesmen when they don't deliver the promised services. In other words, she incurs a lot of 'transaction costs'. It makes more sense for Bev to employ some of these technicians on an ongoing basis on an agreed salary. She can simply fire them if they don't perform. Look at it from the point of view of, say, D the electrician. He too faces costs in finding people who need his services, in concluding contracts and in enforcing them. He also finds that his income rises and falls according to seasonal and other factors. It would make sense for him to become an employee in Bev's firm, with a guaranteed monthly income. Thus the firm expands to embrace all sorts of specialists. Bev is able to do the transactions within the firm, where she is boss, instead of doing them in the open market.

However, things may not stay that way. The firm may get so big that the cost of managing further transactions within the firm may exceed the cost of doing them in the open market. Or else Bev may find that there is wastage of the labour employed (Coase 1937, 394–5). Labour laws may increase the costs of employing workers. New technologies may reduce the cost of outsourcing jobs. (My university once employed a small army of cleaners, but now has engaged a cleaning company to clean our buildings. The university once did its own printing, but now uses a printing company. Some universities even outsource teaching on their off-shore campuses.) Most building companies these days prefer to use sub-contractors rather than employ their own skilled workers. The expansion and contraction of firms depends, ultimately, on transaction costs.

Coase's next major insights were that: (1) law has much to do with transaction costs; and (2) transaction costs spread to society as a whole. What may appear as a problem between two parties may actually have economic consequences for the wider community. Coase explained these insights through his searching analysis of common law decisions on nuisance.

Try to imagine a world with zero transaction costs. It will look very much like the world of Robinson Crusoe in Daniel Defoe's famous novel. Crusoe, the sole survivor of a shipwreck, finds himself on an uninhabited island. Since there is no one else on the island he commands all of its resources. Crusoe hunts animals and grows crops, builds a home and lives a life that is constrained only by the laws of nature. He has zero transaction costs because he has no one to transact with.[1] Crusoe lives in what Richard Epstein called the world of the single owner. 'The single owner knows his own preferences and the various distributions of resources under his command . . . His sole task is to order his own preferences and find the right techniques to satisfy them' (Epstein 1993, 556). Law has no meaning in a one-person world, as law is concerned with relations between persons.

Real societies have many persons interacting with each other. Coase argued that if there were no transaction costs it would not matter what the law was. If the law allowed me to pollute my neighbour's land with smoke, my neighbour could pay me to use cleaner fuels, re-tool my factory or even close it down. If the law prohibited me from polluting my neighbour's property, I could buy from her the right to pollute. Either way, we would bargain to the most efficient arrangement under which the activity that was valued most would continue. All that would be needed would be clear property rights and the freedom of contract. Consider the following concrete example. Assume that the law makes the owner of a factory liable for damage caused to neighbours by the factory's emissions. A owns a factory and B owns the adjoining farmland. The smoke from A's factory causes $10 000 worth of damage to B's crop. It is possible for A to prevent this damage by installing a smoke prevention device at a cost of $5000. Hence, it makes economic sense for A to install the device, as otherwise she will lose $10 000 in a damage payout. Now let us assume that the law is the reverse. A is not liable for damage caused by pollution from the factory. It makes sense for B to offer $5000 to A to install the device. In fact he may decide to offer $6000 as inducement. A is likely to accept the offer and install the device because B is bearing the cost and she is gaining a profit of $1000. B cuts his loss from $10 000 to $6000. In either case, the device will be installed and the efficient solution will be achieved. What if B does not have $6000 to pay A? This is not a serious problem, because he is saving a crop worth $10 000, so he can borrow the money against that value. We are assuming, of course, that transaction costs are zero and that the markets are working smoothly.

---

1 Crusoe is eventually joined by Friday, whom he rescues from a band of cannibals that use the island occasionally for human barbeque picnics, and later by Friday's father and a Spanish sailor whom Crusoe and Friday rescue on another occasion.

Coase's counterintuitive insight was to recognise the reciprocal nature of such problems:

> The question is commonly thought of as one in which A inflicts harm on B and what has to be decided is: how should we restrain A? But this is wrong. We are dealing with a problem of a reciprocal nature. To avoid the harm to B would inflict harm on A. The real question that has to be decided is: Should A be allowed to harm B or should B be allowed to harm A? The problem is to avoid the more serious harm. (Coase 1960, 2)

However, the real world is not free of transaction costs. Even in our simple example, the parties have to measure the extent of harm, agree on the dollar value and negotiate to reach a bargain. They also need to ensure that the bargain that is struck is carried out. It is usually very expensive to enforce the bargain if either party dishonours it. Just think of lawyers' fees! Again, if the pollution harms not just one neighbour but all persons residing within surrounding areas, it will be impossible to strike bargains with all of them. The problem may be caused by the cumulative effect of emissions from many factories and motor vehicles, making bargaining even more difficult. The existence of these transaction costs makes the initial allocation of rights matter.

Assume that the rule is that a factory owner must compensate every person harmed by the factory's emissions. Assume also that the factory is producing textiles used by the community at large. If the cost of striking bargains with every affected person is less than the benefit from being able to continue operating the factory, the owner will incur the bargaining cost and keep the factory running. If the bargaining cost is higher than the value gained by continued production, the factory owner is likely to close down the factory. The closure affects not only the factory owner but also the general public. Unless the common law courts (or the legislature) change the rule to limit the factory owner's liability the local production of textiles may cease permanently. This is the problem of social cost. The general point is that legal rules that allocate rights and duties have a critical bearing on the efficiency of the economic system. As Coase pointed out, where it is too costly to rearrange legal rights by market transactions, 'the courts directly influence economic activity' (1960, 19).

The problem of initial entitlements

According to the Coase theorem, in a zero transaction cost world it does not matter whether A has the right to pollute B's land or B has a right not to be polluted by A. If A has the right to pollute B can pay her to stop the pollution, and if A has a duty not to pollute she can pay B to acquire the right to pollute. In both cases, A and B will reach the most efficient solution and there will no cost imposed on society. In other words, in a zero transaction cost world the initial allocation of rights between A and B does not matter to society in an economic sense. Although there is no *social cost*, there will be a *private cost* to A or B depending on how the law allocates rights and duties. If A has a right to pollute, B will have to spend money to get A to stop the pollution, or endure the loss. If B has the right not to be polluted, A has to buy the right to pollute, or spend money to prevent the pollution. Initial entitlements matter in the real world.

The economic approach has been criticised for its alleged neglect of the issue of initial entitlements. This is not actually true, as a number of L & E scholars have addressed the issue. The contribution of Calabresi and Melamed in 'Property rules, liability rules and inalienability: one view of the cathedral' (1972) is seminal on this topic.

It is obvious that we cannot travel back in time and reset the initial property or liability arrangements. Such an attempt would take us all the way to the primordial existence of our hominid ancestors in small family groups. Even if a time-travelling machine was available today, such an attempt would be utterly futile as the entitlements that we established would soon change. We have no choice but to work from the current distribution of entitlements. Then we can consider questions like the efficiency or justice of the distribution and how entitlements can be protected or changed.

The logical first question is: why have entitlements at all? Imagine that there is a large and valuable area of land called Hundred Acres. No one has any right over this land, not even the state. There are 100 cattle producers who use this land to graze their cattle. Unless they all agree on a scheme of sharing the use of the land there will be conflict and the stronger will gain larger shares at the expense of the weaker. Might will become right. Now assume that the law provides that all persons have equal rights to enter and use Hundred Acres. A different problem arises which, in game theory, is known as the 'Tragedy of the Commons'. (This term was coined by Garrett Hardin in his article 'The tragedy of the commons' published in 1968 in the journal *Science*.) In this scenario, each of the cattle producers will try to increase their own gain (say, by raising more cattle), while the cost will be borne by all the cattle producers. Unless they agree to a scheme of fair and sustainable use, the land will be over-grazed and degraded. The tragedy of the commons is not just a theory; it happens. It is the reason that in many traditional societies the use of commons is regulated by custom, and in modern states by statutes. Over-fishing, over-hunting, unrestrained logging, unregulated irrigation are contemporary examples of limited resources being depleted by unlimited entitlement. The tragedy of the commons is averted by creating separate entitlements or property rights. Thus, there is a strong efficiency argument for establishing some form of property rights.

The next question concerns how entitlements are established or should be established. Calabresi and Melamed identified three possible principles: efficiency, distribution and other justice reasons.

Efficiency reasons

Some societies in history have embraced the idea that the most efficient way is to abolish private property and instead to have a government that administers all resources for the benefit of all the people. The system involves central planning and command and control of methods of plan implementation. Most of the societies that trialled the system have abandoned it. The chief reason for its failure is the inability of a central authority to command and deploy effectively all the knowledge of resources, needs and preferences of people. The administrative option is too inefficient.

Other societies have, to varying degrees, adopted the market mechanism, under which resources find their way to persons who most value them. The system will leave current entitlements as they are and try to reduce transaction costs that inhibit more efficient use of property. Consider the typical prosperous society of our age. Wealth is unequally distributed. Some people have inherited wealth and others have wealth created through their own skills and industry. This is not seen as a problem as long as there are no legal or other constraints on exchange transactions. The property owner who inherits a farm from a parent but has no interest in farming might sell the land to one who wants to farm it, and then use the money to invest or buy what she values. If the farmland has become unproductive, a property developer might buy it for a residential development. One way or another, according to the efficiency argument, the society will be better off.

Distributional reasons

Distributional reasons are all the reasons except efficiency reasons. Societies historically have distributed entitlements in different ways, not necessarily on grounds of efficiency. Plato and Aristotle justified the social stratification of their time, by which some human beings (slaves and women) were the property of others and status determined how property and wealth were distributed. Even today, some societies distribute entitlements according to caste or class status. Liberal democracies have progressively reduced the legal and social barriers to entitlements, but they have not embraced equality of wealth as a goal. As Calabresi and Melamed pointed out, absolute equality is impossible to achieve. If everyone has equal liberty to make noise, noise lovers will be better off than silence lovers. If everyone is entitled to the fruits of their labour, the more intelligent, skilful and industrious persons will become wealthier. Beautiful people will have advantages over those less well endowed (Calabresi & Melamed 1972, 1098–9). Equality of wealth can be maintained only by constant redistribution of wealth, which will be destructive of the incentives to create wealth.

Market oriented liberal-democratic states have usually engaged in limited forms of wealth redistribution. Most of them have recognised the notion of 'merit goods', which refers to the essential goods that a person needs to have a decent chance of improving their condition in an exchange economy. They include healthcare, education, housing and sustenance. This wealth redistribution is usually provided by free services and income supports funded through the tax system.

Other justice reasons

Calabresi and Melamed defined distributional reasons as all reasons that are not efficiency reasons. Hence, distributional reasons include justice reasons. In fact, most distributions that depart from efficiency are rationalised on grounds of justice. Plato and Aristotle defended a system of distributive justice that allocated wealth, public offices and honour according to merit. The virtuous and the wise person received more entitlements than the sinner and the fool. In modern society, demands for wealth redistribution are presented as claims for social justice. It not entirely clear what Calabresi and Melamed meant by 'other justice reasons'. An example that they provided is the entitlement to make noise or to have silence. Society might determine that the interest of the silence lover is more worthy than the interest of the noise lover. Calabresi and Melamed seemed to understand 'other justice reasons' as a subset of distributional reasons (1972, 1105).

Protection and regulation of entitlements

Most liberal democratic societies allocate entitlements variously on grounds of efficiency and distributional considerations. Allocations have little value unless they are protected by law. Ownership of a piece of land has value because the law of trespass and nuisance prevents others from interfering with its use. The liberty to drive on the highway is secured by road rules and the law of negligence. The right to personal safety is secured by the criminal law and tort law. Calabresi and Melamed identified three types of rule that protect entitlements:
1. property rules
2. liability rules
3. inalienability rules.

Property rules and liability rules

Property rules, as Calabresi and Melamed conceived them, protect entitlements in two ways: (a) they protect entitlements against all attacks through the criminal law; and (b) they enforce voluntary contracts by which entitlements are exchanged. In a world without transaction costs the property rules may be all that is required. In the real world people face two kinds of common problems: holdouts and free riding (see discussion below). Hence, there is a need for liability rules. The essential difference between property rules and liability rules boils down to this. Under property rules entitlements are transferred by voluntary contract. Under liability rules the state intervenes to bring about the transfer. Calabresi and Melamed argued that although property rules are usually more efficient, there are circumstances where prohibitive transaction costs prevent the achievement of the desired goal through contract. In some other cases contracting is simply not feasible. They give two examples to illustrate the argument: eminent domain and accident compensation.

The use of the eminent domain doctrine, according to Calabresi and Melamed, is more efficient than market transactions in a limited type of case where holdouts and free riding are likely. The doctrine of eminent domain (which is called 'compulsory purchase' in England and 'resumption' in Australia) allows the state to acquire private lands for public purposes on the payment of compensation determined by the state. In this hypothetical case, the residents of a town desiring a public park wish to buy an extent of land owned by several persons in equal parcels. If the townspeople value the land at $10 000 000 and the owners value it at $8 000 000, the transaction is likely to happen. However, one or more owners may hold out for a higher price, or one or more of the town residents may refuse to contribute their share of the purchase price, hoping for a free ride. If the cost of reaching unanimous agreement is too high the public park will not be established. This kind of problem can be overcome if the state compulsorily acquires the extent of land, at an administratively determined rate of compensation, and then sells it to the townsfolk (Calabrese & Melamed 1972, 1106–7). It is more efficient economically, but not necessarily more just. Some owners, for example, may value their parcels more highly because of sentimental reasons and they will not be justly compensated.

Most people live their lives without ever encountering eminent domain problems. However, the issue of compensation for accidental harm is ever present in our lives. I risk accidental harm every time that I drive out of my house. I might negligently cause damage to another motorist or a pedestrian, or suffer damage by the negligence of another road user. I cannot possibly know who I will hurt or who will hurt me. I also cannot know in advance how much damage I will cause to another, or how much damage I will suffer from another person's negligence. This is not something that can be contractually settled beforehand. I cannot make contracts with every other road user, stating: if you break my arm you should pay me $1000 and if you fracture my skull you must pay me $5000. The solution is provided by third-party determination of compensation if and when the accident occurs. The third party is usually a court or the legislature. In the common law system, the court determines the amount of compensation according to established precedents. In some cases, the legislature fixes rates of compensation, as in the case of workplace injuries.

Inalienability rules

An inalienable right is one that is regulated by law and cannot be waived or altered by contract. An inalienable right can be dealt with only as permitted by law. In every society there are laws that ban persons giving away particular entitlements or that limit the way a person can deal with their entitlements. In most societies people cannot sell themselves into slavery. Most societies ban trade in human organs. Many societies prohibit euthanasia that allows suffering patients to terminate their lives. Heritage laws prevent certain buildings being torn down or even modified. Conservation laws prevent certain lands being subdivided and ban owners from logging trees that they own. Animal protection laws prohibit cruel forms of animal sports. Minors are banned from buying alcoholic drinks or watching pornographic movies. The list goes on.

Conservation limits placed on land use may be seen as a way of preventing environmental harm to the community at large. Since the harm is difficult to cost in relation to each individual, liability rules are unhelpful. The goal can be achieved by a prohibition. Sometimes the harm to others cannot be measured in money, as in the case of cruelty to animals or selling oneself to slavery. These kinds of acts harm others by shocking their conscience or moral sense. The harm is real, but immeasurable. Inalienability rules are seen as more efficient in these cases. Calabresi and Melamed pointed out that inalienability rules often have distributional effects: 'Prohibiting the sale of babies makes poorer those who can cheaply produce babies and richer those who by some non market device get free an "unwanted" baby' (1972, 1114). Laws that create parklands within towns make nearby house owners better off but will make land more scarce and expensive for others.

Choosing between property rule and liability rule

Calabresi and Melamed used their analysis to consider, from an efficiency point of view, when a court should apply the property rule and when it should use the liability rule. Consider the pollution case where P (the plaintiff) sues D (the defendant) over damage caused to P's crop by D's factory. There are four possible judgments the court can make:

1.   D must not pollute P's property unless P allows it. The court will grant an injunction to P and P acquires a tradable right. He may be paid by D in return for giving D permission to pollute. The court has chosen the *property rule*. This rule is efficient where it is cheaper for D to prevent the pollution than for P to do so.

2.   D may pollute but must compensate P for the damages caused. Here the court applies the *liability rule*. It holds that D commits nuisance, but awards only court-determined damages. This option is more efficient where there are many persons affected by pollution, i.e. there are many Ps. The transaction costs of getting the agreement of all victims are very high and some of them may hold out for more. The liability rule overcomes the problems of holdouts and free riding.

3.   D may pollute at will and can only be stopped if P buys the right from D. The court applies the property rule, but in D's favour. D can trade off her pollution right. This is more efficient where P is in a better position to prevent the harm.

4.   P may stop D from polluting, but if he does he must compensate D. The court applies the liability rule, but in favour of D. Calabresi and Melamed illustrated a case where this rule would be the most efficient. A factory in a rich neighbourhood uses cheap coal. It also employs many poor workers. Under Rules 1 and 2, the factory is likely to shut down and workers will lose their jobs. Rule 3 will be efficient if the harm to the rich homeowners

is greater than the cost of switching to clean coal. The homeowners can agree to buy off D. However if there are holdout problems among the homeowners, it will be more efficient for the court to calculate the cost of switching to clean coal and impose it on the homeowners as damages under Rule 4. The problem with Rule 4 is that very few common law courts would claim to have power to make such strange orders.

The Calabresi and Melamed article provides an analytical framework that assists courts and law makers to understand more clearly the choice of rules available to them. They may sacrifice efficiency for distributional or social justice reasons, but do so with a better understanding of potential costs.

Efficiency of the common law hypothesis

The efficiency of the common law hypothesis postulates that the common law system tends to produce more efficient rules than legislatures would. This was first suggested in Coase's article, 'The problem of social cost', and the view was later developed by Posner and others. Most judges would be surprised to hear that economics plays an important part in their decisions. They hardly ever talk about economics in their judgments and always try to rationalise their decisions by reference to precedent, logic and common sense. Coase, Posner and others in the L & E tradition think that judicial common sense is actually a form of economic thinking. In fact, Coase believed that common law judges are more aware than some economists of the 'reciprocal nature of the problem', and that 'they take economic implications into account, along with other factors, in arriving at their decisions' (1960, 19). The courts may not use economic language but the economic aspects of the judgment are revealed by the use of concepts such as 'reasonable use' or 'common or ordinary use' of land (Coase 1960, 22). As Coase demonstrated, this is particularly evident in nuisance cases where courts have taken into consideration the character of the locality. If a person takes up residence in an industrial neighbourhood and complains of disturbance by plant and machinery, the court is likely to be unsympathetic. Similarly, a court refused to stop a building operation to preserve the peace and quiet of a nearby hotel (*Andreae v Selfridge & Co* [1938] 1 CH 1). Conversely, in *Sturges v Bridgman* (1879) 11 Ch D 852, the court stopped a confectioner from disturbing a doctor's consultation room next door, although the confectioner had been using his machinery for 60 years before the doctor moved in. The court in that case seemed to think that the neighbourhood was residential rather than industrial, and judgment for the confectioner would have discouraged residential development.

Judge Posner, who has done more systematic study of the economics of common law than any other writer, has noted:

> Many areas of the law, especially but not only the great common law fields of property, torts, crimes and contracts, bear the stamp of economic reasoning. Granted, few judicial opinions contain explicit references to economic concepts. But often the true

grounds of legal decision are concealed by the characteristic rhetoric of opinions. Indeed, legal education consists primarily of learning to dig beneath the rhetorical surface to find those grounds, many which may turn out to have an economic character. (1998, 27)

The economic undertones are also noticeable in the way lawyers argue their cases. Lawyers support their interpretations of established law on grounds of public policy and not private sympathy. They will say that their interpretation yields the best outcome for society generally, and will rarely appeal for sympathy for the client. Poverty does not release a person from legal obligations.

Why would common law judges consciously or subconsciously promote economic efficiency in making or modifying rules of law? An easy answer is that judges, who are drawn from a class of society that is naturally partial to commerce and industry, favour economically efficient solutions. In short, judges have a capitalist bias. There is almost certainly some historical truth in this. As Posner pointed out, the common law acquired much of its modern shape during the 19th century, when *laissez faire* thinking was ascendant in England (1998, 275). However, Posner argued that the common law system tends to promote efficiency, irrespective of judges' personal views.

Efficiency promoted by judicial neutrality

Posner and others have argued that the neutrality of the court tends to favour efficient rule making. Common law judges are limited by the scope of the cases and the claims presented to them. They cannot engage in redistributing wealth in the way that legislatures do. The common law judge's duty is to restore the parties to the position they would have been in had the breach of the law not occurred. In other words, a common law judge dispenses rectificatory justice and not distributive justice. This means that the courts can only grant compensatory damages. A drives his car negligently into B's car. B has to spend $1000 to restore the car to its pre-collision state. The court will award B only the sum that she spent, and perhaps other incidental costs. The court will not consider extraneous matters such as the personal character of A, the income levels of the two parties or the deservedness of A or B.

Common law as a general rule does not permit judges to award punitive or exemplary damages. Punitive damages are sums awarded to the plaintiff, in addition to the plaintiff's actual loss, as a way of punishing the defendant or deterring the defendant from future wrongdoing. This means that the court does not actually compel persons to observe the law, but only makes defendants pay the opportunity costs of plaintiffs if they choose to violate the plaintiffs' rights. In a contract for the sale of goods, the seller is not compelled to deliver the goods but only to pay damages if she does not. The seller may decide not to deliver the goods but to pay damages, if the damages are less than what she gains by retaining the goods. Posner argued: 'If that price is lower than the value the violator derives from the unlawful act, efficiency is maximised if he commits it, and the legal system in effect encourages him to do so' (1998, 565). The point here is that in the usual case, the common law of contract and tort imitates the market. The contract, in essence, says: deliver the goods or compensate the buyer's loss. The court simply determines the fact of non-delivery and the amount of the buyer's loss. One may ask: if that is the case, why do sellers usually deliver their goods as promised, even when they are able to gain a better price elsewhere? The obvious reason is that a seller who acquires a reputation for unreliability will soon be without customers. This is a cost that the seller has to consider, but the court leaves that decision to the seller.

A court that engages in distributive justice makes political decisions, and hence will not be seen as impartial. Such a court will soon lose its credibility and public confidence. This is the basic reason why courts leave questions of redistribution to the legislature. The law in different ways secures the impersonality and impartiality of the judicial process. In many countries courts have constitutionally guaranteed independence. The rules of natural justice militate against bias and arbitrariness. Common law courts are further insulated from pressure group politics by the rules concerning standing and costs. Under common law rules of standing, a citizen can sue or intervene in an action only to vindicate a private right – that is, a right that the person has over and above the right that every member of the public has. (See, for example, *Australian Conservation Foundation v Commonwealth* (1979) 146 CLR 493, 526–7.) In common law countries such as the United Kingdom, Australia and New Zealand, the party that loses the case has to pay the litigation costs of the party that wins. This means that the person who brings an action thinks that they have more to lose by inaction than the potential cost of losing the action. It also means that the party who elects to defend an action calculates that they have more to lose by conceding the claim. The point that Posner and others make is that the exclusion of busybodies and political activists insulates the courts from distortions that interest group politics can introduce to the judicial process.

Posner believes that the adversarial nature of the common law procedure, which mimics market operations, also promotes impartiality. The case is essentially a private contest between self-interested combatants. The responsibility for presenting the two sides of the case with evidence and legal submissions rests with the parties and their lawyers. The 'invisible hand of the market has its counterpart in the aloof disinterest of the judge' (Posner 1998, 566). A party may be disappointed by a decision but has no reason for personal grievance against the judge. Posner likened this to a customer who fails to find what he is looking for in a shop. The customer may be disappointed but has no reason to be angry at the shopkeeper. This analogy is not exact. The customer in the marketplace can shop around and find what he wants, but the litigant cannot go forum shopping. The former has a choice, but not the latter.

Posner concluded that, since courts are inhibited from redistributing wealth, they focus on expanding wealth:

If, therefore, common law courts do not have effective tools for redistributing wealth – in other words, reslicing the economic pie among contending interest groups – it is to the benefit of all interest groups that courts, when they are enforcing common law principles rather than statutes, should concentrate on making the pie larger. (1998, 571)

Evolutionary explanation of common law efficiency

In every law school introductory course, students are taught the way the common law develops through precedent setting by the appeal courts. They are trained to separate the *ratio decidendi* (the principle or rule that decides the case) from *obiter dicta* (incidental remarks). Most importantly, students are asked to distinguish present cases from established common law rules and to understand how the courts adapt or modify existing law to new conditions. In other words, students are introduced to the mechanics of the evolution of law.

A rule that is efficient may become inefficient under new conditions. It is natural that the people who have to bear the cost of this inefficiency will seek to persuade the court to change the rule. Here is a good example. The doctrine of privity of contract and the doctrine of consideration set out two fundamental rules of the English law of contract. The doctrine of privity states that a contract cannot confer rights or obligations on any person who is not a party to the contract. The doctrine also states that only a party to a contract can sue under the contract. This is common sense and works efficiently most of the time. If not for this doctrine, everybody would be at risk of having duties imposed upon them by the contracts of others. However, it is clearly unjust in some kinds of cases. If A agrees with B to pay B's mother C a sum of money in return for some service B provides, and A fails to pay, C cannot sue to recover the sum. B can sue, but only if she herself has suffered some loss by A's failure to pay C. The efficiency of the doctrine of consideration is even less clear. According to this doctrine, a contract is not valid if no value (consideration) is owed by each party to the other party. D's promise to E to pay a sum of money has no force unless E owes something to D under the contract. It is noteworthy that in civil law countries, the contract system works efficiently without the requirement of consideration.

It is the practice in the building industry for a building company to take out an insurance policy that covers not only the building company but also all its sub-contractors and suppliers who enter the building site. A worker employed by a sub-contractor was injured and the sub-contractor had to pay out a substantial personal injury claim. The insurer refused to indemnify the sub-contractor because he was not a party to the insurance contract and had not provided consideration. It was evident that these two rules were no longer consistent with the expectations of people in the building industry, and that if enforced they would impose major costs on the industry. In *Trident General Insurance Co Ltd v McNiece Bros Pty Ltd* (1987) 165 CLR 107, the High Court of Australia recognised the economic reality and modified the doctrines to allow the sub-contractor to be indemnified. If the court had held for the insurer, the cost to the industry would have led to the precedent being challenged again and again or being overturned by statute.

The first modern writer to recognise the evolutionary efficiency of the common law was FA Hayek, who argued that common law is an adaptive system that gives effect to the expectations established within the community (1973, 96–7). Some economists, though, doubted the tendency of the common law to evolve towards efficiency. They reasoned that most parties settle their disputes outside court because of the high cost of litigation, so inefficient rules remain in the law (Landes 1971; Gould 1973; Tullock 1971). Paul Rubin argued that sufficient economic incentives remain for litigants to seek revision of inefficient rules. This would be the case especially when a rule imposes continuing costs on a particular segment of society, such as government agencies, firms, labour unions or insurance companies (Rubin 1977, 53). If, for example, a rule placed an unusually heavy burden of care on doctors, in excess of the normal practices and procedures of the profession, there would be a strong incentive for doctors and their insurers to have the rule changed by repeated litigation. Trade unions would have strong economic reasons to seek to change factory accident liability rules in their favour. A government that had a railway monopoly might wish to limit its liability for lost property. In Australia, the media had strong economic reasons to have the common law defence of qualified privilege (to an action for defamation) extended to cover political communications. They succeeded in *Theophanous v Herald & Weekly Times Ltd* (1994) 182 CLR 211. Rubin concluded that the evolutionary pressure towards efficiency comes from the behaviour of litigants rather than judges. (If people do not litigate judges have no cases to decide.) He drew the following conclusions from his cost-benefit analysis of accident liability cases (1977, 61):

1. When neither party is interested in precedent, there is no incentive to litigate and hence no pressure on the law to change.
2. When only one party is interested, that party will litigate until a favourable decision is obtained; the law in such cases favours parties with such an ongoing interest.
3. When both parties have an ongoing interest in a type of case, there will be pressure toward efficiency.

GL Priest, who generally agreed with Rubin, developed a stronger version of the evolutionary thesis. He argued that efficient legal rules are more likely to endure regardless of the attitudes of individual judges or the disinterest of litigants about the allocative effects of rules. Let us assume (falsely) that most judges are opposed to efficient rules. Yet more disputes arise under inefficient rules than under efficient rules, because inefficient rules place greater costs on those who must obey them. Therefore, inefficient rules are more likely than efficient rules to be relitigated. The courts hear more cases involving inefficient rules than efficient rules. Thus, efficient rules are more likely to remain outside the reach of judges. Priest concluded that 'as a consequence, judges will be unable to influence the content of the law to fully reflect their attitude towards inefficiency' (1977, 65).

Public choice theory: the economics of legislation

The common law is not the sole source of law in modern society. The evolution of the law through common law adjudication is a slow process. A court cannot address a question of law until it arises in an appropriate case, and this may take a long time. The common law method is also unsuitable for the making of laws establishing and regulating government departments and agencies.

The common law method has another serious limitation. When a common law court makes a change to the law, it has retrospective effect. It changes the legal rights of the parties to the action, as well as the rights of other persons who are not before the court. The common law court cannot change the law to take effect only in the future. This is the reason that common law courts do not usually make radical changes, but only make changes that people have anticipated because of changed social conditions. The decision of the High Court of Australia in *Mabo v Queensland (No. 2)* (1992) 175 CLR 1 overturned a long standing precedent to recognise the validity of customary land rights of Australia's indigenous peoples. The decision corrected historic injustices on indigenous peoples, but it had far reaching effects on property rights of persons who were not before the courts. The High Court could not sort out the many consequences of its decision and it was left to the Australian Parliament to enact detailed legislation to settle the law in the field.

Legislation therefore has a major role in modern society. Legislatures, though, do not limit themselves to the making of general rules, but engage in reallocating or redistributing wealth in ways that courts cannot achieve. A branch of economics known as public choice theory is focused on studying legislative processes to understand the economics of democratic law making. Public choice theory is closely identified with a group of economists led by James Buchanan and Gordon Tullock of the George Mason University in Virginia, and Mancur Olson of the University of Maryland at College Park. Buchanan received the Nobel Prize in Economic Science in 1986 for his pioneering work in this field. Buchanan and Tullock's *The Calculus of Consent* and Olson's *The Logic of Collective Action* stand out as classics in the field.

If a decision affects only two parties, the parties can reach a mutually acceptable agreement. If the decision of two parties affects (has an externality on) third parties, ideally their agreement should also be obtained. In other words, unanimity is the best way to reach the best outcome for all concerned. However, unanimity is not possible when a society needs to take collective decisions affecting the whole population or large sections of it. As we have seen, the cost of negotiation even within small groups can be prohibitive because of holdout and free rider problems, and even the problem of finding all the persons who are affected by the decision. Liberal-democratic societies therefore elect representative legislatures and governments to make decisions for the good of society. It is generally accepted that democratic processes are imperfect, and that elected representatives often act in their self-interest or the interest of their supporters as opposed to the interests of the general public. They are known to act on short-term political expediency rather than longer term public good. Yet most people also accept that representative government is better than the alternatives. Public choice theorists have confirmed these intuitive impressions of democratic institutions and provided new insights about the way collective decisions are made. Among their most interesting findings are those concerning the phenomena of *logrolling* and *rent seeking*.

Logrolling

The studies of public choice economists have cast doubts on the genuineness of democratic collective choices, through their exposure of the way in which majority coalitions are formed under simple majority voting systems. Public choice theorists argue that majority coalitions tend to grow out of distributional struggles for shares of the social pie, which often produce bargains among interest groups pursuing different ends. These 'distributional coalitions', as Olson called them, represent collective choice only in the limited sense of producing legislative majorities (Olson 1982, 44). The reality is that decisions are made through vote trading – or in American parlance, 'logrolling'.

According to Buchanan and Tullock, logrolling takes one of two forms. First, it occurs within legislative bodies, where legislators trade votes to achieve their separate purposes. Senator A will vote for Senator B's proposed farm subsidy scheme in exchange for Senator B's support for Senator A's proposal to limit textile imports. The second form of logrolling occurs in the electorate at large. Political parties present competing policy packages to the electorate, each calculated to secure a winning combination of different voter groups. They will typically offer benefits to critically important voting blocs such as pensioners or families with young children. Voters who stand to gain a large personal benefit (say from an increased pension or a special subsidy) may vote for a party whose program they oppose in other respects. Buchanan and Tullock put it this way:

> Logrolling may occur in a second way, which we shall call implicit logrolling. Large bodies of voters may be called on to decide on complex issues, such as which party will rule or which set of issues will be approved in a referendum vote. Here there is no formal trading of votes, but an analogous process takes place. Political 'entrepreneurs' who offer candidates or programs to voters make up a complex mixture of policies

designed to attract support. In doing so they keep firmly in mind the fact that the single voter may be so interested in the outcome of a particular issue that he will vote for the one party that supports this issue, although he may be opposed to the party stand on all other issues. Institutions described by this implicit logrolling are characteristic of much of the modern democratic procedure. (1962, 134–5)

Olson's work on group behaviour also challenged the conventional theory that particular distributions made by legislatures are the results of genuine collective choice. In *The Logic of Collective Action* Olson argued that smaller, homogeneous groups tend to prevail in the distributional struggle. Even more significantly, Olson claimed that larger interest groups emerge because of the application of 'selective incentives', such as compulsion (negative), or the offer of private benefits (positive) as inducements for joining and sharing the cost of lobbying enterprises (1965, 133–4). Olson argued that in large groups (such as consumers), where an individual's contribution makes no perceptible difference to the group as a whole or to the burden or benefit of any single member, there will be no cooperative effort to pursue a common interest unless there is coercion or some outside inducement (1965, 44). In his later work, *The Rise and Decline of Nations* (1982, 37), Olson summarised the implications of this finding for democracy:

[A] society that would achieve either efficiency or equity through comprehensive bargaining is out of the question. Some groups such as consumers, tax payers, the unemployed, and the poor do not have either the selective incentive or the small numbers needed to organize, so they would be left out of the bargaining. It would be in the interest of those groups that are organized to increase their own gains by whatever means possible. This would include choosing policies that, though inefficient for the society as a whole, were advantageous for the organized groups because the costs of the policies fell disproportionately on the unorganized. (In the language of the game theorist, the society would not achieve a 'core' or Pareto-efficient allocation because some of the groups were, by virtue of their lack of organization unable to block changes detrimental to them or to work out mutually advantageous bargains with others.) With some groups left out of the bargaining, there is also no reason to suppose that the results have any appeal on grounds of fairness.

The general findings of Buchanan, Tullock, Olson and others may be summarised in another way. Even if it is assumed that a legislative majority on a particular question represents a popular majority on a question of policy, such majority is likely to include large numbers who dislike the policy but nevertheless support it as the price for obtaining a majority on some other policy that they value more. Thus, in respect of measures aimed at producing collective goods or material outcomes, there is little likelihood of genuine majority agreement, except in the rare instances where individuals, or the community as a whole, receive a roughly equal gain without costs accruing disproportionately to particular classes.

Rent seeking

Economic rent refers to gains made without productive effort and not through mutually beneficial exchange. It is different from the rent that a house owner charges a tenant under a tenancy agreement. In a tenancy there are benefits to both parties. In its technical economic sense, rent seeking occurs when a person or group gains a benefit under the law while the cost is borne by other sections of society or the public at large. If a company gains a monopoly to supply a product, it makes monopoly profits while the consumers bear the rise in cost that results from the elimination of competition. The farm lobby that persuades the legislature to restrict imports gains the benefit of extra profit without extra effort. All kinds of regulations can impose social costs without social benefit.

Assume that product X can be legally manufactured only under a licence issued by a government authority. The authority grants a licence to A, subject to the condition that A's factory is located in a town some distance from the port from which A must transport imported raw materials. A may decide to take his plant to the town because his additional cost can be recovered by increasing the price of his product. The value of the licence is worth more than the added transport costs. The transport cost is a wasteful impost on the community unless there is a compensating benefit. Some benefit may flow to the townsfolk through increased employment, but its cost is borne by others. In all these cases there is a social cost. Resources that may be used for the greater benefit of society are expended on unproductive distribution.

The kinds of economic rents that regulations can create vary. They include unnecessary qualifications or assets stipulated by the regulator, and the expenses of lobbying regulators. In some countries, regulations lead to enormous corruption in the form of bribery. An authority can get rich simply by requiring a licence to do what is otherwise lawful.

Efficiency, wealth maximisation and justice

The economic approach of the L & E school has critics on both the left and the right of the ideological spectrum. On the right, scholars of the Austrian school of economics reject efficiency as a basis for judicial determination of property rights. They have several objections. First, judges have no competence to determine questions of costs. Second, if judges select rules on the basis of efficiency in different kinds of cases, as suggested by Coase, Calabresi and others, the law will become uncertain. Third, efficiency analysis is based on a misunderstanding of the market process. It assumes that the world is in a state of equilibrium, whereas it actually changes over time. Markets are a process of discovery, and the best means of facilitating discovery is to have firm property rules. Fourth, determining entitlements according to efficiency is simply immoral.

The last argument is noteworthy. The Coase theorem claims that in a zero transaction cost world it does not matter whether a factory owner has the right to damage her neighbour's crop or the neighbour has the right not to have his crop damaged. Walter Block asked the question: what would happen if the damage is not to a commercial crop but to the neighbour's garden that he treasures for sentimental reasons? The plants in the garden may be commercially valueless, so he cannot possibly raise a loan to pay the factory owner to stop the pollution (Block 1977, 111–12). A more telling example is Harold Demsetz's claim that it does not matter whether the state (taxpayers) hires volunteers into the military or the state (taxpayers) conscripts them and allows them to buy their way out of the military; the same persons will end up in the military (1967, 348). Wrong, said Block. There may be pacifists who simply do not want to fight but have no money to buy out of the military. Besides, the conscription alternative amounts to first enslaving or kidnapping a person and then demanding a ransom for release! (Block 1977, 112) One option is moral and the other immoral. Block wrote: 'It is evil and downright vicious to violate our most cherished and precious property rights in an ill conceived attempt to maximise the monetary value of production' (1977, 115).

Ronald Dworkin, a liberal in the social democratic sense, made a similar argument. Dworkin's essential point is this. A person against whom judgment is given should have done something wrong. 'So, decisions can be justified only by deploying some general scheme of moral responsibility the members of the community might properly be deemed to have, about not injuring others, or about taking financial responsibility for their acts' (Dworkin 1998, 285). In doing or not doing something we are guided by moral or legal rules. I have a right to play my trumpet and my neighbour has a right to study algebra in silence. In this situation, I would play the instrument softly or at times when my neighbour is not studying. I exercise restraint not because I calculate the relative costs of playing or not playing but because I respect the 'live and let live' morality that underlies nuisance law. This is not denied by L & E scholars. However, if the conflict has occurred and the court is asked to resolve it, how should it give judgment? The L & E view is that (assuming that neither the trumpet player nor the student has an inalienable right) it makes more sense for the court to make an efficient ruling. The 'efficiency of the common law hypothesis' predicts that in the long run the courts in fact gravitate to efficient rulings.

Many critics on the left present a different argument – that maximising wealth does not make society necessarily better off. In the example that we considered earlier, the carpenter who built the table made a profit, the rich customer who bought it gained value but the student who needed it most could not have it. The transaction made society wealthier by the economic calculus, but perhaps not better off in a moral sense. The argument against wealth maximisation is an argument for social justice in the sense of fairer distribution of wealth.

L & E scholars have two general answers. First, they concede that efficiency is an important consideration, but not the only consideration. Legislatures commonly – and courts less commonly – make rules dictated by moral, ideological or partisan reasons. Efficiency analysis is still useful, as it informs judges and legislators of the economic trade-offs that are involved in doing so. Second, they give pragmatic reasons for embracing wealth maximisation as a guide to law making. They claim that societies whose laws are more conducive to wealth maximisation have done better economically. More importantly, as Posner suggested, 'wealth maximisation may be the most direct route to a variety of moral ends' (1990, 382).

10

Evolutionary Jurisprudence

Like the winds, that come we know not whence, and blow withersoever
they list, the forms of society are derived from an obscure and distant
origin; they arise, long before the date of philosophy, from the instincts,
not from the speculations, of men. The croud of mankind, are directed in
their establishments and measures, by the circumstances in which they
are placed; and seldom are turned from their way, to follow the plan of
any single projector.

Adam Ferguson (1966 (1767), 122)

Introduction

The second half of the 20th century witnessed a resurgence of evolutionary theory
in both the natural sciences and the social sciences. The most significant feature
of this movement has been the extension of the Darwinian theory of evolution –
or, more accurately, the neo-Darwinian synthesis – to human culture in order
to explain such phenomena as scientific and technological development, the
emergence of formal and informal social institutions, language acquisition, and
even mind and consciousness. Evolutionary accounts of legal emergence have
figured prominently throughout the 20th century in cultural anthropology and
within branches of economics, most notably the Austrian and the institutional
economics traditions. Although American jurisprudence was quick to embrace
evolution after Darwin, legal scholars in the 20th century have only paid spo-
radic attention to evolutionary accounts of law (Ruhl 1996a, 1412–13). The
situation has changed somewhat with the persistent efforts in law and biology
by scholars associated with the Gruter Institute for Law and Behavioral Research
(Elliot 1997, 596) and the nascent complexity and law movement (Ruhl 1996a,
1996b). Outstanding work is also flowing from the efforts of Owen Jones and
his colleagues at the Society for the Evolutionary Analysis of Law (SEAL) based
in the Vanderbilt University (Jones 1999, Jones and Goldsmith 2005). However,
this body of learning has yet to establish its presence in mainstream law school
curricula.

It is not widely appreciated that the recent blossoming of the evolutionary theory of culture has a distinguished pedigree that pre-dated Darwin's breakthrough and, indeed, provided Darwin with the intellectual tools that helped him to uncover the idea of natural selection (Hayek 1982, 1, 152–3). The work of these pre-Darwin scholars is particularly significant in legal theory as they drew their greatest inspiration from the shining example of the common law, and proceeded to establish a solid foundation for an evolutionary jurisprudence. The recent developments in evolutionary scholarship allow us to build on this foundation a richer account of law in both its customary and statutory forms. Such a jurisprudence may be developed by drawing together the 18th century evolutionist thought, the neo-Darwinist synthesis, evolutionary epistemology, the emerging science of complexity and self-organisation and the central ideas developed in institutional economics. That task is beyond the scope of this chapter, but I hope to kindle interest in such a project by clarifying the central ideas of the 18th century evolutionists and assessing their relevance in the era of pervasive legislation in the light of recent developments in the aforementioned fields. In what follows, I will discuss the key ideas of the 18th century evolutionary viewpoint, consider the development of that viewpoint in the 20th century and draw some normative implications from the evolutionary approach.

The need for an evolutionary jurisprudence

The idea that all law stems from the will of an identifiable law maker remains influential, despite being contradicted by the natural history of the human race and by what we know of contemporary society. It would be a rare cultural anthropologist who would deny that law existed before there were legislators or courts. Although legislation and judicial precedents form the major sources of law today, it is evident that law formation is a complex and dynamic process grounded in social realities that are beyond the comprehensive control of any authority. Despite its best efforts, the state has failed to monopolise the enterprise of law. As the frontiers of human experience expand, rules become modified by practice to meet the coordination needs of the new field of experience. This phenomenon has been observed throughout history and is illustrated in our age by the continuing evolution of the common law and the emergence of new rules of behaviour in fields such as transnational commerce and new technologies.

Mainstream jurisprudence typically responds to the presence of such rules by ignoring them, by denying them the name 'law' or by treating them as the vicarious achievements of the official legal system. Jurisprudence that limits its concerns to the description of state law and consigns non-state law to other disciplines admits failure. Sophisticated analytical positivists such as Herbert Hart, Neil MacCormick and Joseph Raz abandoned the dogma that law is any command of a sovereign political authority that has capacity to enforce its commands, in favour of the idea of a legal system that establishes the ways in which norms become laws that attract the coercive attention of the state. However, the concept of a legal system developed by these writers does not explain satisfactorily the nature of the legal system as part of the overall dynamic order of society. In particular, it leaves to other disciplines the following questions: (1) how do legal systems arise and change over time? (2) how do we account for the continuing emergence of rules that not only exist side by side with state law but also supply some of the normative content of new state law? It is proposed that these questions should be addressed within jurisprudence and that the evolutionary approach outlined in this chapter is appropriate to that task.

Argument from design versus the principle of the accumulation of design

The human intellect tends to divide the world into two categories, the natural and the artificial, with nothing in between. Structures like machines, buildings and organisations are identified as artificial because they are products of human intelligence and labour. Other physical and biological structures that were not created by human beings – such as rivers and mountains, planets and animals – are classed as natural things. The diversity, complexity and beauty of nature, particularly the way plants and animals fit their environments, have intrigued thinkers through the ages. Who or what brought about these amazing adaptations? The minds of our ancient ancestors could only come up with the anthropomorphic answer that they were the work of a supernatural Intelligent Artificer. Hume's Cleanthes, in the *Dialogues Concerning Natural Religion*, put it this way: 'The curious adapting of means to ends throughout all nature, resembles exactly, though it much exceeds, the productions of human contrivance; of human design, thought, wisdom, and intelligence . . . hence we are led to infer . . . that the Author of nature is somewhat similar to the mind of man' (1947 (1779), 143).

This argument from design would not have mattered much in legal theory had there not been three different types of law: (1) legislation, (2) customary law, and (3) higher natural law. Legal enactments of human agencies were considered artificial, and later came to be known as positive law. There was another kind of law that had existed from time immemorial with no evidence of human authorship. Every society, including the oldest, has its inheritance of laws that cannot be attributed to human legislators. The ancients had little choice but to assign these to the natural category. Hayek thought that the Greeks recognised a separate category of structures established by convention, which included things such as custom, law, language, morals and money, only to lose it in terminological confusion. This category comprised things that were neither natural nor artificial but were, as Ferguson described, 'indeed the result of human action, but not the execution of any human design' (1966 (1767), 122). There was certainly another close encounter with this third kind of law by the later medieval schoolmen, but they, like the Greeks before them, eventually classed it as natural (Hayek 1982, 1, 20–1). Whichever way the law was classified, it was thought to have been designed, like everything else.

The classification of the inherited customary law with things natural created two major problems for legal theory. As mentioned, there was a third type of law with a long standing claim to the name 'natural law'. This natural law comprised the fundamental, universal, and immutable principles of justice and morality, the violation of which was said to deprive human (positive) laws of their validity – on the principle that unjust law is not law (*lex injusta non est lex*) or, alternatively, that it is the corruption of law (*non lex sed legis corruptio*). The first problem was that the equation of the inherited customary law with this higher unchanging natural law further obscured the evolutionary nature of customary law. Custom was adaptive, not immutable like the higher natural law. The second problem was that this classification suggested that customary law, being natural law, was inviolable by human legislators. This was incompatible with the legislative power of sovereign rulers, who could set aside customary law by legislative acts. In societies where legislation is uncommon and customary morality and customary law are hard to separate, the problem is not serious. It is very different where the ruler's power to make and unmake the law co-exists with a substantial body of inherited customary law (common law), as was the case in England. Hobbes and Locke, the 17th century social contract theorists, recognised this problem. Their response was to move customary law from the category of the natural to the artificial. Earlier custom was regarded as the work of a supernatural mind, but now it was the work of human law makers. Though the classification had changed, the argument from design remained.

Both Hobbes and Locke thought that law began only with the establishment of sovereign political authority by the social contract that brought society itself into existence. Indeed, the very purpose of the social contract, they said, was to escape the condition of lawlessness, which according to Hobbes made life 'solitary, poor, nasty, brutish and short' (Hobbes 1946, 82). Locke's state of nature was a little more benign, but still 'full of fears and continual dangers' (1960, 368) because, in the absence of established and known laws and organised executive power, each individual was their own law maker, judge and executioner (1960, 369). According to both theorists, the social contract established a supreme legislature to which was entrusted the exclusive power to make law. Though both believed in the existence of a higher natural law, they insisted that the only source of human law was the sovereign person or assembly. Locke denied custom any legal force, treating the legislature as antecedent to all positive law (1960, 373–4). According to Hobbes, customs were 'antiently Lawes written, or otherwise made known, for the Constitutions, and Statutes of their Soveraigns; and are now Lawes, not by vertue of the Praescription of time, but by the Constitutions of their present Soveraigns' (1946, 175). Hobbes insisted that law should not only be designed but, to be valid, its designer or Author should be sufficiently known

(1946, 178). Thus, with respect to law, social contract theory further entrenched the argument from design.

It is generally thought that until Charles Darwin and Alfred Russell Wallace stumbled upon the idea of the evolution of species by natural selection, there was no alternative to the argument from design. The basic idea of natural selection is very simple, though its implications are endless. Animals give birth to offspring who have varying qualities. Offspring who are better adapted to their environment tend to survive to produce more offspring like themselves, while those who are ill adapted tend not to survive to a reproducing age. Over very long periods of time, this statistical game leads to the gradual evolution of some species and the extinction of others. One of the principal insights from this idea is that the incredibly complex life forms that we observe and their remarkable adaptation of means to ends can result from this simple algorithmic process without the intervention of an Intelligent Artificer. This insight discloses what is known as the principle of accumulation of design, according to which the R & D that complex and adaptive structures require are attained through the slow build up of their design features in the course of natural selection (Dennett 1995, 68). It was certainly Darwin and Wallace who demonstrated this principle in relation to biological evolution. However, as shown in the next section, the principle of accumulation of design was discovered in relation to social evolution more than 100 years before the publication of Darwin's *The Origin of Species,* by 18th century scholars in England and Scotland.

The common law beginnings and the Darwinians before Darwin

The fact that the first understandings of the principle of accumulation of design occurred in 18th century England is, perhaps, not surprising. The English common law provided one of the most unambiguous illustrations of the principle in action. Statutes (*lex scripta*) were a major source of law in the nations of continental Europe even before the Napoleonic Codification. The laws of these nations combined the written Roman law, local statutes and local custom. The dominance of the *lex scripta* obscured the evolutionary character of the law. In England, by contrast, the common law reigned in its classical form without serious challenge from the Roman law or legislation. The evolutionary nature of the common law was noticed by the great Chief Justice Sir Matthew Hale, who wrote that law is 'accommodate to the Conditions, Exigencies and Conveniences of the People [and] as those Exigencies and Conveniences do insensibly grow upon the People, so many Times there grows insensibly a Variation of Laws, especially in a long Tract of Time' (1971 (1713), 39). Hale was speaking of the self-ordering nature of the common law, which enabled it to maintain itself as a system while undergoing change. He identified the two properties of the common law that show its evolutionary character. The first is that the common law has no author or designer but grows endogenously (arises from within) over long periods of time through the build up of precedents. The second is that the common law is part of the process by which society adapts to changing conditions.

Mandeville's *Fable of the Bees*

The first of the 18th century evolutionary thinkers was Bernard Mandeville, a Dutch physician and satirist practising in London, to whom Hayek paid the extraordinary compliment that he made Hume possible (Hayek 1978, 264). In 1705 Mandeville published a parody titled *The Grumbling Hive; or Knaves turn'd Honest*. In a series of 200 doggerels, Mandeville mocked the moralists of high society who viewed all selfish acts as vices. He suggested that if that was true society's good must be the result of vice because people always act in their self-interest. How else does one explain the success of the vibrant English commercial society of his time? The following typical verse captures his message:

> Thus every Part was full of Vice,
> Yet the whole Mass a Paradice;
> Flatter'd in Peace, and fear'd in Wars
> They were th'Esteem of Foreigners,
> And lavish of their Wealth and Lives,
> The Ballance of all other Hives.
> Such were the Blessings of that State;
> Their Crimes conspired to make 'em Great;
> And Vertue, who from Politicks
> Had learn'd a Thousand cunning Tricks,
> Was, by their happy Influence,
> Made Friends with Vice: And ever since
> The worst of all the Multitude
> Did something for the common Good.

Philosophers, politician and churchmen were outraged, but that only made the pamphlet more popular. In 1714, Mandeville republished it with a commentary and a serious essay under the title *The Fable of the Bees: or Private Vices, Publick Benefits*. In 1728 he wrote a second part consisting of six dialogues, and the two parts were published together in 1733. Mandeville's message was that if people were acting in their own interests, culture must be the unintended cumulative result of individual strivings (1924 (1733), vol. 1, 44). He identified the principle of the accumulation of design. In the third dialogue, Cleomenes says, 'That we often ascribe to the Excellency of Man's Genious, and the Depth of his Penetration, what is in reality owing to length of Time, and the Experience of many Generations, all of them very little differing from one another in natural Parts and Sagacity' (1924, vol. 2, 142). In the sixth dialogue, Cleomenes compares the process by which the law attains its sophistication to the mechanical process of weaving stockings (1924, vol. 2, 32). Compare these with Dennett's comment: 'What Darwin saw was that in principle the same work [previously attributed to a designing agent] could be done by a different sort of process that *distributed* that work over huge amounts of time, by thriftily conserving the design work that had been accomplished at each stage, so that it didn't have to be done over again' (1995, 68).

Hume's evolutionary view of society and law

In Chapter 3, I discussed Hume's epistemology (theory of knowledge) briefly, in comparing his empiricism with Kant's transcendental idealism. Here we take another look at his view of human knowledge, to see how it leads to an evolutionary explanation of the emergence of social systems and law. In *A Treatise of Human Nature* Hume argued that reason alone can never give rise to any original idea, and that the basis of our knowledge is nothing more than custom or accumulated experience (1978 (1739–40), 157). As discussed in Chapter 3, Hume observed that there are only perceptions present to the mind. The objects that cause our perceptions are not knowable directly. What we do not perceive directly, we infer on the principle of cause and effect. Causation is a relation and not a thing. Wherever there is fire, we feel heat. Hence we infer that fire causes heat. Yet, however hard we try, we cannot show the essence that connects the two. We cannot infer that one object causes another on the first occasion that we perceive them. (A child will fearlessly go near a fire the first time.) It is only our past experience of the repeated conjunction of one event with another that gives rise to the expectation that where one is found the other will also be found. Hence, our expectation that the future will resemble the past is based on nothing better than custom (Hume 1978, 104–6). Hume rejected the notion of innate ideas. We can construct theories and test them by laboratory experiments, but this process too is based on the 'general habit, by which we transfer the known to the unknown, and conceive the latter to resemble the former' (Hume 1975 (1748), 107). Scientific theorising depends in part on experience, and in part on blind speculation. Hume declared that 'experimental reasoning itself, which we possess in common with beasts, and on which the whole conduct of life depends, is nothing but a species of instinct or mechanical power, that acts in us unknown to ourselves' (1975, 108).

This theory of knowledge led Hume to his view that social institutions grew out of convention or custom and were not the result of design or agreement. Conventions were formed not by reason but by the accumulation of experience. Hume rejected the social contract theory concerning the establishment of law and society. He argued that law and society could not have been established by a promise, as the institution of the promise was itself based on convention. In short, the social contract theorists were guilty of putting the cart before the horse!

Hume retained the natural–artificial dichotomy, and placed justice in the artificial category. However, he was at pains to explain that justice belonged to a subset of artificial things that arose from convention as opposed to reason. He wrote: 'Tho' the rules of justice be *artificial*, they are not *arbitrary*. Nor is the expression improper to call the *Law of Nature*; if by natural we understand what is common to any species, or even if we confine it to mean what is inseparable from the species' (1975, 484). The rules of justice arise out of a sense of mutual need. This shared sense does not result from verbal exchanges but through the coincidence of behaviour, as when 'two men, who pull the oars of a boat, do it by an agreement or convention, tho' they have never given promises to each other'. Thus, rules of justice, like other conventional things such as language and currency, 'arise gradually, and acquire force by a slow progression, and by our repeated experience of the inconvenience of transgressing it' (1975, 490). Hume struck upon the evolutionary idea that rule formation is a process of habit meshing that occurs through the tendency of punishing encounters to extinguish and rewarding encounters to reinforce behavioural patterns. (Compare Campbell 1965, 32–3.)

Hume regarded law as antecedent to government for, though men can maintain 'a small uncultivated society without government, 'tis impossible they shou'd maintain a society of any kind without justice and the observance of the three fundamental laws concerning the stability of possession, its translation by consent and the performance of promises' (1975, 541). Government was needed not to make law, but to administer the law impartially (1975, 537).

Adam Smith and original passions

Like Hume, Adam Smith rejected social contract theory and treated social order, law and government as the outcomes of 'the natural progress which men make in society' (1981 (1776), vol. 2, 710). The starting point of Smith's philosophy is the concept of the 'original passions of human nature'. One of these passions is fellow feeling or sympathy. Though man is selfish by nature 'there are evidently some principles in his nature, which interest him in the fortune of others, and render their happiness necessary to him, though he derives nothing from it except the pleasure of seeing it' (Smith 1976 (1759), 9). Sympathy is the origin of the ideas of beneficence and of justice. The absence of beneficence or sense of justice in a person evokes disapprobation. However it is only unjust conduct that inspires the stronger feeling of resentment and leads to the demand for retribution.

How does the sense of justice give rise to the rules of justice? Rules arise because our sense of justice fails us when we most need it. We cannot make reasoned judgments before every action, not only because of the lack of time but also because we are driven by our passions. Afterwards, if we have acted unjustly, we are prone to forgive ourselves (Smith 1976, 157). This flaw in our nature is overcome by other instincts which, through the observation of the conduct of others, 'insensibly lead us to form to ourselves certain general rules concerning what is fit and proper either to be done or to be avoided' (1976, 159). We avoid self-deception through rule following, and rule formation occurs insensibly by the coincidence of individual behaviour. Smith could have been more reductionist in his search for the origins of rules, in the manner of later game theorists who attributed the evolution of cooperation to the dominance of the 'tit for tat' or 'eye for an eye' strategy (Axelrod 1990). However, he deserves credit for noticing that cooperation is the outgrowth of not only the instinct of retribution but also the instinct of sympathy.

Smith's theory is strikingly Darwinian and, in fact, avoids a mistake commonly made even by modern Darwinists. Smith argued that although social life is impossible without the rules of justice, it is not this consideration that animates the rules of justice initially, but our natural passions (1976, 89). The human species did not acquire its sense of justice and make itself social rules because these rules helped the species to prosper; rather, the race prospered because its members inherited a sense of justice and the instinct for rule following. Smith also brought out the underlying unity of the social, economic and legal evolution throughout his work. A clear demonstration of this unity is offered in his speculation concerning the emergence of the division of labour and money. The division of labour, Smith maintained, is not the product of human wisdom that foresees its great advantages, but 'is the necessary, though very slow and gradual consequence of a certain propensity in human nature which has in view no such utility; the propensity to truck, barter, and exchange one thing for another' (1981, vol. 1, 25). This propensity to exchange brings about the practice of contracting. The initial form of contract, barter, is a severely limited form of exchange. A person must have a stock of things that others commonly want (oxen, salt, pelts etc) in order to obtain what they themselves want through exchange. No exchange will take place where people have no need of what is offered. This problem activates a Darwinian type selection, whereby certain kinds of metals serve as substitutes and by a process of elimination become standard currency for exchange. The emergence of this practice accelerates the development of both commerce and commercial law. The need to certify the weight or value of the metals leads to the practice of official coinage, and hence, we might add, to the law of financial institutions (Smith 1981, vol. 1, 41–6).

Ferguson's theory of unconscious rule following

The idea that social patterns emerge through the cumulative effects of adaptive behaviour of individuals responding instinctively to local conditions was systematically developed by Adam Ferguson in *An Essay on the History of Civil Society*, published in 1767. Ferguson clearly perceived that human beings are able to do the right thing without knowing the reason why it is right. We derive general rules of morality, law, language and so forth by observing the repeated occurrence of particular actions. How does a child or an illiterate peasant gain the capacity to reason or even to speak their language? It is not by memorising bits of information, but by subconsciously grasping the relevant underlying principles of reasoning and of language (Ferguson 1966 (1767), 34).

Ferguson argued that the sense of legal right inheres in human nature: 'Every peasant will tell us, that a man hath his rights; and that to trespass on those rights is injustice.' If we ask him what he means by 'right' we force him 'to substitute a less significant, or less proper term, in place of this; or require him to account for what is an original mode of his mind, and a sentiment to which he refers, when he would explain himself upon any particular application of his language' (1966, 34).

Ferguson was conscious that human learning was radically different from other animal learning, as the human race can accumulate knowledge from generation to generation (1966, 5). Yet, like Hume and Smith, he anticipated the Darwinian insight that all human knowledge gains are achieved without prescience: 'Every step and every movement of the multitude, even in what are termed enlightened ages, are made with equal blindness to the future; and nations stumble upon establishments, which are indeed the result of human action, but not the execution of any human design' (1966, 122). With Hume and Smith, he rejected patriarchal and contractarian theories of the state, observing that they 'ascribe to a previous design, what came to be known only by experience, what no human wisdom could foresee, and what, without the concurring humor and disposition of his age, no authority could enable an individual to execute' (1966, 123).

Summary

In summary, the pre-Darwin evolutionists developed in relation to social phenomena the following key ideas:

1. Human beings inherit certain instincts, dispositions and passions as part of the natural characteristics of their species. These would be identified today as genetically transmitted qualities that have been selectively retained, but this knowledge was unavailable to 18th century thinkers.

2. Human beings also inherit, through cultural means, a fund of knowledge. This knowledge is embodied in the form of convention or custom that results from a process of insensible accumulation of the experience of successive generations.

3. New knowledge (that is, knowledge not acquired through deductive inference from conventional knowledge) is acquired without prescience, through blind theorising. This type of knowledge becomes conventional knowledge if not falsified by experience.

4. Social and legal rules are formed through the blind process of habit meshing, involving the selective retention of rewarding behavioural tendencies. Initially, as we have no prescience, we do not possess the knowledge of the general rules of social life, but only know how to act in specific situations guided by instincts. We gain knowledge of the general rules when regularities of behaviour are observed.

5. Initially, state authority is not the source of law; rather, authority becomes necessary because there is law to enforce.

Eighteenth century evolutionism compared with the German historical approach

The German historical school was founded by Gustav Hugo, but its most influential figure was Friedrich Carl von Savigny (1779–1861), one of the prominent jurists of the 19th century. The historical school was part of the Romantic movement in art and philosophy, which was a revolt against empiricist rationalism. In jurisprudence it took the form of the rejection of legal positivism in favour of law as folkways. The German historical school identified the law not with the state but with the character of the people. There are important similarities between the historical school and the evolutionary approach that we discussed. There are also critical differences.

According to the evolutionists, law is not derived from organised society but, rather, the emergence of law brings about social order. Savigny and his followers completely reversed this order of cause and effect. According to them, law was derived from the common consciousness of a people (*Volksgeist*) who already exist as an 'active personal subject' (Savigny 1867, 15). In other words, law is the product of a society that already exists. Savigny rejected the idea that law emerges insensibly as custom, and claimed that the opposite is true. The law lives in the common consciousness, which is 'diametrically opposite to bare chance'. Moreover, the law lives in this consciousness not as rules but as 'the living intuition of law in their organic connection'. When the need arises for a rule to be conceived in a logical form, 'it must be formed by a scientific procedure from that total intuition' (Savigny 1867, 13). What Savigny meant by 'scientific procedure' is a process whereby the specific rules of law reveal themselves through symbolic acts. Initially, we recognise the law 'when it steps forth in usage, manners, custom' (1867, 28). Later, two other 'organs' of the people's law appear in the form of legal science and legislation. Savigny thought that at some point in the history of the community, 'the law forming energy departs from the people as a whole', so that the law will live only in these two organs (1867, 40). In other words, once the legal experts and law makers take over the law, popular consciousness ceases to be a significant source of law.

The major difference between the German historical school and the evolutionary theory is this. The *Volksgeist* as the source of law eventually runs out of steam. In evolutionary theory, law continues to be shaped by endogenous bottom-up pressures even after the arrival of the jurists and legislators. In fact, as I explain in the following pages, deliberate law making by legislators is not free from evolutionary pressures and the algorithmic process of design accumulation works incessantly at all levels, influencing legislative and juristic activity.

The Austrian school and spontaneous order

The independent discovery of the process of evolution of species through natural selection by Charles Darwin and Alfred Wallace occurred in the middle of the

19th century. The excitement and controversy that ensued, if anything, distracted scholarly attention from the older evolutionary tradition in the social sciences. The carriage of that tradition into the 20th century owes much to the work of the Austrian school of economics, which sprang chiefly from the work of Carl Menger (1840–1921). Although the English and Scottish scholars are hardly mentioned in Menger's work, his view of the emergence of social order is remarkably similar. In his critique of the historical school, Menger wrote:

> National law in its most original form is thus, to be sure, not the result of a contract or of reflection aiming at the assurance of common welfare. Nor is it, indeed, given with the nation, as the historical school asserts. Rather, it is older than the appearance of the latter. Indeed, it is one of the strongest ties by which the population of a territory becomes a nation and achieves state organisation. (1963, 227)

The initial impetus for the revival of evolutionary thinking in the 19th century was the realisation by the economists Jevons, Walras and Menger that the search for inherent value of goods and services was doomed. Menger went furthest in grasping that the price of a good or service was the unintended result of the actions of millions of interacting persons pursuing their own disparate ends (1963, 146). So, too, are many other social structures. Menger realised that the formation of economic arrangements is part and parcel of the spontaneous emergence of social structures. Structures such as law, language, the state, money and markets result from the same process of social development (Menger 1963, 147). They are inter-dependent parts of an overall self-ordering complex system similar to a living organism (1963, 129–30). Menger appreciated that not all social structures are unintended outcomes and that the analogy between social and organic phenomena is incomplete. The social order has many deliberately designed aspects. There is a vast volume of enacted statute law in the modern states. There are also many deliberately made organisations, such as corporations and government agencies. Menger argued that the organic comparison, incomplete as it is, has profound implications for the method of the social sciences. It demonstrates that we cannot make precise predictions about social phenomena, but can only determine their general features and the processes by which they emerge. It also demonstrates that the capacity of a government to produce specific outcomes by deliberate intervention in the workings of society is severely limited, because it cannot precisely predict or control the behaviour of its innumerable members.

The theory of complex orders blossomed in the 20th century through the work of the Austrians Ludwig von Mises and Friedrich Hayek and their followers, who continued to investigate the epistemological problem neglected in classical theory – namely, the disequilibrium of the market and imperfect information of actors. The idea of complex systems or spontaneous order was systematically developed by Hayek, who worked out most of its implications for economics and jurisprudence. Hayek distinguished spontaneous order (*cosmoi*) from made order or organisations (*taxeis*). Spontaneous order was found in complex systems, in which constituent members have freedom of action but are coordinated in their interactions by the observance of general rules. These general rules are themselves the unintended results of the coincidence and meshing of behaviour on the part of members responding to local stimuli in the pursuit of disparate ends.

In Israel Kirzner's work on the equilibrating process of markets, we find further refinements of the theory of spontaneous order. Although Kirzner did not use evolutionist language, the evolutionary implications of his work are clear. Following von Mises and Hayek, Kirzner criticised the neo-classical equilibrium model as failing to show how markets actually work. In a universe of perfectly informed wealth maximisers there would be no scope for entrepreneurship or discovery. The consequences of market events are foreordained within a given set of market data, and genuine unprogrammed change can only result from exogenous (external) shocks to the system (Kirzner 1997, 35). In short, in the equilibrium scenario of mainstream economic theory, there cannot be evolution in the adaptive sense but only change in the computational sense. Kirzner recognised that actors in the market are imperfectly informed and lack prescience. Hence, their entrepreneurial activity has less to do with search than with discovery. Search presupposes existing knowledge of the value of information sought and the cost of acquiring it, whereas discovery consists of noticing information that is costless, but which has been previously overlooked (Kirzner 1997, 32). What is previously overlooked represents an opportunity for pure profit. The human propensity to sense such opportunities leads to the systematic correction of errors that is the feature of the market process. Paradoxically, markets tend to equilibrate not because choices are clear to individual decision makers, but because 'of the unsystematic human efforts to cope with open-ended uncertainties of the great unknown' (Kirzner 1997, 27).

Scientific explanations

Understandings concerning spontaneous order developed by the 18th century evolutionists and the Austrian school have been deepened by research programs in many scientific disciplines that focus on the study of complexity and self-organisation. Complexity theory seeks to explain how order found in dynamical systems emerges without design. Living systems, whether they are single cells in our body, whole organisms or societies, need to be both dynamic and stable because life is not sustainable in static or chaotic states. (A static man is a corpse or a statue.) Complex systems allow flexible behaviour of their parts while withstanding the resulting perturbations (Kauffman 1995, 89; Levy 1992, 1, 27). They occur, in the words of Kauffman, 'at the edge of chaos'.

As observed previously, complex systems, of which societies are prime examples, result from the regularities that arise in the course of interaction among individual agents pursuing their disparate ends. These regularities themselves come under selection pressures, and survive to the extent that they are retained by surviving groups. The evolutionary process is further complicated by the fact that selective retention of living systems occurs simultaneously at different levels in nested hierarchies. The environment that selects the genotype (genetic structure) of an organism includes its phenotype (the observable physical structure), the physical surroundings and the cultural environment. Each of these levels has levels within them. Simpler lower level systems coagulate to form complex upper level systems, which in turn provide the ecologies for future selection at the lower levels, causing systems at the lower levels to change further (Campbell 1987a, 54–73; Hahlweg 1989, 58–62). The survival of the system depends on its capacity to maintain stability through this two-way feedback. This makes the task of controlling living systems to produce desired results that much harder. These observations apply equally to the complex order of society.

Role of purposive action in legal evolution: the contribution of institutional theory

Scottish and Austrian schools highlighted the emergence of social structures as the unintended results of human action. Twentieth century scholars concerned with law and economics focused their efforts on the role of purposive human action in legal evolution. The idea that law is the creation of human agencies is deeply ingrained in the popular mind and is hardly novel. Legal obligations may arise under contract or under customary law, such as the law of tort and common law crime. Rights concerning person and property are directly or indirectly delineated by these two kinds of law. Institutionalists have been interested in the study of the evolution of both these forms of legal obligations. In relation to contract, institutionalists started with the rudimentary form of contract and examined the ways in which contract forms have changed over time (Macneil 1980), and how contract leads to the emergence of firms (Coase 1937; Williamson 1979; *et al.*).

The significance of the work of the institutional economists lies in their integration of purposeful action in the evolutionary process in a way that highlights human design and effort in legal evolution. Yet the differences between the spontaneous order tradition and the institutionalists should not be exaggerated. There is no fundamental inconsistency to be found between the two approaches. Many institutionalists consider the abstract principles of spontaneous order to be equally applicable to designed social organisations. The spontaneous order tradition does not deny the role of human actions in legal evolution. What it denies is that human beings act with prescience, not that they act with intent. Human designs, its theorists maintain, are but hypotheses that stand the test of history or are edited by it. Conversely, there is no denial in the work of the institutionalists of the fallibility of human design and the unpredictability that attends all human action. What they seek to demonstrate is that purposive human action has a great deal to do with legal evolution, a fact not denied by spontaneous order scholars. The key differences between the approaches concerns focus. While the spontaneous order tradition looks at the abstract nature of the process of legal change, the institutionalists study the actual actions that cause such change. We need to be careful not to extrapolate from the work of the institutionalists a theory that human beings are in command of their destiny. Provided we do not do this, their work helps us anchor the evolutionary thinking developed by the Scots and Austrians to concrete developments in modern market based economies and to gain a deeper appreciation of the type of pressures that influence the directions of legal evolution.

There are three branches of institutional theory that are particularly relevant to the study of legal evolution. The first is associated with the 'old institutionalist' scholars who highlight the role of purposive human action in legal evolution. The second represents evolutionary game theory, and the third focuses on the role of history in determining the choices available to human agents seeking legal change. The central concern of the latter school, known also as the new institutional economists (NIE), is the problem of path dependency in institutional change.

The start of institutionalism has been identified with Thorstein Veblen's 1898 essay 'Why is economics not an evolutionary science?' (Seckler 1975, 11). Veblen argued that the idea of the economic person as a free choosing agent should be abandoned. An economic actor is one caught in an institutional web handed down inter-generationally and subject to change through exogenous shocks such as war, famine, disease and technological change (Seckler 1975, 8). The institutions themselves are transformed in response to changing conditions in industrial society, but there is always a time lag in adaptation that leaves some institutions maladapted to modern life. According to Veblen, deliberate law making is a game of 'catch up'. In contrast, Commons took a more optimistic view of the human capacity to direct the course of institutional evolution.

JR Commons and artificial selection in legal evolution

The starting point for JR Commons was the individual transactions between persons. These discrete transactions cumulatively lead to the emergence of legal structures. In *Legal Foundations of Capitalism* (1924), Commons argued that economic and legal evolution involves artificial selection 'like that of a steam engine or a breed of cattle, rather than like that of a continent, monkey or tiger' (1924, 376). What he meant was that law-making authorities (legislators and judges) are continually selecting those laws that serve known purposes, and eliminating those that are detrimental to them. Unlike Hayek, who regarded the cultural universe as comprising made orders (*taxeis*) that are created for known purposes and spontaneous orders (*cosmoi*) that have no purpose, Commons saw that universe in terms of *going concerns*. Going concerns consist of a series of transactions of individuals interacting for particular purposes. They include the corporation, the church, the club, the family, the government and the state. A going concern exists before it is legally recognised in the form of the intentions and transactions of its members. Its internal rules have built up through customs, practices, habits, precedents, methods of work and such like. Law is born when functionaries of the state find a going concern 'already in a trembling existence and then proceed "artificially" to guide the individuals concerned and give it a safer existence' (Commons 1924, 145). The law evolves as courts and legislators seek to fix problems and to eliminate impediments that prevent going concerns from achieving their purposes. The law maker's task is thus similar to that of a mechanic fixing a car. They determine the organisation's purpose, find out the problem and then modify the applicable working rules (Commons 1924, 145).

The analogy of law making with animal breeding and manufacture is misleading, as Vanberg (1997) pointed out. Legal evolution could be said to be artificial only in the sense that it results from actions of human agents, as Ferguson stated. It is not artificial in the sense that law makers can have requisite knowledge, resources and command of process to engineer the law to attain precise ends (Vanberg 1997, 112). Commons' view that laws evolve through purposive human acts of selection is highly contestable. Human acts are elements in a complex selecting environment. One person's act by itself can never be a selector in relation to the law. Indeed, the selecting environment will usually be made up of countless acts, many of which express no preference at all for the selected law. This is obviously the case with customary law but, on examination, is equally true of legislation. Deliberate enactments, whether made by legislators or by judges, undoubtedly change the law, but they too are ultimately selectively retained (or eliminated) by an environment that consists only partly of purposive human actions – many of which say nothing about the laws in question. Thus, judicial precedents are revised from time to time, and so are legislative enactments that do not stand the test of time.

In Common's theory, the working rules of a going concern result from the problem of scarcity. Law makers, whether they be judges, executives or legislators, are engaged in 'proportioning the inducements which collective power creates' (Commons 1974, 365). Commons was unclear on the principle that guides this proportioning. He suggested that officials are guided by 'the sense of fitness and unfitness arising out of habit and custom, which is but the sense of the proper and the improper proportioning of limiting and complementary factors needed to bring about what is deemed to be the best proportioning of all' (1974, 366). As to the sense of fitness, he stated that it is 'that feeling of harmony and unity attained by fitting the immediate transactions under discussion to the whole scheme of life as perceived and habitually accepted' (1974, 366). Though unclear, this explanation of law making draws Commons closer to the spontaneous order paradigm. Compare, in this respect, Hayek's view that the effort of the judge who decides the hard case is part of the process of adaptation of society to circumstances by which the spontaneous order grows. This is because the judge's function is not to create new order but to 'maintain and improve a going order' (Hayek 1982, 1, 119). The judge performs this function by 'piecemeal tinkering' or 'immanent criticism' (Hayek 1982, 118). A dispute comes before a judge when a person's expectations are defeated or when contending parties hold conflicting expectations. Where an existing rule provides no clear answer the judge must supply a rule that will tend to match expectations and not promote conflict. Hayek's judge is directed back to the abstract rules of the spontaneous order upon which expectations were initially founded, in order to devise a rule that is in harmony with that order. Thus, for both Hayek and Commons, the duty of the magistrate is to supply a rule that fits the ongoing order.

Vanberg argued that the value of Commons' work lies in its demonstration that we are not passive sufferers of a given evolutionary destiny, but that we can and should assert a positive influence on the direction of legal evolution, as the German school of ordo-liberalism proposes (Vanberg 1997, 114). Vanberg acknowledged that neither the Scots nor the Austrians had a wholly agnostic view of evolution (1994, 465–6).

Evolution of organisations

The spontaneous order tradition does not deny that there are organisations based on deliberately created rules. What it maintains is that, ultimately, these organisations are subject to the same principle of unforeseeable and unintended consequences as grown orders. Organisations are themselves elements that interact in the overall spontaneous order that no authority can control. What about the government? There are many selectionist explanations of the emergence and ubiquity of headship institutions or governments. H Guetzkow, Harold Leavitt, Alex Bavelas, DT Campbell and others thought that most societies, through selection pressure, tend to produce a single coordinator or communications clearing house (Guetzkow 1961, 187–200; Campbell 1965, 29). Campbell identified the selective advantages of the economy of cognition (information sharing), the economy of specialisation (division of labour) and the economy of mutual defence (1965, 44–5). Whatever may have been the causes, it is evident that government, having legislative power and near monopoly of coercive power, is a common occurrence in social evolution.

Governments are not the only kinds of organisations found in a large society. There is a wide range of private voluntary organisations directed to all manner of purposes. Until Ronald Coase's 1937 essay on 'The nature of the firm', the question of why individuals form organisations and surrender their market power in exchange for central planning had received little attention. (Coase's theory is discussed in more detail in Chapter 9.) Coase's investigation of this puzzle led to new insights concerning the role of purposive action in legal evolution. Coase argued that the firm was a long-term contract among previously independent owners of labour, capital and raw materials who agreed to place themselves under the management of an entrepreneur in preference to engaging in free exchange to produce goods or services. Whether a firm would arise in this manner depends on the marginal cost of using the price mechanism (Coase 1937, 390). Where production reaches a certain scale and complexity normal contracting becomes impractical, as too many contracts are needed to marshal labour, capital and raw materials in a highly competitive and volatile market. At this point it makes economic sense for persons to organise themselves into a firm and become employees of the firm. A firm thus formed will not expand indefinitely, because at some point the capacity of management to efficiently deploy factors of production suffers. Coase concluded that 'a firm will tend to expand until the costs of organising an extra transaction within the firm become equal to the costs of carrying out the same transaction by an exchange on the open market' (1937, 394–5).

Coase's theory was neglected for more than 30 years, until Williamson elaborated it by aligning changes in organisational structure to changes in the transactional environment. Williamson explored the conditions under which firms resort to markets to secure services or make long-term employment contracts. Factors that influence the formation of a firm include uncertainties caused by opportunistic behaviour of others, the recurrence of similar transactions in a business (a furniture business needs a carpenter full time) and the specificity of human and physical capital (Adelstein 1998, 63). Williamson used Macneil's taxonomy of contractual forms to argue that firms oscillate between classical, neo-classical and relational contracts along the chain of production as they seek to maximise profits (Williamson 1979, 248). The classical contract is the discrete contract, where two strangers come together just for the purpose of the contract and can reasonably foresee the consequences of their bargain. In these cases, the courts usually hold parties strictly to the terms. The neo-classical contract occurs where parties have ongoing concerns but may not be able to predict accurately the consequences of particular bargains. Thus, the importer and the exporter of an agricultural product on a long-term contract may leave room for future adjustments of prices. Relational contracts are observed where economic factors create strong ongoing interdependencies within a wider community (Macneil 1980).

The selectionist nature of organisational evolution, even when it is the consequence of purposive actions, was emphasised by Alchian (1950), Friedman (1953) and Becker (1962). They argued that even if entrepreneurs in real life do not engage in profit maximisation through marginal analysis, as assumed in the neoclassical theory, the model holds good when it is viewed in relation to industries as opposed to single firms. All three theorists took the Humean view that a theory may hold good even if its assumptions are unproved (Friedman 1953, 9, 14; Becker 1962, 12). Even if individual entrepreneurs are not driven by profit maximisation, within an industry firms that survive are those whose conduct approximates to the model of profit maximisation. As Alchian contended, we cannot know in advance what subjective preference in relation to risk will yield the better results; we only know with hindsight what actions have yielded the higher profits (Vromen 1995, 22). In a pervasively uncertain world characterised by omnipresent chance, the winners are not always those who act rationally on the best market intelligence, but may be those who are less prudent but more daring. The trick, as Alchian saw it, is to back away from the trees – representing the optimising calculus of individual units – so we can better discern the forest of impersonal market forces operating in disequilibrium (1950, 213). The critical lesson here is that it is more useful to look at what has worked than to look at what is proposed. It is not surprising, therefore, to find entrepreneurs placing reliance on patterns (rules) of behaviour that appear to have been successful. Rules of behaviour, of course, may prove unsuccessful over an extended period, as the environment to which they are adapted is continually changing. Hence, there is a continual revision of plans as a consequence of the disappointment of earlier plans (Kirzner 1962, 381).

Evolution of commercial law

The emergence of rules of conduct in commercial dealings through purposive actions of individual actors has received much attention in law and economics literature. The mainstream view of contract is that it is not law in its own right but is the outcome of law, or at best derivative law, binding only on the parties to the contract. Thus *pacta sunt servanda* (promises must be kept) is the law, and the content of the promise is the outcome of the law. However, it is evident that private contracts are a major source of law in the field of commerce. Standard form contracts devised to suit the convenience of particular groups of traders become trade norms when adopted by a critical mass of traders (Rubin 1995, 155). National and international trade and industry associations contribute to law formation by formulating rules based on trade customs. These are imported wholesale into contracts by parties. In the field of commerce, contract and custom interact in a mutually reinforcing way. Just as successful contractual terms become custom through widespread adoption, successful customary practices are selected for application to particular transactions by express adoption in contracts (Benson 1998, 89). Contract is seen as part of the selection process by which the law evolves. There is perhaps no clearer example of this process than the so-called Incoterms (International Commercial Trade Terms), initially formulated by the International Chamber of Commerce in 1936. The Introduction to the Incoterms states that their purpose 'is to provide a set of international rules for the most common trade terms in foreign trade'. They are periodically revised (most recently in 2000) to reflect changing customs in international trade. Conversely, they set standards that become customary through adoption by traders all over the world.

The role of contracting in legal evolution is closely tied to private dispute resolution. Private dispute resolution processes such as commercial arbitration, mediation and negotiation are based on contracts under which contracting parties agree to resolve disputes by enlisting the services of private arbitrators or conciliators. There is some debate on the question of whether private dispute resolution can produce clear rules. Landes and Posner, for example, argued that profit maximising private judges have little incentive to clarify the rules upon which they determine disputes, as clarity would reduce the incidence of disputes (Landes & Posner 1979, 238–9). Others, such as Fuller (1981), Benson (1998) and Lew (1978), contended that incentives exist for the private judges to clarify and justify their decisions. The success of trade and industry associations in attracting dispute resolution business is explained not only by their technical expertise but also by the reliability and predictability of their decisions. At any rate, it seems reasonable to assume that traders submitting disputes to commercial ADR organisations do not see themselves as entering a lottery conducted by persons having no regard to the law and customs of the trade.

Evolution of liability rules concerning tort and crime

The emergence of liability rules in tort and criminal law has been the subject of studies by Calabresi and Melamed (1972), Adelstein (1998) and others. Building on Coase's insight concerning the effect of transaction costs on what transactions will actually take place among agents, Calabresi and Melamed developed a unified theory of property rights and tort liability, in which the state is seen as the allocator of power to impose costs on others, without compensation or liberty to be free from such imposition (Adelstein 1998, 64). Coase's theorem stated that in zero transaction cost conditions the initial allocation of rights will not matter, as they will gravitate to those who value them most. Posner argued that where transaction costs are prohibitive, efficient allocation of rights will occur only if the state initially allocates them to the actor who values them most. Calabresi and Melamed argued that the state is engaged in just such an exercise in establishing property rights and liability rules. Their thesis is discussed in Chapter 9.

There is no suggestion by these institutionalists that the state is capable of, or indeed motivated to, engage in efficiency analyses of liability rules. The liability rules of tort and crime were developed by common law courts through the process of litigation, which resembles much more closely the spontaneous order model of legal evolution (Ruhl 1996a, 1996b). Similarly, the delictual (tort) liability in Roman law pre-dated codification and arose in ancient custom. The point is that a selectionist explanation – similar to that advanced by Alchian, Friedman and Becker with regard to the emergence of the firm – may be applied to deliberately created liability rules. While legislatures may be motivated by various considerations, including the vote delivering capacities of interest groups, inefficient rules will be subject to constant selection pressures. However, while we may remain optimistic about this process, there is no guarantee that the end results will be efficient rules. Evolution is a non-linear dynamical process that presents many pitfalls, from which subjects may not recover easily, if ever. The integration of this factor into institutional theory is the major contribution to evolutionary jurisprudence of the new institutionalists. The new institutionalists reconnect old institutionalism to the spontaneous order tradition of the Scottish and Austrian schools.

Pathways of legal evolution: the lessons from new institutionalism

Game theory models indicate that conventions or self-executing patterns of behaviour emerge in populations of interacting agents, who adjust their behaviour over time in response to the payoffs that various choices have historically produced. Axelrod's idea that cooperation results from 'tit for tat' strategy among agents suggests that, over repeated encounters, agents will learn to avoid punishing behaviour and to repeat rewarding behaviour (Axelrod 1990). As agents are mostly strangers in larger societies, they depend on a process of social learning through reliance on patterns of behaviour that appear to be successful. Accordingly, game theory models take as given the idea that patterns of behaviour that appear to be successful increase their representation in the population (Mailath 1998, 84).

However, practices that appear to be successful in some communities are not found in others. This does not contradict the assumptions of the game theory models, but alerts us to the presence of costs that prevent the adoption of good practice in some communities. North claimed that game theory provides an inadequate account of 'the complex, imprecise and fumbling way by which human beings have gone about structuring human interaction' (North 1990, 15). This criticism is too harsh, but North was certainly right to point out that we will not get far in understanding social evolution if we disregard the critical role of institutions in the process. As the Scots and the Austrians realised, the origins of some of the most fundamental social norms are lost in the mists of time and some norms pre-date the emergence of human capacity to express them in words. They arose, not from rational calculations, but from regularities of action and the advantages they conferred on groups who happened to observe the regularities without any foresight of those advantages (Hayek 1982, 1, 19). The search for origins of social cooperation is doomed, but we can learn from observation some aspects of its growth and change over time. New institutional economics has made an important contribution to evolutionary legal theory by highlighting the problem of path dependence in institutional change.

We need to know precisely what is meant by 'institution' in institutional theory before proceeding further. The word 'institution' has many meanings. It derives from the Latin *institutum*, which means in this context: (a) ordinance, decree or regulation; (b) practice, custom, usage or habit; and (c) precedent (Lewis 2000, 427). Institutional theorists mean by 'institution' all of the above, as well as other informal constraints that give structure to society.

Evolution is a process of blind variation and selective retention. The variations that can occur, though, are themselves constrained by history and environment.

This is a consequence of the principle of accumulation of design that the Scots discovered. As Gould put it, 'The constraints of inherited form and developmental pathways may so channel any change that even though selection induces motion down permitted paths, the channel itself represents the primary determinant of evolutionary direction' (1982, 383). Natural history is a constant reminder that biological evolution often proceeds down one-way streets and, as presently observed, so does cultural evolution.

The human race, because of its intellectual abilities and cultural institutions, has a limited capacity to change its evolutionary course. However, human development is heavily dependent on cultural inheritance. Although, in comparison to biological emergence, the break outs in social evolution occur more frequently and more visibly, the process remains fundamentally the same – the accumulation of design. A major part of the cultural inheritance of a society is in the form of institutions that constitute the framework of rules within which social life is played out (North 1990, 4–5). Laws are not the only institutions that shape social life. There are other formal and informal constraints, such as conventions, ethical codes, etiquette, religious beliefs and superstitions. The higher order institutions – such as the constitutional dispersal of power, the representative principle, judicial independence, due process, property ownership and freedom of contract – crucially shape lower order institutions. Institutions are critical to legal evolution for three reasons: (1) they are important as historical determinants of evolutionary pathways; (2) they form part of the current selective environment; and (3) they establish the agencies through which legal change is effected.

Once a law (or less formal rule or practice) is established, individuals and organisations adapt to it and arrange their lives in the expectation that it will remain in force for a reasonable period. As public choice studies demonstrate, laws become difficult to repeal when the individuals and organisations that rely on them have greater bargaining power in the political system than those that are harmed by them. Such 'lock ins' result from the dependence of economic actors on the incentive structures created by the established institutional framework (North 1990, 7–8). Thus, already established laws predispose the legal order to evolve in particular directions. Laws that impose price controls on goods and services may, for example, engender black markets, the suppression of which requires further controls on trade. The immense volume of laws in the form of statutes, regulations, orders, discretions and official polices that makes up the welfare state shows how the legal system can gather momentum of its own after it is set on a particular course, producing consequences which no one foresaw or desired. In a world of perfectly informed persons and zero transaction costs, dysfunctional laws will be quickly revised or, more likely, will not get enacted at all. However, in the real world people work with very imperfect subjective models of their environment, which rely to a large extent on their cultural inheritance. The extent to which the models get revised depends on the feedback they receive, and the feedback depends partially on the institutions themselves.

Normative implications

The idea of evolution, in the sense of blind variation and selective retention, suggests a tautology: what is retained is retained and what is eliminated ceases to exist. According to this, our moral standards are themselves products of selection pressures, and hence we have no independent yardstick by which to evaluate the direction of evolution. However, it does not follow from our lack of freedom from the evolutionary process that we cannot or should not make judgments concerning evolutionary directions or provide inputs to the process. Deliberate inputs are perfectly compatible with accumulation of design. As Vanberg argued, 'there is no contradiction between the notion of deliberate institutional design and the notion of a competitive evolutionary process, just as there is no contradiction between the notion of deliberate organised production and the notion of a spontaneous market process in which such deliberate production experiments compete' (1994, 437). In fact, evolution itself renders redundant the question of whether human beings should seek to influence their own evolution. We have evolved into a race of incorrigible theorists, designers and constructivists. As evolutionary epistemologists, led by Popper, claim, cultural evolution is part of a continuum with biological evolution, representing a process of knowledge growth through trial and error (Popper 1963). While it is clear that design inputs are integral to the process of cultural evolution, it remains to consider what normative lessons concerning interventions the evolutionary process itself offers. There are two aspects of the evolutionary process that have normative implications. The first is the selection–competition aspect, and the second the orderliness aspect.

The trial and error process by which human problems are solved may be improved by the proliferation of hypotheses and their testing in competitive conditions. Just as scientific hypotheses seek to explain physical reality, normative rules of the legal system may be regarded as hypotheses about social reality. These hypotheses, as the spontaneous order theorists assert, are generated by the regularities of the behaviour of individual agents adapting to local conditions. The social system also generates, through its scientific and political activity, numerous hypotheses in the form of legislation. The process of theory production and testing is encouraged by open political systems, where competitive conditions are secured by constitutional rules. Constitutional safeguards of the freedoms of communication and association, the representative principle in government, and rule of law conditions, directly and indirectly create the competitive conditions that encourage knowledge growth through trial and error. Information exchange occurs not only through formal discussions but also through the conduct of persons pursuing their own different ends. Hypotheses are generated through the equilibrating process resulting from the revision of behaviour by agents responding to trial and error feedback. Freedom of contract and the freedom to hold, enjoy and dispose of property are seen as critical to the process of information exchange through conduct. The prevalence of abstract and impersonal rules of conduct, as opposed to discretionary powers fixing rights and duties in the individual case, is a clear advantage. It provides stable areas of autonomy that allow agents to utilise knowledge that they alone possess, enabling richer hypotheses to emerge through experience. Unlike patternless interventions, abstract rules also provide contestable standards that are susceptible to revision.

The recognition of the spontaneous nature of social evolution carries normative implications. As Kauffman pointed out, spontaneous order undergirds all stages of evolution, including the capacity to evolve (1995, 71). Static things such as tables and chairs, or even completely programmed things such as clocks, do not evolve. Nor does matter, in chaotic conditions. An adaptive system needs to maintain stability while allowing its members local freedom. This is the character of all spontaneous order, including human societies. If the members are fully controlled the system will lose its adaptive capacity and ultimately die. If they obey no rules, the system will die by descending into chaos. In society, coordination and stability are achieved through abstract laws that allow members to utilise knowledge about their own circumstances. The paradox is that adaptive order is actually made possible by the simplicity and generality of laws. If there are no rules at all there are no prospects for coordination of individual actions, and if the law dictates the behaviour of each person in great detail the system will be less, not more, adaptive. This is a point that Hayek made in the first volume of *Law, Legislation and Liberty* (1982, vol. 1, 49). More than two decades on, scientists investigating complexity and the laws of self-organisation are coming to similar conclusions from experimental data (Kauffman 1995, 86–92). In his incisive book, *Simple Rules for a Complex World* (1995), Richard Epstein argued that our complex social world works best on a handful of simple rules.

Eighteenth century evolutionary thought, as later amplified by the Austrian school, brought to light the nature of legal emergence as a process of accumulation of design, much like the work of the unseen hand or the blind watchmaker. It introduced the idea that while we may certainly engage in social problem solving through legislation, we can do so only within the constraints imposed on us by the spontaneous nature of social order. This viewpoint informs us that by attaining legislative power, the human race did not gain an unambiguous advantage. Legislative power, once born, often falls into the hands of individuals and groups who use it in their own political interests. The information that is used in self-interested law making is seriously limited. Legislation to achieve particular ends frequently takes the form of *ad hoc* commands made by officials to whom discretionary power is delegated. As we have seen, this form of law incorporates even less information. Where legislative power is exercised by assemblies that are periodically elected by the people, the potential for abuse is reduced. However, as the public choice literature illustrates, the electoral process tends to become a marketplace where legislative power is bought and sold among politicians and voting groups.

As North and other institutional historians have pointed out, bargaining democracy has become entrenched because of the increasing returns that it provides to organised groups that have evolved to take advantage of it, and the prohibitive transaction costs of changing it even at the margins. However, evolution time and time again surprises us by the unexpected and unintended break out of systems from their established pathways. Although the cost of directly changing the institutional environment remains high, the cost of exit has been falling in relative terms, owing to the globalisation process, liberalisation of international trade law and new technologies. Exit provides powerful feedback to national governments and the constituencies that elect them. Yet there is no reason for us to be passive observers, optimistically awaiting evolutionary corrections that are impossible to predict. We could be pro-active in constitutional design without pretending that we can fully command our destiny.

PART 4
RIGHTS AND JUSTICE

11

Fundamental Legal Conceptions: the Building Blocks of Legal Norms

Previous chapters have focused on theories about definitions and descriptions of the law as it is or as it ought to be, and of how law is made or emerges in society. This chapter examines another vital aspect of law: namely, the internal structure of legal norms and the basic conceptions that are used in legal statements. In other words, we look for the building blocks of legal statements, the conceptions without which a law maker cannot make a law. This discussion is centred on the remarkable contribution on this subject made by Wesley Newcomb Hohfeld (1879–1918).

Not every kind of statement makes law. Assume that King Rex is the absolute ruler of a country. The rule of recognition accepted by the country's officials and citizens grants Rex the power to make law according to his will. He simply has to express it and his will becomes law. One morning on awaking, Rex says to no one in particular, 'I hope the weather will be nice this morning so I can ride my horse'. This is obviously not a law but a hope. At breakfast he tells his Queen, 'I wish my subjects will be well behaved and law abiding today'. This is also not a law but simply a wish. That afternoon he proclaims at the Royal Council: 'It is henceforth the law that no trader shall sell a standard loaf of bread for more than one dollar'. This is a law because it creates a legal duty and a legal right. The trader has a duty not to sell a loaf for more than one dollar and the customers have the right to receive a loaf by paying one dollar or less.

Law informs people of what they *may* do, what they *must* do and, most importantly, what they *must not* do. A person may make a will to bequeath an estate. The master of a ship must go to the aid of a vessel in distress. A motorist must not drive over the speed limit. It is generally thought that norms work by creating *rights* and imposing *duties*. Person A has a duty not to steal other persons' property. Property owners have a right not to have their property stolen. When I make a will, I instantly create rights in the beneficiaries to have my property conveyed to them on my death according to my instructions. The executor then has a duty to convey the property to the beneficiaries according to my instructions.

Hohfeld argued that there is more to law than just rights and duties, and that legal rules can be understood accurately only if we discern the most basic legal categories or conceptions and the relations among them. Consider the following five statements:

1.   I have a *right* to be paid my wages under the contract of service.
2.   I have a *right* to walk in my yard.
3.   I have a *right* to leave my property to another by will.
4.   I have a *right* not to be arrested without a warrant.
5.   I have a *right* to be respected by my colleagues.

The word 'right' is used in each of these sentences. A moment's reflection reveals that the term 'right' has a different meaning in each sentence. The right to be paid wages according to a contract is a *claim*, which Hohfeld called a right in the strict sense (2001, 13). The right to walk in one's yard is a *privilege* or *liberty*. The right to bequeath property by will is a *power* to bestow rights on others. The right not to be arrested without a warrant is *immunity*. What about the right to be respected by one's fellows? It is not a legal right at all, but a moral claim.

Hohfeld argued that these distinctions have always been present in the law (2001, 12–13). However, they are also neglected from time to time by judges and commentators, causing error and confusion of the law. Hohfeld was not the first to realise this, but he provided the most accurate and compelling analysis of the fundamental legal conceptions that most clearly expose juristic errors. It is useful, though, to start with the first systematic attempt in English jurisprudence to analyse and categorise basic legal conceptions – that of Jeremy Bentham.

Bentham and the classification of legal mandates

Bentham, whose general theory of law I discussed in Chapter 2, was one of the greatest analytical jurists. Bentham noted that although the law is commonly thought of as the commands of a sovereign, it does not always take the form of a command to do or refrain from doing some act. Hence, he substituted the word 'mandate' for 'command' in explaining the different kinds of law that a person encounters in society. In his book *Of Laws in General*, Bentham argued that there are only four kinds of mandates that the law can prescribe: (1) command, (2) non-command, (3) prohibition, and (4) permission (1970 (1782), 97). He offered the following four mandates as illustration:

1.   Every householder shall carry arms (command).
2.   No householder shall carry arms (prohibition).
3.   Any householder may forbear to carry arms (non-command).
4.   Any householder may carry arms (permission). (1970, 95)

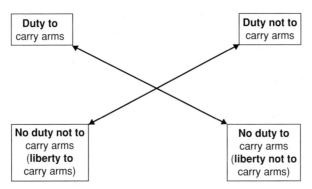

Figure 11.1 Bentham on liberty and duty

Mandates (1) and (2) create duties: the *duty to* carry arms and the *duty not to* carry arms. At any given time it must be one or the other duty, but not both. I cannot have a duty to carry arms and also a duty not to carry arms. Consider mandate (3). It means one of the following two positions:

(a)   There was in force mandate (1) requiring every householder to carry arms and now, by virtue of mandate (3), householders are exempt from carrying arms. Therefore mandate (3) repeals mandate (1).

(b)   Alternatively, it may mean there was no previous mandate requiring a householder to carry arms, and mandate (3) simply declares and confirms the law as it stood before.

Consider now mandate (4). This is the reverse situation. It means one of the following:

(a)   There was in force mandate (2) prohibiting householders from carrying arms and now, by virtue of mandate (4), householders are allowed to carry arms. Therefore mandate (4) repeals mandate (2).

(b)   Alternatively, it may mean there was no previous mandate prohibiting householders from carrying arms, and mandate (4) simply declares and confirms the law as it stood before.

Whichever is the case, it is clear that mandates 1 and 2 impose duties either to carry or not carry arms, and mandates 3 and 4 confer liberties either to carry or not carry arms. The position as regards possible mandates can be illustrated as shown in Figure 11.1.

Liberties and powers

The most fundamental principle of law in the common law world – indeed, the starting point of the law – is simply this. A person may do any act that the law does not forbid and may refrain from doing any act that the law does not require to be done. In other words, the natural liberty of a person is limited only by valid law. The corollary of this principle is that no person or authority may interfere with the liberty of a person except by authority of law (*Entick v Carrington* (1765) 19 Howell's State Trials 1029, 1066). Bentham identified two kinds of liberty.

Liberty 1: Where liberty does not affect any other person

Bentham called these self-regarding liberties. I have a liberty to walk in my yard. The exercise of this liberty does not violate any other person's rights. My neighbour's rights are not affected and, as Hohfeld later stated, my neighbour (and everyone else) has *no-right* that I not walk in my yard. Remember, though, that we have no unrestricted liberty even within our own homes. My liberty to play music on my sound system in my house is limited by the law of nuisance that protects my neighbour's entitlement to a quiet night's rest. Hence, I have no liberty to play my music as loudly as I wish at all times.

Liberty 2 (Power): Where liberty affects the rights of another

Some laws authorise persons to do acts that affect the rights of others. The criminal law authorises a person to inflict harm on another in self-defence. A police officer with a warrant may detain a suspect. A judge may summon a witness. In each case a person's right or liberty is interfered with by authority of law. Bentham wrote: 'When the acts you are left to perform are such whereby the interests of other individuals is [*sic*] liable to be affected, you are thereby said to have a power over those individuals' (1970, 290). *Power* is therefore a liberty whereby the power holder can change the legal condition of another.

Corroborated and uncorroborated liberties and powers

Bentham realised that some liberties will not exist without some form of legal protection. He called such protection corroboration (1970, 290–1). Consider this case. I have the liberty to walk in the public park. Now, this liberty is negated if the park warden prevents me from entering the park. If the park warden lets me in, I would also like to walk freely without the fear of being waylaid and robbed. The law protects my liberty to walk in the public park by imposing duties on others. Duties carry corresponding rights. (Try to think of a duty that is not owed to someone.) The park warden has a duty not to prevent my entry. (Therefore I have a right that the park warden let me enter.) Other persons have duties, cast by the criminal law (and tort law), not to harm or impede me in my activity. (Therefore I have rights that others not harm me.) These duty–right relations support or corroborate my liberty to walk in the public park.

Although in many cases it is practically difficult to enjoy a liberty without them, corroborating rights are not theoretically necessary for a liberty to exist. There are many liberties that can practically exist without direct or immediate protection of the law. Bentham called these uncorroborated liberties. Hart's example, which I have embellished, is instructive on the point (Hart 1973, 176). Imagine that you have an annoyingly inquisitive neighbour. He is often looking over the fence to see what you are doing, who visits you, what you wear to work, when you return at night and with whom. Your neighbour breaks no law, which means that he has a liberty to keep looking. In Hohfeld's terminology you have 'no-right' that he does not look over the fence. Equally, you have no duty not to prevent him observing your activities by any lawful means. The neighbour cannot complain if you erect a screen on your property to shut off his view. Remember, though, that you can only use lawful means. It may be cheaper for you to make him stop his habit by threatening violence than by building a screen. The trouble is that you have a duty under the law not to threaten violence. However, this duty does not directly correlate to his liberty to look. It correlates to his right not to be threatened.

Bentham thought that powers, being a special case of liberties, may also be corroborated or uncorroborated. He considered three scenarios, which I will supplement with examples.

1. The law does not assist in the exercise of power

The power is uncorroborated in this case. The common law allows a property owner to use self-help to abate a nuisance on a neighbouring property. Thus, I can enter the vacant land of my neighbour and clear it of rotting rubbish that is threatening my health. However, there is no duty on the part of the neighbour to assist me, or even not to resist me. She may not open the gate to let me enter. I may not have the physical resources to remove the rubbish. My power in this case depends on my own capacities. I can, of course, seek a court order against the neighbour, but then I am not exercising my own power but invoking the court's power.

2. Law imposes a duty not to oppose the exercise of power

Here we have a weakly corroborated power. Assume that the law grants power to the town council to enter the above described land and abate the nuisance. In this case the property owner has a duty not to oppose the council's action, but has no positive duty to assist it.

3. Law imposes a duty not to oppose and also a positive duty to assist

Some legal powers are accompanied by duties imposed on citizens to assist the power holder in exercising the power. Bentham described this as the highest and most perfect degree of power (1970, 291). An example is found in the common law rule that makes it an offence to refuse assistance to a constable in the execution of her duty to maintain or restore the Queen's Peace. The power to ask for assistance has its origin in the ancient practice of 'hue and cry', which was confirmed by the *Statute of Winchester* (1285). The Statute required all able bodied men to join the hue and cry in pursuit of a fleeing criminal. (Movie fans may be interested to know that the sheriff's posse that chases fleeing outlaws in the 'Wild West' was based on the same common law rule.) Most states in the US have long standing statutory penalties for refusing to assist police in apprehending felons (Blue 1992, 1475–6).

Bentham did not work out all the implications of his analysis of the elements of law. It was left to WN Hohfeld's remarkable essay to identify all the fundamental legal conceptions and their inter-relationships, and thus reveal the logical structure of legal statements.

Hohfeld's analysis of jural relations: the exposition of fundamental legal conceptions

Wesley Newcomb Hohfeld was Professor of Law at Stanford University when he published the first of his two famous articles under the title 'Some fundamental legal conceptions as applied in judicial reasoning'. They were published in volumes 23 (1913) and 26 (1917) of *The Yale Law Journal*. Yale University was so impressed by the first article that it recruited him to the Yale Law School. Hohfeld intended to develop his ideas further and publish them as a book, but his untimely death in 1918 at the age of 39 ended the project. The two articles were published as a book in 1919 and republished in 2001. The references in this chapter are to the latter book.

Hohfeld studied chemistry before turning to law, and brought to his legal study the chemist's instinct for breaking down compounds into their molecules and atoms. Hohfeld was gripped by the classic puzzles in legal theory about *rights in rem* and *rights in personam* in relation to equitable interests. A right *in rem* is traditionally thought to exist with respect to a thing and be applicable against the world at large, whereas a right *in personam* is thought to exist in relation to particular individuals. The rights I have over my house and land are rights *in rem* that I assert against the world at large, and my right to be paid the agreed salary is a right *in personam* that I have against my employer, the university. What, then, is the beneficiary's right under a trust? Trustee T holds a house in trust for beneficiary B, who is a minor until he reaches majority. Does B have a right *in rem* in relation to the house, or a right *in personam* against T? Most writers say that B has only a right *in personam*, some say that it is a right *sui generis* (a unique type by itself) and still others can't make up their minds. Hohfeld realised that these and similar confusions resulted from a misunderstanding of the fundamentals of legal conceptions and jural relations. Once these confusions are cleared it becomes plain that what we call rights *in rem*, for instance, are in fact separate rights that a person has in relation to every other person individually and severally. Hohfeld argued that other artificial dichotomies and constructs will also dissolve when the true nature of legal conceptions and relations is understood.

The most serious impediment to clear thinking and true solution of all legal problems, Hohfeld argued, was 'the express or tacit assumption that all legal relations can be reduced to "rights" and "duties" and that these latter categories are therefore adequate for the purpose of analyzing even the most complex legal interests, such as trusts, options, escrows, "future" interests, corporate interests, etc' (2001, 11). As explained earlier in this chapter, Hohfeld distinguished four different conceptions that lawyers tend to lump under the term 'right'. He aimed to disentangle and clarify the four conceptions. The most effective way of doing this, Hohfeld concluded, was to construct a logical system connecting the four conceptions to their correlatives and opposites. He thought that such a system would display the sum total of the fundamental legal conceptions.

Hohfeld broke the term 'right' into four distinct basic conceptions:

- *Claim right* or right in the strict sense – I will be using the term right for simplicity.
- *Privilege or liberty* – Hohfeld preferred the term 'privilege' to 'liberty' because he felt that 'liberty' had wider connotations. In current usage, 'liberty' is probably more precise than 'privilege'. Hence, following Glanville Williams, I will be using the term *liberty* to refer to Hohfeld's *privilege,* noting that the two may be interchanged without violence to the system (Williams 1956, 1131–2).
- *Power* – like Bentham, Hohfeld regarded power as a special case of liberty. He considered this distinction to be critical for accurate legal thinking.
- *Immunity* – immunity is a special case of right and, again, it is important to distinguish the two for clear understanding of the law.

Each of these conceptions makes sense only when we take account of their correlatives and opposites. I will briefly set out the jural relations between these conceptions before addressing some of their important logical implications and questions raised by commentators.

Jural correlatives

Each of the conceptions 'right', 'liberty', 'power' and 'immunity' has an indispensable correlative. The jural correlative can be technically defined as follows:

> In any legal relation between two parties concerning a single act or omission, the presence of one conception in one party entails the presence of the correlative *in the other party*.

Thus, if A has a right that B pays him $10 under the contract, B has a duty to pay A $10. The vertical arrows in Figure 11.2 represent the correlatives.

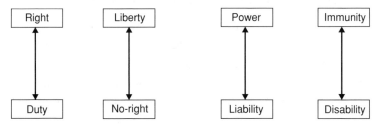

Figure 11.2 Jural correlatives

Jural opposites

Each of the conceptions 'right', 'liberty', 'power' and 'immunity' has a jural opposite. The technical definition of jural opposite is as follows:

> In any legal relation between two parties concerning a single act or omission, the
> presence of one conception in one party means the absence of the jural opposite *in that
> party*.

Thus A, who has a right that B pays him $10, does not also have a *no-right* in that
regard. B, who has a duty to pay $10, does not have a *liberty* not to pay. This
follows from the law of non-contradiction. As Aristotle stated: 'It is impossible
for the same man to suppose that the same thing is and is not. One cannot say of
something that it is and that it is not in the same respect and at the same time'
(1968 (350 BC), 163). Thus, Socrates lives, or he does not. He cannot both live
and not live at the same instant, although he can live in one instant and be dead
the next. The kangaroo is a mammal, or it is not. Jupiter is a planet, or it is not.
A has a right or no-right, but not both. B has a duty or no duty (which is liberty),
but not both.

The diagonal arrows in Figure 11.3 represent the jural opposites.

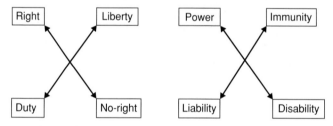

Figure 11.3 Jural opposites

Jural contradictories

Hohfeld identified only the jural correlatives and opposites. Glanville Williams
perceived a third set of jural relations, which he termed *contradictories* (1956,
1135). The technical definition of *contradictory* is as follows:

> In any legal relation between two parties concerning a single act or omission, the
> presence of one conception in one party means the absence of the contradictory in the
> other party.

Thus, if A has a *right* that B pays her $10, B cannot have a *liberty* not to pay A
because B has a *duty* to pay A. The jural contradictory follows logically from the
jural opposite.

The horizontal arrows in Figure 11.4 represent the jural contradictories.

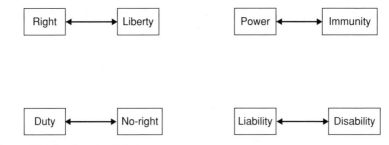

Figure 11.4 Jural contradictories

The interconnectedness of the fundamental legal conceptions

Hohfeld's analysis shows that 'right', 'duty', 'liberty' and 'no-right' are connected in a fundamental way with each other. The existence of one brings about the existence of the others. The conceptions 'power', 'liability', 'immunity' and 'disability' are similarly connected. The totality of these connections is illustrated in Figure 11.5. The vertical arrows show the correlatives, the diagonal arrows indicate the opposites, and the horizontal arrows the contradictories.

Consider the box on the left. A has a right under the contract that B pays her $10:

> Correlative: A has a *right* that B pays her $10 and B has a *duty* to pay $10 to A.
>
> Opposite: Since A has a *right* to be paid $10, A cannot have *no-right* to be paid.
>
> Contradictory: Since A has a *right* to be paid $10, B cannot have a *liberty* not to pay.

Now consider the box on the right. A has power to arrest B:

> Correlative: A has *power* to arrest B and B is *liable* to be arrested by A.
>
> Opposite: Since A has *power* to arrest, A cannot have *disability* to arrest.
>
> Contradictory: Since A has *power* to arrest B, B has no *immunity* from arrest.

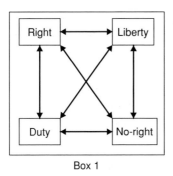

Box 1

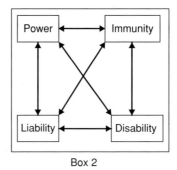

Box 2

Figure 11.5 All the jural relations

Each legal relation is a relation between two individuals concerning a single action or omission

Like the engineer who disassembles a machine to learn how it works, Hohfeld aimed to break down laws into their basic elements to see how the law actually works. He found that the law works through legal relations between individuals in relation to single actions or omissions. I use the term 'individual' in a special sense to include corporate entities such as trading companies, government agencies and the legislature itself. At one level there are Hohfeldian relations within each corporate entity. Directors, managers and shareholders of a company have rights and owe duties to one another. Individual members of parliament have similar rights, duties, powers and immunities. At another level these corporate bodies act as individual corporate entities.

There are important implications of the basic premise of the Hohfeldian analysis. First, a jural relation exists between two individuals. It is never between a person and a thing. I have no jural relation with my motor car, although I claim to own it. I have jural relations with A, B, C and every other individual in the world with respect to my motor car. No person may take it without my permission. In orthodox theory, if I am the owner of Blackacre, I am regarded as having a right *in rem* against the whole world with respect to Blackacre. If I sell Blackacre, the purchaser will gain the same right *in rem* against the world. It is commonly thought for this reason that a right *in rem* is not personal, but is a right that attaches to the land. In one sense it does. Yet what is the actual effect of having a right *in rem*? It is that the owner has a right in relation to every other individual in the world with respect to a thing. In other words, the owner has millions of separate rights *in personam* against each and every individual in the world. She has a right that A does not trespass, B does not trespass, C does not trespass, and so on indefinitely. Sir William Markby observed, in his classic work *Elements of Law with Reference to Principles of General Jurisprudence*:

> If we attempt to translate the phrase [*in rem*] literally, and get it into our heads that a *thing*, because rights exist *in respect of it*, becomes a sort of *juristic person*, and *liable to duties*, we shall get into *endless confusion*. (1905, 165)

Second, ownership of a thing is generally described as a bundle of entitlements over the thing. Hohfeld's system unbundles the entitlements. My right that A, B, C and all others not enter Blackacre without my permission is one entitlement. My liberty to enter and enjoy Blackacre is a distinct entitlement. My right to be free of trespass is obviously helpful to my liberty to enjoy Blackacre, but they are nevertheless separate entitlements.

Third, it is important to keep in mind that the same set of facts may give rise to separate jural relations. The failure to do so leads to common error. A is walking in the public park and is obstructed by B, who physically restrains her. Two distinct jural relations are at work simultaneously:

- A has *liberty* to walk in the public park and B has *no-right* that A does not walk in the public park.
- A has a *right* not to be physically restrained by B and B has a *duty* not to physically restrain A.

Fourth, it is critical that we recognise that a dispute between two parties can give rise to distinct and successive legal relations. This is a point that Finnis missed when he said that we need to ask about remedies before we can say that a person has a right (1972, 380–1). Austin identified a two-tier system of rights. A primary right is one that a person initially has under the law. A seller has a primary right to be paid the price of goods under a contract of sale. If not paid, the seller gains secondary remedial rights to recover the price or to receive damages (Austin 1869, 788). Peter Birks, the leading British private law theorist in the modern era, identified a third level of rights: namely, the rights that the court creates in giving judgment. The judgment creates a new right in place of the primary right. The plaintiff may have claimed $10 000 in damages but may receive $9000 in judgment. She now has a right to receive the latter sum:

> To take the contractual example, on the primary level are the rights born of the contract; on the secondary level are the remedial rights born of the breach; and at the tertiary level is the right born of the judgment itself, which is the right enforced by the process of execution. (Birks 2000, 30)

Birks' analysis is also incomplete from the Hohfeldian viewpoint. This is hardly surprising, since British private law scholars have studiously ignored Hohfeld's system. A Hohfeldian analysis of Birks' example actually yields four levels of legal relations:

1. Each party to the contract has *primary* entitlements. For example, the buyer has a right that the seller delivers the article and the seller has a right that the buyer pays the seller the agreed price.

2. Assume that the seller fails to deliver the promised article, in breach of the contract. The breach gives rise to new *secondary* entitlements. The buyer (depending on local law) may have a power to rescind the contract and treat it as ended. If the buyer has suffered damages, she will gain a right that the seller pay the damages. Differences between the parties concerning the *secondary* entitlements may be settled through negotiation or compromise. The terms of the settlement (which amounts to a contract) may establish new rights and duties that replace the pre-existing relations.

3. If the issues concerning secondary rights are not resolved, the aggrieved party usually has some recourse to a court of law. We say that, in Hohfeldian terms, the plaintiff has a power to sue the defendant. This may be regarded as a *tertiary* entitlement.

4. If the dispute is tried by a court and judgment is entered for the plaintiff, the plaintiff gains new entitlements according to the terms of the judgment. It is usually in the form of the award of a specific amount of damages,

and exceptionally in the form of a right to specific performance by the defendant. These rights represent *quaternary* entitlements.

More examples are discussed later but, before proceeding further, we must firmly keep in mind that Hohfeld's system breaks down jural relations to their most basic level, which is the relation between two individuals with respect to a single action or omission.

Right–duty correlation

A person has a right only because some other person has a duty that *correlates* to that right. One cannot exist without the other. They represent the two aspects of one relation, just as 'heads' and 'tails' represent two sides of a coin. The baker has a right to be paid for the loaf that the customer buys because the customer has a duty to pay for the loaf. The factory owner has a duty to not pollute the neighbour's land because the neighbour has a right that the factory owner does not pollute his land. A highwayman has a duty not to rob the traveller because the traveller has a right not to be robbed. As Finnis commented, it is critically important to bear in mind that a right is never to do an act or not do an act. It is a claim that another person must do an act or not do an act (1972, 380).

Some writers have argued that there are duties that do not correlate to anyone's rights, such as the citizen's duty to pay tax. I will presently discuss their views, which I believe are mistaken.

Liberty–no-right correlation

It is noticeable that a liberty does not carry a correlative duty on the part of another. A, as owner of Blackacre, has liberty to walk on it. It means that others have no-right that A does not walk on Blackacre. Others, of course, have duties not to interfere with A's liberty. B, for example, has a duty not to prevent A from entering Blackacre and thus prevent her walking on it. The critical point is that B's duty correlates to A's right not to be obstructed from walking on Blackacre, and not to A's liberty to walk on Blackacre. This is illustrated in Figure 11.6.

As Finnis showed, the failure to maintain this distinction has led even eminent jurists to serious error in applying Hohfeld's analysis (1972, 377–8).

Power–liability correlation

As Bentham previously explained, power is a special kind of liberty. The exercise of power creates new legal relations by imposing duties and creating rights in others. A simple liberty has no such effect. A's exercise of her liberty to walk in the public park does not *create* B's duty not to obstruct A. B always had the duty not to obstruct A if she chose to walk in the park. In contrast, the police officer's arrest of the suspect brings about a restriction of the suspect's legal liberty to move as he pleases. The arresting police officer exercises a power, not

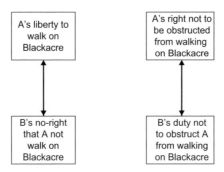

Figure 11.6 Liberty and right disentangled

a simple liberty. The person to whom a lawful power is applied is said to have a *liability*.

The special meaning of liability

Lawyers understand liability in the sense of a legal penalty or disadvantage. A person who commits a serious crime is liable to be sentenced to imprisonment. A factory owner who causes harm to a neighbour's crop is liable to pay damages. Just as power is a special kind of liberty, liability is a special kind of duty that flows from the exercise of power. However, Hohfeld used the term *liability* in an expanded sense. A person may have a Hohfeldian liability to receive a benefit. The maker of a last will exercises power to bequeath her estate as directed in the will. The beneficiaries have liability (in the Hohfeldian sense) to receive the benefits. The minister has power to grant a licence to fish in the lake. The fisherman has liability to be granted the licence to fish in the lake. Hohfeld cited a number of US decisions where judges have used the term liability in this broad sense (2001, 26–7).

Change of legal relations by natural causes and by the exercise of legal powers

Legal power must not be confused with physical power. Hohfeld was aware that legal rights and duties can change as a result of two kinds of events – those that do not involve volitional acts of human beings, and those that do:

> A change in a given legal relation may result (1) from some superadded fact or groups of facts *not under the control of a human being (or human beings)*; or (2) from some superadded fact or group of facts *which are under the volitional control of one or more human beings*. As regards the second class of cases, the person (or persons) whose volitional control is paramount may be said to have the (legal) power to effect the particular change of legal relations that is involved in the problem. (2001, 21; emphasis added)

The following examples will clarify the distinction:

1. A ship is damaged in the high seas by the physical force of a storm and is in danger of sinking with all on board. The master of every passing ship

has a duty to go to the assistance of the ship in distress. The seafarers in the ship in distress (and its owner) have a correlative right that those able to help them provide help. The storm did not create new rights and duties but activated rights and duties that existed in law.

2.   The law prohibits a person from possessing a firearm except under the authority of a licence granted by the minister. The minister grants Farmer X a licence to possess a rifle. The minister exercised a power in conferring a new liberty on X to possess a rifle. Previously X had a duty to not have a firearm in his possession. The minister's decision created new rights and duties.

Do unlawful acts involve the exercise of Hohfeldian power?

C uses physical force to rob D of the money she is carrying. C had a duty not to rob D. However C, by his exercise of physical power, brought about new legal rights and duties. Consequently, D has a right that C returns the money and D has a correlative duty to return the money. Therefore, can we say that D was actually exercising a Hohfeldian *power*? The answer is 'No'. Hohfeld did not directly address this puzzle, but his answer is easily derived from the logic of his scheme.

It is clear that Hohfeld limited the conception of power to the capacity to change *legally* the existing legal relations and entitlements. He noted, with respect to power, that 'the nearest synonym for any ordinary case seems to be [legal] ability' (2001, 21). This is a necessary conclusion from the logic of Hohfeld's analysis. Remember that a power is a type of liberty. The opposite of the *liberty to* do an act is the *duty not to* do the act. It follows from the law of non-contradiction that C cannot have liberty (power) to do something and also a duty not to do it. A person has duty d, or does not have duty d, at the same time in relation to the same act or omission.

The robber C had a duty not to rob D. It was not his physical power that brought about the new legal relations, but his breach of duty. *Power* therefore must be understood as the legal capacity of a human agent to effect a change in legal relations. This means power is the *legal* competence to confer new rights and impose new duties.

Kinds of powers

People experience powers and liabilities in their daily lives. Some powers are readily identified, but there are other powers that go unnoticed. The power of Parliament to enact the *Road Traffic Act*, the power of the minister under the *Road Traffic Act* to make regulations setting speed limits, the power of the town council to permit a public meeting in the town square and the power of the testator to confer by will rights on beneficiaries are easily recognised as legal powers. Similarly, it is not difficult to see that under an agency contract the agent is given power to make decisions that are binding on the principal. Yet there are other competencies that are usually not identified as powers.

People give their friends and relatives gifts. As Hohfeld pointed out, in somewhat laboured language, the simple act of gift giving is an exercise of power (2001, 22). When a person gives a friend a gift of a book, she conveys the property in the book from herself to the friend. (In legal terms, the transfer of property occurs by the abandonment of the property by the owner and its appropriation by the recipient.) Similarly, the making of contracts involves the exercise of powers. X posts a letter to Y in which he offers to sell his car for $5000. X thereby creates a legal power in Y to create a binding contract that imposes a duty on X to deliver the car on the payment of $5000. X's initial offer is itself an exercise of power, because it has created a new legal relation between X and Y that did not exist before. (The making of the offer is the exercise of power to confer a power.) Y's power will terminate if X revokes the offer before it is accepted. Or it might expire after a reasonable time. The act of revocation of the offer is also an exercise of power, because it terminates Y's power to complete the contract. Let us assume that Y pays a deposit of $100 as consideration for X's promise to keep the offer open for one week. Now X has no power during that week to revoke the offer, so he has a disability to revoke the offer within one week (Hohfeld 2001, 23–4).

Immunity–disability correlation

Immunity is an exemption from the force of the law – specifically from the exercise of power. It is a subset of the right that I have that another person not exercise power to change my existing rights. Its opposite is disability. A diplomat has 'diplomatic immunity' not to be charged and tried in the court of a foreign country in which she enjoys diplomatic status. Thus, the Ambassador of country C in Australia who causes an accident by reckless driving in Sydney may successfully invoke her diplomatic immunity when charged for the offence in an Australian court. A donor who donates a part of his income to a recognised charity may claim an exemption (immunity) from income tax on that part of the salary. The so-called 'right to remain silent' is an immunity enjoyed by an accused person that prevents the police or the prosecution from forcing the accused to give evidence against herself.

Hohfeld regarded immunity in a more expansive way. Every disability of a person under the law creates immunity. He began with the following example. X, who is a landowner, has the power to alienate her land to Y or to any other person but Y, and every other person has no power to alienate X's land. Hence, X has immunity from having her property in the land transferred to another without her consent. Now, if judgment has been given against X authorising the Sheriff to sell her land to satisfy the debt she owes the bank, she loses the immunity, but only as against the Sheriff. The Sheriff has power granted by law to transfer her title to another. X therefore has a liability correlative to the Sheriff's power (Hohfeld 2001, 28). X continues to have immunity against all other persons. X also has immunity against the Sheriff with respect to her other properties.

It is evident that in a free society citizens have a vast range of Hohfeldian immunities. The rights and liberties of a citizen are immune from interference unless the power to interfere is granted by law. Lord Chief Justice Camden's memorable words in *Entick v Carrington* spelled out the general immunity enjoyed by all citizens:

> The great end, for which men entered into society, was to secure their property. That right is preserved sacred and incommunicable in all instances, where it has not been taken away or abridged by some public law for the good of the whole ... By the laws of England, every invasion of private property, be it ever so minute, is a trespass. No man can set his foot upon my ground without my license, but he is liable to an action, though the damage be nothing; which is proved by every declaration in trespass, where the defendant is called upon to answer for bruising the grass and even treading upon the soil. If he admits the fact, he is bound to show by way of justification, that some positive law has empowered or excused him. The justification is submitted to the judges, who are to look into the books; and find if such a justification can be maintained by the text of the statute law, or by the principles of common law. If no excuse can be found or produced, the silence of the books is an authority against the defendant, and the plaintiff must have judgment. ((1765) 19 *Howell's State Trials* 1029, 1066)

Immunity, then, is my right that another not interfere with my existing right or liberty except under the authority of the law. Disability is the duty of a person not to interfere with a right or liberty of another except under the authority of law.

Connecting the two 'boxes' in Hohfeld's system

Take another look at Figure 11.5. The vertical, diagonal and horizontal arrows indicate the interconnectedness of the conceptions in each 'box'. Are the conceptions within the box on the left (Box 1) conceptually connected to the conceptions in the box on the right (Box 2)? In other words, are the two boxes fundamentally related? The answer is 'Yes'.

Hohfeld was keenly aware of the correspondence between the conceptions in Box 1 and Box 2. He wrote, near the end of his famous 1913 essay:

> Perhaps it will also be plain, from the preliminary outline and from the discussion down to this point, that a power bears the same general contrast to an immunity that a right does to a privilege [liberty]. A right is one's affirmative claim against another, and a privilege is one's freedom from the right or claim of another. Similarly, power is one's affirmative control over a given legal relation as against another; whereas an immunity is one's freedom [liberty] from legal power or 'control' of another as regards some legal relation. (2001, 28)

Hohfeld did not fully explain that the conceptions in Box 2 are in fact special cases of the conceptions in Box 1; however, judging by the above passage, he was almost certainly aware of it. Dias noted that Box 1 represented the jural relations at rest, while Box 2 showed jural relations in the making (1976, 64–5).

Dias thus introduced a time dimension to the analysis. Imagine that you are standing at a point in time and looking back at Box 1 and looking ahead at Box 2. You see within Box 1 a set of existing jural relations among already established rights, duties, liberties and no-rights. Looking at Box 2 you see the way new rights, duties, liberties and no-rights are being established through the exercise of power. Sumner observed that the conceptions in Box 2 were the second order counterparts of the conceptions in Box 1 (1987, 29–31). Brazil gave a more comprehensive and thoroughgoing explanation of the fundamental sameness of the two boxes (1996, 276–7). The insights that these authors provide leads to the following analysis.

In a two-party relation:

- power is the *liberty to* impose a duty or confer a liberty
- liability is the *no-right* that a duty not be imposed or a liberty not be conferred
- immunity is the *right* that a duty not be imposed or a liberty not be conferred
- disability is the *duty not* to impose a duty or confer a liberty.

This analysis leads to a further question. The conceptions in Box 2 can be logically reduced to the conceptions in Box 1. Can the conceptions in Box 1 be further reduced to a single dichotomy of liberty (duty), or as Brazil contended, to the dichotomy of duty (no-duty)? In other words, are the conceptions of right and no-right in Box 1 redundant? The answer is that they are not, because they represent logical implications of having a liberty or a duty.

Reduction (or abstraction) for its own sake is intellectually interesting and has explanatory value. However, over-reduction can deprive us of useful knowledge by obliterating important distinctions. A farmer who owns a cat, three dogs, four horses and a dozen cows can truthfully say that he owns 20 mammals, but he will thereby suppress useful information. We have learned that it is possible to reduce power to liberty; immunity to right; liability to no-right; and disability to duty. We have deepened our understanding of the conceptions in Box 2 by noticing their pedigree in Box 1. Having gained this insight, it makes a lot of practical sense for us to retain Box 2 and its contents.

Some logical puzzles in Hohfeld's system

The logic of Hohfeld's system has been assailed by generations of academics with, in my view, little result. Nevertheless, we can sharpen our understanding of Hohfeld's analysis by examining some of these challenges.

Are there duties that do not correlate to rights?

Some writers have claimed that certain duties of a public nature have no correlative rights. Jeremy Bentham argued that duties such as the duty not to counterfeit money, the duty to pay taxes and the duty to perform military service do not correlate to anyone's rights. As Hohfeld's analysis demonstrates, this is plainly wrong if the constitutional status of the state as a rights bearer is acknowledged. A state that has the legal monopoly to issue currency has a legal right that persons not counterfeit its currency. Where the law permits private individuals or firms to issue currency, the position is identical. The authorised currency issuers have a right that others not counterfeit the private currency. In each case the duty correlates to the right of the person who is authorised to issue the currency. In the case of the duty to pay tax, the state has the right that citizens pay taxes. Where the law allows conscription (compulsory military service), the duty to provide military service correlates to the state's right to have the service rendered. There is no mystery in any of this once the Hohfeldian system is properly grasped.

White's claim concerning duties unrelated to rights is typical of the continuing misunderstanding and misapplication of Hohfeld's thesis. White considered the cases of the duty of the state to punish an offender, the duty of a football player to stop the opposing centre forward and the citizen's duty to expose a felony. He said that the application of the Hohfeldian analysis to these cases would lead to the ridiculous propositions that the offender has a right to be punished, the centre forward has a right to be stopped, and the felon has a right to be informed on (White 1984, 60). None of this follows from Hohfeld's analysis, and White revealed a monumental misunderstanding of Hohfeld's system. The duty of the judge to impose punishment on an offender is not owed to the offender. It is a duty owed to the state as representing the citizens. Alternatively, the duty is owed to each and every citizen. *A public duty is owed to the public*. The offender has a liability to be punished that correlates to the judge's power to impose punishment.

The case of the football player's duty to stop (more accurately, to try to stop) the opposing centre forward is very illuminating. Contrary to White's claim, the case illustrates the power of Hohfeld's analytical method. How does the duty to oppose the other side arise? It could be from moral obligation or from contract. Assume that the game is only a social event. Even then, each player owes a moral duty to their team mates and to the spectators to contest the opposition. The duty is primarily owed to team mates and supporters, not to the opponent. However, there may even be a duty owed to the opponents to try your best to oppose them, because if you do not try there will be no game. Now consider a professional game, where a great deal of money is involved and the player is paid a salary to perform well. In this case, the contracted player's duty to do their best against the opposition is owed to the employer. What is the Hohfeldian relation between two opposing players? Each player has, within the rules of the game, the liberty to overcome the opponent and the opponent has no-right that the player does not do so. The side that displays superior strength, skill and wisdom and enjoys a fair share of luck usually prevails. It is the existence of these liberties, constrained by duties to play by the rules, that makes the game a compelling spectacle.

As to the citizen's duty to inform on a felon, every member of the public has a correlative right in that regard under the law, although they may not have the means of enforcing it. In fact, as previously noted, the duty of a citizen to assist in the apprehension of a wrongdoer is an ancient common law obligation stretching back to the practice of hue and cry. The duty is not owed to the wrongdoer but to fellow citizens.

Holmström-Hintikka claimed that responsibilities constitute a type of duty that has no corresponding rights:

> Responsibilities may be considered obligations – or duties – without corresponding rights. The physician is responsible for her patient with respect to providing a particular treatment, the expecting mother is responsible for the well being of the fetus, the pet owner is responsible for the quality of life of his pet. None of these responsibilities correspond to a right for the beneficiary and yet laws may be created to impose such responsibilities, laws which if broken lead to punishment. (1997, 54–5)

The first example in the above passage is plainly wrong. The physician's duty of care is owed to the patient, who has a correlative right. Take the second example, of the expecting mother's responsibility for the wellbeing of the foetus. Why would the law of a particular society make it a criminal offence to harm a foetus? It may be the case that the foetus is considered to be a rights bearing entity that is worthy of protection. In that event the duty is owed to the foetus. It does not matter in the Hohfeldian scheme that the foetus is incapable of enforcing its right. Alternatively, the state, in criminalising the act or omission, is creating a duty that is owed to the state or to every member of society. The same reasoning applies exactly to the case of cruelty to animals. The animal may be regarded as a rights bearer or the society may consider that persons owe the state or each member of society a duty to desist from animal cruelty because of the offence it causes to the society's moral values. In that case, the correlative right resides in each member of society. It does not matter that many members of society are indifferent to animal cruelty and would not wish to enforce their right. A right may exist in law without the right holder desiring it. It is open to a citizen who takes offence to prosecute the violator, either by complaining to the state law enforcers or by launching a private prosecution.

The theory that public duties have no correlative rights proceeds from two significant oversights. The first is that there is nothing unusual about laws that impose on an individual the identical duty in relation to each and every member of a specified group or of the entire public. Thus, I have a duty of care towards each and every member of the public when I am driving my car. Every member of the public has a correlative right that I take reasonable care not to harm them. Every member of the public has an individual duty not to trespass on my land. I have a correlative right against each and every members of the public that they not trespass on my land. Hohfeld's analysis has the virtue of breaking down the misleading dichotomy between public and private duties.

The second oversight concerns the fact that, in Hohfeld's analysis, the question of the existence of a right is distinct from the question of the availability of a remedy for the violation of that right. The duty of the police officer to keep traffic moving confers a correlative right on the motorists, though they may have no immediate remedy if the police officer fails to do her duty. Even where an effective remedy is available – as where an injured party may sue for damages – the activation of that remedy brings about new sets of jural relations. Thus, I have a power to sue for damages and the tortfeasor has a liability to be sued. Once judgment is entered in my favour, I have a new right that correlates to the defendant's duty to pay me the awarded damages. As previously discussed, a *primary* right, in Hohfeldian analysis, is independent of consequent entitlements that result from its violation.

Liberties without rights

The conventional understanding before Hohfeld was that legal liberty was a special kind of physical liberty that was protected by rights. If a liberty was not secured by appropriate rights it was not thought of as a legal liberty. Hohfeld, as we have seen, argued that the existence of a liberty did not depend on legal protection. He demonstrated his reasoning in relation to JC Gray's now-famous hypothetical concerning a shrimp salad. Gray wrote:

> The eating of shrimp salad is an interest of mine, and if I can pay for it, the law will protect that interest, and it is therefore a right of mine to eat shrimp salad which I have paid for, although I know that shrimp salad always gives me the colic (1909, 15–16).

Gray, according to Hohfeld, made two errors. First, he spoke of 'right' in the sense of liberty. Second, he implied that the liberty to eat the shrimp salad existed because of the protection given by law. Hohfeld described the legal situation this way:

> A, B, C and D, being owners of the salad, may say to X: 'Eat the salad if you can; you have our licence to do so, but we don't agree not to interfere with you.' In such a case the privileges [liberties] exist, so that if X succeeds in eating the salad, he has violated no rights of any of the parties. But it is equally clear that if A had succeeded in holding so fast to the dish that X couldn't eat the contents, no right of X would have been violated. (2001, 16)

People enjoy many liberties with no accompanying legal rights preventing others from interfering with the liberty. These kinds of interferences are known as *damnum absque injuria* (loss without injury). Glanville Williams gave a series of examples of these situations. One is this. You and I are walking together and we see a gold watch lying ahead of us. I have liberty to run to pick it up, but so have you. The one who picks it up first acquires title that is good against all but the true owner (Williams 1956, 1143). We encounter less dramatic instances of this nature often in life. X and Y are looking for a parking space in the car park. They see one and they both have liberty to take the space. The one who reaches it first gets to park. At our university cafeterias, there are two conventions. One is the 'first come first served' principle. The other is the convention of queuing. Students have equal liberty of hurrying to take a place in the queue ahead of others. In the evenings some of our students play rugby football. Players have liberty to force their way to the opponents' try line to score. Equally, opponents have liberty to prevent the attacking players from reaching the try line. The liberties of both sides are identical.

The reader will notice, in each of the above examples, that a person will not be able to exercise the liberty in a practical sense if they do not enjoy an array of basic rights. In the car park example, X and Y have liberty to take the parking spot, but each has a duty to avoid a collision in doing so. Hence, each has a right that the other takes due care. The liberty would be defeated in a practical sense if this right did not exist. In the example of the cafeteria queue, each student has a liberty to join the queue but has a duty not use force in doing it. Every student joining the queue has a right not to be pushed aside. In the rugby game, the players are restricted in the way they can attack their opponents' try line or defend their own try line. Every player has a duty not to commit foul play such as striking the head of an opponent or tripping an opponent. The game would become impossible to play without a set of rights and duties. So, was Hohfeld wrong?

Hohfeld's contention was that a right cannot be logically derived from the existence of a liberty. 'Whether there should be such concomitant rights (or claims) is ultimately a question of justice and policy; and it should be considered, as such, on its merits. The only correlative logically implied by the privileges or liberties in question are the "no-rights" of "third parties".' (Hohfeld 2001, 17) Hohfeld was correct on this question. However, in the real world of social life, many liberties exist only because they are protected by a perimeter of legal rights. It is the experience of humankind that where there is lawlessness there are no rights and duties and where there are no rights and duties liberties are at best precarious.

Is liberty divisible?

We have already noted that the conceptions in Box 1 (in Figure 11.5) can be expressed in a positive or negative form.

- When we speak of right we include both the right that another person *do an act* and the right that another person *not do an act*. I have a *right to* be paid my wages. I have a *right not to* be assaulted. These rights correlate to the *duty to* pay my wages and the *duty not* to assault me.
- When we speak of liberty we include both *liberty to* and *liberty not to*. I have a *liberty to* walk in my yard and a *liberty not to* walk in my yard. These liberties correlate to the *no-right* that I not walk and *no-right* that I walk.

In the Hohfeldian scheme, liberty and duty are opposites. Either I have a liberty to walk in the park or I have a duty not to walk in the park. Since liberty is the absence of duty, it cannot be both. Here, though, is a puzzle.

- X has *liberty to* give money to a charity. X also has *liberty not to* give money. In other words X has neither a *duty to* give nor a *duty not to* give. He has a choice.
- X has a *duty to* pay tax. Does X also have a *liberty to* pay tax?

There are two possible answers. One is to follow Williams and say that X has a liberty to pay tax even when he is duty bound to pay tax. Williams' argument is that the term *liberty* as used by Hohfeld refers to two distinct conceptions: (1) *liberty to* and (2) *liberty not to*. Then the opposites are as follows:

Liberty to   ⟷ Duty not to
Liberty not to ⟷ Duty to

This shows that there is no opposition between *liberty to* do something and a *duty to* do it. Thus X will have liberty to pay tax and duty to pay tax (Williams 1956, 1138–40).

The second possible answer is that if X has a duty to pay tax it makes little sense to say that he has a liberty to pay tax. This view regards choice as an essential feature of liberty. As Williams himself noted, a philosopher would regard the idea of liberty to do one's duty as 'a poor kind of joke' (1956, 1139). A's liberty to walk in the park necessarily implies A's liberty not to walk in the park. Professor Gray's liberty to eat the shrimp salad implies that he has a liberty not to eat it. When the law imposes a duty, this choice is taken away. One must do what the law demands – like pay tax. X of course needs certain other liberties in order to be able to pay tax, such as the liberty to write a cheque and the liberty to travel to the post office to mail the cheque. These are not liberties to pay tax but general freedoms that allow us get through daily life.

I prefer the second answer, because it reflects the conventional and philosophical understanding of the conception of liberty and because it retains the simplicity of Hohfeld's system without practical harm.

Value of Hohfeld's system

Hohfeld's aim was to show that many common errors and misconceptions about law could be eliminated if lawyers understood the fundamental legal conceptions and gained precise understanding of the nature of jural relations. In particular, he hoped that his analysis would expose the problems posed by artificial constructs such as the idea of the right *in rem*. Hohfeld did not claim originality for his insights, but argued that he was presenting systematically the ideas that the abler minds in the judiciary and the academy were already applying to the law. He showed through citations that the essentially interpersonal nature of rights *in rem* was keenly appreciated by John Austin, Sir William Markby, Oliver Wendell Holmes, Lord Chancellor Viscount Haldane, Lord Summer, and Justice

Brandeis of the US Supreme Court (Hohfeld 2001, 60–4). Hohfeld devoted the second instalment of his work (published in 1917 in *The Yale Law Journal*) to an extended survey of judgments and commentaries that showed how some judges and jurists got it conceptually wrong and how others got it right.

As previously discussed, the recurrent errors concerning the term 'rights *in rem*' flow from its association with a thing. If A owns Blackacre he has a right against each and every individual that each does not commit trespass. The critical point that tends to get lost is that, although the subject of the right is Blackacre, the right exists in relation to every separate individual in the world. If A sells Blackacre to B, B will have the same (or similar) rights *in rem* against every separate individual. Hohfeld proposed a new dichotomy to replace the categories of rights *in rem* and rights *in personam* and, to this end, coined the terms 'multital right' and 'paucital right' (2001, 52–3). *Paucital* rights are those that a person has in relation to one individual or a group of identifiable individuals. A has a right that B pays her $10 under the contract. This is a paucital relation between A and B. Company director C owes duties to the shareholders of the company. This too is a paucital relation, because it exists between C and each individual member of a finite and known group of individuals. In contrast, D, as the owner of Whiteacre, has multital relations with every other individual in the world severally. Here D has rights against an indeterminate group of persons.

This analysis enables us to see that multital rights need not relate to physical things. X, when driving on the motorway, has a right that every other person shows care not to cause an accident. Y, who is the holder of a patent, has a right that no other person shall manufacture articles using the patented design. Z has a right that no person publishes a libel against him.

Hohfeld's system is an unambiguous help in thinking clearly about the law. His terminology has not gained the currency that he hoped. This is mainly because lawyers and legal scholars are too wedded to the terms 'right' and 'duty'. Yet, as Hohfeld himself demonstrated, the better lawyers intuitively grasp and apply the Hohfeldian analysis without necessarily embracing his lexicon. When a lawyer submits that her client has a *right* to grow cabbages in her garden and that her neighbour has *no right* to let his goat eat them, she will usually mean that the client has a Hohfeldian liberty to grow cabbages and that the neighbour has a Hohfeldian duty not to let his goat eat the cabbages. Good lawyers and good academics will get it right even if they do not know that Hohfeld ever lived or wrote! Yet, as Hohfeld and, later, Williams showed, even great legal minds are prone to error when they depart from the Hohfeldian system, knowingly or unknowingly. The study of the Hohfeldian analysis has dropped out of the curricula of many law schools, as has analytical jurisprudence generally. This is an unmitigated misfortune for legal education.

12

Justice

Justice is a universal aspiration, and the sense of injustice is a powerful human emotion. It is strongest when a person's own interests are harmed, but is also aroused in civilised people when they witness wrongs done to others. Widespread and unrequited injustice inevitably leads to conflict. A society that does not have justice as a governing principle is an unstable society that will be held together, if at all, by force. Justice is also a perennially controversial idea in human affairs. People are united in their belief in justice as an ideal, but are divided on what justice means or requires. Many conflicting claims for material goods are made in the name of justice because of its emotive power. Justice has no universally valid definition. It means different things to different people and its requirements may change over time. Different kinds of justice are not always in harmony. One person's claim for legal justice may conflict with another person's demand for distributive justice. The legal requirements of procedural justice may constrain the pursuit of substantive justice, as explained further below.

Justice is not exclusively a jurist's concern. It is at the centre of moral and social philosophy. I will not attempt the futile task of surveying, within a book chapter, the vast body of legal and philosophical literature on justice from the time of Plato to the present day. My aim is to explore the main connections between law and justice. Some of these connections were examined in Chapters 5 and 6, in relation to natural law theory and the question of separating law and morality. In Chapter 5, I discussed the jurisprudential tradition that proposes that law must meet certain moral criteria to warrant the obedience of citizens. In Chapter 6, I addressed the idea that the law by its nature is a moral institution – that it has what Fuller called an inner morality and what Dworkin termed integrity. This chapter will consider a broader range of relations between law and justice.

Justice according to law and justice of the law

Most of the time people look to the law for justice. Sometimes, though, people appeal to justice against the law. The demand for justice is made in the form of a legal or moral claim. In one sense every legal claim is a claim of justice. A person accused of a crime claims the right to a fair trial or procedural justice. People's demand for punishment of a criminal act is a demand for justice. The claim of a craftsman to be paid the agreed price for an artefact fashioned for a customer is a demand for justice. A pedestrian's claim for damages for personal injury caused by a road accident is a claim for justice. A citizen's claim to equality before the law (in a country that has a constitutional assurance of equality) is a claim of justice. In fact, every claim of right based on existing law is a demand for justice according to law, or simply legal justice. Legal justice requires that every person and every authority act according to established law. Legal justice, in this sense, has little to do with the moral justness of the law. A court that enforces a morally unjust law upholds legal justice, though not moral justice. As presently explained, legal justice has two dimensions – substantive and procedural.

There is a core body of legal rules that most societies expect persons to observe as a matter of basic justice. The rules in the criminal law against murder, assault and other wilful acts harming person and property belong to this class, and so do the fundamental rules of private law that impose obligations to perform contracts and make reparations for damage caused by negligent acts. These are what Adam Smith called rules of justice and FA Hayek termed *nomoi*, or the rules of just conduct. They are abstract and impersonal rules and are not directed to the achievement of specific ends such as the distribution of wealth. In the ancient and medieval societies, the law did not do much more than lay down the rules of just conduct. Rules of just conduct are so called because they are indispensable to social life, have generally grown with the society and are recognised by most people as rules that ought to be followed.

In the past, the law generally reflected the rules of social life as they had evolved. The notion that the law is a means of changing society is relatively modern. (See discussions in Chapter 4 and Chapter 10.) The law of our age is very different. In addition to its ancient function of stating the rules of just conduct, law has become the means for making various types of material allocations to different groups, often at the expense of other groups. Income extracted by taxes on the rich pays for the welfare of the poor. Subsidy schemes favour some industries as against others. Consumer protection laws are designed to favour consumers at the expense of sellers and manufacturers. In contrast, import controls favour local manufacturers at the expense of consumers. The claims for wealth transfers are presented almost invariably as pleas for justice in the moral sense, although in reality some claims may simply reflect the bargaining power of the claiming group. The law does not recognise every moral claim for justice. Hence, persons who make moral claims naturally wish to have their claims converted to legal rights so that they become matters of legal justice. Moral claims are transformed into legal claims by legislative acts of parliaments or judicial decisions. The kind of justice that is sought in this manner is commonly called distributive justice or social justice. It should be noted that self-interest is not the only reason why some people demand legal change. There may be moral, ideological, economic or cultural reasons for seeking legal change. The demands for stricter environmental laws, less stringent anti-terror laws and laws prohibiting cruelty to animals are a few random examples of such claims.

When we look beyond the realm of the rules of just conduct (the impersonal rules that most people accept and willingly observe), we see serious differences of opinion about the justness of particular laws. Should the law permit a trading monopoly? Should families with young children be given income support out of taxes paid by others? Should private schools be subsidised by taxpayers who can only afford to send their children to public schools? Should farm incomes be subsidised when small industries are not? Should farmers be asked to limit land use without compensation in order to combat climate change? Should a car manufacturer be protected from foreign competition so that its employees will not lose their jobs?

The major problem with distributive justice concerns how we determine what just distribution is. We may say that it is just deserts – that a person must be given what they deserve. This answer takes us nowhere, since it poses the same question in a different way. How do we decide who deserves what? Justice may be defined as fairness, but then we need to define what fairness is. In his 'Critique of the Gotha Programme', Karl Marx stated the communist principle of distribution as: 'From each according to his ability, to each according to his needs' (1965 (1875), 325). Marx thought that this principle would work in a society of ideal citizens. Even if we concede for argument's sake that it will work in an ideal society, it seems unachievable in our own. An omniscient, omnipotent and disinterested ruler will be required to determine the capacities and needs of individuals but, as history and common sense tell us, such a ruler is inconceivable. Hence, liberal philosophers have abandoned the quest for just distribution and sought to formulate the rules of a just political system.

In the following pages I will discuss different conceptions of justice and the debates that they have generated in legal philosophy. Figure 12.1 provides a 'map' of the intellectual landscape that I will explore. The graphic is offered only as a rough guide. The reader will notice that there is considerable overlap between subdivisions.

Justice as virtue

The concept of justice has a central place in moral philosophy. In its widest and most profound sense it means righteousness, or living in harmony with the

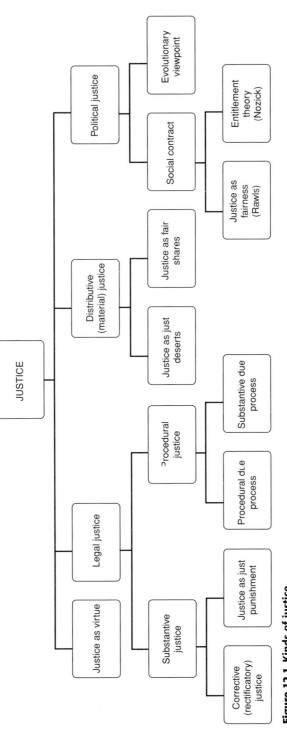

Figure 12.1 Kinds of justice

higher cosmic laws. Justice in this sense corresponds to the *Dharma* in Hindu and Buddhist philosophy and to *Jen* in Confucian thought.

Platonic justice

In his book *The Republic*, the Greek philosopher Plato (c. 427–348 BC) developed a detailed theory of the just person and the just state. In Book I of *The Republic* Plato set up a debate between Socrates and Thrasymachus the Sophist. Socrates argued that injustice only leads to conflict and disharmony, whereas justice promotes harmony (Plato 1974 (360 BC), 97). Similarly, he argued that injustice produces conflict within the individual so that 'it renders him incapable of action because of internal conflicts and division of purpose, and sets him at variance with himself and with all who are just' (1974, 97).

Plato took the teleological view that everything and everyone has an appointed purpose within the scheme of the universe and therefore each has a peculiar excellence. Justice means to serve that purpose and strive for that excellence. A horse has a purpose, so has a man. There is an ideal horse that represents the excellence of being a horse. It is better to be a good horse than a bad horse. The eye and the ear each has its purpose and its peculiar excellence. An excellent eye provides better vision than a defective eye. An excellent ear provides better sound than a flawed ear. Likewise, Plato argued that the human mind has a purpose and its peculiar excellence. The mind's function is to provide control, attention and deliberation, which are essential to rational living: 'It follows therefore that a good mind will perform the functions of control and attention well, a bad mind badly' (1974, 100). Plato concluded that justice is the peculiar excellence of the mind and injustice its defect (1974, 100). The excellence of the mind consists in balancing and harmonising its three different tendencies: reason, appetite and spirit. In later parts of *The Republic* Plato developed his theory of the just state, which was a state that consisted of different classes performing different functions, making up an efficient system in harmony with the cosmic law. There were three major classes in his ideal state, representing reason, appetite and spirit. The entrepreneurs, who produced goods and traded them, symbolised appetite; the auxiliaries, or the military, who provided security, represented spirit; and the guardians, who were philosophers, provided reason. The guardians guided the state and ensured the justice of the system. (See discussions and references in Chapter 5.)

Aristotle's theory of justice as virtue

Aristotle (384–322 BC) regarded justice as inseparable from virtue. Aristotle's theory of justice as virtue is set out in detail in his master work, *Nicomachean Ethics*, thought to have been published in 350 BC. Aristotle understood virtue in the teleological sense as right conduct in accordance with universal law. He divided virtue into moral virtues and intellectual virtues. Moral virtue is to

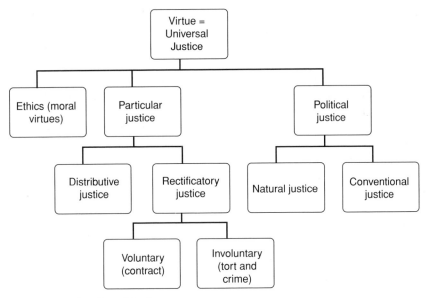

Figure 12.2 Aristotle and justice

'act according to the right principle' (Aristotle 1976 (350 BC), 93). Intellectual virtue, in particular the virtue of prudence, enables a person to determine the right principle (1976, 101–2). The right principle, according to the prudent person, turns out to be the mean between two extremes (1976, 101–2). For example, the virtue of courage is the mean between the vices of rashness and cowardice. The virtue of modesty is the mean between the vices of boastfulness and shamefulness. The virtue of temperance is the mean between the vices of profligacy and insensitivity. Like Socrates and Plato before him, Aristotle believed that all things and all beings have a purpose and a rightful place in the universal scheme of things. A virtuous person performs their role, and gives others their due place. Aristotle's scheme of justice is set out in Figure 12.2.

Universal and particular justice

Aristotle also divided virtue from another angle. Virtue consists of ethics and justice in the general or universal sense. Ethics, according to Aristotle, is moral virtue (1976, 91). Moral virtue can be practised within oneself and need not be practised in relation to others. A person can be courageous, temperate and modest without affecting others. Justice, on the contrary, is virtue as practised in relation to others. Aristotle wrote: 'there are plenty of people who can behave uprightly in their own affairs, but are incapable of doing so in relation to somebody else' (1976, 174; Miller 1995, 69). A person who practises virtue privately as well as towards others is just in the universal sense. Universal justice is the whole of virtue (Aristotle 1976, 174). Apart from universal justice, there is also particular justice, which is not the whole of virtue but a part of it. Injustice in the particular sense is injustice that causes harm to others. A person can be unjust in the universal sense without being unjust in the particular sense (Aristotle 1976, 174–5). A man who refuses financial help to another is unjust in the universal sense but not in the particular sense, for he commits no positive harm (Aristotle 1976, 175). However, a person who is guilty of particular injustice is also guilty of universal injustice, because the former is part of the latter. The following examples illustrate the point.

1.   A is prone to excessive beer drinking. Yet he performs his duties by his family, friends and his employer and causes no harm to anyone. He lacks the virtue of temperance, which is part of universal justice, but is not guilty of injustice in the particular sense.

2.   B displays all the ethical virtues in her private life. She is temperate, courageous, modest, is not over-ambitious, and so forth. She has one fault, which is that she neglects to repay her debts on time. B causes harm to the creditor and commits a particular injustice. Since particular injustice is part of universal injustice, she is also guilty of the latter.

Distributive and rectificatory justice

Aristotle divided particular justice into two kinds: distributive and rectificatory. Distributive justice is the just 'distribution of honour or money or such other assets as are divisible among the members of the community (for in these cases it is possible for one person to have either an equal or unequal share with another)' (1976, 177). It should be remembered that in Aristotle's teleological scheme all persons were not equal. Each person and class of persons had a particular station in life and a particular function. Women and slaves had very inferior positions in this scheme of things (see discussion in Chapter 5). Aristotle said that just distribution is equal distribution, but by 'equal' he really meant 'proportional'. Thus, if A is worth 2 and B is worth 1 in the scheme of society, in distributing 6 apples A should be given 4 and B only 2. Virtuous, wise and courageous persons should receive more than immoral, ignorant or cowardly persons. The rationale of distributive justice is that 'if the distribution is made from common funds it will be in the same ratio as the corresponding contributions [to the funds] bear to one another' (Aristotle 1976, 179). In other words, persons who contribute more to the production of the common wealth get more from it in return.

The trouble with this argument is that in Athenian society not everyone had an equal chance to contribute to the common stock, and some persons' contributions (such as the work of slaves) did not count at all. In practice, the patterns of distribution were established by persons who held political power. As discussed presently, contemporary notions of distributive justice are based more on the needs of persons than on the contributions they make to the social wealth. However, traces of Aristotelian distribution remain in the modern age. The Queen of the United Kingdom grants peerages and honours to her subjects on the basis of merit determined by the government. The Governor-General of Australia awards honours to Australian citizens. In many Commonwealth jurisdictions, selected senior lawyers are appointed as Queen's Counsel or Senior Counsel.

Rectificatory justice, according to Aristotle, operates in relation to private transactions. It is not about shares of the public goods but about wrongs done by one person against another. There are two branches of rectificatory justice, which correspond to voluntary and involuntary transactions. Voluntary transactions refer to contracts for the sale of property, letting and hiring, pledging, lending money with or without interest, and so forth (Aristotle 1976, 177). Involuntary transactions are those that constitute crimes and torts in present day legal language. Here the parties are treated as equal and the question is not about distribution but about rectifying wrongs. 'For, it makes no difference whether a good man has defrauded a bad man or vice versa, nor whether a good or a bad man has committed adultery; all that the law considers is the difference caused by the injury; and it treats the parties as equals, only asking whether one has committed and the other suffered an injustice, or whether one has inflicted and the other suffered a hurt' (Aristotle 1976, 180).

Political justice

Political justice is achieved through a just constitution and rules of justice. There are two kinds of rules of justice: (1) natural and universal, and (2) legal or conventional (Aristotle 1976, 189). Universal rules of justice are common to all societies and to all times, because they are just by nature. The laws against murder, assault, theft and rape, for example, are found in every civilised society and they represent universal rules of justice. Apart from these, there are laws that are peculiar to particular societies and circumstances. The punishment for a crime, for example, may differ from society to society. These laws represent conventional rules of justice.

One of the puzzles in Aristotle's treatment of justice is his equation of legislation with justice. It is clear that, by legislation, Aristotle meant just law. He wrote: 'Since the lawless man is, as we saw, unjust, and the law-abiding man just, it is clear that all lawful things are in some sense just; because what is prescribed by legislation is lawful, and we hold that every such ordinance is just' (1976, 173), This statement can be understood only in the context of Aristotle's theory of the just constitution (*politeia*). Aristotle was the first philosopher to recognise explicitly the superiority of the rule of virtuous law as against the rule of virtuous men. His experience of the politics of the Greek city states convinced him that all rulers ultimately are corrupted by self-interest. In his other great work, *The Politics*, Aristotle posed his famous question: 'Is it more advantageous to be ruled by the best man or by the best laws?' He was countering the monarchist argument that a government bound by general laws is not the most efficient. Aristotle concluded:

> Yet surely the ruler cannot dispense with the general principle which exists in law; and he is a better ruler who is free from passion than who is passionate. Whereas the law is passionless, passion must ever sway the heart of man. (1905, 136)

Aristotle argued that 'even if it be better for certain individuals to govern, they should be made only guardians and ministers of the law' (1905, 139). He was speaking of just law, and not the law that bends to the private will of rulers:

> He who bids [that] the law rule, may be deemed to bid God and Reason alone rule, but he who bids [that] man rule adds an element of the beast; for desire is a wild beast, and passions pervert the minds of rulers, even when they are the best of men. The law is reason unaffected by desire. (1905, 140)

Thus, for Aristotle, law in its true sense is law that is just.

Monarchists were not the only opponents of the rule of law. Whereas monarchists thought that the rule of a wise person is better than the rule of impersonal law, the believers in extreme democracy argued that a system where every decision is taken by popular assemblies unfettered by law is best. Aristotle observed that in the Greek city states that practised extreme democracy, the rule of law was displaced by the rule of momentary majorities. There were two serious problems with such a system. First, in this type of democracy personal or group interest may prevail over the general interest of the community, and hence lead to political injustice. Second, there will be no certainty of the law, as every right and duty is determined by the unpredictable whims of a transient majority, which in practice becomes the rule of demagogues who happen to dominate the assemblies. Aristotle argued that these kinds of systems lack a constitution, 'for where the laws have no authority, there is no constitution' (1905, 157).

Political justice, then, is governance under just or virtuous law. How does a just political order ensure governance under just law? It is achieved through constitutional arrangements that separate the legislative function from the executive function. The constitution has a supreme place in Aristotle's political justice. It is different from, and superior to, the laws that legislators make. It sets out the principles that guide the making of law, and governance according to law. In *The Politics*, Aristotle described the just constitution thus:

> A constitution (*politeia*) is the organisation of offices in a state, and determines what is to be the governing body, and what is the end of each community. But laws are not to be confounded with the principles of the constitution: they are the rules according to which the magistrates [officials and judges] should administer the state and proceed against offenders. (1905, 147)

The distinction between law making and the administration of the state is spelt out in Book VI of *Nicomachean Ethics*. Law making is the subject of legislative science, and the administration of the state is the province of political science (Aristotle 1976, 213–14). Aristotle used political science in both a broad sense and a narrow sense. Political science in the broad sense encompasses both legislative science and political science in the narrow sense. Legislative science concerns the making of rules of justice. Political science in the narrower sense is concerned with the details of administering the law. Aristotle further divided political science into deliberative science and judicial science (1976, 214). Deliberative science is the science of routine politics. Judicial science is the science

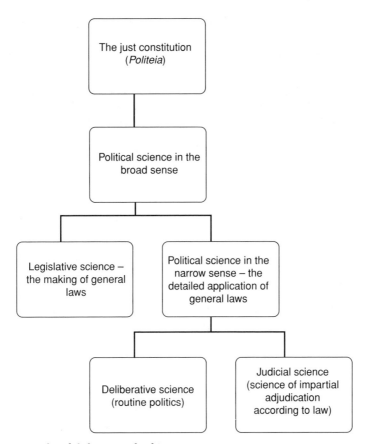

Figure 12.3 Aristotle's just constitution

of impartial adjudication according to law. Both legislative science and political science are based on prudence or practical wisdom (*phronesis*). Prudence is one of the cardinal intellectual virtues.

Let us take a contemporary situation. Parliament, in its practical wisdom, makes a law that prohibits citizens from bribing a public official. This is an exercise in legislative science. The investigation and prosecution of a person who gives or receives a bribe is left to the law enforcing agencies of the government, such as the police. In Aristotle's terminology, this is within the province of political science in the narrower sense. The actual trial of the accused person and the imposition of punishment, if found guilty, is done according to judicial science. Thus, Aristotle's just constitution (*politeia*), illustrated in Figure 12.3, was one that recognised the distinction between legislative, executive and judicial functions of the state (cf. Aristotle 1905, 175).

When Aristotle equated legislation with justice he did not mean that every human enactment is just, for he knew that this was often not the case. Legislators can make mistakes and, even under a just constitution, there may be corrupt law makers. What he meant was that in the just constitution laws will be generally just, whereas a deviant constitution will generally produce unjust laws (Aristotle 1905, 127; Miller 1995, 81). A just constitution is one that serves the community's good, therefore the rules of justice will serve the community's good. Rules of justice must possess the qualities of generality and clarity and certainty in order to serve the public interest (Aristotle 1976, 190, 282, 338; Miller 1995, 81). These are the qualities that enable the state to perform the function of organising or structuring the polis and of instructing and habituating the citizens (Miller 1995, 81–2).

Aristotelian justice in contemporary democracy

Political justice, in one respect, has improved remarkably since the time of Aristotle. Political justice did not extend to slaves and children in Athenian society. It must be remembered that Aristotle shared the teleological worldview of his times, which regarded different classes of persons as serving different purposes in an overall scheme of nature. Slaves, in this scheme, were property. Children were extensions of the parent:

> Justice on the part of a master or father [towards a slave or child respectively] is not the same as, although analogous to, the forms already discussed. There cannot be injustice in an unqualified sense towards that which is one's own; and a chattel, or a child until it is of a certain age and has attained independence, is as it were a part of oneself; and nobody chooses to injure himself (hence there can be no injustice towards oneself); and so neither can there be any conduct towards them that is politically just or unjust. (Aristotle 1976, 189)

Slavery has been abolished in most parts of the world today, and children enjoy legal rights under domestic and international law. Liberal democracies, in theory, regard all persons as equal before the law and entitled to equal justice.

Political justice has changed in other ways in liberal democracies. Aristotle's legislative science has been eclipsed by the realities of electoral politics. Parliaments carry out a certain amount of careful law making, often on the recommendations of national law reform commissions or in response to treaty obligations flowing from the work of international agencies such as the International Law Association (ILA) or the United Nations Commission on International Trade Law (UNCITRAL). However, a great deal of legislation is shaped by the pressures of electoral politics, which advance short-term and sectarian goals at the expense of the long-term public interest. In parliamentary systems based on the Westminster model, the executive government generally controls the legislature, with the result that parliament has lost its deliberative and prudential role in the making of law. The legislative program is set and executed by the prime minister and cabinet, who control the majority faction within parliament. So-called 'conscience votes' are rarely allowed in this system. Members of the

United States Congress are not subject to this degree of party discipline but, as I discussed in Chapter 9, the practice of vote trading or 'logrolling' subordinates legislative science to political expediency.

I will discuss modern theories of political justice later in this chapter.

Legal justice

Legal justice is justice *according to law*. It is not about the justice *of the law*. I may regard a tax law that forfeits half my income to the state as morally unjust, but legal justice demands that I pay it. An employee might think that her wages are too low for the work she does, but legal justice will not compel the employer to pay her more than the agreed wage or the statutory wage. As illustrated in Figure 12.4, legal justice has two branches: (1) substantive legal justice, and (2) procedural legal justice. These two kinds of legal justice are interdependent and derive from the same basic value – the duty to obey valid law. Procedural legal justice is again divisible into procedural due process and substantive due process.

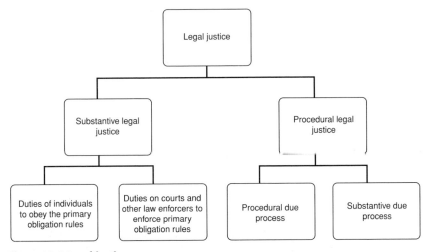

Figure 12.4 Legal justice

Substantive legal justice

Substantive legal justice demands that persons do as the law commands. It is primarily concerned with the conduct of individuals, but also places obligations on judges and other officials responsible for the enforcement of the law of the land.

Substantive legal justice is mainly related to private law, criminal law and the rights conferred by statutes or the constitution. Private law, in this context, includes the laws of contract, tort and restitution as well as substantive statutory entitlements. Crimes are punishable acts but – except for the category of crimes against the state (treason, sedition, rioting, counterfeiting, bribery etc) – they concern wrongs done to individuals. Torts and crimes committed against persons or their property, breaches of contract and the failure to return what belongs to another give rise to legal injustice in the substantive sense. Substantive legal justice represents not only what Hart called primary obligation rules but also his secondary obligation rules (or rules of recognition) placed on officials to enforce the primary obligation rules.

A state that is committed to legal justice provides remedies for injustices under substantive law. Aggrieved persons usually are entitled to ask a court or other competent tribunal to adjudicate their claims for legal justice and to enforce their legal rights. These tribunals have the duty to determine claims according to the substantive law and thereby uphold legal justice. Thus, substantive legal justice concerns rights and duties of individual citizens in relation to each other and the state, and the duties of authorities to enforce primary legal relations.

Procedural legal justice

There is another branch of legal justice, best described as procedural legal justice. It is better known in American jurisprudence as due process of the law. Procedural legal justice reinforces substantive legal justice. The existence of substantive legal justice depends to a large extent on procedural legal justice. Procedural legal justice also has two aspects: (1) procedural due process and (2) substantive due process.

Procedural due process

Substantive legal justice requires persons to respect each other's substantive legal rights. In a harmonious and stable society people largely respect rights and perform their duties. However, from time to time there is a need to resolve disputes. These disputes may arise from wilful or negligent acts or omissions that violate rights, or from disagreements about what the law requires. The courts, as a rule, conduct criminal trials. Civil disputes may be resolved through private negotiations or arbitration, but the state usually provides recourse to the courts for the ultimate adjudication and enforcement of rights. The judicial process provides means of clarifying the law and of vindicating rights when they are violated. This is an essential condition for the practical prevalence of substantive legal justice.

Procedural due process requires that a person's rights and duties under the law are determined according to fair procedures. A person who is accused of a crime should be given a fair trial. An administrative decision that affects the rights and obligations of a citizen should not be taken without the concerned citizen being given a fair hearing by an impartial arbiter. Thus, a holder of a trading licence must be given reasons and a fair hearing before the licence is taken away, and an applicant for a building permit should be heard fairly if the permit is to be refused. The entire body of law governing procedure and evidence in courts is designed to ensure procedural justice.

In the sphere of administrative action, the common law rules concerning natural justice, procedural fairness and jurisdictional error are designed to secure procedural justice in the making of decisions that affect the rights and duties of citizens. There is no better short summary of this jurisprudence than that offered by Professor Stanley de Smith in his classic work *Judicial Review of Administrative Action*:

> The relevant principles formulated by the courts may be broadly summarised as follows. The authority in which a discretion is vested can be compelled to exercise that discretion, but not to exercise it in any particular manner. In general, a discretion must be exercised by the authority to which it is committed. That authority must genuinely address itself to the matter before it: it must not act under the dictation of another body or disable itself from exercising a discretion in the individual case. In the purported exercise of its discretion it must not do what it has been forbidden to do, nor must it do what it has not been authorised to do. It must act in good faith, must have regard to all relevant considerations, and must not be swayed by irrelevant considerations, must not seek to promote purposes alien to the spirit of the legislation that gives it power to act, and must not act arbitrarily or capriciously. Nor where a judgment must be made that certain facts exist can a discretion be validly exercised on the basis of an erroneous assumption about those facts. These several principles can conveniently be grouped in two main categories: failure to exercise a discretion, and excess or abuse of discretionary power. (1980, 285–6)

Substantive due process

Procedural due process, as we have seen, is about the defence and vindication of rights that exist. Substantive due process is about the way in which existing rights and liberties can be lawfully abolished or altered.

Substantive due process is said to be the very foundation of the law in the English legal tradition. It flows from the fundamental doctrine of the law: that a person may do anything that the law does not forbid and may refrain from anything that the law does not require. Chief Justice Camden's memorable exposition of this doctrine in *Entick v Carrington* (1765) 19 Howell's State Trials 1030 was set out in the previous chapter (see 'Immunity–disability correlation'). As Camden explained, the important corollary of this rule is that an official who wishes to deny citizens their right or liberty must find the authority of a substantive law. This ancient doctrine remains at the heart of English jurisprudence to this day. It was reiterated by Justice Laws in *R v Somerset County Council; ex parte Fewings and Others* [1995] 1 All ER 513, 524:

> For private persons, the rule is that you may do anything that you choose that the law does not prohibit . . . but for public bodies the rule is opposite, and so of another character altogether. It is that any action to be taken must be justified by positive law . . . the rule is necessary in order to protect the people from arbitrary interference by those in power over them.

Substantive due process in the United Kingdom simply means that a person's rights must not be violated except under the authority of the common law or an Act of Parliament. The Parliament of the United Kingdom is said to be sovereign, and it may, in theory, take away the most basic rights and liberties of a person by an ordinary Act of Parliament, or even authorise a delegate do so. This is because the UK Parliament is unrestrained by a written constitution that guarantees basic rights to citizens. (The UK adopted much of the *European Convention on Human Rights* by enacting the *Human Rights Act 1998*, but Parliament may overturn the mandates of that Act if it so wishes.) In contrast, substantive due process imposes many more restrictions in countries where legislatures are not sovereign but subject to constitutional limitations.

In countries where the power of the legislature is limited by a constitution of superior force, substantive due process has greater importance. Congress and the state legislatures in the United States have limited powers under the US Constitution. The position is similar in Australia. The US Constitution makes the due process of law an explicit requirement. The due process clause of the Fifth Amendment (ratified in 1791) commands that no person shall 'be deprived of life, liberty, or property, without due process of law'. This clause is directed to the actions of officials of the federal government. However, the due process clause of the Fourteenth Amendment (ratified in 1868) declares: '[N]or shall any State deprive any person of life, liberty, or property, without due process of law'. This clause limits the powers of the state legislatures, as well as their governments.

The requirements of the 'due process of law' in the Fifth and Fourteenth Amendments dictate not only how the law *is enforced* but also how the law *is made* and what sort of law *can be made*. The central idea of substantive due process is that a person's rights and liberties must not be impinged upon, except by an enactment that is law not just in name and form but also in substance. The classic formulation of the doctrine of substantive due process is found in the US Supreme Court's judgment in *Hurtado v California*:

> Law is something more than mere will exerted as an act of power. It must not be a special rule for a particular person or a particular case . . . but the general law . . . so that every citizen shall hold his life, liberty, property and immunities under the protection of the general rules which govern society, and thus excluding, as not due process of law, acts of attainder, bills of pains and penalties, acts of confiscation . . . and other similar special, partial and arbitrary exertions of power under the forms of legislation. Arbitrary power, enforcing its edicts to the injury of the persons and property of its subjects, is not law, whether manifested as the decree of a personal monarch or an impersonal multitude. (110 US 516, 535–6 (1884))

The Australian Constitution does not have an express guarantee of substantive due process. However, several constitutional provisions – such as the just terms clause that requires compensation to be paid for property taking (s 51(xxxi)), the establishment clause prohibiting religious discrimination (s 116), the clause guaranteeing freedom of interstate trade (s 92) and the requirement of a trial by jury on indictment (s 119) – promote substantive due process. The High

Court of Australia has drawn several substantive due process implications from the separation of judicial powers from other powers. The chief among these is the recognition of a constitutional ban on bills of attainder (*Polyukhovich v Commonwealth* (1991) 172 CLR 501, 539, 631, 686).

Distributive justice as social justice

The aim of distributive justice is to bring about and maintain a just distribution of benefits and burdens in society. Campbell, for example, said that 'it remains illuminating to say that justice has to do with the distribution amongst persons of benefits and burdens, these being loosely defined so as to cover any desirable or undesirable thing or experience' (1988, 19). Barry said: 'When we ask about the justice of an institution we are inquiring into the way in which it distributes benefits and burdens' (1989, 355). The means of determining what amounts to just distribution, and the means of achieving and maintaining such a distribution, are the burden of theorists who define justice in this way. Distributive justice is also known as social justice, because the duty of bringing about just distribution is thought to be a social obligation. Many thinkers outside the law consider justice purely in the distributive sense. As Campbell noted, 'most modern theories of justice have little to say about justice in law despite the fact that justice might appear to be *the* legal virtue' (1988, 23).

Distributive justice and legal justice

Legal justice and distributive justice, as already noted, differ in a number of ways. The most important difference is that distributive justice is concerned with outcomes or end states, whereas legal justice is about the observance of rules of conduct. A person is legally just whose conduct is lawful and a person is unjust whose conduct is unlawful. Legal injustice always arises from the conduct of a person. A person who suffers harm suffers no *legal injustice* unless another person is responsible for the harm. Consider the case of a person who gambles at the casino and loses most of their savings. Their situation is *unfortunate* but not *unjust*. This is because their loss is not caused by the illegal act of a person but by a combination of factors for which no individual is responsible. If, however, they lose money because of fraud or theft, they are clearly the victim of legal injustice.

Distributive justice is not a legal proposition but a moral, philosophical or political ideal. The word 'justice' can be used in different senses. Whichever way the term is defined, it suggests the idea of a claim or right. A person seeks justice not as charity but as entitlement. The question is whether the entitlement is legal or moral. The modern welfare state has converted many moral claims into legal rights. Minimum wages, pensions and health care are examples of legalised moral claims. However, there is no state – outside the small number that remain organised on Marxist-Leninist principles – that recognises a general legal obligation to establish and maintain a particular pattern of distribution within society. Distributive justice remains in the moral sphere, except to the extent of piecemeal incorporation of some of its claims into the formal legal system.

Distributive justice and equality

The starting point of most social justice theories is the proposition that all persons should share equally the benefits and burdens in society. Any departure from the principle of material equality has to be justified. The question of whether inequalities can be defended was, for Barry, the inescapable issue of justice (1989, 4). Honore saw only two reasons to depart from the standard of equal shares: (a) a person's own choice, and (b) a person's conduct (1970, 63). Campbell said that 'every theory of justice must seek to explain or justify the basic presumption of the equality of persons as well as demonstrate legitimate grounds for differential treatment' (1988, 32). Rawls stated the general conception of justice this way:

> All social values – liberty and opportunity, income and wealth, and the social bases of self-respect – are to be distributed equally unless an unequal distribution of any, or all, of these values is to everyone's advantage. (1999, 54)

There are two meanings of equality we must consider. One is abstract equality, which is a feature of legal justice. It does not matter whether the driver of a speeding car is the prime minister or an errant schoolboy. They are equally liable under the offence of speeding. It does not matter that one party to the contract is a millionaire and the other party is a pensioner. The party in breach is liable in damages. The law, to the extent that it is abstract and impersonal, does not recognise personal circumstances. This is legal justice. The other kind of equality is the equal sharing of benefits and burdens. This is the basis of social, or distributive, justice theories.

Distributive justice and social security

It is important to distinguish the aim of distributive justice from what is known as social security. Social security safety nets usually comprise unemployment insurance, age and disability pensions, health care and education subsidies and such like. Some of the most prominent critics of the idea of distributive justice, among them FA Hayek and Milton Friedman, accepted the need for social security as a safety net. Friedman was well known for his advocacy of safety nets, including state provided education vouchers for children and state insurance against catastrophic illness (Friedman 1962, 85–98). Hayek wrote:

> There is no reason why in a free society government should not assure to all protection against severe deprivation in the form of a minimum income, or a floor below which nobody need to descend. To enter into such an insurance against extreme misfortune

may well be in the interest of all; or it may be felt to be a clear moral duty of all to assist, within the organised community, those who cannot help themselves. So long as such a uniform minimum income is provided outside the market to all those who, for any reason, are unable to earn in the market an adequate maintenance, this need not lead to a restriction of freedom, or a conflict with the Rule of Law. (1982, 2, 87)

Distributive justice is a more far reaching goal: namely, to reorder economic relations to achieve a just distribution of all benefits and burdens in society. It is the idea that society as a whole has a moral duty to bring about just distributions of the benefits and burdens of social life. Theorists who define justice as just distribution tend to treat rectificatory justice as an aspect of just distribution.

Theorists who consider justice as just distribution have the burden of demonstrating the criteria by which just distribution is determined. Most people agree on safety nets, but beyond that threshold distribution of burdens and benefits becomes contentious. How is this distribution determined and by whom? Karl Marx expressed the socialist principle of distribution in the maxim: 'From each according to his ability, to each according to his needs'. Marx was thinking of a stateless communist society of angelic citizens who embrace the maxim without compulsion. In the real world of self-interested individuals, such a scheme will have to be coercively implemented by omniscient, well-meaning and disinterested politicians – if such a breed can be found. Hence, social justice theorists have sought to develop other criteria that are more realistic. Two main concepts have emerged from their work: (1) justice as just desert, and (2) justice as fairness. The obvious questions are: what is 'just desert', and what is 'fair'? We must turn to these theorists for answers.

Justice as just desert

Just desert is what a person deserves. What does a person deserve? Some writers have embraced the notion that just desert is giving to each his own. This only postpones the answer. What is 'his own' other than his legal entitlements? Ulpian's statement that 'Justice is a constant and unfailing disposition to give everyone his legal due' is not helpful, since he was talking about legal right and not moral claims (*Digest* I.I.11; Justinian 1904 (529–534, 4).

A writer who attempted to give some definition to the idea of 'just desert' outside legal right was Joel Feinberg. Feinberg's concern was with personal desert. This is desert in the sense of how a person deserves to be treated by others. We may say that the reckless driver who hits a lamp post deserved the damage, but that is not personal desert. Feinberg identified two kinds of personal desert: polar desert and non-polar desert. Polar desert is where a person deserves either good or ill, as in retributive (criminal) justice or reparation of harm. The accused person is punished or set free. In an action for tort the defendant or plaintiff must bear the loss. Feinberg mentioned three kinds of polar desert: (1) rewards and punishments; (2) reparation, liability and other modes of compensation; and (3) praise, blame and other informal responses. The division in non-polar situations is not between persons who deserve good and those who deserve ill, but between those who deserve good and those who do not. Feinberg mentioned two kinds of non-polar desert: (1) award of prizes; and (2) assignment of grades (1963, 75). The winner of the Wimbledon men's tennis final is richly rewarded. The loser may feel bitterly disappointed but he cannot complain of being punished or made to suffer ill. Feinberg said that 'non-polar desert is central to what philosophers have traditionally called the concept of distributive justice' (1963, 76).

Consider the case of the award of the gold medal for the high jump at the Olympic Games. According to the competition rules the gold medal is awarded to the athlete who jumps the highest. The winner, as Feinberg contended, is not necessarily the person who *deserved* the prize. The best jumper may have suffered an injury during the competition that prevented her clearing the winning height. University teachers are all too familiar with the case of very good students who fail to gain a good grade because of personal circumstances or mishap at the examination, such as anxiety or memory loss. In one sense they may be deserving of the highest grade, though according to the institutional rules they are not. Feinberg's key point was that there is an important difference between desert in the sense of deserving a reward and the entitlement to receive the award. The idea of desert in university grading is that students who show greatest proficiency in the subject deserve the highest grades. The grading system is designed with this desert in mind. However, once the rules are made, fairness demands that the grades be awarded according to the rules. The question is no longer who deserves the highest grade but who is entitled to the highest grade. Feinberg concluded that 'desert is a moral concept in the sense that it is logically prior to and independent of public institutions and their rules' (1963, 97).

Feinberg's discussion makes an important conceptual clarification about the moral or non-legal nature of just desert. It helps us to understand what just desert means in situations such as prizes, awards and competitions, but not in relation to the distribution of benefits and burdens across society. Hence, distributive justice theories usually turn to the idea of fairness.

Justice as fairness: Rawls' theory of justice

The most influential theory of distributive justice is that of the American philosopher John Rawls (1921–2002). Rawls held chairs in philosophy at Cornell University and the Massachusetts Institute of Technology before moving to Harvard University, where he worked for more than 40 years. Rawls' theory of justice as fairness was set out in his seminal work *A Theory of Justice*, first published in 1971, but its elements were already in place by 1963 (Rawls 1963, 100–5).

Rawls' theory of justice is a theory of just political institutions. It is not a theory of distributive justice based on the wants or needs of individuals or groups. He explained it this way:

Put another way, the principles of justice do not select specific distributions of desired things as just, given the wants of particular persons. This task is abandoned as mistaken in principle, and it is in any case, not capable of a determinate answer. (1963, 102)

Rawls' theory, then, is about the justice of political arrangements. It is a theory of distributive justice only in a limited sense. It does not call for fair shares of the social pie, but rather seeks to maximise equal liberty of individuals without disadvantaging the least endowed groups in the community.

Why distribute at all?

Imagine a free society of individuals who are constrained only by the rules of legal justice, such as the laws of crime, tort and contract. Every person either produces their own material goods or obtains them by legal exchange with others. Some goods – such as security of person and property (police services) – may be difficult to secure, so individuals may band together to hire a protection agency that is able give everyone security. They may end up creating what Nozick called a minimal or night-watchman state, to which the members of society pay fees (called taxes) in return for protection (Nozick 1974, 26–8). The night-watchman state does not redistribute rights but simply protects them. Where is the injustice in such a community? Distribution achieved by voluntary transactions between two free persons can hardly be called unjust. The plumber needs money and I need my taps fixed. We satisfy each other's needs by contract. Agreement between people with similar bargaining strength represents the purest form of justice.

The need for distribution, according to Rawls, arises from the fact that people gain more by social cooperation than by living alone by their own efforts (Rawls 1999, 4). Let us say that a person living alone will be able through their own efforts to gain utilities worth X. They gain utilities worth Y by cooperating with each other. The net gain for all is $Y - X$, which, let us say, is S. The question, then, is how to distribute S. There are different kinds of social cooperation. Members of primitive societies survive by cooperative hunting, gathering and defence. Since I live in a market exchange society I cooperate with others (in fact, directly and indirectly, with millions of others), mainly through contract. I don't have to do my own plumbing, car repairs, medical treatment, gardening, and my tax returns because I get others to do these things at an agreed price. I also need not grow my own food or make my own wine because I can buy them at my local supermarket and wine store. This means that I can use my time for other things that I wish to do, like reading a book or watching cricket. The markets on which I rely work because of the rules of just conduct that most people voluntarily observe, as in performing contracts and respecting each other's person and property. Rawls' point that I am better off in society than by myself is valid, but so is everybody else. The case for distribution is still not clear. Rawls argued that people differ on how the gain from cooperation should be divided, and therefore it is necessary to have an institutional structure that distributes the surplus fairly, according to a set of principles that all can agree on. He wrote: 'There is a conflict of interest since persons are not indifferent as to how the greater benefits produced by their collaboration are distributed, for in order to pursue their ends they each prefer a larger to a lesser share' (1999, 4).

The problem of distributing the surplus is clearer in a primitive society. A caveman who hunts by himself with primitive weapons may only take small game with great effort. He will not share that meat with anyone but his own family. A hunting party of cavemen may bring down a large animal that will provide everyone with meat for a month or more. The cooperation has made everyone substantially better off. Traditional rules will determine who gets which share of the meat. The need for rules for distributing the surplus created by a market exchange society is less clear. People buy the benefits they receive. The persons who gain from the existence of a market exchange society may have already paid for their gains, raising the question: should they pay again? Rawls did not address this issue. Let us leave this question for later, and examine Rawls' theory on the assumption that there is a surplus that needs to be distributed.

The new social contract: two principles of justice

Many philosophers who have tried to work out the terms of a just social order have been attracted to the idea of the social contract. Rawls said that his aim was to present a conception of justice which 'generalises and carries to a higher level of abstraction the familiar theory of the social contract as found, say, in Locke, Rousseau and Kant' (1999, 10). Imagine a number of persons living in an original condition where each person fended for themselves through their individual efforts, with no cooperation among them. Imagine also that they each realised that they could do much better for themselves if they cooperated at some level on agreed terms. What kinds of rules of association would they agree on? This is not the way human societies actually grew. The evidence suggests that society is not the product of deliberate designing, but the result of habits and traditions that grew gradually and imperceptibly among people coming into daily contact with each other. Nevertheless, philosophers have found the idea of an original condition a useful device to speculate on the kinds of rules that people in their primordial state would find agreeable as the basis of social cooperation. This is the kind of condition that Hobbes and Locke called the state of nature. Hobbes described the state of nature as one in which every person was at war with every other person. Life in this state, he famously said, was 'solitary, poor, nasty, brutish and short' (Hobbes 1946 (1651), 82).

Hobbes thought that the persons who wished to escape the state of nature would agree to establish a sovereign government, to which each individual would concede their autonomy in exchange for the sovereign's commitment to protect their life, liberty and property. Locke's state of nature was not so harsh, but also had the fatal flaw that each person was their own law maker, judge and law enforcer. The people under Locke's social contract create a government with limited power, which is:

> ... bound to govern by establish'd standing Laws, promulgated and known to the People, and not by Extemporary Decrees; by indifferent and upright Judges, who are to decide Controversies by these Laws; And to employ the force of the Community at home only in the execution of such Laws, or abroad to prevent or redress Foreign Injuries, and secure the Community from Inroads and Invasion, And all this to be directed to no other end, but the Peace, Safety, and publick good of the People. (Locke 1960 (1690), 371)

Rawls also adopted the social contract device to construct his theory of justice. He did not take us back to the state of nature, but to an even more primordial state in which we are ignorant about ourselves. We do not know our stations in life, and what knowledge, abilities and skills we have. In fact, we have no knowledge that allows us to predict what the future holds for us. Rawls then speculated on what kind of political arrangement we will adopt, from among the many alternatives available in a situation where no one knows whether they will end up at the top or the bottom of the social heap. He concluded that people negotiating behind this veil of ignorance will agree to the following principles, which he called the principles of justice:

> *First Principle*: Each person is to have an equal right to the most extensive total system of equal basic liberties compatible with a similar system of liberty for all.
>
> *Second Principle*: Social and economic inequalities are to be arranged so that they are both:
> a) to the greatest benefit of the least advantaged, consistent with the *just savings principle*; and
> b) attached to offices and positions open to all under conditions of fair equality of opportunity (1999, 266).

The First Principle is a straightforward endorsement of the classical liberal ideal that an individual should have the greatest degree of freedom that is compatible with the equal freedom of others. It is most famously expressed in John Stuart Mill's aphorism that 'the only purpose for which power can be rightfully exercised over any member of a civilised community, against his will, is to prevent harm to others' (2002 (1869), 8). Absolute freedom is impossible when we live in society. My freedom to swing a baseball bat ends where your head begins. If I have total freedom to practise my baseball swing in a crowded bar, I will destroy the freedom of other patrons to drink their beer in peace. My freedom to drive on a suburban road at high speed will limit the freedom of others to use that road. Unrestrained freedom of speech can lead to incitement to violence against others, to the destruction of reputations and the subversion of fair trials. In a society that values freedom for all, there cannot be absolute freedom.

The Second Principle is not so straightforward. First, what is the *just savings principle*? It is the principle of justice between generations. Each generation must leave to the next not only its political institutions but also sufficient assets and resources:

> Each generation must not only preserve the gains of culture and civilisation, and maintain intact those just institutions that have been established, but it must also put aside in each period of time suitable amount of real capital accumulation. This saving may take various forms from net investment in machinery and other means of production to investment in learning and education. (Rawls 1999, 252)

In practice, this means that there is a limit to how much can be transferred (through taxes and subsidies) to the least advantaged people in the current generation.

It must be noted that inter-generational transfer of moral, cultural and economic capital happens anyway, in the normal course of social life. Most parents invest heavily in the upbringing and education of children. Some parents strive to leave some legacy to their children. In some traditional cultures, like the one in which this author was raised, parents make enormous personal sacrifices to ensure the education of their children. Consider the case of commerce and industry. Businesses are ongoing operations that can grow over many generations. A corporation has a life beyond the lifetimes of its directors and shareholders. A government cannot and does not build roads and bridges only to benefit the current generation. Again, what is the current generation? The reality is that generations are intermingled in a continuum. The next generation is already with us, shaping economic activities even as we progress to retirement. Its members are already partially in command.

The meaning of the Second Principle

Leaving this issue aside, what does the Second Principle mean? First, it assumes that social and economic inequalities are unavoidable in society. Second, it assumes that social and economic inequalities can be 'arranged' by political action. So, what are the conditions that justify inequality? According to Rawls, they must: (1) be of the greatest benefit to the least advantaged; and (2) provide a fair equality of opportunity to all to gain 'offices and positions'.

Fair equality of opportunity

What is a fair equality of opportunity? Rawls considered two possible interpretations. The first is an interpretation in terms of what Rawls called a system of natural liberty. This is a system that eliminates all legal barriers to the attainment of offices and positions but does nothing to assist persons in gaining them. There are no positions reserved for nobility and all careers are open to talent. It presupposes equal liberty for all and a free market that allocates goods according to supply and demand. Rawls rejected this system, as it does not help people disfavoured by social circumstances and chance (1999, 62–3). Children of affluent and educated parents, for example, are more likely to be well educated than are children of poor working class families. Chance brings windfalls to some and adversity to others. According to Rawls, a system of natural liberty does not offset these factors. This is not entirely true. There is no reason to presume that human qualities such as friendship, charity and benevolence are lacking in the state of natural liberty.

The second option is what Rawls called a 'liberal interpretation'. The reader should be aware that Rawls used 'liberal' here not in the sense of classical liberalism or libertarianism (which is closer to what he calls natural liberty) but in the North American sense of social democratic liberalism. Liberals in the American sense think that formal equality is not enough and that some affirmative action is required to deliver actual equality. In Rawls' words, liberals recognise 'the importance of preventing excessive accumulations of property and wealth and of maintaining equal opportunities of education for all . . . and the schools system, whether public or private, should be designed to even out class barriers' (1999, 63). Rawls thought that the liberal interpretation was superior to the natural liberty interpretation but was still inadequate: 'For one thing, even if it works to perfection in eliminating the influence of social contingencies, it still permits the distribution of wealth and income to be determined by the natural distribution of abilities and talents . . . shares are determined by the outcome of the natural lottery, and this outcome is arbitrary from a moral perspective' (1999, 64). Even if every person is given the same opportunities for education, some persons will have advantages over others because of their inborn characteristics. Take a class of students having the same state provided benefits, such as free tuition and living allowances. Some will do better than others because of personal qualities such as superior intelligence, better work ethic, effort and motivation. In other words, some students will make more out of their equal opportunity than others. Inequalities will arise inevitably over time, and the offspring of the more industrious and successful students will have greater opportunities than those of the less successful.

Rawls believed that more should be done to promote equal opportunity by limiting wealth accumulation. Limits can be placed by devices such as inheritance and gift taxes and restrictions on rights of bequest (1999, 245). These are meant to prevent the concentration of wealth, which tends to enhance inequality of opportunities. The other way is through income tax, which allows the state to make transfers to the least advantaged and hence increase their opportunities (Rawls 1999, 246).

The difference principle

It should be remembered that Rawls was trying to explain the principles that people in the *original position* will accept, in the state of ignorance about their future condition. He argued that they will find the fair equal opportunity principle to be inadequate even when it is given the liberal interpretation as explained above. The people behind the veil of ignorance will wish to make sure that if they find themselves at the bottom of the pile, they have an assurance that those at the top cannot get further ahead by making their position even worse. Hence, they will insist on what Rawls calls the difference principle.

According to the difference principle, 'the social order is not to establish and secure the more attractive prospects of those better off unless doing so is to the advantage of those less fortunate' (Rawls 1999, 65). Let us say that A represents the better off people in society and B represents the worst off people. No change in the rules should be made that makes A better off unless it also makes B better off. A rule may be made that makes A worse off and B better off. What does the difference principle mean in practice, in the kind of market exchange society that many people live in?

Rawls thought that markets are efficient means of allocating resources, but that they leave some people worse off and do not meet their basic needs. Hence, the difference principle requires a suitable minimum income to be guaranteed for everyone (1999, 245). This is done by taxing the rich and transferring some of the income to the poor. Once the suitable minimum is determined, the market may allocate the rest of the income. In fact, Rawls took the classical economic view that it is more efficient to meet the needs of the least advantaged by minimum income guarantees than by devices such as wage regulation (1999, 245).

Priority of basic liberties

Rawls granted what he calls lexical priority to the First Principle over the Second Principle. Lexical (or serial) priority is explained as follows:

> This is an order which requires us to satisfy the first principle in the ordering before we can move on to the second, the second before we consider the third, and so on. A principle does not come into play until those previous to it are either fully met or do not apply. A serial ordering avoids, then, having to balance principles at all; those earlier in the ordering have an absolute weight, so to speak, with respect to later ones, and hold without exception. (Rawls 1999, 38)

Rawls believed that people in the original position will wish to ensure that their basic liberties are given priority over equal opportunity and the regulation of inequalities. He also believed that the people would rank the Second Principle over the principle of efficiency, and rank fair opportunity over the difference principle (1999, 266). The overall ranking, therefore, can be stated as follows:

1. equal basic liberties
2. fair equality of opportunity with respect to offices and positions
3. arrangement of inequalities so that they are to the greatest benefit of the least advantaged
4. principle of efficiency and the maximisation of the sum of advantages.

An important question then is: what are basic equal liberties that are given priority? Rawls proposed a non-exhaustive list:

- political liberty (the right to vote and to hold office)
- freedom of speech and assembly
- liberty of conscience and freedom of thought
- freedom or integrity of the person, including freedom from psychological oppression and physical assault and dismemberment
- the right to hold personal property
- freedom from arbitrary arrest and seizure as defined by the concept of the rule of law.

When the elements of the two principles, the priority rules and the basic liberties are considered as a system, it is apparent that the people in the original position, according to Rawls, would vote for a political system remarkably like the market oriented welfare state democracies of the Western world.

Entitlement theory of justice: Nozick's response to Rawls

Rawls' theory of justice is widely regarded as the most important contribution to political and moral philosophy since the 19th century. However, it is not without its critics, whether from the left, right or centre of the ideological spectrum. Critics on the left, for whom material equality is the primary value, regard Rawls' theory as too individualistic and liberal. Brian Barry, a liberal in the American sense, made a critical departure from Rawls' original position in his magisterial work *A Treatise on Social Justice* (1989).

Rawls' theory of justice is based on the hypothetical social contract reached by a group of self-interested individuals in a state of ignorance about their futures. They engage in a game of risk minimisation. Barry questioned whether this kind of game could yield truly moral principles of justice. Barry's model does not place the parties to the hypothetical social contract behind a veil of ignorance but only asks them to be impartial. Barry envisaged a process whereby the issues of justice are decided by persons who are aware of their positions in society and may defend it to a reasonable point. In Barry's original position, 'each person has a veto over proposed principles, which can be exercised unless it would be reasonable for that person to accept a principle' (Barry 1989, 372).

Rawls received his sternest examination from the classical liberal and libertarian thinkers, among whom the most prominent critic was the American political philosopher Robert Nozick (1938–2002). Nozick was Pellegrino University Professor at Harvard University until he succumbed to cancer at the early age of 63. Nozick wrote his book *Anarchy, State and Utopia* as a libertarian response to Rawls' *A Theory of Justice*. Nozick, like Rawls, belonged to the social contract tradition in political philosophy. Unlike Rawls' social contract, struck by persons working behind the veil of ignorance, Nozick's social contract is the outcome of an evolutionary process involving free bargaining among individuals through the course of time.

The night-watchman state

The state, in John Locke's theory, is born out of the need to overcome the insecurity that results from every man being the judge and enforcer of his own natural rights (Locke 1960, 368). Individuals escape this state of nature by creating a supreme authority under a trust or social contract that obligates the authority to protect life, liberty and estate of individuals. Nozick showed that, even without a Lockean social contract, an ultra-minimal state can arise through free contracting for protection services without violating anyone's rights. Imagine a state of natural liberty where each individual has a right to their own livelihood and there is no government. Each person relies on their own resources to protect their rights. Some are stronger than others, so person and property are insecure. In such conditions, it is natural that persons will form associations that are capable of providing their members with protection that individually they cannot provide for themselves. These protective associations provide protection only to their members. They defend members against violence by outsiders and settle disputes that arise between members by determining and enforcing the rights of each member. Successful protective associations may then offer their services to outsiders, who may or may not have their own protective associations. The more effective protective associations will absorb the less effective ones over the course of time, and eventually a dominant protective association will emerge. This association is what Nozick called an ultra-minimal state. It has no power to alter the rights and duties of members but only to protect and enforce them. It also has no power over non-members (independents) unless they violate the rights of the members. By the same token, its power does not extend to the protection of independents. Hence, it has no distributive role. The members of the dominant association may recognise that they have a moral duty to offer protection to these non-members who happen to be within their territory. This leads to the emergence of the minimal state, which Nozick called the night-watchman state. The night-watchman state eventually assumes a *de facto* monopoly of coercive powers over all persons within a territory, whether they are members or not.

The ultra minimal state has no distributive function. Those who purchase its services gain its protection, but not others. There is no transfer of wealth. In contrast, the night-watchman state that offers protection to all, including independents, *appears* to perform a redistributive function. Members pay for the protection of non-members. Nozick argued that despite this appearance, the night-watchman state is not a redistributive state (1974, 27). How so? Remember that the night-watchman state arises without the violation of anyone's rights, purely through contract. It exists to protect rights and not to violate rights, even of independents. The independents may use self-help to vindicate their rights against members. The night-watchman state may ask the independents to use fair procedures before they act against a member, because members have rights to fair procedure. In other words, it prohibits the use of what it deems to be unfair procedures. This may seriously affect the way the independents go about their lives. They may, for example, have to take extra expensive precautions because they cannot use self-help to redress their wrongs. The members of the night-watchman state must therefore compensate the independents for this disadvantage. Nozick said that it may be cheaper on the whole for the members of the night-watchman state to offer protective services to independents to cover disputes that they have with members (1974, 110). If this is the case there is no redistribution.

Nozick concluded that the minimal state is the most extensive state that can be justified and that any state more extensive violates people's rights (1974, 149).

Entitlement theory of justice

Nozick started his entitlement theory of justice by denying that anyone is entitled to engage in distribution of property. The philosophical foundation of his theory of justice in a free society is revealed in the following passage:

> There is no *central* distribution, no person or group entitled to control all the resources, jointly deciding how they are doled out. What each person gets, he gets from others who give to him in exchange for something, or as a gift. In a free society, diverse persons control different resources, and new holdings arise out of voluntary exchanges and actions of persons. There is no more a distributing or distribution of shares than there is a distributing of mates in a society in which persons choose whom they shall marry. (1974, 149–50)

Nozick understood distribution purely in the sense of entitlement: thus 'the complete principle of justice would say simply that a distribution is just if everyone is entitled to the holdings they possess under the distribution' (1974, 151). Justice in holdings is represented by the following three rules:

1. A person who acquires a holding in accordance with the principle of *justice in acquisition* is entitled to that holding.
2. A person who acquires a holding in accordance with the principle of *justice in transfer*, from someone else who is entitled to the holding, is entitled to the holding.
3. No one is entitled to a holding except by (repeated) applications of 1 and 2. (Nozick 1974, 151)

These rules look backwards to see how a person came to hold the property, and in that sense are historical principles. A person may come upon a thing by purchasing it, by producing it, by receiving it as a gift, by gambling, by finding it, and so on. In legal terms, the transferee gets good title to a thing if the transferor had the right to pass property in the thing. It is possible that at some point in the past a person obtained the property by theft, fraud or some other unlawful means. The current owner may be an innocent receiver in a chain of transactions that was started by a person who stole the property. How far back the law will look is a matter for each legal system, but all legal systems provide some means of rectifying past injustices. The common law and equity, for example, allow the tracing of property by the owner. Nozick therefore added a fourth principle:

4.   A person who acquires a holding according to the principle of *rectification of injustice* is entitled to the holding (1974, 153).

Nozick added what he called a version of the Lockean Proviso. Locke's theory of property postulates that a person acquires a previously unowned thing by mixing his labour with the thing. A person who cultivates an acre of land that does not belong to any other person acquires it. Locke, however, stated a proviso that those who acquire things from nature must leave 'enough and as good in common' for others. Thus, if there is only one source of water in the desert a person cannot acquire it to the exclusion of all others. Nozick stated that any adequate theory of justice in acquisition will contain a similar proviso:

> A process normally giving rise to a permanent bequeathable property right in a previously unowned thing will not do so if the position of others no longer at liberty to use the thing is thereby worsened. (1974, 178)

Nozick contrasted historical principles with end-state principles. The aim of end-state principles is not merely to see that persons came to hold things in a lawful manner but also to determine a pattern of distribution of things across society according to some distributive principle. These principles can take many forms, such as: to each according to merit; or according to usefulness to society; or need; or marginal product; or the weighted sum of these qualities. The principles of historical entitlements do not ensure patterns of distribution, but on the contrary have a tendency to upset established patterns.

Nozick's criticism of Rawls' theory of justice

Rawls' case for distributive justice in its simplest form is that a system of social cooperation makes everyone better off than a system of non-cooperation in which each person fends for themselves by their own effort. Principles of justice are required to distribute the surplus that results from social cooperation. People in the original position will decide on the two principles that Rawls stated. Nozick challenged this theory on several grounds, and the most important among them are explained in what follows.

The principles that people settle on in the original position are not necessarily fair

This is an argument that Barry made, but it was previously identified by Nozick. People who have no knowledge of where they stand in society or what abilities they possess will naturally seek to minimise their risk in case they happen to be the least endowed. Nozick's argument was: what has this to do with fairness and justice? Unanimity is not justice. Once the veil of ignorance is drawn they may find the system very unjust. Nozick employed the following illustration to make the point. I have simplified it for easy reading.

In the first scenario, a class of 10 students complete an examination and are given scores between 0 and 10. Let us say that the sum of all the scores given is 60. They are not told what scores each of them has received and are asked to determine unanimously what score each student should receive. The only condition is that the total of all the scores awarded must not exceed 60, which is the total of marks gained by the group as a whole. The students do not know how clever they are in relation to each other or how well each has prepared for the exam. In other words they are placed in a Rawlsian original position. The likely decision is to divide the total into equal shares so that each student gets 6. If the students are asked not to determine individual scores but a principle for distributing the scores, they would opt for the equality principle, namely dividing the whole by the number who sat the exam. The second scenario is the same as the first, except that the students are told the score each of them was actually awarded by the examiner. They are nevertheless given the right to overrule the examiner and award themselves the final scores. If self-interest is the sole criterion, the students will still not agree to anything but equality (Nozick 1974, 200).

The point Nozick made is the same one that Barry noticed. The conditions that Rawls created in the original position make self-interest the criterion for determining the principles of justice. Nozick's further point was that these conditions do not allow historical or entitlement principles to be considered. (The people do not even know their own histories.)

> The nature of the decision problem facing persons deciding on principles in an original position behind a veil of ignorance limits them to end-state principles of distribution. The self-interested person evaluates any non end-state principle on the basis of how it works out for him; his calculations about any principle focus on how he ends up under the principle. (Nozick 1974, 201)

The problem of procedural principles in Rawls

A procedural principle is a principle that governs a decision-making process. Whatever emerges from following the procedure is considered to be just. The procedural principle Rawls used is that of a contract concluded by persons in the original position. He wrote: 'The idea of the original position is to set up a fair procedure so that any principle agreed to will be just. The aim is to use the notion of pure procedural justice as a basis for theory' (1999, 118).

Nozick noticed a heavy irony in Rawls' use of the contract process to generate his principles of justice. The contract process yields a principle that is anti-contract. Rawls' principles of justice do not deny the freedom of contract. However, the difference principle takes precedence over contract and thus limits contractual freedom. Freedom of contract is permitted only if it improves the conditions of the least advantaged persons in the community. Nozick's essential point is this. If the contract is a fair process to determine the principles of justice, contract should also be capable of being one of the principles of justice so determined. 'If processes are good enough to found a theory upon, they are good enough to be the possible result of the theory. One can't have it both ways' (Nozick 1974, 208–9).

Immorality of taking natural assets into account

Nozick reserved his harshest criticism for Rawls' position that the distribution of natural assets is arbitrary from a moral point of view. Natural assets are the inborn or self-developed qualities of a person, such as intelligence, psychological motivation, strength of character, single-mindedness and endurance. Rawls' view of these assets is revealed by the following passage:

> While the liberal conception seems clearly preferable to the system of natural liberty, intuitively it still appears defective. For one thing even if it works to perfection in eliminating the effects of social contingencies, it still permits the distribution of wealth and income to be determined by the natural distribution of abilities and talents. Within the limits allowed by the background arrangements, distributive shares are decided by the outcome of the natural lottery; and this outcome is arbitrary from the moral perspective. There is no more reason to permit the distribution of income and wealth to be settled by the distribution of natural assets than by historical and social fortune. (Rawls 1999, 63–4)

Rawls refused to recognise even conscientious effort as a basis of distribution. He said: 'It seems clear that the effort a person is willing to make is influenced by his natural abilities and skills and the alternatives open to him' (1999, 274). This led Rawls to the conclusion: 'The difference principle represents, in effect, an agreement to regard the distribution of natural talents as in some respects a common asset . . . Those who have been favoured by nature, whoever they are, may gain from their good fortune only on terms that improve the situation of those who have lost out' (1999, 87).

As Nozick pointed out, this approach amounts to attributing everything noteworthy about a person to 'external' factors (1974, 214). He doubted that any coherent conception of a person would remain after the person is stripped of talents, assets, abilities and special traits (1974, 228). An individual's talents benefit society anyway. A talented person is likely, all being equal, to be more productive than a talentless person. A talented person may be of greater service to others. A physician may have a higher income than a law professor. Part of the difference may be attributable to the difference in talents. It is more likely, though, that the difference correlates to the greater usefulness of the physician to the community. In other words, the difference in the incomes is based on a difference that is not arbitrary from the moral point of view (Nozick 1974, 218).

Nozick and social security

One of the frequent criticisms of Nozick's entitlement theory of justice is that it has no place for any form of socially provided safety net. The question, then, is whether the society can retain the loyalty of the poor who for one reason or another (such as old age and disability) cannot look after themselves. According to Nozick's theory, 'the state may not use its coercive apparatus for the purpose of getting some citizens to aid others' (1974, ix). The theory only excludes coercive means. In a minimal state social security will be a voluntary exercise. This presumably may take various forms, such as charities and privately funded social insurance. Nozick was aware that the apparent callousness towards the needs and suffering of others would turn many away from his theory. What he sought was a consistent theory of the state that did not violate the rights of citizens as defined by the rules concerning justice in holdings.

Another frequently heard criticism concerns Nozick's supposed failure to show why his entitlement theory is right. This is not true, as his entitlement theory is based on the Lockean moral theory of natural rights. Nozick rejected utilitarian arguments for entitlements because they lead to end-state justice, which is inconsistent with his Lockean view of natural rights. His reasoning commenced in the state of nature before the birth of government. Individuals had natural rights to their lives, liberty and property. (Imagine trying to live without liberty and property.) Property is acquired in the first instance by persons taking possession of things that are not already owned. This is his principle of justice in acquisition. Property thereafter changes hands according to the principle of justice in transfer and the principle of rectification. Nozick theorised how a minimal state may arise that does not violate these rights through free contracting. One may disagree with the Lockean theory of natural rights. However, anyone who adopts the Lockean view will find in Nozick's *Anarchy, State and Utopia* one of the most systematic, logical and coherent expositions of the principles of justice that flow from this view.

Evolutionary theory of justice

I discussed in the previous two sections the two main contending theories of justice that emerged in the late 20th century. They are both located within the social contract tradition in political philosophy. The subject of justice must not be concluded without considering an alternative approach, based not on contract but on the evolutionary view of human society and institutions. The evolutionary tradition was discussed in Chapter 10, but its specific contribution to the question of justice remains to be examined.

The evolutionary point of view on justice was first presented by the Scottish philosopher David Hume in his monumental work *A Treatise of Human Nature*, which was published in 1739 when Hume was just 28 years old. Hume, like Locke, was one of the great British empiricists. However, unlike Locke, Hume regarded the fundamental laws of social life and principles of justice not as natural but as fashioned by accumulated experience.

Hume and the conventional (artificial) nature of justice

Hume developed his theory of justice through a number of stages, and we will do well to distinguish them.

Virtue is determined by motive

Hume commenced his treatment of justice with the observation that the justice of an act does not consist of the act itself but the motive behind it: 'The external performance has no merit. We must look within to find the moral quality' (Hume 1978 (1739–40), 477). Since we cannot read minds, we deduce motives from our observation of actions. Our attention is usually fixed on the signs to the neglect of motive, but on occasion we revise our judgment of an act when the motive comes to light. We may think that a person who walks away with a gold coin belonging to another person has acted unjustly, until we realise that the person was genuinely mistaken because she owns an identical-looking gold coin.

Hume argued that the virtue of an act cannot be in the act itself, but in an antecedent motive. 'We blame a father for neglecting his child. Why? Because it shews a want of natural affection, which is the duty of every parent. Were not natural affection a duty the care of children cou'd not be a duty . . . ' (Hume 1978, 478). Humanitarian acts of a philanthropist are regarded as virtuous because of the antecedent principle of humanity. Hume concluded:

> In short, it may be establish'd as an undoubted maxim, *that no action can be virtuous, or morally good, unless there be in human nature some motive to produce it, distinct from the sense of its morality* (1978, 479).

Hume took the view that certain virtuous motives are common in human nature. In other words, certain virtues are hard wired in us. Hume called these virtuous motives 'impelling passions' (1978, 483). Particular individuals may not have a particular virtuous motive or impelling passion, such as gratitude, but may practise it in order to acquire it or to hide the lack of it. (Some, like robbers and swindlers, do not care to hide their lack of virtue.) Nature, though, hardwires us in certain ways. Hume explained:

> A man naturally loves his children better than his nephews, his nephews better than his cousins, his cousins better than strangers, where everything else is equal. Hence arise our common measures of duty, in preferring one to the other. Our sense of duty always follows the common and natural course of our passions. (1978, 483–4)

The conventional (artificial) nature of justice

It follows from the previous observations that actions are just or unjust according to motivation. It is circular reasoning to say that an act is just because of the justice of the act. So what motivates just conduct in a society? Hume, along with most political philosophers, agreed that persons can achieve more in society than in a state of individual existence. Rules of justice are born out of the necessity of society. People possess three kinds of goods: (1) internal satisfaction of the mind; (2) external advantages of the body; and (3) possessions acquired by labour or good fortune (Hume 1978, 487). A person may control the first two, but the protection of possessions requires mutual respect. I do not take your possessions so long as you do not take mine. Thus, there is an overwhelming motivation to settle on certain rules of justice. The rules of justice are therefore not natural, but founded on convention. How is this settlement reached? Locke and Hobbes and Rawls constructed a hypothetical scenario of a social contract. Hume rejected this approach in favour of an evolutionary explanation.

Evolutionary nature of the rules of justice

Hume realised that human beings have always lived in society, however far back we go in the history of the species. They could not have lived in a state of nature, as envisaged by Hobbes and Locke. Conventions are as old as society. The state of nature can only be a convenient fiction for philosophers (Hume 1978, 493). Paleoanthropology confirms this view.

Hume maintained that the convention is not in the nature of a promise or contract, because promises themselves are founded on conventions. What is the nature of a contract? It is that the parties must fulfil their duties under its terms. However, the duty to perform contractual obligations cannot be founded in the contract itself, for that would lead to hopeless circularity. (A contract must be observed because the contract requires that it be observed!) Hence it has to be based on some other reason, such as mutual convenience.

According to Hume, conventions arise not through the deliberations of an assembly but by the gradual and insensible realisation among interacting individuals of the advantage of observing certain rules. Hume compared the growth of rules of justice to the emergence of language and the institution of money as substitute for goods:

> Two men, who pull the oars of a boat, do it by an agreement or convention, tho' they have never given promises to each other. Nor is the rule concerning the stability of possession the less deriv'd from human convention, that it arises gradually, and acquires force by a slow progression, and by our repeated experience of the inconveniences of transgressing it. On the contrary, this experience assures us still more, that the sense of interest has become common to all our fellows, and gives us a confidence of the future regularity of their conduct: And 'tis only on the expectation of this, that our moderation and abstinence is founded. (1978, 490)

For Hume, then, conventions are practices formed over time through the regularities of behaviour that lead persons to rely on those practices in going about their lives. I leave my house to go to work in the knowledge that it will not be plundered by others. Likewise, others expect me not to harm their possessions. The stability of possessions thus established gives rise to the idea of justice and injustice as well as property, right and obligation (Hume 1978, 490–1). 'A man's property is some object related to him. This relation is not natural but moral and founded on justice' (Hume 1978, 491).

Hume drew three major conclusions from this idea of justice:

1.   Regard to the public interest or a strong sense of benevolence is not the origin of justice, but selfishness and the scarcities of things provided by nature. People are compelled to accept the rule concerning the stability of possessions in order to survive. If things are in abundance and people are naturally generous, justice has no use (1978, 495–6).

2.   Justice is not founded on reason or the discovery of universal, eternal and immutable obligations. The sense of justice is not founded on ideas but on impressions (1978, 496).

3.   The impressions that give rise to the sense of justice are not natural, but arise from 'artifice and convention' (1978, 496).

Adam Smith on justice

Adam Smith (1723–90) is best known for his book *An Inquiry into the Nature and Causes of the Wealth of Nations*, published in 1776. It set out the philosophy and the principles of markets and free trade, and stands as the most influential book in the history of economic thought. Smith's other great work, *The Theory of Moral Sentiments*, published in 1759, is less well known outside philosophical circles. Yet it is one of the most important treatises in moral philosophy written in the English language. In Parts II and III of the book we find Smith's most important contribution to moral philosophy. They deal with the two main 'outward' moralities: justice and beneficence.

Original passions and the role of sympathy

Like his friend David Hume, Adam Smith took an evolutionary view of human morality. The starting point of moral discourse for both Hume and Smith was the instincts or 'original passions' of man. These are qualities that are hardwired in human beings. Current evolutionary psychology offers explanations of how these instincts may have become ingrained in the human psyche. Smith, Hume and other evolutionist thinkers in the 18th century did not have the benefit of discoveries in biological and psychological evolution or in post-Mendelian genetics (Tooby & Cosmides 1992; Jones 1999, 288; Dennett 1996, 79–80). Yet these discoveries have reinforced Smith's initial premise: that human beings are psychologically endowed with certain instincts or original passions. Smith began his *Treatise* by asserting that one of the original passions of a human being is sympathy or fellow feeling. This was a sharp departure from Hume's position that every benevolent feeling arises, in the ultimate analysis, out of self-love. Smith argued that though man is selfish by nature, 'there are evidently some principles in his nature, which interest him in the fortune of others, and render their happiness necessary to him, though he derives nothing from it except the pleasure of seeing it' (Smith 1976 (1759), 9). Smith's 'sympathy' is a broad concept that includes the capacity to empathise with both the misfortunes and the fortunes of others.

Smith initially distinguished between two types of moral judgment. The first is the judgment of the *propriety or impropriety* of a person's passions in responding to events. Assume that A steals B's wallet containing a small sum of money. B is properly upset and resentful. However, if B reacts with excessive grief, as if he has lost his entire fortune, his behaviour may be judged by others to be improper. Or else, if B is boastful of some achievement or good fortune, his reaction will be judged by others to be improper. The second type of moral judgment relates to the *merits and demerits* of actions. This is judgment about the proper reward or punishment for an act (Smith 1976, 93).

The impartial spectator

How should judgments about propriety or just deserts be made? Smith argued that moral judgments are those made from the point of view of the impartial spectator. Why the impartial spectator? Smith's argument proceeds as follows. Sympathy or fellow feeling is a universal instinct. A person can have sympathy for another only if the person can imagine the feelings of the other. We cannot get into the mind of another. So we imagine their feelings by the way we ourselves would feel in their situation. 'To approve or disapprove, therefore, of the opinions of others is acknowledged, by every body, to mean no more than to observe the agreement or disagreement with our own' (Smith 1976, 17). Assume that W sees A stealing B's wallet and observes B's unhappiness. W has sympathy for B because W knows that she would feel the same way if she was the victim. However, a person can never fully associate with the feelings of another. W's resentment of A's act is likely to be somewhat weaker than B's own resentment of it. Hence, overreaction will not meet with W's approval. The aggrieved person, therefore, is advised to attune his passion to the level of an impartial spectator if he is to gain their sympathy. 'He can only hope to obtain this [sympathy] by lowering his passion to that pitch, in which the spectators are capable of going along with him' (Smith 1976, 22). Thus, moral judgment about propriety and impropriety of an action is that of the impartial spectator, who has no particular positive or negative relation to the parties directly involved. Likewise, proper judgment about reward or punishment for the act of theft is that of the impartial spectator. B may feel that A deserves life imprisonment, but he will not find much sympathy for this from the impartial spectator.

In Part I of the book, Smith discussed at great length the degrees of different passions that are consistent with propriety. Smith identified passions that arise from the appetites of the body or sensory factors (hunger, sexual urge, pain), from imagination (romantic love), unsocial passions (hatred and resentment), social passions (generosity, kindness) and selfish passions (self-centred grief and joy). The impartial spectator will draw the line of propriety at different points in relation to different passions. Two categories of passions are particularly significant in Smith's moral system. First, a person who controls the passions that arise from bodily appetite displays the virtue of *temperance*, for which they gain public approbation. Second, a person who is kind, generous and helpful engages in the virtue of *beneficence*. Whereas temperance is mainly about self-control and does not directly concern others, the effects of *beneficence* – like those of *justice* – extend to others.

Emergence of the rules of justice

Sympathy is the origin of the ideas of beneficence and of justice. The absence of beneficence or of the sense of justice in a person evokes disapprobation. However, it is only unjust conduct that inspires the stronger feeling of resentment and leads to the demand for retribution. This is a critical distinction. Beneficence involves positive action, whereas justice is concerned with the breach of negatively expressed prohibitions. That one should show charity to a victim of misfortune is a principle of beneficence. That one should not steal another's property is a rule of justice. Smith rejected the notion of social justice. He wrote: 'Beneficence is always free, it cannot be extorted by force, the mere want of it exposes to no punishment; because the mere want of beneficence tends to do no real positive evil' (1976, 78). A person could be just without being beneficent. 'We may often fulfil all the rules of justice by sitting still and doing nothing' (Smith 1976, 82).

According to Smith, the sense of justice also is rooted in sympathy. The impartial spectator identifies with the pain of the victim of violence and approves of their desire for punishment, though not to the same extent as the victim desires. How does the sense of justice, which is hardwired in us, give rise to rules of justice? The answer is found in another aspect of human nature – the tendency to self-deceit. As previously mentioned, Smith had an evolutionary view of the emergence of social order. Rules arise because our sense of justice fails us when we most need it. This is when we have to judge our own actions. We cannot stop and make reasoned judgments before every action, not only because we often act on the spur of the moment but also because our judgments are coloured by our own passions. If we reflect on our actions afterwards, we are prone to forgive ourselves. This flaw in our nature is overcome by other instincts that allow us to identify the proper rules of conduct. 'Our continual observations upon the conduct of others, insensibly lead us to form to ourselves certain general rules concerning what is fit and proper either to be done or to be avoided' (Smith 1976, 159). The coincidence of these individual perceptions leads to the crystallisation of moral rules of just conduct. Rules were not originally established by a designer with prescience, but through the accumulation of experience. Smith wrote:

> We do not originally approve or condemn particular actions because, upon examination, they appear to be agreeable or inconsistent with a certain general rule. The general rule, on the contrary, is formed, by finding from experience, that all actions of a certain kind, or circumstanced in a certain manner, are approved or disapproved of. (1976, 159)

This is the quintessential evolutionary argument. However, the persistence of general rules involves another element. Rules of justice exist because most people observe them voluntarily most of the time. The element of observance is supplied by the virtue of self-command – the virtue that Smith considered to be the fountain of all other virtues (1976, 241). Knowledge of the rules of conduct alone will not secure their observance. Self-interest seduces people to violate the rules that they know and approve. It is self-command that suppresses our immediate temptations and directs us to the observance of the rules of justice.

Smith's account of the emergence of rules is consistent with modern game theory, which attributes the evolution of cooperation to the dominance of the 'tit for tat' strategy (Axelrod 1990). According to Smith, it is the anticipation of disapproval, or 'tit for tat', that leads us to form the rules of proper conduct. The rules that are so formed have a customary character. In Part V of the book, Smith discussed another kind of custom or fashion – particular local usages. These usages, when they coincide with the natural principles of right and wrong 'heighten the delicacy of our sentiments, and increase our abhorrence of everything which approaches to evil' (Smith 1976, 200). Smith, however, was of the view that particular usages are often destructive of good morals, for they are 'capable of establishing, as lawful and blameless, particular actions, which shock the plainest principles of right and wrong' (1976, 209). He gave, as a particularly barbaric example, the custom of infanticide in Greek cities, which even Plato and Aristotle failed to condemn.

The central implications of the evolutionary view of justice

There are three major implications of the evolutionary view of the rules of justice. The first is that they are general and impersonal. The second is that they concern the conduct of persons. The third is that they impose negative obligations.

Distillation through experience is a process of generalisation or abstraction. The fruits of experience are preserved 'not as a recollection of particular events, or explicit knowledge of the kind of situation likely to occur, but as a sense of the importance of observing certain rules' (Hayek 1982, 2, 4). A rule of conduct can be universalised only in the negative form, unless the rule relates to a very narrow type of circumstance. It is impossible to express the rules against murder, rape, theft, trespass, and non-performance of contracts in positive terms if they are to protect all persons currently living and yet to be born. Universality can be achieved only by the 'Thou shall not . . . ' formula. Even when it appears that a rule requires positive action, it will be seen on closer examination to be capable of negative formulation. The rule that requires contracts to be performed is a rule that prohibits actions contrary to the contract. The rule that requires a surgeon to provide post-surgical care to a patient is actually an application of the rule against negligence, measured by the standard of care expected of a surgeon. Even in the rare cases where the common law imposes positive duties, such as the seafarer's duty of rescue at sea, there is a special relationship at play where the duty bearer is in a unique, hence quasi-fiduciary, position in relation to the beneficiary. The law can be generalised into the injunction: 'Do not abandon a person whose life uniquely depends on you, if you can save that person without endangering your own life'.

Only norms that can be universalised can become recognised as rules of justice, but not all such norms are so recognised. As Hayek noted, Kant's categorical imperative – to act only by rules that you will apply to all – is a necessary but not sufficient condition of justice (1982, 2, 43). The difference between justice and beneficence is rooted in the very structure of the evolved complex order that is society. The rules of justice are the coordinating principles of social life without which the social structure collapses. They are determined by the nature of the spontaneous order of society. The difference between rules of justice and norms of beneficence may be seen from another angle. Rules of justice forming the same system are generally accommodated to each other, and hence may be enforced without violence to one another. Rules of justice also can be enforced without violence to beneficence, but beneficence cannot be enforced without violence to justice.

Rules of just conduct concern a person's relations with others. A rule that is concerned with a thing will be a rule of justice insofar as it also concerns some other person. Thus, the rules against pollution are rules of justice where they prevent harm to others. However, the state has a history of legislating rules that prohibit conduct where the harm to others is not clear. Examples include prohibitions of pornography that involves no harm to others, alcohol consumption and, in some societies, homosexual acts. These are attempts to enforce temperance or religious norms rather than justice.

Successful and harmonious societies display justice, beneficence and temperance. A society in which those less fortunate receive no sympathy or assistance is unlikely to be stable. Nor would one in which licentiousness and intemperance reign, as the fate of the Roman Empire showed. This message was not lost on evolutionist thinkers. Beneficence carries rewards in the form of psychological fulfilment, reciprocal beneficence and enhanced reputation that fosters trust in future dealings. Society also benefits from beneficence to the extent that it promotes trust and eases dependence on the state. Smith's argument was that although the absence of beneficence excites disapprobation, attempts to extort it would be even more improper (Smith 1976, 79). He wrote: 'To neglect it altogether exposes the commonwealth to many gross disorders and shocking enormities, and to push it too far is destructive of all liberty, security, and justice' (1976, 81). Smith realised that while beneficence is highly desirable, it cannot be exacted without jeopardising the more fundamental morality that is justice. Beneficence is the 'ornament which embellishes' the building, whereas justice 'is the main pillar that upholds the whole edifice' (Smith 1976, 86). While both justice and beneficence form the moral capital of society, the state is effective only in the promotion of justice. Beneficence can only be promoted by 'advice and persuasion' (Smith 1976, 81).

We need to keep in mind that justice means different ideas to different persons. The evolutionists understood justice as the observance of the fundamental rules of conduct established by the accumulated experience of humankind. Care for the victims of misfortune was left to beneficence. The modern welfare states have chosen to exact beneficence from citizens by the coercive transfer of wealth among persons, in the form of benefits paid out of tax revenue and regulations that favour particular groups at the expense of others. This has been done in the name of justice – not in the sense understood by the evolutionist thinkers or by natural rights theorists such as Locke and Nozick, but in the sense of fair distributions of the wealth of society that theorists such as Rawls and Barry proposed.

References

Abrahams, MH 1989, 'Construing and deconstructing', in A Rajnath (ed.), *Deconstruction: a critique*, Palgrave Macmillan, London.

Adelstein, RP 1981, 'Institutional function and evolution in the institutional process', 76 *Northwestern University Law Review*, 1–99.

——1998, 'American institutional economics and the legal system', in *The New Palgrave dictionary of economics and the law*, vol. 1, Macmillan, London.

Alchian, AA 1950, 'Uncertainty, evolution, and economic theory', 58 *Journal of Political Economy*, 211–21.

Anzilotti, D 1928, *Di corso di diritto internazionale*, Athenaeum, Rome.

Aquinas, T St 1947, *Summa theologica (literally translated by Fathers of the English Dominican Province; with synoptical charts)*, vols 1–3, Burns & Oates, London.

Aristotle 1905 (350 BC), *The politics*, tr. B Jowett, Clarendon Press, Oxford.

——1968 (350 BC), *The metaphysics*, tr. H Tredennick, Heinemann & Co., London.

——1972 (350 BC), *De partibus animalium (Parts of animals)*, tr. AL Peck, W Heinemann, London.

——1976 (350 BC), *The ethics of Aristotle: the Nicomachean ethics*, tr. JAK Thomson, Penguin Books, London.

Austin, J 1869, *Lectures in jurisprudence or the philosophy of positive law*, 3rd edn, J Murray, London.

——1995 (1832), *The province of jurisprudence determined*, Cambridge University Press, Cambridge.

Axelrod, R 1990, *The evolution of cooperation*, Penguin, London.

Bakewell, CM 1907, *Source book in ancient philosophy*, Charles Scribner's Sons, New York.

Barry, B 1989, *A treatise on social justice*, vol. 1, Harvester-Wheatsheaf, London.

Becker, GS 1962, 'Irrational behavior and economic theory', 70 *Journal of Political Economy*, 1–13.

Benson, BL 1989, 'Spontaneous evolution of commercial law', 55 *Southern Economic Journal*, 644–61.

——1990, *The enterprise of law: justice without the state*, Pacific Research Institute for Public Policy, San Francisco.

——1992, 'Customary law as a social contract', 2 *Constitutional Political Economy*, 1–27.

——1998, 'Evolution of commercial law', in *The new Palgrave dictionary of economics and the law*, vol. 1, Macmillan, London.

Bentham, J 1970a (1782), *Of laws in general*, The Athlone Press, University of London, London.

——1970b (1789), *An introduction to the principles of morals and legislation*, The Athlone Press, University of London, London.

——1998, *Legislator of the world: writings on codification, law, and education*, ed. P Scholfield & J Harris, Clarendon Press, Oxford.

Bernstein, L 1992, 'Opting out of the legal system: extralegal contractual relations in the diamond industry', 21 *Journal of Legal Studies*, 115–58.

Birks, P 2000, 'Rights, wrongs and remedies', 20 *Oxford Journal of Legal Studies*, 1–37.

Block, W 1977, 'Coase and Demsetz on private property rights', 1(2) *Journal of Libertarian Studies*, 111–15.

Blue, JC 1992, '*High Noon* revisited: commands of assistance by peace officers in the age of the Fourth Amendment', 101 *The Yale Law Journal*, 1475–90.

Boyle, J 1987, 'Thomas Hobbes and the invented tradition of positivism: reflections on language, power and essentialism', 135 *University of Pennsylvania Law Review*, 383–426.

Brazil, B 1996, 'Connecting the Hohfeldian boxes: towards a technical definition of liberty', in S Ratnapala & GA Moens (eds), *Jurisprudence of liberty*, Butterworths, Sydney.

Buchanan, JM 1980, 'Reform in the rent-seeking society', in JM Buchanan, RD Tollison & G Tullock (eds), *Toward a theory of rent seeking society*, Texas A & M University Press, College Station.

——& Tullock, G 1962, *The calculus of consent*, University of Michigan Press, Ann Arbor.

Buckland, WW 1963, *A text book of Roman law from Augustus to Justinian*, Cambridge University Press, Cambridge.

Cain, PA 1990, 'Feminism and the limits of equality', 24 *Georgia Law Review*, 803–47.

Calabresi, G & Melamed, AD 1972, 'Property rules, liability rules and inalienability: one view of the cathedral', 85 *Harvard Law Review*, 1089–1128.

Campbell, DT 1965, 'Variation and selective retention in socio-cultural evolution', in HR Barringer, GI Blanksten & RW Mack (eds), *Social change in developing areas: a re-interpretation of evolutionary theory*, Schenkman Publishing Co., Cambridge MA, 13–49.

——1987a, 'Evolutionary epistemology', in G Radnitzy & WW Bartley (eds), *Evolutionary epistemology, theory of rationality and sociology of knowledge*, Open Court, La Salle IL, 47–89.

——1987b, 'Blind variation and selective retention in creative thought as in other knowledge processes', in G Radnitzy & WW Bartley (eds), *Evolutionary epistemology, theory of rationality and sociology of knowledge*, Open Court, La Salle IL, 91–114.

Campbell, T 1988, *Justice*, Macmillan Education, Basingstoke.

Cardozo, BN 1928, *The paradoxes of legal science*, Columbia University Press, New York.

Carlyle, RW & Carlyle AJ 1903–38, *A history of medieval political theory in the West*, vol. 1, Blackwood, Edinburgh.

Chroust, A-H 1944, 'The philosophy of law of St Augustine', 53(2) *The Philosophical Review*, 195–202.

Cicero, MT 1928 (54–51 BC), *De republica de legibus*, tr. CW Keyes, Heinemann, London.

Coase, RH 1937, 'The nature of the firm', 4(16) *Economica*, 386–405.

——1960, 'The problem of social cost', III *The Journal of Law and Economics*, 1–44.

Commons, JR 1924, *Legal foundations of capitalism*, AM Kelley, Clifton NJ.

——1974, *Legal foundations of capitalism* (reprinted with preface by Joseph Dorman), AM Kelley, Clifton NJ.

Comte, A 1975 (1830–42), *Cours de philosophie positive*, Hermann, Paris.

Cornell, D 1990, 'The doubly-prized world: myth, allegory and the feminine', 75 *Cornell Law Review*, 643–99.

D'Entrèves, AP 1951, *Natural law: an introduction to legal philosophy*, Hutchinson's University Library, London.

Darwin, C 1985 (1859) *On the origin of species by means of natural selection*, Penguin Classics, London.

Davies H & Holdcroft D 1991, *Jurisprudence: texts and commentary*, Butterworths, London.

Demsetz, H 1967, 'Towards a theory of property rights', 57(2) *American Economic Review*, 347–59.

Dennett, DC 1995, *Darwin's dangerous idea: evolution and the meanings of life*, Allen Lane, The Penguin Press, London.

——1996, *Kinds of minds: towards an understanding of consciousness*, Weidenfeld & Nicolson, London.

Derrida, J 1972, 'Structure, sign and play in the discourses of the human sciences', in R Macksey & E Donato (eds), *The structuralist controversy: the languages of criticism and the sciences of man*, Johns Hopkins University Press, Baltimore, 247–72.

——1976, *Of grammatology*, tr. GC Spivak, Johns Hopkins University Press, Baltimore.

——1981, *Positions*, Athlone Press, London.

——1992, 'Force of law: "The mystical foundation of authority"', in D Cornell, M Rosenfeld & DG Carlson (eds), *Deconstruction and the possibility of justice*, Routledge, New York, 3–67.

Dias, RWM 1976, *Jurisprudence*, 4th edn, Butterworths, London.

Draetta, U, Lake, RB & Nanda, VP 1992, *Breach and adaptation of international contracts: an introduction to lex mercatoria*, Butterworths, Salem NH.

Durkheim, E 1964, *The division of labour in society*, The Free Press, New York.

Dworkin, R 1977, *Taking rights seriously*, Duckworth, London.

——1998, *Law's empire*, Hart Publishing, Oxford.

Ehrlich, E 1936, *Fundamental principles of the sociology of law*, Harvard University Press, Cambridge MA.

Elliot, ED 1997, 'Law and biology: the new synthesis?', 41 *Saint Louis Law Journal*, 595–624.

Epstein, RA 1993, 'Holdouts, externalities and the single owner: one more salute to Ronald Coase', 36 *Journal of Law and Economics*, 553–86.

——1995, *Simple rules for a complex world*, Harvard University Press, Cambridge MA.

Feinberg, J 1963, 'Justice and personal desert', *Nomos, VI Justice*, Atherton Press, New York.

Ferguson, A 1966 (1767), *An essay on the history of civil society*, Edinburgh University Press, Edinburgh.

Finley, L 1988, 'Nature of domination and the nature of women: reflections on *Feminism unmodified*', 82 *Northwestern University Law Review*, 352–86.

Finnis, J 1972, 'Some professorial fallacies about rights', *The Adelaide Law Review*, 377–88.

——1980, *Natural law and natural rights*, Clarendon Press, Oxford.

Fish, S 1989, *Doing what comes naturally*, Duke University Press, Durham NC.

Frank, J 1949, *Courts on trial: myth and reality in American justice*, Princeton University Press, Princeton NJ.

Frank, WA 1997, *Duns Scotus on the will and morality*, The Catholic University of America Press, Washington DC.

Freeman, MDA 2001, *Lloyd's introduction to jurisprudence*, Sweet & Maxwell, London.

Friedman, M 1953, *Essays in positive economics*, University of Chicago Press, Chicago, Part I: 'The methodology of positive economics'.

——1962, *Capitalism and freedom*, University of Chicago Press, Chicago, Ch. 6: 'Role of government in education', 85–98.

Fuller, LL 1958, 'Positivism and fidelity to law: A Reply to Professor Hart', 71(4) *Harvard Law Review*, 630–72.

——1964, *The morality of law*, Yale University Press, New Haven CT and London.

——1969, *The morality of law*, rev. edn, Yale University Press, New Haven CT and London.

——1981, *The principles of social order*, Duke University Press, Durham NC.

Gable, P 1980, 'Reification in legal reasoning', 3 *Research in Law and Sociology*, 25–46.

Gaius 1905 (130–180) *Institutes of Roman law by Gaius*, tr. E Poste, Clarendon Press, Oxford.

Gell-Mann, M 1995, *The quark and the jaguar: adventures in the simple and the complex*, Abacus, London.

Gilligan, C 1982, *In a different voice: psychological theory and women's development*, Harvard University Press, Cambridge MA.

Gluckman, M 1967, *The judicial process among the Barotse of Northern Rhodesia*, Manchester University Press, Manchester.

Gould, JP 1973, 'The economics of legal conflicts', 2 *Journal of Legal Studies*, 279.

Gould, SJ 1982, 'Darwinism and the expansion of evolutionary theory', 216 *Science*, 380–7.

Gray, JC 1909, *Nature and sources of law*, Macmillan, New York.

Grotius, H 1927 (1625), *De jure belli ac pacis*, tr. FW Kelsey, Oxford University Press, Oxford.

——1957 (1625), *Prolegomena to the law of war and peace*, tr. FW Kelsey, Liberal Arts Press, New York.

Guetzkow, H 1961, 'Organizational leadership in task oriented groups', in B Bass & L Petrullo (eds), *Leadership and interpersonal behavior*, Holt, Rinehart & Winston Inc., New York, 187–200.

Gurvitch, G 1947, *Sociology of law*, Kegan Paul, Trench, Trubner & Co., London.

Gwartney, J, Stroup R & Lee, D 2005, *Common sense economics: what everyone should know about wealth and prosperity*, St Martin's Press, New York.

Haakonssen, K 1996, *Natural law and moral philosophy: from Grotius to the Scottish Enlightenment*, Cambridge University Press, New York.

Hägerström, A 1953, *Inquiries into the nature of law and morals*, tr. CD Broad, Almqvist & Wiksell, Stockholm.

Hahlweg, K 1989, 'A systems view of evolution and evolutionary epistemology', in K Hahlweg & CA Hooker (eds), *Issues in evolutionary epistemology*, State University of New York Press, New York, 45–78.

Hale, Sir Matthew 1971 (1713), *The history of the common law*, University of Chicago Press, Chicago.

Hardin, G 1968, 'The tragedy of the commons', 162 *Science*, 1243–8.

Harris, JW 1980, *Legal philosophies*, Butterworths, London.

Hart, HLA 1958, 'Positivism and the separation of law and morals', 71(4) *Harvard Law Review*, 593–629.

——1961, *The concept of law*, Clarendon Press, Oxford.

——1965, 'Book review of *Morality of law* by Lon Fuller', 78 *Harvard Law Review*, 1281–96.

——1973, 'Bentham on legal rights', in AWB Simpson (ed.), *Oxford essays in jurisprudence. Second series*, Clarendon Press, Oxford, 171–201.

——1983, *Essays on jurisprudence*, Oxford University Press, Oxford.

——1997, *The concept of law*, 2nd edn, Oxford University Press, Oxford.

——1998, 'Kelsen's doctrine of the unity of law', in SL Paulsen & BL Paulsen (eds), *Normativity and norms: critical perspectives on Kelsenian themes*, Clarendon Press, Oxford, 553–81.

Hayek, FA 1973, *Rules and order*, Routledge & Kegan Paul, London.

——1978, *New studies in philosophy, politics, economics and the history of ideas*, University of Chicago Press, Chicago.

——1982, *Law, legislation and liberty*, 3 vols, Routledge & Kegan Paul, London.

Heidegger, M 1993, *Basic writings: from 'Being and time' 1927, to 'The task of thinking' 1964*, ed. DF Krell, with general introduction and introductions to each selection, Routledge, London.

Hobbes, T 1946 (1651), *Leviathan or the matter, forme and power of a commonwealth ecclesiastical and civil*, Basil Blackwell, Oxford.

Hohfeld, WN 2001, *Fundamental legal conceptions as applied in judicial reasoning*, ed. D Campbell & P Thomas, Ashgate Dartmouth, Aldershot.

Holmes, OW Jr 1871, 'Book notices', 6 *American Law Review*, 723–5.

——1897, 'The path of the law', 10 *Harvard Law Review*, 457–78.

——1963 (1881), *The common law*, Harvard University Press, Cambridge MA.

Holmström-Hintikka, G 1997, 'Rights and responsibilities', *Rights: Proceedings of the 17th world congress of the International Association of Philosophy of Law and Social Philosophy*, Franz Steiner Verlag, Stuttgart, 45–55.

Honore, AM 1970, 'Social justice', in RS Summers (ed.), *Essays in legal philosophy*, Basil Blackwell, Oxford.

Hooker, R 1977, 'Of the laws of ecclesiastical polity', in *The Folger Library edition of the works of Richard Hooker*, vol. 1, Harvard University Press, Cambridge MA.

Hume, D 1947 (1779), *Dialogues concerning natural religion*, Bobbs-Merril Co., Indianapolis.

Hume, D 1975 (1748), *Enquiries concerning human understanding and concerning the principles of morals*, 3rd edn, Clarendon Press, Oxford.

——1978 (1739–40), *A treatise of human nature*, Clarendon Press, Oxford.

——1985 (1742), *Essays moral, political and literary*, Liberty Classics, Indianapolis.

Hutcheson, JC 1929, 'The judgment intuitive: the function of the hunch in judicial decision', 14 *Cornell Law Quarterly*, 274–88.

Jones, O 1999, 'Law, emotions and behavioural biology', 39 *Jurimetrics*, 283–9.

Jones, O and Goldsmith, T 2005, 'Law and behavioural biology', 105 *Columbia Law Review*, 405–502.

Justinian 1904 (529–34), *The digest of Justinian*, vol. 1, tr. CH Monro, Cambridge University Press, Cambridge.

Kant, I 1883 (1783), *Prolegomena and metaphysical foundations of natural science*, Bell, London.

——1930, *Critique of pure reason*, G Bell & Sons, London.

——1947, *The moral law, or Kant's groundwork of the metaphysics of morals*, tr. HJ Paton, Hutchinson's University Library, London.

Kauffman, S 1995, *At home in the universe: the search for the laws of self-organisation and complexity*, Viking, London.

Kelman, M 1987, *A guide to critical legal studies*, Harvard University Press, Cambridge MA.

Kelsen, H 1935, 'The pure theory of law: its method and fundamental concepts, Part II', 51 *Law Quarterly Review*, 517–35.

——1945, *General theory of law and state*, Harvard University Press, Cambridge MA.

——1967, *Pure theory of law*, 2nd edn, University of California Press, Berkeley and Los Angeles.

——1998 (1923), 'Foreword to the second printing of "Main problems in the theory of public law", in SL Paulsen & BL Paulsen (eds), *Normativity and norms: critical perspectives on Kelsenian themes*, Clarendon Press, Oxford, 2–22.

Kennedy, D 1976, 'Form and substance in private law adjudication', 89 *Harvard Law Review*, 1685–1778.

——1978, 'The structure of Blackstone's Commentaries', 28 *Buffalo Law Review*, 205–382.

Kern, F 1970, *Kingship and law in the Middle Ages: studies*, Harper & Row, New York.

Kirzner, IM 1962, 'Rational action and economic theory', 70 *Journal of Political Economy*, 380–5.

——1997, *How markets work: disequilibrium, entrepreneurship and discovery*, Institute of Economic Affairs, London.

Landes, WM 1971, 'An economic analysis of the courts', 14 *Journal of Law and Economics*, 61–107.

——& Posner, R 1979, 'Adjudication as a private good', 8 *Journal of Legal Studies*, 235–84.

Leach, E 1977, *Custom, law and terrorist violence*, Edinburgh University Press, Edinburgh.

Levy, S 1992, *Artificial life: the quest for a new creation*, Pantheon Books, New York.

Lew, JDM 1978, *Applicable law in international commercial arbitration: a study in commercial arbitration awards*, Oceana Publications, Dobbs Ferry NY.

Lewis, CT 2000, *Elementary Latin dictionary*, Oxford University Press, Oxford.

Llewellyn, K 1960 (1930), *The bramble bush: on our law and its study*, Oceana Publications, Dobbs Ferry NY.

——1962, *Jurisprudence: realism in theory and practice*, University of Chicago Press, Chicago.

Locke, J 1960 (1690), *Two treatises of government*, ed. P Laslett, Cambridge University Press, Cambridge.

Long, AA & Sedley, DN 1987, *The Hellenistic philosophers*, vol. 1, Cambridge University Press, Cambridge.

Lucretius 1947 (50 BC), *De rerum natura (On the nature of natural things)*, tr. C Bailey, Clarendon Press, Oxford.

Lundstedt, VA 1956, *Legal thinking revised: my views on law*, Almqvist & Wiksell, Stockholm.

Luscombe, DE 1982, 'Natural morality and natural law', in *The Cambridge history of later medieval philosophy*, Cambridge University Press, Cambridge.

Lyotard, F 1984, *The postmodern condition: a report on knowledge*, University of Minnesota Press, Minneapolis.

MacCormick, N 1979, *Legal reasoning and legal theory*, Oxford University Press, Oxford.

MacKinnon, CA 1987, *Feminism unmodified: discourses on life and law*, Harvard University Press, Cambridge MA.

Macneil, IR 1980, *The new social contract: an inquiry into modern contractual relations*, Yale University Press, New Haven CT.

Mailath, GJ 1998, 'Evolutionary game theory', in P Newman (ed.), *The new Palgrave dictionary of economics and the law*, vol. 1, Macmillan, London.

Malinowski, B 1922, *Argonauts of the Western Pacific: an account of native enterprise and adventure in the archipelagos of Melanesian New Guinea*, Routledge & Kegan Paul, London.

Mandeville, B 1924 (1733), *The fable of the bees, or private vices, publick benefits*, vols 1 & 2, Clarendon Press, Oxford.

Markby, W 1905, *Elements of law with reference to the principles of general jurisprudence*, 6th edn, Clarendon Press, Oxford.

Marx, K 1968 (1875), 'Critique of the Gotha Programme', *Karl Marx and Frederick Engels: selected works in one volume*, Lawrence & Wishart, London, 319–35.

——& Engels, F 1973 (1845), *The German ideology*, International Publishers, New York.

Menger, C 1963, *Problems of economics and sociology (Untersuchungen über die Methode der Socialwissenschaften und der Politischen Oekonomie insbesondere)*, University of Illinois Press, Urbana IL.

——1985, *Investigations into the method of the social sciences with special reference to economics*, New York University Press, New York.

Mill JS 1997 (1869), *Subjection of women*, Dover Publications, Mineola NY.

——2002 (1869), *On Liberty*, Dover Publications, Mineola NY.

Miller, FD Jr 1995, *Nature justice, and rights in Aristotle's politics*, Clarendon Press, Oxford.

Nietzsche, FW 1954, *The portable Nietzsche*, selected and tr. W Kaufmann with introduction, prefaces and notes, Viking Press, New York.

North, DC 1990, *Institutions, institutional change and economic performance*, Cambridge University Press, Cambridge.

Nozick, R 1974, *Anarchy, state and utopia*, Basic Books, New York.

Olivecrona, K 1939, *Law as fact*, Oxford University Press, Oxford.

Olson, M 1965, *The logic of collective action*, Harvard University Press, Cambridge MA.

——1982, *The rise and decline of nations*, Yale University Press, New Haven CT.

Paulsen, SL 1998, 'Hans Kelsen's earliest legal theory: critical constructivism', in SL Paulsen & BL Paulsen (eds), *Normativity and norms: critical perspectives on Kelsenian themes*, Clarendon Press, Oxford, 23–43.

Plato 1974 (360 BC), *The republic*, Penguin Books, Harmondsworth.

——1980 (360 BC), *The laws*, tr. TL Pringle, The Chicago University Press, Chicago and London.

Pollock, Sir Frederick 1890, *Oxford lectures and other discourses*, Macmillan, London.

Popper, KR 1963, *Conjectures and refutations*, Routledge & Kegan Paul, London; Basic Books, New York.

——1972, *Objective knowledge: an evolutionary approach*, Clarendon Press, Oxford.

——1993, *The open society and its enemies*, vol. 1, Routledge, London.

Posner, AR 1990, *The problems of jurisprudence*, Harvard University Press, Cambridge MA.

——1998, *Economic analysis of law*, 5th edn, Aspen Law & Business, New York.

Pospisil, L 1958, *Kapauku Papuans and their law*, Yale University Press, New Haven CT.

Poster, M 1989, 'Why not to read Foucault', 31 *Critical Review*, 155.

Pound, R 1930, 'The new feudal system', 25 *Commercial Law Journal*, 397–403.

——1940, *Contemporary juristic theory*, Pamona College, Claremont CA.

——1943, "Sociology of law and sociological jurisprudence', V(1) *The University of Toronto Law Journal*, 1–20.

——1954, *An introduction to the philosophy of law*, Yale University Press, New Haven CT.

Priest, GL 1977, 'The common law process and the selection of efficient rules', 6 *Journal of Legal Studies*, 65–82.

Pufendorf, S 1991 (1673), *On the duty of man and citizen according to natural law*, tr. M Silverthorne, Cambridge University Press, Cambridge.

Radbruch, G 1950 (1932), *Legal philosophy in the legal philosophies of Lask, Radbruch, and Dabin*, tr. K Wilk, Harvard University Press, Cambridge MA.

——2006 (1946), 'Statutory lawlessness and supra-statutory law', 26(1) *Oxford Journal of Legal Studies*, 1–11.

Rawls, J 1963, 'Constitutional liberty and the concept of justice', in CJ Friedrich & JW Chapman (eds), *Nomos, VI Justice*, Atherton Press, New York, 98–125.

——1999, *A theory of justice*, rev. edn, Oxford University Press, Oxford (first published 1971).

Raz, J 1979, *The authority of law: essays in law and morality*, Oxford University Press, Oxford.

——1980, *The concept of a legal system: an introduction to the theory of legal system*, Clarendon Press, Oxford.

——1986, 'The purity of the pure theory', in R Tur & W Twining (eds), *Essays on Kelsen*, Clarendon Press, Oxford, 79–97.

——1995, *Ethics in the public domain*, Oxford University Press, Oxford.

Rock, P 1974, 'The sociology of deviancy and conceptions of moral order', 142 *The British Journal of Criminology*, 139–49.

Rommen, HA 1955, *The natural law*, B Herder Book Co., St Louis and London.

Rorty, R 1982, *Consequences of pragmatism*, University of Minnesota Press, Minneapolis.

Ross, A 1968, *Directives and norms*, Routledge & Kegan Paul, London.

Rothbard, M 1985, *For a new liberty: the libertarian manifesto*, Libertarian Review Foundation, New York.

Rousseau, J-J 1968 (1762), *The social contract*, Penguin Books, Harmondsworth.

Rubin, EL 1995, 'The nonjudicial life of contract: beyond the shadow of the law', 90 *Northwestern University Law Review*, 107–31.

Rubin, PH 1977, 'Why is the common law efficient', 6 *Journal of Legal Studies*, 51–63.

Ruhl, JB 1996a, 'The fitness of law: using complexity theory to describe the evolution of law and society and its practical meaning for democracy', 49 *Vanderbilt Law Review*, 1407–90.

——1996b, 'Complexity theory as a paradigm for the dynamical law-and-society system: a wake up call for legal reductionism and the modern administrative state', 45(5) *Duke Law Journal*, 849–928.

Russell, B 1962, *History of Western philosophy*, George Allen & Unwin Ltd, London.

Sandel, MJ 1982, *Liberalism and the limits of justice*, Cambridge University Press, Cambridge.

Saussure, F 1989, *Course in general linguistics*, Open Court, La Salle IL.

Savigny, FK von 1867, *System of the modern Roman law*, Hyperion Press, Westport CT.

Seckler, D 1975, *Thorstein Veblen and the institutionalists: a study in the social philosophy of economics*, Macmillan, London.

Smith, A 1976 (1759), *The theory of moral sentiments*, Clarendon Press, Oxford.

——1981 (1776), *An Inquiry into the Nature and Causes of the Wealth of Nations*, vols I & II, Liberty Classics, Indianapolis.

Smith, BH 1988, *Contingencies of value*, Harvard University Press, Cambridge MA.

Smith, SA de 1977, *Constitutional and administrative Law*, 3rd edn, Penguin Books, Harmondsworth.

——1980, *Judicial review of administrative action*, 4th edn by JM Evans, Stevens, London.

——& R Brazier 1998, *Constitutional and administrative law*, 8th edn, Penguin Books, London and New York.

Sophocles 1984 (c. 441 BC), *The three Theban plays*, tr. R Fagles, Penguin Books, Harmondsworth.

Starke, JG 1998, 'Monism and dualism in the theory of international law', in SL Paulsen & BL Paulsen (eds), *Normativity and norms: critical perspectives on Kelsenian themes*, Clarendon Press, Oxford, 537–52.

Suarez, F 1944 (1612), *De legibus ac deo legislatore: selections from three works of Francisco Suarez, SJ*, vol. 2, Clarendon Press, Oxford.

Sumner, LW 1987, *The moral foundation of rights*, Clarendon Press, Oxford.

Tooby, J & Cosmides, L 1992, 'The psychological foundations of culture', in Barkow, JH, Cosmides, L & Tooby, J (eds), *The adapted mind: evolutionary psychology and the generation of culture*, Oxford University Press, New York.

Triepel, H 1958 (1899), *Völkerrecht und Landesrecht*, CL Hirschfeld, Leipzig.

Tullock, G 1971, *The logic of the law*, Basic Books, New York.

Twining, W 1973, 'The Bad Man revisited', 58 *Cornell Law Review*, 275–303.

Ullman, W 1966, *Principles of government and politics in the Middle Ages*, 2nd edn, Methuen, London.

Unger, RM 1983, *The critical legal studies movement*, Harvard University Press, Cambridge MA.

Vanberg, V 1994, 'Hayek's legacy and the future of liberal thought: rational liberalism vs. evolutionary agnosticism', 5(4) *Journal des Economistes et Etudes Humaines*, 451–81.

——1997, 'Institutional evolution though purposeful selection: the constitutional economics of John R Commons', 8 *Constitutional Political Economy*, 105–22.

Veblen, T 1898, 'Why is economics not an evolutionary science?', *Quarterly Journal of Economics*, July (1898) vol. 14, no. 4, 373–97.

Vinogradoff, P 1927, *Commonsense in law*, Williams & Northgate, London.

Vromen, JJ 1995, *Economic evolution: an enquiry into the foundations of new institutional economics*, Routledge, London and New York.

Weber, M 1968, *Economy and society: an outline of interpretive sociology*, Bedminster Press, New York.

West, R 1988, 'Jurisprudence and gender', 55 *Chicago Law Review*, 1–72.

White, AR 1984, *Rights*, Clarendon Press, Oxford.

William of Ockham 1992 (1340), *A short discourse on the tyrannical government over things divine and human, but especially over the Empire and those subject to the Empire, usurped by some who are called highest pontiffs*, ed. AS McGrade, tr. J Kilcullen, Cambridge University Press, Cambridge.

Williams, G 1956, 'The concept of liberty', 56 *Columbia Law Review*, 1129.

Williams, W 1989, 'Notes from a first generation', *University of Chicago Legal Forum*, 99–113.

Williamson, OE 1979, 'Transaction cost economics: the governance of contractual relations', 22 *Journal of Law and Economics*, 233–61.

Wolfe, A 1992, 'Algorithmic justice', in *Deconstruction and the possibility of justice*, Routledge, New York.

Wolff, RP 1960, 'Kant's debt to Hume via Beattie', 21(1) *Journal of the History of Ideas*, 117–23.

Index